Ummah

Ummah

A New Paradigm for a Global World

Katrin A. Jomaa

SUNY PRESS

Published by State University of New York Press, Albany

Printed in the United States of America

For information, contact State University of New York Press, Albany, NY
www.sunypress.edu

Library of Congress Cataloging-in-Publication Data

Name: Jomaa, Katrin A., author.
Title: Ummah : a new paradigm for a global world / Katrin A. Jomaa, author.
Description: Albany : State University of New York Press, [2021] | Includes bibliographical references and index.
Identifiers: ISBN 9781438482057 (hardcover : alk. paper) | ISBN 9781438482040 (pbk. : alk. paper) | ISBN 9781438482064 (ebook)
Further information is available at the Library of Congress.

10 9 8 7 6 5 4 3 2 1

To Prophet Mohammad and his family, with love

I dedicate this work to every human being who struggles and hopes for a just, integrated, and peaceful world

For seekers of truth and lovers of wisdom wherever they find it

"O humankind, indeed We have created you from male and female and made you peoples and tribes that you may know one another. Indeed, the most noble among you in the sight of God is the best in conduct (most pious). Indeed, God is All-knowing and All-aware." (Qur'ān 49:13)

"Political society exists for the sake of noble actions, and not of living together. Hence they who contribute most to such a society have a greater share in it than those who have the same or a greater freedom of nobility of birth but are inferior to them in political excellence; or than those who exceed them in wealth but are surpassed by them in excellence."[1]

"Let there be from among you (*minkum*) an *Ummah* inviting to goodness (*khayr*) and enjoining righteousness and deterring wrongness (*ya'murūna bil-ma'rūf wa yanhawna 'an al-munkar*) and those are the successful." (Qur'ān 3:104)

Imām Ali says: "He who has a despotic opinion will perish and he who consults men shares with them their minds."[2]

". . . To each among you, We have prescribed a law and a clear way (*shir'atan wa minhājan*). If Allah willed, He would have made you one *ummah*, but that (He) may test you in what He has given you; so strive as in a race in all virtues. The return of you (all) is to Allah; then He will inform you about that in which you used to differ." (Qur'ān 5:48)

"My sense is that multicultural societies can be held together by a political culture, however much it has proven itself, only if democratic citizenship pays off not only in terms of liberal individual rights and rights of political participation but also in the enjoyment of social and cultural rights. The citizens must be able to experience *the fair value of their rights* in the form of social security and the reciprocal recognition of different cultural forms of life."[3]

---

1. Aristotle, *Politics* (1281a 3–8).

2. Ali Bin Abī Ṭālib, *Nahju-l-Balāgha*, Sermon 161, ed. Muhammad 'Abduh (Beirut: Mu'assasat al-'A'lamī lil-Maṭbū'āt, 2003), 500.

3. Jurgen Habermas, "The European Nation-State: On the Past and Future of Sovereignty and Citizenship," 409.

Contents

List of Illustrations xi

Acknowledgments xii

Introduction 1

Chapter 1
Conceptual Meaning of *Ummah* in the Meccan Verses of the Qur'ān 21
Ummah in the Literature 21
Analysis of the word *ummah* in the Meccan verses of the Qur'ān 24
Ummah, Appointed Term (*ajal*), and Associated Responsibility 24
Ummah, Religion, and Forefathers 30
Ummah and *al-Kitāb* 34
Ummah and *Imām* 38
Ummah and the Covenant (*al-Mīthāq*) 42
A Possible Order of a Global *Ummah* Composed of Different *Umam*? 48
Ummah, *Ummī* Prophet, and the Global *Ummah* 50
Ummah and Sovereignty 55
Leadership, the Book, and Justice 55
Land (Territory) 57
Ummah and Nation-State 58

Al-Ummah al-Wāḥidah and Its Differentiation across Human History 62
Ummah of the Prophets 62
Dealing with Religious Diversity 63
Confederates of Evil (*al-Aḥzāb*) 65
The Reformers (*Muṣliḥūn*) 66
Conclusion 71

Chapter 2
Ummah in the Medinan Verses of the Qur'ān 77
The Notion of a Shared *Ummah*: Rights and Obligations 78
Prophet Abraham (*Ibrāhīm*) Was an *Ummah* 80
Defining the Ideology and Outlook of the Muslim *Ummah* through Prophet Abraham 83
The Best Religion (*Dīn*) is Following *Millat Ibrāhīm "al-Ḥanīf"* 93
Al-Manāsik (the Rituals) 100
The Middle *Ummah* (al-*Ummah al-Wasaṭ*) and the Witness (*Shahāda*) 103
Ummah from *Ahl Al-Kitāb* (Jews and Christians) 109
The Best *Ummah* (*Khayr Ummah*) Ever Raised Up for Humankind 114
Ummah of the Book and Governance 122
Conclusion 128

Chapter 3: *Ummah* in the Medina Constitution 133
Al-Mu'minūn ("The Believers") 139
Decrees Addressing the Believers 144
Decrees Addressing the Jews 155
Decrees Addressing *Ahl as-Ṣaḥīfah* (the People of the Constitution) 160
Sacred Land (*ḥaram*) 160
Conclusion 169

Chapter 4
The *Ummah* and Political Governance—Comparative 173
The *Ummah* and the Aristotelian Polis 177
Khalīfa and Political Animal 177

Khalīfa 179
Khalīfa in Early, Classical, and Modern Exegesis 181
Khilāfa in Islamic Literature 191
Aristotelian Polis and Qurʾanic *Ummah* 197
Polis and *Ummah*: Medium Whereby Citizens Exercise Virtuous Activity 201
Difference between Law and *Sharīʿah* 203
Rule of Law (Polis and *Ummah*) 207
Resolving Conflict by Invoking Competing Virtues in Aristotle and the Qur'ān 208
Community and State in Contemporary Political Theory 212
Polis and Constitution versus *Ummah* and *al-Kitāb* 222
Introducing Reforms through the Constitution 223
The Characters of Constitution and the Citizen Mirror Each Other 226
Constitutional Law Transformed into Community Norm 229
Polis and Justice versus *Ummah* and *Wasaṭiyyah* 232
Justice as a "Mean" and the Concept of "*Wasaṭ*" 232
Understanding "Prophet Abraham Was an *Ummah*" through Aristotle's "Unity of Virtues" 237
Ummah Attains Justice through *Shūra* (Collective Judgment of *Khulafāʾ*) 238
Justice Is Manifested in the "Common Good" Resulting from Collective Judgment 243
Ummah and Political Power 245
The Just Leadership versus *Ṭāghūt* 245
ʾUlū 'l-Amr (Those Entrusted with Authority) 249
ʾUlū 'l-amr in the Medina Constitution 255
ʾUlū 'l-amr in the Modern Period 257

Concluding Remarks 263

Appendix 279

Bibliography 287

Index 295

Index of Qurʾanic Citations 331

Illustrations

Figure 1.1	The networked global structure of the *ummah*	48
Figure 1.2	Difference between nation-states and *umam*	60
Figure 1.3	The one *ummah* and its differentiation, and the way to achieve unity	63
Figure 3.1	The embracing united *ummah* (*ummah wāḥidah*): the *Islamic ummah*	144
Figure 4.1	*Ummah* and its different parts	233
Table 4.1	Spheres of governmental and religious authority	260

Acknowledgments

I am very grateful to God for giving me the patience to learn and complete this project, and for putting in my way the gifted teachers and enlightened scholars who help us open new horizons in our thinking process.

I am indebted to Professor Aurelian Craiutu, whose encouragement and enthusiasm inspired me to carry out this project.

A special word of gratitude to Professor Maria Dakake for her generosity and her time reading and thoroughly editing this manuscript in its initial stage. Her suggestions and advice helped me better organize the book and enriched its content. I am also very thankful to all those who gave their time to read or edit this book and whose valuable feedback and contributions made this book richer. Special thanks to Professor Abdulaziz Sachedina, Professor Khaled abou el-Fadl, Professor Asma Afsaruddin, Professor John Walbridge, Professor Cyrus Zargar, Professor Cheryl Foster, Aisha Sharif, Levin Arnsperger, and Daniel Shorr.

Finally, I would like to acknowledge with gratitude the support of my family—my parents, the most intriguing people ever; my mother, Zein; my father, Abdo; and my siblings, whose prayers kept me going. I would also like to acknowledge my loving and supportive husband, Mohammad, who encouraged me to push through the final stages of editing this book and for our valuable discussions, which helped me refine many ideas and table 4.1 in this book.

Introduction

Purpose and Focus of the Book

What alternatives are there to the current global order, competing nation-states within a dominant economic and political order in which powerful nations thrive on the remnants of weaker ones? Sovereign nation-states tightly secure their borders against the "alien other." Diversity, whether racial, ethnic, or religious, is deemed a threat against a peaceful order governed by a central power. Tolerance and pluralism are celebrated as long as they don't intervene with the integrity and power of the state. Controlled inclusion of diversity within nation-states creates "politics of the visual," constructing images of pluralism rather than a serious engagement with diverse political actors.

This book attempts to explore an alternative sociopolitical unit to the nation-state—namely, the *ummah*, based on the Qur᾿ān and prophetic Sunnah. Inspired by the Qur᾿ān, the foundational source for Islamic thought, it first pursues a meticulous analysis of the word *ummah* in the Qur᾿ān. Historically before the rise of the modern nation-state, the *ummah* signified a pluralistic society that stretched over large areas and had a political leadership. In the modern period, *ummah* was reduced to signifying a Muslim community on a national level or an imagined community on a transnational level. Qur᾿ānic interpretation is always affected by the historical context of the exegete's time. The Qur᾿ānic hermeneutical reinterpretation in this research operates in two parallel trajectories. First, considering the importance of historical context, this book consults both selected premodern and modern scholars and compares their discussion of "single" Qur᾿ānic verses about the *ummah* before and after the rise of the nation-state. This takes into account how the historical context might have affected Muslims' understanding and conceptualization of the *ummah*. The comparison reveals the merits and shortcomings of potential conceptualizations of *ummah*. However, this is not a historiography of the *ummah* and how the concept evolved over time; hence medieval scholars are not consistently consulted. The latter would constitute a book by itself and is beyond the scope of this research. The focus of this book is developing a workable definition of the *ummah* that could be compared with the nation-state, hence engaging in modern constructive Muslim political theology. The aim of focusing on the primary sources, the Qur'ān and the Sunnah, as the main sources to decipher the meaning of *ummah* is to avoid much of the historical nuance associated with the classical legal tradition (though it is not neglected). As Fazlur Rahman suggested, for Muslims to engage with the modern world, they need to move beyond what he calls "historical Islam," constructed historically by jurists, and focus on "normative Islam" based on Qur'ān and Sunnah.

Second, which is the unique part of this work, is assembling "all the verses," including *ummah* in the Qur'ān and exploring the Qur'ānic own reasoning of *ummah* as a concept, an attempt similar to Danial Madigan's work "The Quran's Self Image." This part targets the process of the Qur'ān's own revelation, starting chronologically with the Meccan verses followed by the Medinan verses. The aim of this part is exploring the possibility of a hermeneutical reinterpretation that addresses the Qur'ānic internal discourse about its terms and how it tackles them conceptually at a specific period of revelation as well as chronologically. While exegetes have been interpreting individual verses, with occasional references to other verses tackling the same term, this research attempts to combine all the related verses in a thematic study to check the possibility of a novel interpretation of the Qur'ānic term *ummah*.

After researching the different aspects of the term *ummah* in the Qur'ān and proposing a more inclusive understanding of the concept, the following part of the book explores the possibility of activating and implementing the concept within a political setting. First, the earliest historical polity where the concept *ummah* was initially activated and practically manifested during the Prophet's time is analyzed. This is carried out by analyzing the historical document "Medina Constitution" in light of the Qur'ānic reinterpretation of *ummah* proposed in the first section of this book. Last, the book enters into an analogical as well as dialectical reasoning with Western thought, exemplified by Aristotle as well as liberals and their critics in modern time. The *ummah* is compared with the Aristotelian polis that emphasized the active participation of citizens in the administration of justice. Such a comparative discussion contributes to the modern debate between advocates of individual rights (liberals) and advocates of community rights (communitarians). Communitarians focus on encouraging an ethic of responsibility toward society and political power, in contrast with liberals, who emphasize individual rights, sometimes at the expense of one's duty toward the community. While not neglecting individual rights, an ideal communitarian society strikes a balance between individual rights and social responsibilities.[1] Exploring a new understanding of the *ummah* situates it within contemporary discourses on liberal politics and community and creates the space for an alternative vision to the nation-state.

The research conducted in this book is an interdisciplinary study between the fields of theology, history, philosophy, and political science. It tackles the concept *ummah* through multiple perspectives. First it analyzes the concept *hermeneutically* in the Qur᾿ān, then checks its validity *historically* through the prophetic practice in order to carry out a *philosophical* inquiry that explores possible political implications of the *ummah* in the modern period.

Theoretical Background and Current Need for This Study

Secularism, the basic forming ideology of modern nation-states, marginalized political opposition inspired by religious ideologies. Modern liberal theories automatically assume the common public sphere to be the dominion of the secular, hence separate from the private religious, which is considered subjective and irrelevant to the common good of all. In most Western societies, religion has been marginalized or secularized. Thus, it no longer can withstand the monopolizing power of the nation-state. In Fukuyama's terms, modern liberal societies have reached "the end of history" as liberalism has established itself firmly with no rival power or ideology. In Muslim-majority societies, this process is not fait accompli. Despite the establishment of secular nation-states after the colonial period,

1. Amitai Etzioni, "Communitarianism," in *Encyclopedia of Sociology*, 2nd ed., vol. 1 (New York: Macmillan Reference USA, 2001), 356–57.

Muslim societies are still grappling with competing ideologies, specifically secularism and Islamism (different forms of political Islam). This is due to the fact that, contrary to the secularizing process in the West, which was operating in the social, religious, and political spheres, its Muslim counterpart operated only in the political sphere, leaving the social and religious spheres mostly immune to its effects. The difference is attributed to the historical establishment and the nature of political power and religious authority, as well as their relationship, in both societies. While the religious and political institutions were unified in the premodern West, they were separate and acted as parallel actors across most Islamic history. The separation between the aspirations of the masses and their political elite is still a distinctive feature in most Muslim countries in the modern period.

Comparing the Islamic and Western civilizations, Mālik Bin Nabiy argues that the latter is based on technical roots, while the former is founded on the world of the unseen and moral roots. In other words, the Western civilization values time (and life) based on materialistic achievements while the Islamic one values time based on intellectual and moral satisfaction. He thinks the message of Islamic ideology is that "you were the best *ummah* raised to people as you enjoin goodness and forbid evil and believe in Allah . . ." (Qur'ān 3:110). Thus, he claims that Islamic law is complemented by a pure spiritual character that cannot be envisioned in a secular legal order.[2]

Bin Nabiy says that an original idea has a sacred character that represents a truth independent of history. He differentiates between an original idea (*al-fikra al-aṣliya*) and an effective one (*al-fikra al-faʿāla*). He thinks that original Islamic ideas entered their effective period after the early political conquests, which allowed for Islamic civilization to flourish

2. To clarify his point, Bin Nabiy gives a practical example from shari'a. When discussing inheritance laws in the Qur'ān, God adds, "and if the relatives, orphans and poor people were present at the time of distributing the inherited wealth then provide them some of the wealth, and speak to them words of kindness and justice" (Qur'ān 4:8). Bin Nabiy alludes to an interesting point here where he says that inheritance laws could be legislated by any secular civil law, however adding the concept of "doing good" to the law, in this case giving charity to the impoverished people who are not legal recipients of the inherited wealth and speaking kindly to them, makes Islamic shari'a distinctive. In Mālik Bin Nabiy, *Mushkilat Al-Afkār fī Al-ʿĀlam al-Islāmī* (Damascus: Dār Al-Fikr, 2002), 17–25.

and materialize. Only then did Muslims and people of other faith traditions alike believe in the efficacy of Islamic ideas because they witnessed their practical potential in the world. Bin Nabiy claims that European civilization, on the other hand, controlled the world through its effective ideas and not through original ones.[3] Similarly, Fukuyama argues that the large wealth produced by liberal economies is the key point for stabilizing the liberal sociopolitical order. He also thinks that this order has reduced all human interaction to economic activity. He concludes that humanity has reached the end of history because no other ideology could compete with the capitalist liberal order in its efficacy.[4]

> The end of history will be a very sad time. The struggle for recognition, the willingness to risk one's life for a purely abstract goal, the worldwide ideological struggle that called forth daring, courage, imagination, and idealism, will be replaced by economic calculation, the endless solving of technical problems, environmental concerns, and the satisfaction of sophisticated consumer demands. In the post-historical period there will be neither art nor philosophy, just the perpetual caretaking of the museum of human history.[5]

Bin Nabiy would agree with Fukuyama that the modern liberal order is thriving based on its efficacy rather than its originality but would disagree with him that we have reached the end of history. He rather thinks that the Islamic original ideas can reenter history if they retain their efficacy, that is, renew their place among the ideas that create history. The problem is not related to means, but rather to ideologies and systems that activate these ideologies.[6]

In this spirit, *ummah* presents itself as an original idea whose potential has not been fully activated. Several scholars have defined the *ummah* theoretically. For example, Mohammad Shaḥrūr looks for a common root to interpret *ummah* after surveying its various meanings in the Qur'ān.

3. Ibid., 102–6.

4. Francis Fukuyama, "The End of History?," *The National Interest*, Summer 1989.

5. Ibid., last page.

6. Mālik Bin Nabiy, *Mushkilat Al-Afkār fī Al-ʿĀlam al-Islāmī*, 110–13.

He says that "behavioral conduct" is the basis for defining an *ummah*. Shaḥrūr defines *ummah* as a group of rational or irrational beings who share a common behavior; non-human beings share an instinctive behavior, while humans share a conscious behavior represented in what we call "culture." People later have differed in their behavior because of the difference in laws and customs associated with diversity. Difference started with the dialectical relationship between freedom of thought and dominant cultures, as well as the intermixing of different cultures and progressive change within one culture across time.[7] Al-Kawākibī defines the *ummah* as a group of individuals who are brought together under the banner of ethnicity, a nation, a language, or a religion. Through the *ummah*, people can acquire mutual rights and establish a political association in which every individual has the right to publicly voice his opinion.[8]

I think these definitions are quite simplified and reductive; they do not tackle the complexity of the concept to address all its different layers described in the Qurʾān. Collectively, they offer a general overview of a common denominator for the word, a trial that has been conducted by several scholars, but thus far this collective does not provide a comprehensive study that can bring to light the hidden meanings and activate them to be implemented in a sociopolitical context, which is the main objective of this book. This lack of sociopolitical implementation is precisely what Olivier Roy, a French political scientist, argues to be merely a reflection of Western secularization and its focus on individualism: "The definition of a religious community as a voluntary gathering of believers who intend to live according to the definite patterns of their faith—either in harmony with the external society or in opposition to it, but with no possibility of translating it into organizational political terms—is a Western (or more precisely US) view of religion in society."[9]

Mohammad ʿImāra asks a yet unresolved question: what is the nature of political authority in Muslim societies? Is it civic (*madaniyyah*) or reli-

7. Moḥammad Shaḥrūr, *Dirāsāt Islāmiyya Muʿāṣira fi al-Dawla wal-Mujtamaʿ* (Damascus: Al-Ahālī lil-Ṭibāʿa wal-Nashr wal-Tawzīʿ, 1994), 67–72.

8. Mohammad Jamāl Ṭaḥḥān, *al-Ruʿa al-Iṣlāḥiyya lil-Mufakkir al-Nahḍawī Abd al-Raḥmān al-Kawākibī* (Damascus: Ittiḥād al-Kuttāb al-ʿArab, 2007), 245.

9. Olivier Roy, *Globalized Islam: The Search for a New Ummah* (New York: Columbia University Press, 2004), 39.

gious (*dīniyyahh*)? Some scholars regard the *khilāfa* as a religious state based on early tradition, and others regard it as purely political. ʿImāra then poses a question that is basically the core of my research: can the *ummah* in Islam be the source of these authorities, or it is not related at all to them?[10] ʿImāra asserts that political authority is civic (*madaniyyah*) through *shūra* and elections. At the same time, he does not support the secular idea of separating religion and state (*faṣl ad-dīn ʿ3an ad-dawlah*) nor the idea of uniting them as in a theocracy. ʿImāra thinks the uniqueness of Islamic thought is attributed to its *wasaṭiyyah* ("middle status"), which refuses to be biased to the latter extreme positions or reject them totally. It is instead the median of justice between two injustices, the truth between two falsehoods and moderation between two extremes. This middle ground balances between the religious message and politics, as well the religion and state.[11] He adds that Islamic government should be committed to Qurʾānic laws (i.e., it has a religious framework). Yet the state has two components: a fixed religious component and a civic variable one, which portrays a unique relationship between religion and state.[12] ʿImāra then clarifies that the *ummah* should be in charge of electing its leader or representative. He discusses that social life is subject to general laws represented in *"maqāsid al-sharīʿah"* ("aims of Islamic law"), which put forth a general framework within which people can legislate and advance their lives. He considers the latter as general ethics and values determined by God so that people can find the means to approach these values and not stray away from them.[13] He supports the idea that the *ummah* should be the source of delegating powers (*al-ummah maṣdar as-Sulutāt*),[14] yet he does not explain how he comes to this conclusion.

In this book, I derive a conceptual meaning of the *ummah* in the Qurʾān and *Sunnah* in order to understand the *ummah's* role in the socio-political sphere, both religiously and civically. Thereby, the term *wasaṭ*

10. Mohammad ʿImāra, *Nathariyat al-khilāfa* (Cairo: Dār al-Thaqā al-jadīda), 9–11.

11. Mohammad ʿImāra, *Ad-Dīn wal-Dawla* (Cairo: Maṭābiʿ al-Hayʾa al-Miṣriyya al-ʿĀmma lil-Kitāb, 1986), 31.

12. Ibid., 50.

13. Mohammad ʿImāra, *ad-Dawla al-Islāmiyya bayna al3ilmāniyya wal-Sulṭa ad-Dīniyya* (Cairo: Dār al-Shurūq, 2007), 73.

14. Ibid., 65.

is not only interpreted theologically but also activated as a system and practice politically.

What is unique to the modern period and a product of the modern nation-state is so-called "political Islam." A central nation-state that doesn't tolerate opposition, yet is not responsive to the needs and aspirations of its masses and quite separate from them, created sore points of contention. Thereby, the many forms of modern political Islam usually assume a reactionary, violent, and exclusive character quite similar to the nation-state that paved the way for their creation. Even among Islamic thinkers, there is an obsession with the concept of the "Islamic state," which appears to be a modern nation-state with an Islamic title. For example, Ḥasan Ḥanafī asks: what is the political system that Muslims would accept? He then lists and criticizes many forms that Muslims have endorsed across history, starting with the rightly guided caliphate, the Umayyad and Abbasids, to the nation-state that was established with the help of British or world powers. He also considers the religious state oppressive under the guise of religion, where any criticism is rejected because obeying the ruler is considered equivalent to obeying God. At the end, he proposes the free nation-state as the only alternative because it is pluralistic and endorses equal rights for all, while proposing that the European Union would be a good model for Muslims to follow. He also thinks that while some countries such as Indonesia succeeded in promoting the idea of implementing Islamic *sharīʿah*, the latter still remains a symbol that provides temporary relief to people rather than seriously raising their socioeconomic status.[15] Another problem he discusses is the fierce opposition between Islamists and secularists, where each accuses the other for creating all the ills facing society without leaving any possibility for dialogue. He suggests that criticism should be constructive and both groups should work together for the betterment of society rather than focusing on attaining political status.[16] While Ḥanafī analyzes and criticizes the current situation in the Muslim world, he does not offer an original answer to the question he poses.

Wael Hallaq uncovers the root causes of the failure of some Muslim societies to integrate a holistic system that would uphold Islamic val-

15. Ḥasan Ḥanafī, *Al-Wāqiʿ Al-ʿArabī Al-Rāhin* (Cairo: Dār al-ʿayn lil-Nashr, 2012), 471–77.

16. Ibid., 512–15.

ues successfully within a socioeconomic and political setting. As Ḥanafī asserts, implementing *sharīʿah* in some aspects of the Indonesian society is merely symbolic and does not resolve the socioeconomic or political problems of society. Speaking of partially implementing *sharīʿah* is more of a sedative temporarily appeasing the masses without treating the root cause of the illness. In that regard, Hallaq's book is critical for revealing the basis of the problem. He discusses in detail the inherent contradiction in the term "Islamic state," where he uncovers the foundational ideas and goals for establishing a nation-state in the modern world. He then shows how these foundations contradict basic Islamic ethics and principles related to the purpose of human life and value, political governance and its limits, and the rule of law. Hallaq asserts that the predicament of the nation-state is essentially moral; "whereas the Muslim subject strives for moral improvement, the state's subject strives to fulfill sovereign will, fictitiously a representation of the subject's own will but realistically the will of a commanding sovereign."[17] There is no restriction on the use of violence/force in a state that regards itself sovereign under the rule of law through popular will. On the contrary, Islamic governance derives its legitimacy from a sovereign will, God's will and law, that is higher and outside of itself. Hence, its actions could be curbed by that higher will. Therefore, assuming that the nation-state could be converted to an Islamic one erroneously overlooks the fundamental nature of the modern state.[18] Along similar lines, Western scholars such as Jacques Maritain, a French Catholic philosopher, argues that "the concept of sovereignty predicates of a created being—individual or collective—a divine attribute, namely total independence and self-sufficiency."[19] Because God is the only sovereign, Maritain thinks that this concept is "intrinsically wrong."[20] Hence, others contend that "the idea of the sovereign state is bankrupt and our present conception of national sovereignty is obsolete and pregnant with danger.

17. Wael B. Hallaq, *The Impossible State* (New York: Columbia University Press, 2013), 160.

18. Ibid., 157–58.

19. Leon Thiry, "Nation, State, Sovereignty and Self-Determination," *Peace Research* 13, no. 1 (January 1981): 19.

20. Jacques Maritain, *Man and the State* (Chicago: Chicago University Press, 1968), 29.

The time for declarations of independence is long past; what we need today is a universal declaration of universal interdependence."[21]

Secular liberals such as Jurgen Habermas also warns that the nation-state in post-modernity is losing its grip on sovereignty internally and externally. Internally, the nation-state is facing the challenge of multiculturalism whereby a national consciousness based on a culturally homogeneous population has lost its integrative potential at the expense of growing diverse complex societies. Constitutional patriotism cannot offer a strong bond to hold multicultural populations together.[22] Externally, "the globalization of commerce and communication, of economic production and finance, of the spread of technology and weapons, and above all of ecological and military risks, poses problems that can no longer be solved within the framework of nation-states or by the traditional method of agreements between sovereign states."[23] Habermas continues that national sovereignty is undermined by the growth of political institutions on the supranational level, which are replacing the ineffective United Nations.[24]

From the Muslim perspective, the nation-states in the Middle East are also facing serious challenges that are disrupting the regional order as well as the international scene. Rached Ghannouchi, an Islamist theorist and leader of the Tunisian Ennahda party, which formed in the wake of 2011 Arab spring and became part of the government, thinks that the nation-states formed in the Middle East after the Sykes-Picot Agreement were established to serve foreign interests and willpower rather than self-determination of the people.[25] This explains the weakness of popular legitimacy of regimes in the Middle East, where the boundaries forming the states were formed based on colonial interests and practices of divide-and-rule. Colonial powers imposed economic policies that benefited the

21. Leon Thiry, "Nation, State, Sovereignty and Self-Determination," 19, emphasis added.

22. Jurgen Habermas, "The European Nation-State: On the Past and Future of Sovereignty and Citizenship," trans. Ciaran Cronin, *Public Culture* 10, no. 2 (1998): 408–9.

23. Ibid., 398.

24. Ibid., 399.

25. Rached Ghannouchi, *The Islamic Conception of the State*, Conference of the Young Muslims in London, April 1992.

European settlers initially and an elite political group later after independence. The needs of masses in terms of economic development, education, and other needs were neglected. This led to the rise of dictatorships that secured their power through centralized state bureaucracy and military, leading to the deterioration of socioeconomic conditions.[26]

The Islamist response to these imposed malfunctioning nation-states was calling to restore the Caliphate and erase the artificial borders that divided and disintegrated the Islamic *ummah*. This response, however, took two directions. One direction, espoused by the Muslim Brotherhood, integrated their ideology with the Westphalian paradigm by encouraging political activism within the nation-state. A good example would be Ennahda party in Tunisia, which adopts a state-centric logic aiming at forming strong states based on Islamic identity within its borders instead of the pan-Islamic transnational vision of reestablishing the caliphate.[27] The other direction is undertaken by armed violent transnational groups, such as al-Qaeda and Daʿesh, who seek to overthrow all regimes and reestablish the caliphate.[28]

A third novel and unexpected path was initially espoused by neither Islamist groups nor violent ones, but rather by people of different affiliations and religions in a recent phenomenon called "the Arab spring," "the Arab uprisings," or, a better term used by Sadiki, "peoplehood." It represented popular yearning for freedom, dignity, and a moral outcry against authoritarian tyranny and the deteriorating socioeconomic and political order. Larbi Sadiki proposes an analysis of the concept "peoplehood" as a bottom-up mobilization of non-state actors who embody the ideal "for the people" and whose goal is to alter the state hegemony. He adds that this practical concept has both local and global manifestations where connections are formed internally as well as transnationally.[29]

26. Raffaella A. Del Sarto, "Contentious Borders in the Middle East and North Africa: Context and Concepts," *International Affairs* 93, no. 4 (July 2017): 770–71.

27. Mohamed Ali Adraoui, "Borders and Sovereignty in the Islamist and Jihadist Thought: Past and Present," International Affairs 93, no. 4 (July 2017): 925–29.

28. Ibid., 932–33.

29. Larbi Sadiki, "The Arab Spring: The 'People' in International Relations," in *International Relations of the Middle East*, ed. Louise Fawcett (Oxford, UK: Oxford University Press, 2016), 326–27.

> Tunis was the trigger; Cairo built the momentum; Tripoli and Benghazi signaled a kind of "domino effect." From then on, the travel of the Arab Spring took a life of its own. From this perspective, the Arab Spring is just another manifestation of the human desire for freedom, dignity and justice. From an International Relations perspective, we have three ideas from the foregoing. First, there is a dynamic of "deterritorialization" of activism whereby ***new*** political imaginaries, solidarities, language and protest strategies render nationalist borders meaningless. Second, the resulting trans-border newly reconstituted identities, moral protests, and networks hint at the idea of social "movement spillover" . . . captured by the notion of *al-ḥarāk* or "peoplehood."[30]

While Sadiki finds global parallels with the Arab Spring such as the 1979 Khomeini Revolution in Iran, the 1986 People's Power revolution in Philippines, or the 2004 Orange Revolution in Ukraine, he still thinks that the Arab Spring is unique: "This is where the Arab Spring impresses: the Arab region remains a cohesive cultural sub-system."[31] It is quite surprising how Sadiki, while still acknowledging the cultural cohesiveness of the Arab region, missed associating his concept of peoplehood with the concept of the *ummah*, which is widely prevalent in the Arab-Muslim world. Possibly the lack of an English term that would accurately describe the *ummah* made him choose peoplehood as an approximate translation. However, while he still acknowledged that global parallels were all national whereas the Arab spring was transnational, he regarded that phenomenon as a movement spillover that forged *new* political imaginaries and solidarities. I think his latter assumption glossed over the fact that the *ummah* as a political imaginary and solidarity is deeply engrained in the Arab-Muslim conscience since the beginning of Islamic history. I would rather argue that it became dormant in the modern period, and the Arab spring is nothing but a historical moment of revival in which *old existing* political imaginaries and solidarities were activated. That would better explain the

30. Ibid., 328. Emphasis added.

31. Ibid., 331.

fast domino effect that is unique to the Arab region; the cohesive cultural sub-system that Sadiki describes is evidently a practical manifestation of the underlying structure of the *ummah.*

However, that the Arab spring unleashed the political power of the *ummah* and the astonishing power of human agency against oppressive structures is precisely what makes this book timely. The recent events trigger questions about the political role of the *ummah* and confirm the speculations of intellectuals such as Naṣīf Naṣṣār, who argues that the *ummah* as a sociopolitical realization has not been revealed yet in the social history of humankind.[32] The rapid transnational spread of these uprisings speaks of an underlying phenomenon that merits research. While the Arab spring uncovered the political potential of the *ummah*, its aftermath shows that the *ummah* is still grappling with many variables that are critical for the *ummah* to successfully manifest itself politically. Unless these requirements are met, the *ummah* can achieve temporary victories that nonetheless are not sustainable. Therefore, exploring the different facets of the concept would identify how the *ummah* functions, what sustains it, and how it can undertake a successful political role.

In summary, the nation-state system imported through colonialism neither accommodated the needs of the people nor ethnic, religious, and tribal identities characteristic of the Middle East. Moreover, it did not resolve the tension between the Westphalian state and the promotion of pan-Arabism or pan-Islamism.[33] On the contrary, it led to internal unrest as well as the rise of violent extremism, which is not only causing much distress in the region but also affecting the regional as well as the international order. Therefore, whether the problem is cultural or political as in the West or socioeconomic and conflicting with native aspirations as in the Middle East, the nation-state system is in danger as it faces the challenges of globalization by the consensus of both Western and Islamic intellectuals. Different intellectuals call for proposing alternative visions to the nation-state; Habermas ends his article on the European nation-state with

---

32. Naṣīf Naṣṣār, *Mafhūm al-Ummah bayna ad-Dīn wal-Tārīkh* (Beirut: Dār at-Talīʿa, 1978), 5.

33. Raffaella A. Del Sarto, "Contentious Borders in the Middle East and North Africa: Context and Concepts," 781.

the question: "overcoming the nation-state: abolition or transformation?"[34] Similarly, Del Sarto asserts: "it may be worthwhile to explore alternative conceptualizations of the state and its borders."[35] Adraoui also asks: "what would a new Islamist conception of borders look like and is it possible?"[36]

Hallaq urges Muslim intellectuals to engage in nontraditional and creative thinking to propose an alternative social unit that forms the larger sociopolitical order, one in which morality is a central domain. To construct nascent forms of Islamic governance, Muslims need to reinterpret the concept of political community and how *sharīʿah* is activated within that community. Simultaneously, Hallaq suggests that this process should be dialectical, in which Muslims should also engage with their Western counterparts who are dealing with the same ethical dilemma of the modern world.[37] Hallaq's call resonates with Western scholars who are also advocating for Muslims to explore their Islamic heritage to answer the problems of the modern age. For instance, the Western historian Marshall Hodgson concluded his massive work on Islamic history with this question: What does Islam or the Muslim conscience have to say about the problems of the modern age on both local and global scales?[38] In addition, Amitai Etzioni, the founder of new communitarianism, is open to the contribution of Islamic thought on modern political issues when he says, "the communitarian good society combines 'Asian' values (also reflecting tenets of Islam and Judaism that stress social responsibilities) with a Western concern with political liberty and individual rights."[39]

Hodgson emphasizes this need for cross-cultural dialogue, which he thinks is lacking in contemporary Islamic thought. Hodgson says that in the modern period and the age of globalization, the world is connected, and no community can live in isolation without affecting other communities.

---

34. Jurgen Habermas, "The European Nation-State: On the Past and Future of Sovereignty and Citizenship," 413.

35. Raffaella A. Del Sarto, "Contentious Borders in the Middle East and North Africa: Context and Concepts," 783.

36. Mohamed Ali Adraoui, "Borders and Sovereignty in the Islamist and Jihadist Thought: Past and Present," 935.

37. Wael B. Hallaq, *The Impossible State*, 168–70.

38. Marshall Hodgson, *The Venture of Islam*, vol. 3 (Chicago: University of Chicago Press, 1974), 433–35.

39. Ibid., 357.

Also, the religious traditions have lost their assured independence. Hodgson suggests that the meanings of *ummah* and *sharīʿah* need to be reassessed in order to confront creatively the presence of contrasting spiritual traditions of equal status in a single, worldwide society. This must be achieved along two parallel tracks. First, the Muslim community must overcome its exclusivity without sacrificing its formative discipline, that is, its laws and way of life. Second, Islamic heritage must be in dialogue with contemporary modern culture so that it becomes common knowledge of all communities without sacrificing its integrity. This is the only way, Hodgson believes, to resolve the tension between universalism and communalism in Islamic communities, or any other community, if they are to play a creative role and contribute effectively to the world. The community's heritage should be brought into living interaction with worldwide cultural elements.[40]

This book answers the questions posed by the scholars mentioned above. This book engages in a novel reinterpretation of key concepts: the *ummah* and how it is activated as a sociopolitical concept. Moreover, it engages with Western thinking in a dialectical process in order to address the common challenges we face today as a global world. While the nation-state, as a concept and an institution, is facing challenges both in the West and the East, this book is timely, as it proposes an alternative option that, while being inspired by Islamic ideology, can still be applied universally.

Exegetical References

The first two chapters of the book explore the concept of the *ummah* meticulously in the Qurʾān through a thematic analysis of different exegetical works such as At-Ṭabarsī (d. 523/1128), Al-Qurṭubī (d. 671/1273), Ibn Kathīr (d. 774/1373), Mawdūdī (d. 1399/1979), At-Ṭabaṭabāʾī (d. 1401/1981), and Sayyid Quṭb (d. 1385/1966), with a focus on the following five exegetes: At-Ṭabarī (d. 310/923) and Al-Qummī (d. 307/919) from the third century after the Prophet's death; Muhammad ʿAbduh (d. 1322/1905), Sayyid Quṭb (d. 1385/1966), and Muhammad Faḍlallah (d. 1431/2010) from the modern period.

In line with the spirit of this work, which is bridging between East and West, Sunnī and Shīʿī exegetical works are consulted not only to be

40. Marshall Hodgson, "*The Venture of Islam*," vol. 3 (Chicago: University of Chicago Press, 1974), 433–35.

representative of both traditions, but also to make them talk to each other. This is a much-needed endeavor, especially when sectarianism, identity politics, and religious fanaticism have taken their toll in Muslim societies. I think it is incumbent upon academics to raise the level of knowledge, thereby raising the standards of people above abusive political manipulations under the disguise of religion. Nonetheless, from an academic perspective, seeking various exegetes with different sectarian affiliations enriches our understanding of Qur᾽ānic key concepts.

At-Ṭabarī and al-Qummī's exegeses are considered classical references by Sunnī and Shī῾ī scholars, respectively. The classical interpretations are crucial, as they provide a massive literature of prophetic sayings and the earliest reports of the Companions or the family of Prophet Muhammad, both of which are indispensable for understanding the Qur᾽ānic text in the time of its revelation. Moreover, modern exegesis is very helpful for understanding Qur᾽ānic concepts in light of modern concerns. Both ῾Abduh and Faḍlallah, despite their different sectarian affiliation, stress the need to use reason in interpreting religious texts to keep up with changing times, and both of them were actively involved in politics as well. Thus, they provide a perfect asset for this book, as it endeavors to create a dialogue between Islamic concepts and Western ideas, as well as explore the interplay between religion and politics. A short biography of the five exegetes is provided in the following paragraphs.

Al-Qummī's exegesis is a major Shī῾ī classical work. Abū l-Ḥasan ῾Alī b. Ibrāhīm al-Qummī was one of the earliest influential *Imāmī* traditionalists (*muḥaddith*). It is said that his father, Abraham b. Hāshim, was acquainted with the eighth *imām*, ῾Alī b. Mūsā al-Riḍā (d. 202/818). In addition, Al-Qummī was a contemporary of the eleventh *imām*, al-Ḥasan al-῾Askarī (d. 260/873). Al-Qummī has written many books on religious and legal matters, but the only work that remains intact is his *Tafsīr*. The latter work is considered one of the most significant sources for *Imāmī* doctrine because of its early date and its inclusion of several selections from the *Tafsīr* of Abū l-Jārūd. It is said that the *Tafsīr* of Abū l-Jārūd includes long excerpts of an old Qur᾽ān commentary attributed to the fifth *imām*, Muhammad al-Bāqir (d. 119/737).[41]

41. *Encyclopedia of Islam*, THREE, ed. Gudrun Krämer et al. (Leiden: Brill, 2009), s.v. "῾Alī b. Ibrāhīm al-Qummī," American University of Beirut, http://www.paulyonline.brill.nl/subscriber/entry?entry=ei3_SIM-0323.

Abū Jaʿfar Muhammad Ibn Jarīr Ibn Yazīd At-Ṭabarī is most famous as the supreme universal historian and Qurʾān commentator of the Islamic medieval ages. His major works that remain intact to this day are his Qurʾānic *Tafsīr*, titled *Jāmiʿ al-bayān ʿan taʾwīl al-Qurʾān*; and the "History." Al-Ṭabarī's *Tafsīr* is considered the first main work to develop the *tafsīr* methodology.[42] It is regarded as the *Tafsīr* par excellence and his most outstanding achievement as compared to his works on law and tradition. His methodology emphasizes *ijtihād*, or independent exercise of judgment. In his *Tafsīr*, he usually quotes several exegetical opinions and then states his opinion regarding which constitutes the most acceptable view. The commentary comprises most of the exegetical works before him since the beginning of Qurʾānic exegesis as a discipline. Hence his *Tafsīr* preserved critical exegetical material from the early century of Islam.[43] In addition, he tackles the grammatical and lexicographical aspects of Qurʾānic verses and deduces theological and legal inferences from the Qurʾānic text. At-Tabarī was an orthodox Sunnī originally following the *Shāfiʿī madhhab.* However, as his ideas developed, he formed an independent corpus of law and constituted a separate *madhhab* called Jarīriyya (named after his father). Although his school comprised many leading scholars of the age, it did not develop over time into an independent *madhhab* because its principles were not that distinctive from *Shāfiʿism.*[44]

After the rise of the nation-state, in addition to consulting other scholars, there is a focus on three scholars due to their involvement in politics and their witnessing forms of imperialism that will affect their conceptualization of the *ummah*. Muhammad ʿAbduh (1849–1905) was an Egyptian scholar and reformer. He is famous for being the pioneer of Islamic modernism. He was a journalist, theologian, jurist, and, during the last six years of his life, he served as the grand *muftī* of Egypt. ʿAbduh was greatly influenced by Jalāl al-Dīn al-Afghānī (1839–1897), who was an activist supporting the idea of unity in Islam (Pan-Islam) against

42. *The Oxford Encyclopedia of the Islamic World*, ed. John Esposito (Oxford: Oxford University Press, 2009), s.v. "Ṭabarī, Abū Jaʿfar Muhammad Ibn Jarīr Al-."

43. Wadād Al-Qāḍī, "The Term "Khalīfa" in Early Exegetical Literature," *Die Welt des Islams*, New Series, Bd. 28. No. ¼ (1988), 395.

44. *Encyclopedia of Islam, Second Edition*, ed. P. Bearman et al. (Brill, 2009), s.v. "al-Ṭabarī, Abū D̲jafar Muhammad b. D̲jarīr b. Yazīd," American University of Beirut, http://www.paulyonline.brill.nl/subscriber/entry?entry=islam_COM-1133.

European domination and the breakup of the Muslim world into nation-states. He placed great emphasis on the idea of the *ummah* united against European colonization. ʿAbduh founded with al-Afghānī the anti-British journal *al-ʿUrwa al-Wuthqā*, which lasted only eight months. The journal represented the thinking of a generation of enthusiastic writers, including Rashīd Riḍa, who would later edit and complete ʿAbduh's exegetical work *Tafsīr al-Manār*. Initially Riḍa encouraged ʿAbduh to write a *tafsīr*, but he was not interested. So Riḍa started writing it based on ʿAbduh's lectures. The resulting work was approved and corrected by ʿAbduh as needed. After ʿAbduh's death in 1905, Riḍa continued the work, and it was published in 1927 in twelve volumes. ʿAbduh believed that revelation and reason do not contradict one another, but rather complement each other. Thus, he believed that Islam is compatible with modernity but that there was a problem with religious education and the *ʿulamāʾ* because they relied upon *taqlīd* ("imitation"). Muslim scholarship was heavily based on citing authority (*Isnād*) and passive satisfaction with rigid norms. ʿAbduh advocated emancipation from the *taqlīd* mentality while still retaining Islamic authenticity. Because of his involvement in politics, he was sent to exile twice. After his return to Cairo, he concentrated his efforts on education and renewal of Islamic theology.[45]

Sayyid Quṭb Ibrāhīm Ḥusayn Shādhilī (1906–1966) was an Egyptian intellectual who contributed to the modernization of Islamic political thought in the twentieth century. He was also a novelist, poet, literary critic, and an activist, as he was a member of the Muslim Brotherhood during the 1950s and 1960s. Among his several books is the thirty-volume influential commentary of the Qurʾān, "*Fī Ẓilāl al-Qurʾān*." Quṭb challenged traditional clergy by advocating free engagement with Islamic primary texts.[46] Quṭb was an important link between the Muslim Brotherhood and the Free Officers, who toppled the monarchy in 1952. He had a personal relationship with Gamal Abdel Nasser, where he used to attend meetings of the Revolutionary Command Council (RCC) after their confiscation of power. Because of their different visions about the

45. *The Oxford Encyclopedia of the Islamic World*, ed. John Esposito, s.v. "ʿAbduh Muhammad."

46. *Encyclopedia of Modern Political Thought*, ed. Gregory Claeys (Thousand Oaks, CA: CQ Press, 2013), s.v. "Qutb, Sayyid," University of Rhode Island, http://dx.doi.org.uri.idm.oclc.org/10.4135/9781452234168.n266.

Egyptian society, the relations between the Free Officers and the brotherhood degenerated after the Free Officers seized power.[47] Quṭb criticized contemporary Islamic societies as living in a state of *jāhiliyya* ("ignorance or barbarism). While *jāhiliyya* is a term used to describe pre-Islamic Arabia, Quṭb used the term to denote rejecting divine revelation in favor of the individual's sovereignty.[48] Hence, he criticized Nasser for exploiting the postcolonial Egyptian state as a means to maintain his authoritarian rule. Quṭb developed a political theory based on ultimate sovereignty of God (*ḥakīmīyah lillah*) and Islamic principles of justice based on *sharīʿah*. Initially he postulated that the latter principles would be manifested in an Islamic state after people receive proper Islamic education. Nonetheless, after being imprisoned by the Egyptian government for several years, later in his life he started advocating social and political activism through a dedicated Muslim vanguard. His revolutionary ideas to reestablish a pure Islamic order has inspired several Islamist and revivalist groups.[49]

Muhammad Ḥusayn Faḍlallah (1935–2010) was a Lebanese *ʿālim* and political activist. He received his religious education in the city of Najaf in Iraq. Faḍlallah believed that the task of a Muslim intellectual is to "bridge the deep divide that exists between youth and religion" because of the gap that exists between *ʿulamāʾ* and young people. In contrast to his principal teacher, Abū al-Qāsim Khūʾī, who was against the involvement of the *ʿulamāʾ* in politics, Faḍlallah was deeply involved in the sociopolitical affairs of his country, Lebanon, particularly within its Shīʿī community. In 1964, he started his activities in an impoverished area of Beirut by establishing cultural youth clubs and free community centers and clinics. Faḍlallah rejected the idea of separating religion and politics and advocated the need for a disciplined political party to serve Islam. His sermons and teachings inspired young people to resist the Israeli military occupation of Lebanon; hence he is known as the spiritual leader of Ḥizbullāh. In 1984, Khomeini gave him the legitimizing honor of being

47. *The Oxford Encyclopedia of the Modern Islamic World*, ed. John Esposito (New York: Oxford University Press, 2001), s.v. "Quṭb, Sayyid," University of Rhode Island, http://www.oxfordislamicstudies.com/article/opr/t236MIW/e0663.

48. *Encyclopedia of Modern Political Thought*, ed. Gregory Claeys, s.v. "Qutb, Sayyid."

49. *The Oxford Encyclopedia of the Modern Islamic World*, ed. John Esposito, s.v. "Quṭb, Sayyid."

marjaʿ al-taqlīd ("source of imitation"). Faḍlallah believed in an economy, social structure, and politics governed by Islamic ethics, but he did not advocate a specific type of political regime. Faḍlallah criticized the political theory of *wilāyat al-faqīh* ("rule of the jurisconsult") because he thought it results in autocratic personal power. He rather advocated the practice of *marjaʿīyat at-taqlīd* ("authority of the source of imitation"), which limits personal power by endorsing pluralism. Faḍlallah advocated substantive dialogue and peaceful coexistence between Muslims, Christians, and other religious groups. He criticized religious sectarianism and called for an open and humanized *fiqh* ("jurisprudence").[50]

Acknowledging the historical dynamics witnessed by different scholars and thinkers after the rise of the nation-state is critical for this research because the latter political environment affects the exegete's ideological trajectory. Thereby it aids in clarifying how the pertinent historical context might have impacted the way modern scholars conceptualized the *ummah* and how different their understanding is from premodern scholars.

50. *The Oxford Encyclopedia of the Islamic World*, ed. John Esposito, s.v. "Faḍlallah, Muhammad Ḥusayn."

Chapter 1

Conceptual Meaning of *Ummah* in the Meccan Verses of the Qur'ān

Ummah in the Literature

In common parlance, the term *ummah* often refers to the Muslim community. However, looking at the literature, we find different usages for the word and different explanations for its meaning. Riḍwān as-Sayyid cited eight meanings for the word *ummah* in classical Arabic dictionaries, whereas six of those meanings are mentioned in the Qur'ān. The common meanings are: a group of people, followers of a prophet, a specific religion, exemplary human being, unrivaled individuals, and a period of time.[1] There is no comprehensive study that relates all of those meanings to one another or, in other words, attempts to find a causal relationship among the different meanings in the Qur'ān that would highlight the specific connotation of the word *ummah* relative to other similar terms.

Naṣīf Naṣṣār, an Arab intellectual from the modern period, says that the concept of the *ummah* is one of the greatest social ideas, an idea that is most complicated, mysterious, and charming. However, the idea of the *ummah* is different from its practical manifestation in social and historical realities. Thus, Naṣṣār argues, the dialectic between the idea of the *ummah* and its different forms of existence will continue until all the hidden content of the *ummah*, as an idea, is practically revealed in the

1. Riḍwān as-Sayyid, *Al-Ummah wal-Jamāʿa was-Sulṭa* (Beirut: Dār Iqraʾ, 1984), 43–45.

social history of humankind.[2] I find this statement particularly interesting because it reflects two realities; one is the abstract theoretical dimension of the term, and the other is its practical expression in history. It also suggests that the full realization of the *ummah* has not come about yet and that research carried out on the *ummah* has not exhausted all of its possibilities. Exegetes resort to interpretation (*taʾwīl*) to define and understand the concept. However, this method still leaves many question marks about the concept.[3] On the other hand, Muslim exegetes did not study the concept in a methodological, organized manner to explore the different aspects and meanings of *ummah*. Their orientation was focused on the relationship between the concept of a community and *sharīʿah* (religious law), so they overlooked the theoretical understanding of the *ummah* before receiving religious law.

The latter statement is evident in the way exegetes differed in their understanding of *ummah* in the premodern and modern periods. For example, the prominent historian and classical Qurʾānic exegete At-Ṭabarī (839–923 AD) thinks that the original meaning of *ummah* is a group of people practicing one religion based on the Qurʾānic verse "Humankind were one *ummah* then Allah sent Prophets with glad tidings and warnings, and with them He sent down the Scripture in truth to judge between people in matters wherein they differed . . ." (Qurʾān 2:213). There are different interpretations of the time during which people were all one community. Some exegetes consider this time to be between the prophets Adam and Noah. Others consider this time to be at the beginning of creation in the spiritual realm before physical existence when all the offspring of Adam were presented before him and they acknowledged their submission to God. At-Ṭabarī argues that, irrespective of the knowledge of that time in which all humans were one *ummah*, the crucial point is that they were one *ummah* by one faith, "the religion of the truth." Only after humans differed among themselves about the truth did Allah send the Prophets to guide them, as the above verse shows.[4] However, in the modern period, there is a shift in understanding why people were one *ummah*. For example, the scholar and reformer Muhammad ʿAbduh

2. Naṣīf Naṣṣār, *Mafhūm al-Ummah bayna ad-Dīn wal-Tārīkh* (Beirut: Dār at-Talīʿa, 1978), 5.

3. Naṣīf Naṣṣār, *Mafhūm al-Ummah bayna ad-Dīn wal-Tārīkh*, 13.

4. Abu Jaʿfar Muhammad Bin Jarīr at-Ṭabarī, *Jāmiʿ al-Bayān*, vol. 3 (Beirut: Dār al-Fikr, 1995), 220–27.

(1849–1905) discussed at length what could be meant by *ummah wāḥidah* and concluded that people were guided by their *fiṭrah* ("the innate nature of humans inherent to acknowledging the one creator and submitting to him"), that is, guidance derived of reason (*hidāyat al-ʿaql*). However, when people are left to their own discretion without divine guidance, each starts following his or her personal motives, and thereby dissent and conflict occurs. Hence, there was a need for prophets to guide people and organize their life according to an unbiased divine book.[5] Similarly, the scholar and Qurʾānic exegete Faḍlallah (1935–2010) says that the verse refers to people before they received divine revelation in the forms of divine books and laws through messengers. What united them as one *ummah* was a common creed rather than one religion (i.e., a comprehensive doctrine with its divine laws such as Judaism, Christianity, or Islam). That creed is basically *fiṭrat-Allah*.[6] Then guidance was not based on a specific religious law because they had not received a detailed religious message. Prophet Adam did not bring religious law, unlike the other prophets such as Moses, Jesus, and Muhammad.[7] From that perspective, the word *ummah* relates to the root "*umm*" ("mother"), symbolic of the *fiṭrah* state.

In the premodern period, there is more emphasis on exclusivity, whereby the only means people could be united is by following one true religion (religious law). In the modern period, the understanding is widened to include all humans who are united by their reason and *fiṭrah*. This shift shows how the modern period, witnessing more interaction and globalization, has affected the exegetes' understanding of Qurʾānic concepts. This new hermeneutical reinterpretation opens up the possibility for exploring a richer and more open understanding of the concept and underpinning its theoretical roots before confining it to a specific religious law.

Naṣṣār deduces, based on research into Islamic sources performed so far on the concept of *ummah* in the Qurʾān, that the Qurʾanic perception of the *ummah* is mainly rooted in the dialectic relationship between community and its religious path. The adopted solution for this dialectic

5. Muhammad ʿAbduh and Muhammad Rashīd Riḍā, *Tafsīr al-Manār*, vol. 2 (Egypt: Dār al-Manār, 1954), 278–95.

6. "So set your purpose for religion as a human by nature upright—*fiṭrat-Allah*—in which He has created humans. There is no altering (*the laws of*) Allah's creation. That is the right religion, but most men know not" (Qurʾān 30:30).

7. Muhammad Ḥusayn Faḍlallah, *Min Waḥy al-Qurʾān*, vol. 4 (Beirut: Dār al-Malāk, 1998), 142–46.

is based on the perception of the *ummah* as a community agreeing on following a specific way or path. In this case, the concept of the path takes precedence over the concept of the community, whereby the community becomes known and determined by the path it follows.[8] From this understanding, we find the common expression "the Muslim *ummah*," where *ummah* is determined by the path or religion it follows. Frederick Denny, a Western scholar who has studied the concept of *ummah* in the Qur᾽ān, argues that the *ummah* holds a prominent role in Islam that has no precedent in any other world religion. In his view, the *ummah* had its theoretical foundations in the Qur᾽ān before it crystallized as a social and political entity in Islamic history.[9]

In this chapter, I examine the theoretical aspect of the *ummah*, mentioned by both Naṣṣār and Denny, in the Meccan Qur᾽ānic verses. It is worth noting that there is no mention of "Muslim *ummah*" in the Meccan verses because it was not formed historically during that period of revelation. The Muslim *ummah* was first crystallized later in Medina. This is important for the research objective of this chapter, which explores the concept as a general term without being confined to a specific religious law or path. There are sixty-two verses in the Qur᾽ān where the word *ummah* or its derivative forms are mentioned. This chapter is devoted to the Meccan verses, where I start with the first verse revealed in Mecca; then I group the relevant verses according to a main theme uniting them, such as that of religion, *al-kitāb*, *Imām*, and so forth. The exact chronological order of the Meccan verses had to be sacrificed in order to develop my argument.

Analysis of the Word *Ummah* in the Meccan Verses of the Qur᾽ān

Ummah, Appointed Term (*ajal*), and Associated Responsibility

The first mention of the word *ummah* in the Meccan verses is in *sūrat al-᾽A῾rāf*. "And every *ummah* has its appointed term (*ajal*); when

8. Naṣīf Naṣṣār, *Mafhūm al-Ummah bayna ad-Dīn wal-Tārīkh*, 21.

9. Frederick Denny, "Community and Salvation: The Meaning of the Ummah in the *Qur᾽ān*" (PhD diss., University of Chicago, Illinois, 1974), 3–4.

their term comes, neither can they delay it nor can they advance it an hour" (Qur'ān 7:34). The second time in which *ummah* is related to the context *ajal* in Meccan verses is in *sūrat al-Ḥijr*; "And never have We destroyed any town [for its wrongdoing] but there was a known decree (*kitāb maʿlūm*) for it. [But remember that] no *ummah* can ever anticipate [the end of] its term (*ajalaha*) and neither can they delay [it]" (Qur'ān 15:4–5). There is no striking difference in the interpretation of both premodern and modern scholars regarding these verses.[10] Faḍlallah says the root of the word comes from the verb "*amma*," meaning to lead and leading, which occurs through purpose and intention.[11] Thus, *ummah* is the group that has a common purpose.[12] Purpose shows very clearly in *sūrat al-Qaṣaṣ*; "And when he arrived at the watering (place) in Madyan, he found there an *ummah* of people watering (their flocks), and apart from them he found two women who were keeping back (their flocks). He said: 'What is the matter with you?' They said: 'We cannot water (our flocks) until the shepherds take back (their flocks): And our father is a very old man'" (Qur'ān 28:23). The use of the word *ummah* in this verse shows that the term is related to fulfilling a particular purpose; the *ummah* has a job of watering the flocks. The two women were apart from them because they were not engaging in the same action.

The following verses in *al-ʾAʿrāf* mentioning *ummah* are:

> (Allah) will say: Enter into the Fire among *umam* (pl. of *ummah*) of the jinn and humankind who passed away before you. Every time a new *ummah* enters, it curses its sister *ummah* (that went before) until they will be gathered all together in the Fire. The last of them will say to the first of them: "Our Lord! These misled us, so give them a double torment of the

---

10. At-Ṭabarī interprets *Ummah* in this context as a group of people unified against the one God's messengers and rejecting their advice in At-Ṭabarī, *Jāmiʿ al-Bayān*, vols. 8, 9. Muhammad ʿAbduh interprets *Ummah* as a group of people (*jamāʿa mina-n-nās*) in Muhammad ʿAbduh and Muhammad Rashīd Riḍā, *Tafsīr al-Manār*, vol. 1, 478.

11. At-Ṭabarī's interpretation of verse 15:4–5 also implies a common purpose that unified the people into an *Ummah*, which was rejecting God's messengers. In At-Ṭabarī, *Jāmiʿ al-Bayān*, vols. 8, 9.

12. Faḍlallah, *Min Waḥy al-Qurʾān*, vol. 10, 105.

> Fire." He will say: "For each one there is double (torment), but you know not." Then the first of them will say to the last of them: you had no advantage over us; so taste the chastisement for what you have earned. (Qur'ān 7:38–39)

Premodern exegetes regarded the first *ummah* as the ancestors of the last *ummah* (a new generation): At-Ṭabarī (models exemplary in *milla*)[13] and Al-Qummī (same religious path).[14] However, the modern exegetes interpreted both *umam* as living in the same epoch. ʿAbduh, who witnessed forms of European colonialism, said it could refer to those in power relative to the followers or those less privileged.[15] Fadlallah adds that both *umam* are united intellectually under the banner of *kufr* ("denying the truth"); nevertheless, emotionally they are adversaries who cannot accept their common abode.[16]

In all cases, the last *ummah* blindly follows either the ways of ancestors or those in power on whom it puts the blame and responsibility of its suffering. The Qur'ānic message here rejects blind following (whether in creed or personal choices) by placing equal responsibility on both *umam* and emphasizing the need for intellectual independence. This dialogue shows that each *ummah* is responsible for its own actions and choices. Even in terms of those oppressed in relation to the oppressors, the Qur'anic verses state:

> Verily! As for those whom the angels take (in death) while they are wronging themselves, the (angels) say (to them): "In what (condition) were you?" They reply: "We were weak and oppressed on earth." They (angels) say: "Was not the earth of Allah spacious enough for you to emigrate therein?" Such men will find their abode in Hell—What an evil destination! Except the weak ones among men, women and children who

13. At-Ṭabarī, *Jāmiʿ al-Bayān*, vol. 5, 228.

14. Abū l-Ḥasan ʿAlī b. Ibrāhīm al-Qummī, *Tafsīr al-Qummī*, vol. 1 (Beirut: Dār as-Surūr, 1991), 258.

15. Muhammad ʿAbduh and Muhammad Rashīd Riḍā, *Tafsīr al-Manār*, vol. 8 (Egypt: Dār al-Manār, 1954), 414.

16. Faḍlallah, *Min Waḥy al-Qur'ān*, vol. 10, 120–22.

cannot devise a plan, nor are they able to direct their way. (Qur'ān 4:97–98)

These verses, along with the earlier verses from *sūrat al-A'rāf*, make it clear that there is an individual as well as a collective responsibility for those belonging to an *ummah* because one cannot belong to an *ummah* without making a deliberate choice to be a part of it. This is evident from the concurrent historical events at the time of the latter verses' revelation (*'asbāb an-nuzūl*). At-Ṭabarī reported that these verses were revealed when the Prophet along with the believers were ordered to migrate from Mecca, their hometown, to Medina. Muslims were persecuted and oppressed in Mecca because they rejected their ancestors' religion of idol worship and instead submitted to God. The divine order to migrate to Medina was from one perspective a relief from oppression and at the same time a trial testing the determination and faith of Muslims. Those who claimed submission to God yet refused to migrate were considered deniers until they agreed to do so. Exemption was granted to the weak and the children who could not find the means to implement the action.[17] The same interpretation was endorsed by Al-Qurṭubī.[18]

The modern exegetes added clarifications stemming from their own personal experiences. For example, ʿAbduh, who was exiled from Egypt by the British for six years for supporting the Egyptian nationalist revolt, says that *hijrah* ("migration") was decreed for three reasons: two are related to individuals and one is related to community. First, it is not permissible for a Muslim to dwell in a country where his personal and religious freedoms are forfeited; his staying will result in sinning and harm his integrity. Second, a Muslim who has no knowledge of religious practice should seek this knowledge, even if it leads to his migration. He is obligated to migrate to a place where *ʿulamā'* ("scholars of religion") are available to teach him about his faith and religion. The third reason is related to Muslims as a community (*jamāʿat al-Muslimīn*): Muslims should have a community or strong country that upholds Islam as a religion and a way of life and protects Muslims from their enemies. If this country becomes weak, Muslims are obligated to migrate therein to strengthen it such that

17. At-Ṭabarī, *Jāmiʿ al-Bayān*, vol. 4, 318.

18. Abū Abdallah Muhammad Bin Aḥmad Al-Ansārī al-Qurṭubī, *Mukhtaṣar Tafsīr Al-Qurṭubī*, vol. 1 (Beirut, Cairo: Dār al-Shurūq, 1980), 483.

it can fulfill its obligations. ʿAbduh says that these three conditions were present during the time when Muslims were oppressed in Mecca, and thus it was necessary for them to migrate to Medina.[19] ʿAbduh believed that a society should be able to choose its government based on its history and culture; hence his support of Egyptian nationalism over the British domination. Nonetheless, it is hard to pinpoint whether his religious education influenced his political decisions or vice versa. Sayyid Quṭb[20] supports *hijrah* to the house of Islam (*dār al-Islām*) where a Muslim feels safe to practice his religion and lives a decent life following God's *sharīʿah.*

Faḍlallah also argues for the necessity of Muslims to emigrate from any country where the person is oppressed personally and religiously. The philosophy of migration in Islam is based on freeing human beings from pressure that may hinder personal and religious development. This purposeful transition is meant to advance individuals and weaken, if not remove, oppressive power in society by diminishing such powers' influence. Faḍlallah asserts that migration is part of Islam's intention that seeks the development of individuals and seeks developing a nurturing society, one that is free from oppression and injustices and that reflects Islamic ethics and moral standards.[21]

The premodern exegesis emphasized the individual obligation to migrate as a test from God and a personal relief from oppression. However, the modern exegesis, while still addressing individual benefits, added the importance of establishing a society based on Islamic ethics and *sharīʿah.* Hence there is a shift from the individual to the collective.

While there is a stress on individual obligation for migration in the preceding verses, the historical events proved that personal choice has far-reaching effects on the character and destiny of the *ummah.* Historically, the formation of the Muslim *ummah* in Medina was realized by the individual migration of every single believer, an indispensable act for the well-being of the collective whole. The *ummah* was formed by the collective individual choices of its members. The verses describe the oppressed

19. Muhammad ʿAbduh and Muhammad Rashīd Riḍā, *Tafsīr al-Manār*, vol. 5, 361–62.

20. Sayyid Quṭb, *Fī Ẓilāl al-Qurʾān*, vol. 2 (Beirut, Cairo: Dār al-Shurūq, 1980), 744–45.

21. Faḍlallah, *Min Waḥy al-Qurʾān,* vol. 7, 421–24.

as being unjust to themselves because they chose to favor the oppressor's condition over God's provision of migration and relief.

Combining the previously discussed verses, Faḍlallah's relating the concept of the *ummah* to purpose and direction is reasonable. The first verses relating the *ummah* to an appointed term (*ajal*) urge people to take up their responsibility immediately because the time of one's *ajal* is unknown. The concept of *ajal* implies a deadline in which people are judged. Thus the closer the deadline is approaching, the higher the sense of responsibility and action. This sense of direction, responsibility, and urged action are what characterize the *ummah* as a term distinct from other Qurʾanic and Arabic terms that define a collective of people united by a common culture, place, or heritage, such as *qabīla* ("tribe"), *shaʿb* ("nation"), or *qawm* ("group of people").

Maysam al-Faruqi[22] makes a relevant point in this regard, in which she refutes the Orientalists' understanding of the word *ummah*. Orientalist literature equates *ummah* with a tribe that later took on a religious character, which limits the word to ethnic and linguistic confines. For example, Rudi Paret defines *ummah* as "Ethnical, linguistic or religious bodies of people who are objects of the divine plan of salvation."[23] Al-Faruqi supports her argument against the Orientalists' claim using classical Arabic philology and checking the root meaning of the word *ummah*. The root *amma*, or *amama*, means to seek or go intentionally forward. It also means to walk ahead of someone (group) or to lead, the same root meaning aforementioned by Faḍlallah. Another important root is *umm*, meaning mother, which was used in early Arab society, where matrilineal system prevailed, to denote one's identifying with a specific tradition. At that time, one identified with the maternal tribe's tradition where the husband moves in with the wife's tribe. Al-Faruqi concludes her discussion by saying that all the root meanings make the word *ummah* an active rather than a passive term. *Ummah* becomes a source of identification rather than identity, and she equates *ummah* with a goal.[24] In that sense, *ummah* does not describe

22. Maysam Al-Faruqi, "Ummah: The Orientalists and the Qurʾanic Concept of Identity," *Journal of Islamic Studies* 16, no. 1 (2005).

23. *The Shorter Encyclopedia of Islam*, ed. H. A. R. Gibb and J. H. Kramers (Leiden: E.J. Brill, 1954), s.v. "Ummah."

24. Maysam Al-Faruqi, "*Ummah*: The Orientalists and the Qurʾanic Concept of Identity," 22–24.

a natural trait or physical characteristics, such as ethnicity or color, and thereby cannot accurately represent a tribe, as Orientalists argue. Ethnicity is given, whereas religion is an acquired or elected system of belief.

While al-Faruqi emphasizes the element of choice in the term *ummah*, she highlights the religious dimension as well. She agrees with the primary meaning of the *ummah* used in Muslim literature as "a religious community bound by faith and transcending all other markers of belonging."[25] Al-Faruqi adds the notion that this religion is acquired and voluntarily followed rather than being given or inherited. While I agree with Al-Faruqi on the critical element of choice associated with the term *ummah,* I do not agree with its necessary association with religion. The above Qur᾿anic verses (7:38–39) refer to the dialogue between two different *umam* condemning each other, who are both cast in hellfire irrespective of their religion. It rather lay emphasis on the responsibility of embracing reality and taking active choices in that regard, that is, humans taking responsibility for their life. Religion certainly can be, and has been, transformed into an inherited given identity across history. It can easily be transformed into an inherited identity or traditional customs associated with a certain culture, people, or tribe. In that case, religion is no longer a source of identification, as al-Faruqi asserts. Different religious communities across history have all faced this challenge. According to the Qur᾿ān, that is the main reason why a new prophet was sent after a specific period of time (*ajal*) to people to revitalize their understanding of religion and purify it from the shackles of ossified blind faith. Following the Prophetic period, it became the responsibility of scholars to revive the religion from misguided developments in tradition and focus. Hence, the relationship between the *ummah* and the time (*ajal*) is that the highest potential flourishing of the *ummah* is only realized in those times of revival.

Ummah, Religion, and Forefathers

Religion as an inherited tradition that is blindly followed is admonished in the Qur᾿ān: "When it is said to them: 'Follow what Allah has sent down.' They say: 'No! We shall follow what we found our fathers following.' (Would they do that!) even though their fathers did not understand anything nor were they guided?" (Qur᾿ān 2:170). Thus, the best

25. Ibid., 2.

religion according to the Qurʾān is that which needs exploration and thinking to realize, rather than a religion that takes for granted what has been delivered by the ancestors. The previous verse is followed by rebuking blind followers "And the parable of those who reject guidance is as the likeness of one who calls unto that (flock of sheep) which hears nothing except shouts and cries. Deaf, dumb and blind as they do not understand" (Qurʾān 2:171). It is interesting how the verse uses the parable of a flock of sheep because people (especially when we refer to the masses) are usually led or misdirected by those in power in a very similar way to sheep who are led by a shepherd. They are compelled by external forces as opposed to personal motivation. Thus, the verse suggests counteracting mindless obedience by engaging the senses: listening, exploring, and understanding is what leads to an informed action rather than a blind one. The premodern interpretation of al-Qummī and at-Ṭabarī was literal.

The modern interpretation emphasized the value of reason and conviction before endorsing a specific religion. ʿAbduh, who was against the mindless imitation of tradition and encouraged the use of reason in understanding religious texts, said that a person cannot be a believer unless he thinks about his religion, internalizes it, and reaches conviction (*ʿaqala dīnahu wa ʿarifahu binafsihi ḥatta ʾiqtanaʿa bihi*). He even claims that a person who is trained to submit without using his mind or a person who worships without knowledge is not a believer. According to ʿAbduh, the goal of religion is not to mold human character in a forceful way like an animal is forced and trained to work. Rather, religion is meant to advance mind and soul through knowing the creator and acknowledging his religion. Thus, when a person enjoins good or avoids evil, he understands the benefits of his actions and is aware of their repercussions on his life and existence. His belief is then based on a clear vision and rationale rather than a blind submission to the ways of the forefathers.[26] Along similar lines, Faḍlallah, who also considered reason critical to interpreting religious texts and was himself critical of some historical narrations from the Shiite tradition, says that the Qurʾānic message endorses the attitude of criticizing one's past (*ʿaqlanat al-mawqif minal-māḍī*) because this attitude respects the human's mind and his existence. The human is encouraged to objectively evaluate the rationality of one's past attitudes and positions

26. Muhammad ʿAbduh and Muhammad Rashīd Riḍā, *Tafsīr al-Manār*, vol. 2, 94–95.

before reaching a personal conviction (such as a religion), so that one can counteract potentially irrational emotional attachments to the convictions of forefathers, family, friends, and so forth. Emotional attachments are not equivalent to the truth and do not represent a justification for one's rational choices. The verses emphasize that in choosing a life path, one must exercise reason/cognition (*al-ʿaql*) and maintain conviction through continued contemplation. Cognition represents the foundation for a path based on seeking true knowledge and guidance and a complete awareness of one's responsibilities.[27]

The verses that connect the *ummah* and the concept of inherited religion occur in *sūrat al-Zukhruf*:

> Or have We given them any book (scripture) before this to which they are holding fast? Nay, for they say only: we found our forefathers following a religion or a path (*ʿala ummah*), and, verily, it is in their footsteps that we find our guidance! And thus it is: whenever We sent, before your time, a Warner to any town, those of its people who had lost themselves entirely in the pursuit of pleasures (*mutrafūhā*) would always say, "Behold, we found our forefathers on a certain way and religion (*ʿala ummah*), and, verily, it is but in their footsteps that we follow." (Whereupon each prophet) would say "Why, even though I bring you guidance better than that which you found your forefathers believing in?" They reply: "Verily, we deny that with which you have been sent." (Qurʾān 43:21–24)

The premodern interpretations are once more literally based. Al-Qummī interprets *ʿala ummah* as following a particular sect (*ʿala madhhab*).[28] At-Ṭabarī interprets it as following a particular religion and *milla* ("creed"), which in this case would be idol worship.[29] The modern

27. Faḍlallah, *Min Waḥy al-Qurʾān*, vol. 3, 172–84.

28. Al-Qummī, *Tafsīr al-Qummī*, vol. 2, 287.

29. At-Ṭabarī also mentions a different reading for the word *Ummah*; by changing the vowel of the first letter, it becomes "*ʾimma*," meaning kingship or the imamate of the king and its luxury. However, at-Ṭabarī thinks that the first reading (as *Ummah*) is more relevant in the context of this verse because people typically

interpretations are more critical of the old ways of ancestors and endorse intellectual dialogue. Sayyid Quṭb argues that Islam endorses intellectual freedom and does not accept blind imitation of ancestors. Rather, it calls for thinking and contemplation, for one has to have evidence, then base his choice on certitude.[30] Faḍlallah interprets "*ʿala ummah*" as espousing a certain way of thinking and worship. The logic of blind followers is that history and tradition become sacred in a way that does not allow change, correction of past errors, or self-evaluation. The leaders of those blind followers are usually "*al-Mutrafūn*"[31]: "people extremely spoiled by pleasures of worldly life and who occupy important positions in society." Through these positions, they act as oppressors, opposing any change or reform that could affect their status in society. They seek to preserve the status quo, including antiquated ideas and concepts, and seek to resist intellectual freedom that contradicts their approved ways of thinking or jeopardizes their privileged conditions, even when the introduction of new ideas will better their lives. The question in the last verse, "even if I bring you better guidance than that of your forefathers?," provokes intellectual dialogue, which is critical for reaching a legitimate conclusion about which way to follow. This as well reflects the objective truth brought by messengers, for even their messages should not be followed blindly. However, *al-mutrafūn* prohibit dialogue and endorse a dogmatic attitude of outright rejection.[32]

It is clear that the political conditions facing modern exegetes, whether British colonialism for ʿAbduh, a government that does not tolerate dissent for Quṭb, or sectarian strife and military occupation for Faḍlallah, urged them to provoke intellectual criticism in their writings and thereby call for resisting the status quo. We do not find such an urge in premodern interpretations because the political conditions of the Muslim world were relatively more stable than the modern time.

Combining the verses in this section shows that there is a rationale behind belonging to any *ummah*. The Qurʾānic usage of the word

---

follow a particular religion or path (*minhāj wa ṭarīqa*) rather than follow a path of seeking kingship. In At-Ṭabarī, *Jāmiʿ al-Bayān*, vol. 13, 77–78.

30. Quṭb, *Fī Ẓilāl al-Qurʾān*, vol. 5, 3182.

31. Translated as "luxurious people" by Pickthall, and "wealthy people" by Yusuf Ali, and "those who lead an easy life" by Shakir.

32. Faḍlallah, *Min Waḥy al-Qurʾān*, vol. 20, 225–27.

al-mutrafūn shows the rationale motivating "blind followers": a choice based on preserving one's worldly status in society and maintaining power and control. The verse exposes their real intention, which is not even related to the forefathers but rather to maximize worldly gains. At-Ṭabarī's interpretation is relevant in this case; he reads it as "*ʿala ʾimma*," which he interprets as kingship or luxury.[33] In essence, this implies that there is no "blind" choice; rather, there are always ulterior motives. All the latter confirms that "choice" is an important attribute in defining the concept of *ummah*.

UMMAH AND *AL-KITĀB*

Most Qurʾanic verses dealing with the *ummah* are preceded, followed, or include references to *al-Kitāb*[34] ("the Book") or to synonyms such as *an-Nūr*[35] ("the light"), *al-Ḥaq*[36] ("the Truth"), and *al-Qurʾān*.[37] There is clearly a relationship between the concept of the *ummah* and the book. According to the Qurʾān, the objective truth is present in divine books. However, including *kitāb* in the former verse (43:21) with its general message implies that approaching the divine books with the mentality of preserving the religion of the forefathers or preserving a specific status will be counterfeiting. Sincere intention and an objective dialogue are required for deciphering truth from falsehood. Thereby, the concept of the "Book" is different from inherited religion, as is discussed later in this section.

In *sūrat al-Jāthiya*, each *ummah* has a book: "And you shall see every *ummah* kneeling down; every *ummah* shall be summoned to its book (*kitābiha*); today you shall be recompensed for what you used to do. This our book (*kitābuna*) speaks of you in all truth: for, verily, We have caused to be recorded (copied) all that you ever did!" (Qurʾān 45:28–29).

---

33. At-Ṭabarī, *Jāmiʿ al-Bayān*, vol. 13, 77–78.

34. *Al-Ḥijr* 15:4; *Az-Zukhruf* 43:21; *Al-Muʾminūn* 23:49; *Al-Jāthiya* 45:28–29; *An-Naḥl* 16:64, 16:89; *Ghāfir* 40:1; *Fātir* 35:25; *Al-ʾAʿrāf* 7:169–70; *Al-ʾAnʿām* 6:38.

35. *Al-ʾAʿrāf* 7:157.

36. *An-Naml* 27:79; *Ghāfir* 40:5; *Fātir* 35:24; *Al-ʾAʿrāf* 7:159, 7:181.

37. *Az-Zukhruf* 43:31; *An-Naml* 27:76; *As-Shūra* 42:7; *Yūnus* 10:15.

The interpretations of premodern exegetes Al-Qummī[38] and at-Ṭabarī[39] consider the book a compilation of deeds recorded by angels.

Among the modern exegetes, there are different approaches. For example, Quṭb does not differ from premodern exegesis.[40] On the other hand, Faḍlallah introduces an active term where he interprets the book to represent the "collective responsibility" of each *ummah*. The book embodies its ideas and opinions and unites its members in their decisions and attitudes.[41] This interpretation defines the *ummah* as one entity with a collective will, which is quite different from the premodern exegesis, which simply considers the book as a compiled record of their deeds.

Exegetes[42] think that the usage of the term *kitābiha* ("its book") in the first verse and *kitābuna* ("our book") in the following verse simply implies that the second book is a duplicate copy. However, I think that this distinction is purposeful because the use of the suffix (its book) emphasizes the choice and responsibility of an *ummah* in making its own book and as a result determining its final abode. The second suffix (our book) signifies God's knowledge and his encompassing dominion that is indispensable for judgment and compensation. In that regard, Faḍlallah's interpretation is reasonable, as these verses of *sūrat al-Jāthiya* connect individual responsi-

38. Al-Qummī: the book of the *Ummah* represents their required obligations and deeds (*mā yajib ʿalayhim min ʾaʿmālihim*), *Tafsīr al-Qummī*, vol. 2, 301.

39. At-Ṭabarī: *al-kitāb* represents a copy of the deeds of any *Ummah* written by angels, some called *ḥafaẓa*, *Jāmiʿ al-Bayān*, vol. 13, 201–4.

40. Quṭb, *Fī Ẓilāl al-Qurʾān*, vol. 5, 3233.

41. Faḍlallah, *Min Waḥy al-Qurʾān*, vol. 20, 333–34.

42. Exegetes also think that the book in the above verses could refer to "divine revelation" for two reasons. First, divine revelation also contains stories and deeds of previous nations and information about the future, hence the statement "our book (*kitābuna*) speaks of you in all truth." Second, the use of the verb summoned in the phrase "summoned to its book" implies that each *Ummah* is invited to follow its revealed book that governs its life and dealings; then the *Ummah* will be judged according to whether it followed its own divine book or not. The subsequent verses (45:30–31) clarify a contrast between those who believe in God's signs and others who reject them; hence, as faith is mentioned, the book in the preceding verse could refer to a divine revelation and whether the associated *Ummah* choose to follow or reject it.

bility to the collective responsibility of the *ummah,* similar to what was discussed earlier in *sūrat al-Aʿrāf* (verses 97–98). As an individual will be accountable for a personal book of deeds on judgment day, each *ummah* will be also held accountable before its book.

Other verses that relate the concept of the *ummah* to the book while highlighting the book's function are in *sūrat an-Naḥl:*[43]

> By Allah, We indeed sent (Messengers) to *umam* (plural of *ummah*) before you (Muhammad) but Satan made their deeds fair-seeming to them. So he (Satan) is their guardian today, and they shall have a painful torment. And We have not sent down the Book to you except that you make clear unto them all on which they have come to hold divergent views, and [thus offer] guidance and mercy for people who believe. (Qurʾān 16:63–64)

Premodern exegetes such as At-Ṭabarī[44] and Al-Qurṭubī,[45] as well as modern ones such as Faḍlallah,[46] similarly deduce that the Book in this verse refers to the Qurʾān. Its function is clarifying doubts and misconceptions and providing guidance to the believers. In this verse, they think the book is equivalent to divine revelation where every *ummah* had a messenger and a book sent to it. Satan assumes the opposite function; that is, engendering satisfaction in each *ummah* toward their practices and beliefs such that they cannot accept other ideas as valid. Satan's role is boosting the ego to create separation and conflict. On the other hand, the role of divine books is to resolve differences and create harmony and peace in order to maintain connections between different *umam.* Quṭb[47] confines the Qurʾān, as being the last divine message, to resolving the differences that previous *umam* have disagreed about based on the foundation of

43. The same theme is also in *sūrat Fuṣṣilat* in verses 1–2 and verse 25.

44. At-Ṭabarī, *Jāmiʿ al-Bayān*, vol. 8, 171

45. Abū Abdallah Muhammad Bin Aḥmad Al-Ansārī al-Qurṭubī, *Mukhtaṣar Tafsīr Al-Qurṭubī*, vol. 3 (Beirut: Dār Al-Kitāb al-ʿArabī, 1987), 81.

46. Faḍlallah, *Min Waḥy al-Qurʾān,* vol. 13, 251–52.

47. Quṭb, *Fī Ẓilāl al-Qurʾān*, vol. 4, 2179, 2180.

tawḥīd. He does not interpret the verse generally to include everyone, including Muslims, as the other exegetes alluded to.

However, the Book remains passive without human interpretation, as the saying of *Imām* Ali states: ". . . That Qurʾān interrogate it, it will not speak, but let me tell you about it. Indeed in it is the knowledge of what is to come and the knowledge of the past and it is the cure for your ailments, and the order governing your relationships with each other."[48] This statement shows that the human mind is critical to making the teachings of the book alive and realizable. The above Qurʾānic verse also supports this idea by stating that the Prophet's role is "that [he] make clear unto them all on which they have come to hold divergent views."

Daniel Madigan analyzes the Qur'ān's discourse about itself "*al-kitāb*" in his book *The Qur'ān's Self-Image*. He claims that the concept of the book in the Qur'ān is not what is commonly understood by the notion of a book: a fixed, complete manuscript that is ordered and structured. Madigan argues that the different meanings associated with the word *kitāb* in the Qur'ān, as has been shown in this section, implies a complexity of the Qurʾānic term and points to a unity "that goes deeper than some idea of a heavenly library or archive."[49] By presenting a semantic analysis of the word, Madigan shows that the Qurʾān perceives itself not as a codified text but as an ongoing process of divine writing and rewriting. He supports his argument by the Qurʾānic rejection of the Meccans' request for a physical book that represents Muhammad's calling. The Qurʾān insists that it is rather a gradually unfolding revelation of God responding to developing needs and situations (*al-Tanzīl*). Hence, the word *kitāb* is a symbol of God's authority and infinite knowledge. The finite form of that authority and knowledge is the writing, which Madigan thinks to be the closest translation to the word *kitāb* (with some qualifications). However, the infinite knowledge it is conveying keeps it open and responsive, functioning as the voice of God's ongoing address to humanity. Madigan maintains that Muslims coalesced around the Qurʾān as a direct communication with God while it was still descending on Prophet Muhammad, and this is what united them as an

48. Ali Bin Abī Ṭālib, *Nahju-l-Balāgha*, ed. Muhammad ʿAbduh (Beirut: Muʾassasat al-ʾAʿlamī lil-Maṭbūʿāt, 2003), Sermon 156, 317.

49. Daniel Madigan, *The Qurʾān's Self-Image* (Princeton: Princeton University Press, 2001), 6.

ummah: "the evidence indicates that they coalesced around it while it was still incomplete, still oral, still in process. They committed themselves to believe in a God who had initiated a direct communication with them. They gathered around the recitations as the pledge of God's relationship of guidance to them rather than as a clearly defined and already closed textual corpus."[50] Madigan's analysis confirms the points discussed earlier that divine revelation cannot be treated as inherited religion confined by static laws and regulations. If the book's innate essence is engaging and dynamic, then it inevitably requires an engaging and contemplative follower. Thus, the *ummah* cannot sustain its life without actively engaging with its Book and maintaining its unity through constantly turning to it and abiding by its guiding essence. Nevertheless, it is worth noting that the critical element that preserves such an intrinsic relationship between the *ummah* and its book is precisely the notion of perceiving the book as a dynamic communication with God rather than a codified scripture of archaic beliefs. Madigan's analysis is quite relevant for this research because its conceptual orientation makes it possible to conceptualize a fresh understanding of the *ummah* that corresponds to current conditions.

Ummah and *Imām*

This section examines whether there is a correlation between the *ummah* as a concept and *imām*. The Qur᾽ānic verse correlates *ummah* with a Warner; "Verily we have sent you with the Truth, a bearer of glad tidings and a Warner, and there never was an *ummah* but a Warner (*nadhīr*) had passed among them. And if they reject you, so did their predecessors, to whom came their messengers with clear signs, scriptures, and the book of enlightenment" (Qur᾽ān 35:24–25). There is a consensus among premodern and modern exegetes from the Sunnī tradition, At-Ṭabarī,[51] al-Qurṭubī,[52] and Quṭb,[53] who interpret *nadhīr* as a messenger. Among Shiite exegetes, Al-Qummī interprets *nadhīr* as *Imām*, saying that

50. Ibid., 52.

51. At-Ṭabarī interprets *nadhīr* as a messenger, *Jāmiʿ al-Bayān*, vol. 12, 156.

52. Al-Qurṭubī, *Mukhtaṣar Tafsīr Al-Qurṭubī*, vol. 4, 193.

53. Sayyid Quṭb, *Fī Ẓilāl al-Qur᾽ān*, vol. 5, 2940.

for every time period there is an Imām ("*li-kulli zamān imām*").[54] However, Faḍlallah from the modern period interprets it literally as a warner.[55]

The verse that mentions *imām* in relation to a group of people is "On the day when We shall call every people (*ʾunāsin*) by their (respective) *imām*; So whoever is given his book in his right hand, such will read their book (record), and they will not be wronged in the least" (Qurʾān 17:71).

In this verse, exegetes from both periods across both traditions agreed on similar interpretations for *imām*, yet they differed on their preference for what it could actually mean. First, *imām* can signify a prophet because for every *ummah*, a prophet was sent. Second, it may denote a revealed book such as the Qurʾān, Bible, or Torah, which people may follow in leading their lives. Third, it can refer to an *imām* in the literal sense, meaning a religious leader or scholar to whom people turn for guidance. Fourth, it may refer to the book of their deeds. From the premodern period, At-Ṭabarī,[56] similar to al-Qummī,[57] thinks that the most relevant meaning for this verse is the literal meaning of *imām* because Arabs usually use the word *imām* to refer to a religious leader and a guide. Al-Qurṭubī seems to endorse the fourth interpretation, which is the book of their deeds, so he equates *imām* with *kitāb*.[58] From the modern period, Quṭb[59] does not endorse a specific interpretation. Faḍlallah argues that an initial reading of the verse implies the fourth interpretation; however, he thinks that the first three meanings are also relevant to the context and implication of the fourth meaning. This is because a book of deeds will either contain deeds that are endorsed by or rejected by the teachings of a prophet and

54. Al-Qummī, *Tafsīr al-Qummī*, vol. 2, 210.

55. Faḍlallah, *Min Waḥy al-Qurʾān*, vol. 19, 103.

56. At-Ṭabarī, *Jāmiʿ al-Bayān*, vol. 9, 157–59.

57. Al-Qummī confines the interpretation of *imām* to a religious leader bound by time and place. So people who followed Prophet Muhammad would be in one group (*firqa*), then the followers of *Imām* Ali in another *firqa*, then followers of *Imām* Hussein, then *Imām* Hassan, and so forth. Thus, every group of people would be called by the *Imām* of their time whom they followed, *Tafsīr al-Qummī*, vol. 2, 22.

58. Al-Qurṭubī, *Mukhtaṣar Tafsīr Al-Qurṭubī*, vol. 3, 137. He adds that *imām* could mean "intention" or "mother."

59. Quṭb, *Fī Ẓilāl al-Qurʾān*, vol. 4, 2241.

the divine book sent through him, or judged according to the teachings of a scholar who follows the way of the Prophet and the divine book. So God identifies people with the symbol they associate themselves with, whether it is a prophet, a book, or a leader, any model by which one can lead a life. The people's frame of reference, which guides their lives, is what determines their acts and deeds.[60] Despite that Faḍlallah's interpretation appears to be more inclusive of the human experience in its diversity, I think that the literal interpretation as *imām* by at-Ṭabarī and al-Qummī is more reasonable.

The critical question is: how is the *ummah* as a concept related to *imām*? By literally comparing the verses "every *ummah* shall be summoned to its Book" (Qurʾān 45:28) and "We shall call every people (*ʾunāsin*) by their *imām*" (Qurʾān 17:71), we see that there is no mention of the word *ummah* in the latter verse. The *ummah* is "called to" its book, while people are "called by" their *imām*. The apparent connotation in the previous verses is that people are identified with their *imām*, who can be a prophet, a book, or an *imām*, while the *ummah* is identified with its book. *While individuals are judged according to their subjective choices, an ummah is judged by its book, which is more objective, because it represents a collection of individuals' subjective judgments.* A critical implication follows in defining the concept of the *ummah*; it can be characterized as a community composed of individuals sharing the same book, yet individuals interpret the book differently. A book serves not only to unify an *ummah*, but to provide specific ethics and an order to guide its members. Nonetheless, while the book seems to be the uniting factor for the *ummah*, the book still needs an interpreter and an executer, as *Imām* Ali said earlier: the book will not speak for itself or implement itself. Evidently, the *ummah* needs an *imām* or a leader to maintain its unity.

Taking a closer look at the prophetic practice, we can decipher which concept takes precedence in the definition of the *ummah*. The constitution drafted by Prophet Muhammad in Medina, discussed in detail in chapter 3, was drafted as an attempt to regulate the differences between the conflicting tribes of Medina and establish their affairs peacefully. In essence, this constitution was a means to create a unified *ummah*, an *ummah* composed of different *umam* ("plural of *ummah*"), with each *ummah* adhering to

60. Faḍlallah, *Min Waḥy al-Qurʾān*, vol. 14, 186–87.

its own Book (i.e., Muslim and Jewish scriptures), nevertheless unified by a common constitution (i.e., another book that guides their relationship with each other) and a common leader (Prophet Muhammad). In the Medina Constitution (MC), the first decree states: "This is *kitāb* ("book/writing") from Muhammad the Prophet between the believers and Muslims of Quraysh and Yathrib and those who follow them, join them and fight along with them." The second decree states: "They form an *ummah* apart from the people." Examining the order of the decrees in the MC, it is obvious that the concept of the book and the leader preceded that of the *ummah*. However, the MC ends with: "47—This book (*al-kitāb*) shall not protect the perpetrator of an unjust act or crime from punishment. Whoever goes out shall have security and whoever remains in Medina shall also have security; except one who commits an unjust act or a crime. Allah protects the person who observes undertakings and keeps free of dishonorable acts and offences, and Muhammad the messenger of Allah, Allah bless and honor him." It is interesting that the last decree specifies that the "book," rather than the prophet, will not protect those who commit injustice. Besides, the first decree states that the book is "from Mohammad" . . . "between" the different members rather than "to" the members, thereby implying that this book was not imposed from the leader on the people, but a drafted document that was drafted between them based on their participation and consent. Other decrees such as decree 22 show that people consented to the content of the book: "It is not lawful for any believer approving the contents of this treaty. . . ." The raised points imply that individuals joining the *ummah* are bound by the decrees of its book, rather than a subjective ruling of a leader. Prophet Mohammad is mentioned in the first and last decrees, as the drafter of the constitution, the protector of its decrees, and as the chosen leader. Therefore, I think that the leader takes the role of the executive, ensuring the implementation of the ethics and rulings of the book, rather than the foundation upon which the *ummah* is formed and defined. While the existence of a leader is crucial for the success of *ummah*, the book is predominant in its formation. *An ummah is an active community that is always seeking unity based on its book of guidance and thereby founds its leadership, so it is a collective effort of different individuals.*

Among the Shiite exegetes, al-Qummī, identifies the *ummah* with its *imām*. For example, in *sūrat al-ʾAʿrāf* (verses 38–39) discussed earlier, he interprets the *ʾumam* cursing each other in the fire as *ʾaʾimmat al-jūr* ("oppressive leaders").[61] Also in the Medinan verses (Qur᾽ān 2:143), which are discussed in the next chapter, he interprets *ummah wasaṭ*[62] ("middle *ummah*") as *᾽a᾽immat ʿadl* ("just *a᾽imma*, who are mediators between the Prophet and the people").[63] In earlier verses (43:21–24), al-Qummī interprets *ʿala ummah* as *ʿala madhhab* ("following a particular sect"),[64] that is, people who follow a particular *imām* who follows a particular school of thought. While I do not agree with al-Qummī's identifying an *ummah* by its *imām* for the reasons discussed above, I think that al-Qummī's associating *ummah* with *imām* reflects the Shīʿīte school of thought whereby the *imām* holds a central position for believers. It is interesting, though, that we do not see a similar interpretation in Faḍlallah's exegesis. This exemplifies my earlier point that individuals, despite their abiding by the same scripture or even school of thought in this case, are still subjective in their understanding and judgment. The centrality of the *imām* to al-Qummī is evidenced in his exegesis frequently interpreting the Qur᾽ānic verses in relation to *Imām* Ali and his progeny. This is not the case in Faḍlallah's exegesis.

Ummah and the Covenant (*al-Mīthāq*)

The Qur᾽ān establishes a strong connection between the concept of a divine book and a written treaty or contract between individuals. Any revelation or divine guidance is actually a covenant, called *mīthāq* in Qur᾽anic context, between God and the believers. This is shown in the following verses:

> And (remember) when We took a covenant (*mīthāq*) from the children of Israel, (saying): Worship none but Allah (alone) and be dutiful and good to parents, and to kindred, and to orphans and the poor, and speak good to people and establish prayers and give charity, then you refrained, except a few of you, in rejection. And (remember) when We took your covenant

61. Al-Qummī, *Tafsīr al-Qummī*, vol. 1, 258.

62. This term is discussed in detail in chapter 2.

63. Al-Qummī, *Tafsīr al-Qummī*, vol. 1, 191.

64. Ibid., vol. 2, 287.

(saying): shed not the blood of your (people), nor turn out your own people from their dwellings. Then, (this) you ratified and (to this) you bear witness. (Qur'ān 2:83–84)

From the premodern period,[65] At-Ṭabarī interprets *mīthāq* by dissecting its grammatical roots,[66] thereby showing its relation to a binding document *wathīqa*,[67] a form of law that in this case is the Qur'ān, a book specifying God's commands and his prohibitions. The verses show that the Qur'ānic *mīthāq* not only binds a person from wrong actions but also from wrong speech. The presence of a *wathīqa* is indispensable to verify an individual's verbal pledge. Similarly, from the modern period, Faḍlallah emphasizes that *mīthāq* is a covenant that requires verbal expression (*lā yakūn illa bil-qawl*).[68] Additionally, he suggests that the Qur'ān regards *sharīʿah* as a covenant between God and his worshippers because complying with *sharīʿah* means endorsing its values, similar to one abiding by his pledge. Thus, disobedience becomes equivalent to betraying one's oath, making it a form of self-betrayal.[69]

ʿAbduh relates the covenant to the *ummah* whereby keeping up one's covenant by fulfilling God's commandments will lead to the *ummah's* success. For example, refraining from killing another soul makes a person feel that his soul is the same as the other, thus strengthening the feeling of unity among the members of an *ummah*. Moreover, ʿAbduh adds that shifting the addressee in verse 83 from the early generation of Israel who took a covenant with God (We took *mīthāq* from the children of Israel) to directly addressing the current generation (then you refrained) reflects

65. Both Al-Qummī and Al-Qurṭubī did not address the interpretation of *mīthāq* in Al-Qummī, *Tafsīr al-Qummī*, vol. 1, 79, and Al-Qurṭubī, *Mukhtaṣar Tafsīr Al-Qurṭubī*, vol. 1, 88.

66. At-Ṭabarī, *mīthāq* is equivalent to the form *mifʿāl* of the word *wathīqa* ("binding document"), meaning abiding by a legal document (i.e., law) through taking *yamīn* ("an oath") or making *ʿahd* ("a covenant"), *Jāmiʿ al-Bayān*, vol. 1, 462. At-Ṭabarī adds that the usage of the word *mīthāq* specifically, and not the word oath, for example, is to emphasize guaranteeing the oath (*at-tawāthuq bil-yamīn*), *Jāmiʿ al-Bayān*, vol. 1, 548.

67. The Medina Constitution is also referred to as "*wathīqat al-Madīna*."

68. Faḍlallah, *Min Waḥy al-Qur'ān*, vol. 2, 109.

69. Ibid., 119–20.

a connection between earlier and later generations of one *ummah*. The life of an *ummah* across time can be represented by the life of a person whose actions as a young person affect his life as an adult. Similarly, actions of earlier generations of an *ummah* leave an imprint on later generations and inevitably affect the latter's behavior. So members of an *ummah* are also united throughout history.[70] This modern exegesis takes into consideration the time factor and its effects on the performance on an *ummah*, whereas the premodern exegetes do not address this point. While ʿAbduh was facing the challenges of British imperialism and witnessing the disintegration of the Ottoman Empire, he was more aware and critical of the historical conditions that led the *ummah* in that direction.

The concept of covenant shows as well between the prophets and their lord:

> And (remember) when Allah took the covenant of the prophets (*mīthāq an-nabiyyīn*), saying: "If, after all the revelation and the wisdom (*kitāb wal ḥikma*) which I have given you, there comes to you a messenger confirming the truth already in your possession, you must believe in him and support him. Do you—said He—'acknowledge and take this my covenant as binding on you?' " They answered: "We do acknowledge it." He said: "Then bear witness [thereto], and I am with you among the witnesses." (Qurʾān 3:81)

The premodern exegesis of Al-Qummī[71] and At-Ṭabarī[72] was literal. The modern exegesis again included the *ummah* in its interpretation. ʿAbduh said that the prophets will act as witnesses against their *umam*. Moreover, ʿAbduh says that the essence of the verse is the oneness of

70. Muhammad ʿAbduh and Muhammad Rashīd Riḍā, *Tafsīr al-Manār*, vol. 1, 371–72.

71. Al-Qummī adds that every prophet took a pledge with God to inform his *Ummah* about the coming of Prophet Muhammad, *Tafsīr al-Qummī*, vol. 1, 134.

72. At-Ṭabarī reports a ḥadīth by *Imām* Ali saying that God took the covenant with every prophet to support Prophet Muhammad and ask his people to support him as well. At-Ṭabarī adds that the prophets referred to in this verse are *ʾahl al-kitāb*. At-Ṭabarī continues that the verse not only implies the prophets but their *umam*, followers, as well, *Jāmiʿ al-Bayān*, vol. 3, 450–52.

God's religion (*tawḥīd*), which is the same religion of Abraham and the rest of the messengers.[73] Faḍlallah elaborated on the latter idea by saying that prophets are not humans separate from each other in their ideology, behavior, and goals, and they do not act according to their personal whims. On the contrary, prophethoods represent a series of interconnected stages that complete and complement each other. Each prophet delivers a message that is suited to its time and concurrently completes what the previous prophet delivered and prepares the stage for the message of the following prophet. The verse clarifies these complementary stages through covenants whereby each prophet takes a covenant with God to deliver his message and support the subsequent prophet; a recurring progression takes place across human history. Then the same covenant undertaken by the prophets will be also upheld by their followers. Faḍlallah adds that the use of the word *kitāb* ("book") refers to the realm of theory, and the word *ḥikma* ("wisdom") refers to the realm of practice and implementing God's law.[74]

The following verses relate the concept of the covenant to the *ummah*:

> And be true to your bond with God (*ʿahd Allah*) whenever you bind yourselves by a pledge, and do not break [your] oaths after having [freely] confirmed them and having called upon Allah to be witness to your good faith: behold, Allah knows all that you do. Hence, be not like her[75] who breaks and completely untwists the yarn which she [herself] has spun

---

73. Muhammad ʿAbduh and Muhammad Rashīd Riḍā, *Tafsīr al-Manār*, vol. 3, 350–53.

74. Faḍlallah, *Min Waḥy al-Qurʾān*, vol. 6, 134–36.

75. At-Ṭabarī and Faḍlallah mention the story of a woman in Mecca who was called the "silly woman" because she had a strange habit. The woman used to spin her yarn, and upon its completion she would undo all that she had accomplished. So God used the example of this silly woman to show the effect of breaking one's oath after taking it. They also reported a practice among some Arab tribes who would exploit the use of covenants and verbal oaths to facilitate their betrayal of people. As soon as they received the benefits they were seeking, they would break their covenants. Thus, in these verses God warns people against using covenants as tools of deception. In At-Ṭabarī, *Jāmiʿ al-Bayān*, vol. 8, 218–20, and Faḍlallah, *Min Waḥy al-Qurʾān*, vol. 13, 285–87.

> and made strong—[be not like this by] using your oaths as a means of deceiving one another, simply because some *ummah* may be more powerful than another. Thereby, Allah puts you to a test and [He does it] so that on Resurrection Day He will certainly make clear to you (the truth of) that on which you differed. For, had Allah so willed, He could surely have made you all one single *ummah* (*ummah wāḥidah*); however, He lets go astray him that wills [to go astray], and guides aright him that wills [to be guided]; and you will surely be called to account for all that you ever did. (Qurʾān 16:91–93)

The premodern exegesis of al-Qummī[76] and at-Ṭabarī[77] consider *ummah wāḥidah* as people with one creed (*milla*). The modern exegete Faḍlallah suggests a more rational argument: people would have been one *ummah* on the path of guidance if belief were compulsory. However, because God ennobled humans with free will and provided them with the tools of thinking and judgment, it was inevitable that people would differ and not be one *ummah*. Faḍlallah concludes that variety and difference among people is an existential and purposefully constructed reality (*at-tanawuʿ ḥaqīqa wūjūdiya*).[78] Quṭb interprets the verses in light of nation-state conflict. He argues against states breaking their covenant with each other based on pragmatic state interests (*maṣlaḥat ad-dawla*). He clarifies that this would be considered cheating from an Islamic perspective. He thereby introduces the concept of the Islamic group (*al-jamāʿa al-islāmiyya*) and the need for establishing the Islamic state, which guarantees trusting and peaceful relations between states on a global level.[79] There is a noticeable shift in the modern interpretation of these verses

76. Al-Qummī interprets *Ummah* in this verse as an *imām*: *ʾan takūn ʾaʾimma hiya ʾazka min ʾaʾimmatikum* ("that there will be *aʾimma* who are purer than your *aʾimma*"). Then he interprets the test to be the Imamate of Ali—whether individuals accepted or rejected his Imamate. *Ummah wāḥidah* according to al-Qummī is the *Ummah* that follows the same *madhhab* and same goal, Al-Qummī, *Tafsīr al-Qummī*, vol. 1, 421.

77. At-Ṭabarī, *Jāmiʿ al-Bayān*, vol. 8, 218–20.

78. Faḍlallah, *Min Waḥy al-Qurʾān*, vol. 13, 286.

79. Quṭb, *Fī Ẓilāl al-Qurʾān*, vol. 4, 2191–92.

based on the historical conditions of the exegetes. Faḍlallah, who lived in a nation-state torn by sectarian wars, recognized and accepted that diversity in belief is an ongoing reality. Alternatively, the premodern exegetes saw the world through the lens of the Muslim empires existing then, which made it possible to conceive of an *ummah* united under one belief. Quṭb, on the other hand, was dealing with European colonialism and its exploitation of the weaker Arab nation-states. He felt that the solution was in the establishment of an Islamic state based on the vision of the Muslim brotherhood.

The discussion so far in this chapter has shown that the *ummah* as a Qur'ānic concept is based on choice and the concept of the book (whether divine revelation or a treaty). This section clarified that divine revelation is a form of a covenant between an individual and his creator. Therefore, the concept of the covenant is an added attribute to the Qur'ānic term *ummah*. *A community becomes an* ummah *when it enters a covenant with God to follow a specific book revealed through a messenger. In addition, a group of people agreeing to live together and establish their living through a covenant, a pact, or a treaty also form an* ummah. Their covenant with each other is actually a covenant with God, as shown in the verse "And be true to your bond with God (*ʿahd Allah*) whenever you bind yourselves by a pledge, and do not break [your] oaths after having [freely] confirmed them and having called upon Allah to be witness to your good faith: behold, Allah knows all that you do" (Qur'ān 16:91). This verse shows that any covenant made between people represents in its essence a pledge to God who is the guarantor and the witness. The concept of the witness in relation to the *ummah* is described in *sūrat al-Qaṣaṣ*[80] "And from each *ummah* we shall take out a witness (*shahīd*),[81] and We

80. The theme that each *Ummah* has a witness (*shahīd*) in the Meccan chapters is also visible in *sūrat an-Naḥl*, verse 84.

81. Al-Qummī interprets *shahīd* as *imām*, Al-Qummī, *Tafsīr al-Qummī*, vol. 2, 144. At-Ṭabarī interprets *shahīd* as a prophet who will witness against each *Ummah*, At-Ṭabarī, *Jāmiʿ al-Bayān*, vol. 11, 127. Faḍlallah provides a more inclusive interpretation where *shahīd* can be any person who lived in the *Ummah*, experienced its conditions, and has a good knowledge of its ideas and inclinations. He adds that God does not need a witness because his knowledge encompassed everything, but having a witness represents a proof against unjust people and an assurance of God's justice before everybody, Faḍlallah, *Min Waḥy al-Qur'ān*, vol. 17, 331.

shall say: "bring your proof": then they shall know that Allah (alone) has the Truth, and all what they forged will have forsaken them" (Qurʾān 28:75). The concept of the witness against a specific *ummah* becomes more relevant when speaking of covenants because usually taking an oath requires witnesses to the act. The concept of the witness is introduced in the Meccan verses but becomes clearer in the Medinan verses, which are discussed in the next chapter.

A Possible Order of a Global *Ummah* Composed of Different *Umam*?

Analyzing the verses (16:91–93), we find that the last verse (93) discusses human nature, which is inherently diverse, whereas the second verse (92) employs metaphorical imagery to convey the effective means to deal with differences. The anecdote of the woman spinning her yarn and the specific usage of the words "interwoven yarn" or wool fabric effectively illuminates the concept of an *ummah* based on a covenant or a set of covenants. This *ummah* in its structure resembles the making of a strand of yarn, each thread connected to the other and critical to maintaining the structure of the whole strand. The loss of one thread will result in an imperfect structure. If we imagine each thread representing a single *ummah*, their coming together through bonds of covenants will result in the formation of an inclusive *ummah* that is unified and strengthened by its interconnected relationships, similar to that of an interwoven piece of yarn (figure 1.1). Upholding those

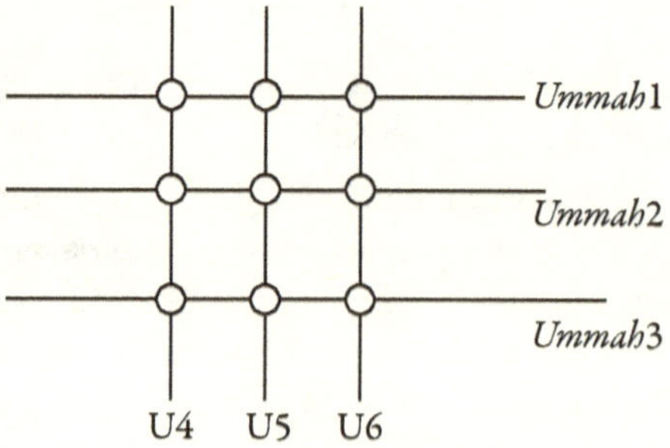

Figure 1.1. The networked global structure of the *Ummah*, each circle represents a covenant between two *umam*.

covenants, or bonds, is critical to the integrity of the whole *ummah*. The verse warns against breaking one of those covenants for the sake of worldly gains. The verse warns that while a strong *ummah* may be deceived by the insignificance of maintaining a relationship with a weak *ummah*, the loss of this bond will weaken both *umam*. Thus, an inclusive *ummah* composed of different *umam* cannot maintain its unity and its strength without upholding its established covenants. In the Medina Constitution, we find three representations of covenantal *ummah*, as is discussed in chapter 2. First is the Muslim *ummah* whose covenant is based on following the Qurʾān, as a divine book. Second is the Jewish *ummah* whose covenant is based on the divine book of the Torah. Third is the inclusive *ummah* of the Constitution (treaty) whose covenant is based on following its decrees, and thereby unifying both *umam*.

There is a similar metaphor in the prophetic *ḥadīth* of how different *umam* across human history have been connected and intertwined. This connection resonates with the earlier verse that describes how all prophets made a covenant with God to support each other, and how the divine message was meant to be delivered through different complementary prophets. Prophet Muhammad said: "My similitude in comparison with the other prophets before me, is that of a man who has built a house nicely and beautifully, except for a place of one brick in a corner. The people go about it and wonder at its beauty, but say: 'Would that this brick be put in its place!' So I am that brick, and I am the last of the Prophets."[82] This *ḥadīth,* similar to the last Qurʾanic verses discussed (16:92–93), shows that each prophet has a specific role in the whole prophetic history. Nevertheless, the prophets' roles are interdependent; the absence of a prophet, like the missing of a thread in the knit, will result in an imperfect structure. The same idea applies to different *umam*: each *ummah* has a specific role in

82. Al-Bukhārī, *Al-Jāmiʿ as-Ṣaḥīḥ, Kitāb al-Manāqib*, *ḥadīth* no. 3535, vol. 2 (Beirut: Dār Iḥyāʾ al-Turāth al-ʿArabī, 1980), 513. It is also narrated in Ṣaḥīḥ Muslim by Jabir binʿAbdullah: "The similitude of mine and that of the prophets is like that of a person who built a house and he completed it and made it perfect, except for the space of a brick. People entered therein and they were surprised at it and said: Had there been a brick (it would have been complete in all respects). Allah's Messenger (may peace be upon him) said: I am that place where the brick (completing the building is to be placed), and I have come to finalize the chain of prophets."

human history; even one's absence cannot be endured if the fulfillment of the divine will for humanity is to be realized.

Ummah, *Ummī* Prophet, and the Global *Ummah*

The latter discussion makes it inevitable to explore the connotation of the word *ummī*, which has the same root as the word *ummah* and appears twice in *sūrat al-ʾAʿrāf.*

"Those who follow[83] the messenger, the *ummī* Prophet, whom they find mentioned in their own (scriptures), the Torah and the Gospel; for he commands them what is just and forbids them what is evil; he makes lawful for them the good (and pure) and prohibits them from what is bad (and impure); he releases them from their heavy burdens and from the shackles that are upon them. So those who believe in him, honor him, help him, and follow the light which is sent down with him, it is they who will prosper" (Qurʾān 7:157).

The premodern exegesis provide three interpretations for the term *ummī.* The most common are people who are illiterate, people who do not read or write, or people who are unscriptured, meaning people who

83. This verse describes the characteristics of believers and the rationale behind their belief, which stands opposite to the blind followers spoken of in earlier verses (2:170–71). It starts with the verb "follow"; however, it shows that there are a series of steps to reach the "conclusion" of following a specific way of life. First, earlier scriptures are referenced in urging people to check the validity of a scripture before deciding to follow it; again here we see the emphasis on exploration before affiliation. Then described are the benefits associated with following the Messenger and the light (revelation) that came to him, and how his message liberates humans from the chains imposed by society, misinterpretation of earlier scriptures, and abuses of power. In the ideal case, belief becomes a constantly active choice rather than a blind faith ruled by dogma. This constantly active choice is equivalent to the continuous act of *tawḥīd* ("Islamic monotheism"). Grammatically, *tawḥīd* is an intensive gerund form of the verb "*waḥḥada*" ("to unify"). That is why belief in the one God (*tawḥīd*) cannot be a dogma, because it involves a continuous act or choice of unifying. The verse emphasizes that only those who are blessed with that kind of belief are the prosperous. It is worth mentioning here that this active belief does not amount to the same idea of religion mentioned by Al-Faruqi earlier.

have no knowledge of the earlier scriptures of the Jews and Christians. All three definitions met the condition of Arabs before Islam. The following verse describing prophet Muhammad sums up both definitions: "Neither did you (Muhammad) read any book before it (this Qur'ān), nor did you write any book with your right hand. In that case, indeed, the followers of falsehood might have doubted" (Qur'ān 29:48). Frederick Denny[84] studied the Western scholars' interpretation of the word *ummī* (unscriptured, heathen, and gentiles) and concluded that the best expression to distinguish the Arabs from Jews and Christians would be unscriptured. The third meaning, which is less common, is mentioned in al-Qurṭubī[85] and At-Ṭabarī.[86] Al-Qurṭubī said that the term *ummī* is related to the *ummī ummah* (i.e., the illiterate *ummah*) where the Prophet said "we are an *ummī ummah,* we don't write and we don't calculate." So the Prophet was described in relation to his *ummah* that was illiterate.

Another interpretation is that the Prophet is described in relation to *Umm al-Qura* ("the mother of the villages"), which is his hometown, Mecca. At-Ṭabarī relates the word *ummī* to the *ummah* of Prophet Muhammad irrespective of literacy. At-Ṭabarī mentioned this interpretation without explaining the relationship between *ummī* and *ummah*, a link that I would like to explore. At-Ṭabarī as well as ʿAbduh[87] from the modern period also mentioned that prophet Muhammad is the only prophet in the Qur'ān to be given the adjective "*al-ummī*." Thus, there must be something more in the word *ummī* than illiterate and unscriptured.

The following verses show that prophet Muhammad may be described as *ummī* in relation to his *ummah*, as at-Ṭabarī stated. In the previous verse, the Prophet is described as "the messenger, the *ummī* Prophet . . . for he commands them what is just and forbids them what is evil . . ." (Qur'ān 7:157), and this is the same description his *ummah* is characterized by in the Qur'ān: "You were the best *ummah*, ever raised up to humankind, for

84. Frederick Denny, "The Meaning of Ummah in the Qur'ān," *History of Religions* 15, no. 1 (August, 1975): 39–42.

85. Abū Abdallah Muhammad Bin Aḥmad Al-Ansārī al-Qurṭubī, *al-Jāmiʿ li-'Aḥkām al-Qur'ān*, vol. 7 (Beirut: Dār 'Iḥyā' al-Turāth al-ʿArabī, 1985), 298–99.

86. At-Ṭabarī, *Jāmiʿ al-Bayān*, vol. 6, 111.

87. Muhammad ʿAbduh and Muhammad Rashīd Riḍā, *Tafsīr al-Manār*, vol. 9, 225.

you command what is just and forbid what is evil and believe in Allah . . ." (Qur'ān 3:110). Because both the Prophet and his *ummah* are described by the same attribute of commanding what is just and forbidding what is evil, there must be a relationship between *ummī* and *ummah*. If this assumption is true, then a reasonable question would be why Prophet Muhammad is the only one described in relationship to the *ummah*. All prophets were sent to specific *umam*, but none of them was given that specific description.

The life of Prophet Muhammad reveals an organic connection between the leader and his *ummah*. We see instances when the opinion of the *ummah* goes against the leader's opinion (in the battle of *'uḥud*), but the Prophet still followed their advice and they lost the battle. Nevertheless, God reveals that despite their mistake, the Prophet should still consult them before making a decision. Prophet Muhammad's perseverance and patience with his people affected their overall behavior. God says in the Qur'ān, ". . . He is the one who supported you with his victory and with the believers" (Qur'ān 8:62). *So, the believers later became an indispensable element for the health and continuity of the message. The emphasis in earlier prophetic periods seemed to be on the individual prophet; later it shifted to the relationship between prophets and the believers who share a symbiotic relationship.* This relationship did not end with the physical death of the Prophet but continued afterward, as exemplified by Muslims' continued blessing of the Prophet and his family in every prayer (it is a crucial part of the ritual *ṣalāt*). Moreover, the relationship is projected to reach its ultimate culmination on the Day of Judgment, where Prophet Muhammad is the only prophet who is given the privilege to grant his *shafā'a* ("intercession") on behalf of his *ummah*. This is shown in the *ḥadīth*: "Every prophet has an invocation that will be answered; and every prophet hastened in his invocation, but I withheld my invocation so that I may intercede for my people on the Day of Judgment . . ."[88]

Another important point that strengthens the link between *ummī* and *ummah* is examining to what *ummah* Prophet Muhammad was sent. Is this *ummah* restricted to Muslims? Or is it restricted exclusively to the Arab Bedouins present at the time of the Prophet who were known to

88. Abū al-Ḥusayn Muslim Bin al-Ḥajjāj al-Qushayrī al-Naysābūrī, *Ṣaḥīḥ Muslim, Kitāb al-Īmān* (Riyāḍ: Maktabat al-Rushd, 2001), 64.

be illiterate, as Al-Qurṭubī claims? The following Qur'anic verse negates the latter two claims:

> Say "O humankind! Verily, I am sent to you all as the Messenger of Allah—to whom belongs the dominion of the heavens and the earth. There is no deity except him (the one God). It is He who gives life and causes death." So believe in Allah and His Messenger, the *ummī* prophet, who believes in Allah and His Words (this Qur'ān, Torah and Gospel, etc. . . .) and follow him so that you may be guided. (Qur'ān 7:158)

This verse, which directly follows the previously studied verse from *sūrat al-A'rāf*, further reveals the meaning of the word *ummī* and, I would argue, links it to the *ummah*. In this verse, it is clear that Prophet Muhammad is sent to all people from the Qur'anic usage of the words "humankind" and "all" and the fact that he believes in all God's words that include all prophets and revelations that preceded him. This verse indicates that the *ummah* Prophet Muhammad was sent to is meant to have the potential to encompass all humankind. Besides his description as a messenger and a prophet, he is specifically described as "*ummī*," which is a characteristic, I suggest, related to his being sent to inspire a potential global *ummah*. His being the last prophet, as attested in Islam, makes the idea more conceivable. Previous prophets were usually sent to a specific people, which is a mission Prophet Muhammad fulfilled as a "prophet" and "messenger," but in addition to serving his own people, he was sent to humankind; that is most likely why we find this third description of him as "*ummī*." Now the picture is complete as *'ar-rasūl, an-nabī, al-ummī'* ("the messenger, the prophet, the *ummī*"). I think that the universal community has the potential to organize itself as a global *ummah* based on interrelated covenants to achieve a peaceful global order of mutual benefit, if it chooses to do so. Thereby, *ummah* as a concept upholds a universal prospective that is not limited to Muslims but is open to anyone who recognizes its merit and acknowledges the benefit in implementing its structure.

Besides, looking at the description following the word *ummī* in both verses, "the *ummī* Prophet, whom they find mentioned in their own (scriptures), the Torah and the Gospel and "the *ummī* prophet, who believes in Allah and His Words (Qur'ān, Torah and Gospel, etc. . . .)," we find a link between the word "*ummī*" and earlier scriptures and their people. From the Prophet's perspective, he has a covenant with God to confirm and support all messengers before him and their scriptures, as discussed earlier. From another perspective, if a prophet is to be sent to a certain people, there must be a connection between him and those people for his message to be meaningful and relate to them. In this case, the verses show that earlier scriptures (Torah and Gospel) specifically speak of the coming of Prophet Muhammad. Thus, there is again here a reciprocal relationship maintained between the messenger and his *ummah*, whether they are literally from his own people and culture or are related to him through previous messengers who shared the same belief and goal. The link between the Prophet's description of "*ummī*" and earlier scriptures and its people is that they are all part of a potential global *ummah* who shares a common destiny and has a common responsibility.

From the modern period, Quṭb defines the *ummah* ideologically as a universal concept. According to Quṭb, the *ummah* represents a group of believers irrespective of their race, gender, color, and nationality. He believes that the Qur'anic view of the *ummah* is based on belief rather than materialistic considerations.[89] Accordingly, Prophet Muhammad is described as *ummī* because his message is complete and is not confined by particular people, land, or generation. All messages before him were local messages addressing specific people and limited to a particular period of time. Every new message included some changes in *sharīʿah* that would suit the development of humanity, in a way that prepared humanity for receiving the final message. The final message came complete in its basic principles, as it completed previous messages and allowed renewal and flexibility in its derived applications. It came to the global *ummah* because it matches the innate nature of all humans (*fiṭrah ʾinsāniyya*). Quṭb describes the *ummī* prophet as one who had a pure *fiṭrah* based solely on God's teachings, untouched by worldly experiences and people's ideas. His message was a message of the *fiṭrah* meant to address the *fiṭrah* of all people.[90] Quṭb's idea provides a theological perspective about the relationship between *ummah* and *ummī*, which supports my earlier argument. Nonetheless, my perspective adds a sociopolitical perspective to the concepts that could be applied universally.

89. Sayyid Quṭb, *Fī Ẓilāl al-Qurʾān*, vol. 1, 113.

90. Ibid., vol. 3, 1379.

Ummah and Sovereignty

Leadership, the Book, and Justice

The following verses from the latter part of *sūrat al-Aʿrāf* will shed some light on the *ummah*'s responsibility: "And of the people (*qawm*) of Moses there is an *ummah* who guide (people) with the truth and thereby establish justice" (Qurʾān 7:159), and a similar verse in the same *sūra*: "And of those whom we have created, there is an *ummah* who guides (others) with the truth, and thereby establish justice" (Qurʾān 7:181). In these verses, it is evident that there is a difference between the meaning of a group of people (*qawm*) and an *ummah*. It shows that not all the people of Moses will be part of his *ummah*, rather only those who are guided by the truth (the Holy Scripture) and who establish justice by it. Here there is an added dimension to the *ummah*—its leadership's purpose is establishing justice. The inclusion of leadership in the concept of the *ummah* is further implied in the following verse of the same *sūra al-Aʿrāf*:

> And We divided them into twelve (*ʾasbāṭan*) tribes, *umam* (plural of *ummah*). We revealed to Moses when his people asked him for water, (saying): "Strike the stone with your stick," and there gushed forth out of it twelve springs, each group of people (*ʾunās*) knew its own place for water. We shaded them with the clouds and sent down upon them *al-Manna* and the quails (saying): "Eat of the good things We have given you." (but they rebelled) and they were not unjust to us but they did injustice to their own souls. (Qurʾān 7:160)

This verse refers to the people of Moses and shows that they were divided into twelve groups that are described using two words: *sibṭ* and *ummah*. The premodern exegetes differed in their interpretation of this verse. Al-Qummī simply interprets it as a means of distinguishing between them.[91]At-Ṭabarī interprets *ummah* in this verse as a group of people divided because of their difference in religion.[92] Al-Qurṭubī says that the word *sibṭ* is used to indicate that each group is known by its

91. Al-Qummī, *Tafsīr al-Qummī*, vol. 1, 270.

92. At-Ṭabarī, *Jāmiʿ al-Bayān*, vol. 6, 120.

leader, the hierarchy facilitating Prophet Moses's ability to communicate with his people; and *ummah* in this verse is used as an adjective for the word *sibṭ* or tribe.[93] From the modern period, ʿAbduh described *sibṭ* as a group of people whose life is governed by a particular order and system. The adjective form of *ummah* indicates that *sibṭ* and *ummah* are groups whose members are united by a specific connection, benefit, or system.[94] Similarly, Quṭb says that each *ummah*, a large group ("*jamāʿa kabīra*"), is distinguished by a well or a place or a kind of food.[95] Faḍlallah says that the word *sibṭ* means a tribe in Hebrew, and he interprets the whole verse to mean that the people of Moses were divided into different tribes or groups, each having their own leader, traditions, and location.[96]

I think that al-Qurṭubī's and Faḍlallah's interpretation that each tribe had its own leader is reasonable because of the use of *ummah* in the verse rather than *sibṭ*. The preceding verse (7:159) shows the function of the *ummah*, which is guiding people by truth and justice and harnessing such in leadership. This verse is a clarification of the practical implementation of justice, even among people of the same religion (in this case, the people of Moses). God divided them into twelve *umam*, each having its independent share of water. I do not agree with at-Ṭabarī that they may have differed in religion because the verse describes Moses as a common prophet. It may be possible though to interpret the wells metaphorically and consider them to represent different sources of knowledge whereby each *ummah* had different interpretations of the same religion. Given such an interpretation, that they had different traditions, what Faḍlallah and ʿAbduh mentioned would seem more feasible. And it follows to associate the *ummah* with a book or a prophet rather than a religion (*dīn*).

There is no verse in the Qurʾān that associates the word *ummah* with *dīn*; it is either associated with a book or a prophet. As mentioned earlier, religion (*dīn*) is subjective and personal, while the concept of a book or a prophet is more objective and universal. This verse shows that the different *umam* of the people of Moses were identified by their leaders and location.

93. Al-Qurṭubī, *Al-Jāmiʿ li-ʾAḥkām al-Qurʾān*, vol. 7, 303.

94. Muhammad ʿAbduh and Muhammad Rashīd Riḍā, *Tafsīr al-Manār*, vol. 9, 365–67.

95. Sayyid Quṭb, *Fī Ẓilāl al-Qurʾān*, vol. 3, 1381.

96. Faḍlallah, *Min Waḥy al-Qurʾān*, vol. 10, 268–69.

This Qur'anic verse also shows that diversity, even among believers of the same creed, need not be negative as long as justice, equal distribution, and general impartiality is maintained between all the different parties. The justice that is a direct result of guidance according to the Truth (divine revelation) is as characterized in the previous verse by an equal distribution of resources and relative independence of each *ummah*. All the exegetes mentioned above advocate that the verses emphasized that each group should have a specific location for water so that no group would usurp the right of another one. Moreover, this verse along with the one preceding it show two attributes to the word *ummah*: the need for leadership, and the need for *guidance by means of the divine revelation and the justice defined therein*. The importance of revelation, as a book that resolves differences between people, is shown in the following verses of *sūrat an-Naml*: "Verily, this Qur'ān explains to the children of Israel most [of that] concerning which they differ. And it is certainly a guidance and mercy to the believers. Verily, your Sustainer will judge between them in His wisdom—for He alone is almighty, all-knowing" (Qur'ān 27:76–78). This verse confirms the same idea discussed in verse 7:159.

Land (Territory)

Another point the verse (7:160) alludes to is the relationship between the land and the concept of the *ummah*. Each of the twelve *umam* had its own "well," which means its own location or land. This relationship was discussed by Ibn Khaldūn in his prolegomenon, where he said "every *ummah* should have a *waṭan* (homeland) which is their place of origin (*mansha'*) and from it they have the priority to the right of sovereignty."[97] The land in this context not only means a geographical location, but rather reflects a strong bond between community and land, land transcending a mere geographical concept.[98] The Qur'anic verse associates the land with their place of drinking, which is a source of life by which they can farm and survive. So the land becomes a means to attain a living instead of merely being a geographical place. Ibn Khaldūn mentions that the land is

97. Ibn Khaldūn, *Muqaddimat Ibn Khaldūn* (Cairo: Lajnat Al-Bayān Al-ʿArabī, 1957–1962), 882.

98. Naṣīf Naṣṣār, *Mafhūm al-Ummah bayna ad-Dīn wal-Tārīkh*, 123.

their place of origin, which implies an emotional attachment to the land of forefathers, culture, and tradition. It is interesting how exegetes such as al-Qurṭubī and Faḍlallah relate the division of *umam* to independent leadership, while Ibn Khaldūn relates the place of origin to sovereignty. Based on the different exegetes, the verse (7:160) implies that sovereignty is achieved by political leadership as well as economic benefit (a source of provision) associated with a territory. Thus, the *ummah* as a concept carries within it an implication of sovereignty realized by both economic and political elements.

Ummah and Nation-State

At this point, it merits comparing the *ummah* with the nation-state. The nation is a community that shares a common history, language, and culture. The state, however, is a territorial society whose sovereign power is constituted in the form of positive law, and citizens are under its jurisdiction within the borders of the territory.[99] The state is the "body politic" and the nation is the people. Originally, people did not have any political power because they transferred it to the king who was the only sovereign and above the law. After the revolution, the sovereign lawgiving authority was taken from the king or dynasty and given to the people as "democracy." When the nation achieves statehood, it became an independent sovereign state apart from other sovereign states, that is, "nation-state."[100]

The process of bordering (creating a territorial defined space) not only refers to sovereignty over a defined space but also links it with collective identity building through symbols and values that create a sense of belonging.[101] The newly constructed form of belonging in which popular national consciousness is crystallized into the "imagined community" replaces the dissolving old religious and ethnic affiliations that bonded earlier communities. This process of creating a positive self-assertion of one's nation around a homogenous culture is linked to renouncing the

99. Jurgen Habermas, "The European Nation-State: On the Past and Future of Sovereignty and Citizenship," trans. Ciaran Cronin, *Public Culture* 10, no. 2 (1998): 399.

100. Leon Thiry, "Nation, State, Sovereignty and Self-Determination," *Peace Research* 13, no. 1 (January 1981): 18–19.

101. Daniel Meier, "Bordering the Middle East," *Geopolitics* (2016), 5.

"foreign other," such as other neighboring nations and minorities within the same nation.[102] "The strategic self-assertion of the modern state against external enemies is transformed into the existential self-assertion of 'the nation.' "[103] Political elites have misused the propaganda of artificial national myth to construe national freedom as an imperial expansion of power. In this manner, domestic conflicts were diffused by military foreign successes outside the borders of the nation. The modern nation-state is facing serious challenges in integrating the new complex communities because of the growing multiculturalism within and outside its borders. It becomes harder to sustain a culturally homogeneous population under globalization and hence to maintain the national myth of supremacy. In addition, constitutional patriotism is losing its integrative role with the growing interconnectedness in a globalized postmodern world.[104]

I think that the major problem of the "construct" nation-state is its foundation whereby national consciousness is built upon a myth of false supremacy and sovereignty. The latter alienated the "other" within its borders as a minority and outside its borders as a foreign subject to military aggression in case it is weaker economically and politically. A global order based on nation-states is basically a group of encapsulated and isolated entities who hold a false sense of self-sufficiency and sovereignty and are related superficially by fear, private interest, or the monopoly of the stronger (see figure 1.2). It becomes clear how globalization is breaking these artificial borders or ideological constructs that separate people from the different "other." Globalization is dissolving the myth of self-sufficiency by exposing the reality of human interdependency. Jacques Maritain argues that "the concept of sovereignty predicates of a created being—individual or collective—a divine attribute, namely total independence and self-sufficiency."[105] Because God is the only sovereign, Maritain thinks that this concept is not only obsolete but "intrinsically wrong."[106]

---

102. Jurgen Habermas, "The European Nation-State: On the Past and Future of Sovereignty and Citizenship," 402.

103. Ibid., 404.

104. Ibid., 407–8.

105. Leon Thiry, "Nation, State, Sovereignty and Self-Determination," *Peace Research* 13, no. 1 (January 1981): 19.

106. Jacques Maritain, *Man and the State* (Chicago: University of Chicago Press, 1968), 29.

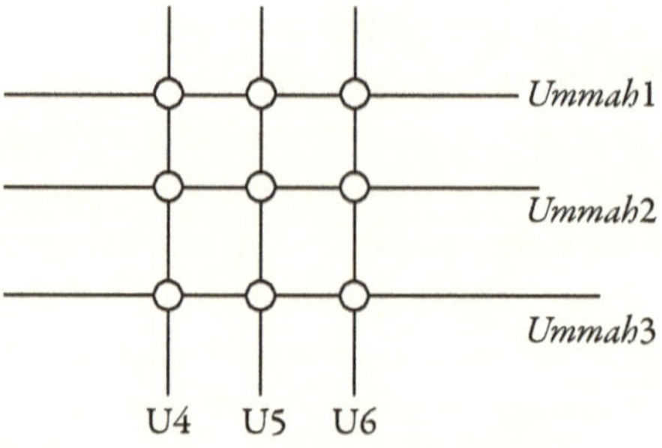

Umam (Interconnected based on covenants, sovereignty based on the book/covenant)

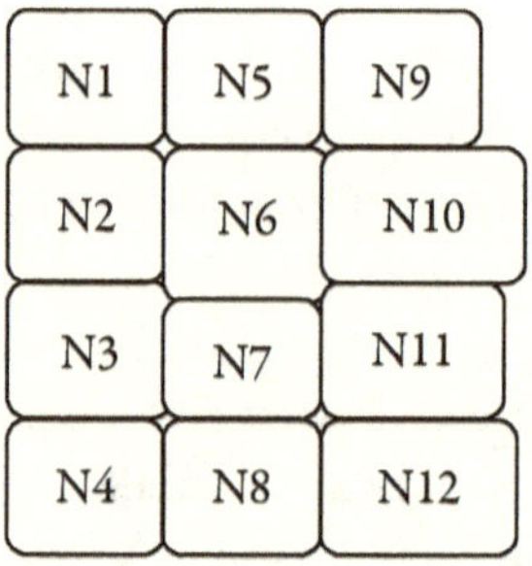

Nation States (Territorial/borders sovereign [false sense of national supremacy, isolated])

Figure 1.2. Difference between Nation States and *Umam*.

The *ummah* as a foundational concept for organizing communities has resolved many of these issues. First, the concept of "absolute" sovereignty belongs to God only. This does not translate into a religious community usurping this right at the expense of others. Rather, it means that a religious community is governed by the divine law, and no human being, including political elites, is above the law. It also means that other religious communities have the right to resort to their own divine law, and that would extend to secular communities as well. Therefore, the *ummah* as a concept does not abolish diversity in its various forms (ethnic, religious, cultural) and does not separate these forms from the political sphere. Within the *ummah*, enjoying political rights is coupled and mirrored by enjoying cultural and religious rights. The book or the constitution uniting the diverse communities of the *ummah* should stipulate rights and obligations of those participating in the makeup of that *ummah*. Chapter 3 delves into an analysis of the first *ummah* established by the prophet in Islamic history clarifying the latter ideas in practice. Western scholars are also inclined toward this direction in thinking, yet without proposing a practical system to make it work; Habermas, for example, suggested that:

> My sense is that multicultural societies can be held together by a political culture, however much it has proven itself, only if democratic citizenship pays off not only in terms of liberal individual rights and rights of political participation but also in the enjoyment of social and cultural rights. The citizens must be able to experience *the fair value of their rights* in the form of social security and the reciprocal recognition of different cultural forms of life.[107]

The *ummah* organizational principle resolves the problem of the need to create a myth that unites different people within a territory that creates a false sense of supremacy. It also prevents the demonization of the "other" in the form of internal minorities or external aliens. Minority as a concept is not only related to numbers residing within a majority group; they also represent the other as a sociopolitical construct. This translates into a dominant sociopolitical structure and a legal system that is designed by and for the benefit of the majority at the expense of the minority. Military aggression outside the borders of the nation-state is simply a mirror of the defective system within its borders.

By creating a sociopolitical and legal structure that mirrors the ethnic, religious, and cultural diversity of society, the *ummah* as a concept and practice breaks the artificial construct of minority versus majority and its associated problems. By resolving the problem from within, it becomes more feasible to create more covenants with bordering *umam*, hence a status of interdependency, similar to the yarn piece/network described earlier in the chapter. The latter is not only based on covenant making but also on an equal positive perception of who the "other" is.

Territory within the *ummah* as a concept is not based on the process of othering to build collective identity to establish sovereignty. Rather, it

---

107. Jurgen Habermas, "The European Nation-State: On the Past and Future of Sovereignty and Citizenship," 409.

is focused on engaging in establishing a peaceful order among its diverse people within its borders; that is why the territorial entity is defined as *ḥaram* (sacred) in the Medinan *ummah*, discussed in chapter 3. In addition, because the territorial aspect of the *ummah* is not obsessed with the other as an outside alien, it is very porous and accepts anyone who wants to join the *ummah* as long as they abide by their constitutional principles. Chapter 3 discusses this aspect in more detail.

Al-Ummah al-Wāḥidah and Its Differentiation across Human History

Ummah of the Prophets

According to the Qurʾān, the *ummah* of the prophets was always unified across human history, as shown in *sūrat al-ʾanbiyā*ʾ; "Verily this is your *ummah*, a single *ummah* (*ummah wāḥidah*) and I am your sustainer so worship me" (Qurʾān 21:92). While the prophets are unified by their worship and submission to their Lord, they were sent to different communities as shown in the verse: "To every *ummah* (was sent) a messenger: when their messenger comes (and delivers his message), judgment is passed on them equally, and never are they wronged" (Qurʾān 10:47). Thus, judgment and justice are established only after people receive the guidance from their messenger. Here again we see the correlation between the concept of an *ummah* and that of revelation, where justice and equity cannot be established without following the guidance sent by a messenger. The fact that all prophets belong to one *ummah* but are sent to different communities best explains the concept of diversity; it does not separate but rather creates an enriching experience. At the same time, every *ummah* has an appointed time, part of the divine plan, as shown in the verse ". . . For every *ummah,* there is an appointed term; when their time comes, neither can they delay it nor can they hasten it an hour."

Unlike the *ummah* of the prophets, the Qurʾān states that humankind used to be one *ummah* but later diverged and separated:

> And [know that] all humankind were once but one single *ummah* (*wāḥidah*), and only later did they begin to hold divergent views. And had it not been for a decree—that had already gone forth from your Sustainer, all their differences would indeed have been settled [from the outset]. (Qurʾān 10:19)

This verse was discussed thoroughly in the introduction of this chapter, showing that the premodern exegesis was inclined toward exclusivity, whereby one *ummah* has one faith. However, the modern exegetes define *ummah wāḥidah* more broadly, as people united by their innate nature (*fiṭrah*).

These verses account for diversity in human history, explain its origin, and elucidate a divine plan behind the phenomenon. They also show how each *ummah* goes through a cycle of strength and decline. The peak of an *ummah* is realized when its messenger establishes justice and equity among its members by judging through divine revelation. The impact of messengers can also be explained metaphorically at the times when messengers are no longer present, where recorded revelation is the primary guide. Using the term messenger (*rasūl*) and not prophet (*nabī*) in the verses may indicate that what is emphasized is the message or revelation more than the conveying messenger.

The first human community represents a prototype of all human communities in history. It shows us that the decline of an *ummah* will be a direct consequence of its deviating from its ideals, and that its ultimate strength will be through abiding by them. While explaining diversity, the verses refer to the original condition of people, that they were one *ummah*, and refers to the condition of the prophets, that they are all worshipers of God. As such, diversity can be imagined as different branches growing from the same tree, just as the one *ummah* (*ummah wāḥidah*) grew into different *umam*. At the same time, those different *umam* can still live together as *ummah wāḥidah* through covenants (see figure 1.3).

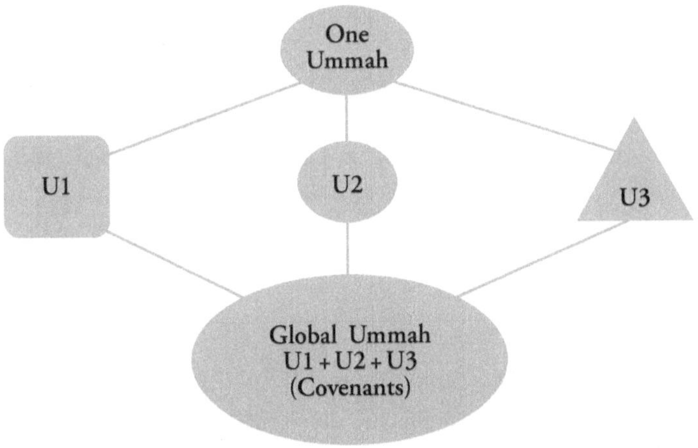

Figure 1.3. The one *ummah* and its differentiation, and the way to achieve unity.

Dealing with Religious Diversity

Verses 21:92 and 10:19 invoke a feeling of unity among different people by reminding them of their common humanity and common creator. Thus, the verses urge people to interact with each other from the aspect of a common humanity rather than from confined aspects such as ethnicity or race. However, people can exploit diversity to provoke conflict; hence the Qur'ān addresses religious conflict: "But do not revile those [beings] whom they invoke instead of Allah, for fear that they revile Allah out of spite, and in ignorance. Thus unto every *ummah* have We made their deed seem goodly. Then unto their Lord is their return, and He will inform them of all that they used to do" (Qur'ān 6:108).

Premodern exegetes Al-Qummī,[108]at-Ṭabarī,[109] and Al-Qurṭubī[110] interpreted the verse literally using reports from the life of Prophet Mohammad. Among the modern exegetes, ʿAbduh and Faḍlallah say that this verse endorses religious tolerance. ʿAbduh argues that Allah has ordered his messenger to reveal his message to people by words and through action. The Prophet should face polytheists' rejection by patience and wisdom because God created human beings with varying degrees of understanding. ʿAbduh continues that humans differ because it is part of their human nature. God sent his messengers as guides and bearers of good news rather than as forceful tyrants. The messengers should not restrict people's freedom to choose their beliefs because God intentionally created free people and did not force them to believe. ʿAbduh asserts, in reflection of God's tolerant character, that believers should not revile others' gods and beliefs. Otherwise, ignorant people will revile God in order to humiliate the believers.[111]

Faḍlallah adds that there is a prohibition of reviling any idea or belief that another person holds sacred, no matter how much this idea or belief contradicts one's own. The one who insults another's belief will end up insulted for his belief, which will result in a vicious cycle of hatred, conflict,

108. Al-Qummī, *Tafsīr al-Qummī*, vol. 1, 241.

109. At-Ṭabarī, *Jāmiʿ al-Bayān*, vol. 5, 403–5.

110. Al-Qurṭubī, *Mukhtaṣar Tafsīr Al-Qurṭubī*, vol. 2, 139.

111. Muhammad ʿAbduh and Muhammad Rashīd Riḍā, *Tafsīr al-Manār*, vol. 7, 663–64.

and enmity. The Qur'anic message thus provides divergent believers with a basis for interacting with each other. It highlights the critical importance of using respectful communication when interacting with others, no matter how contradictory each other's ideas, beliefs, or perceptions. In another aspect, the Qur'ān also provides a rationale for different communities' coexistence; it is part of the divine plan that each *ummah* will see its ideas or beliefs as goodly and right. Thus, insulting the other will not cause them to change their opinion. The only means by which a person can change his attitude is through personal interest. This cannot happen in a tense atmosphere charged with insults and hurt feelings. It can only be realized in a peaceful environment conducive to mutual respect and calm, objective discussion, which opens hearts and minds to thinking and contemplation.[112] Not all modern exegetes interpreted the verse to encourage religious tolerance and peaceful coexistence. For example, Quṭb[113] focused his discussion on the believer, showing how it is appropriate for his manners and belief to be calm and confident without provoking the other's anger.

Confederates of Evil (*al-Aḥzāb*)

The earlier verses showed the believers a peaceful means by which to deal with others who disagree with them. On the other hand, the following verses move beyond personal encounter to public discourse and the creation of parties and confederations to promote a specific idea.

> None can dispute (*yujādil*) about the Signs of Allah but those who are bent on denying the truth. Let it not then deceive you that they seem to be able to do as they please on earth. But (there were people) before them, who denied (the Signs), the People of Noah, and the confederates (of evil) (*al-aḥzāb*) after them; and every *ummah* plotted against their prophet, to seize him, and disputed (against his message) with falsehood, thereby to condemn the Truth; but then I took them to task—and how was then my retribution. (Qur'ān 40: 4–5)

112. Faḍlallah, *Min Waḥy al-Qur'ān*, vol. 9, 266–70.

113. Sayyid Quṭb, *Fī Ẓilāl al-Qur'ān*, vol. 2, 1169.

There is no noticeable difference between the premodern and modern exegesis of these verses.[114] At-Ṭabarī[115] and Al-Qurṭubī[116] said that each *ummah* denied its prophet and plotted against him by forming opposing parties or employing confederates who opposed the truth using false argumentation. The modern exegetes Faḍlallah[117] and Quṭb[118] elaborated that false argumentation means futile argument that is not intended to clarify truths or answer human questions. It is rather motivated by human desires away from sound logical thinking, and is of those who use their powerful positions on earth to divert people from following the truth.

The ones who led that process of defending and promoting falsehood are called *al-aḥzāb*, translated as the confederates of evil. Fazlur Rahman interprets *al-aḥzāb* as "those who split up the community of religion."[119] Depending on its instance in the Qur'ān, it means either the people who reject and oppose God's messengers or those who split into sects after truth has come to them. The Qur'ān speaks of Christians and Jews who split into different sects many centuries since their forming. Those sects originally followed a unitary truth but later separated such that "each sect rejoices in what it has" (Qur'ān 3:103). By referring to previous *umam*, the Qur'ān addresses the Muslim *ummah* as well and thereby speaks in general of any *ummah* as prone to such divisions and opposition.[120]

THE REFORMERS (*MUṢLIḤŪN*)

To counteract the position of *al-aḥzāb*, the Qur'ān speaks of another group who carries out a process of reform to save the *ummah* from strife

114. Al-Qummī was different where he interprets the signs of Allah as the *a'imma* and those who denied the signs are the companions of the prophets who split into different parties, in Al-Qummī, *Tafsīr al-Qummī*, vol. 2, 258.

115. At-Ṭabarī, *Jāmi' al-Bayān*, vol. 12, 54–55.

116. Al-Qurṭubī, *Mukhtaṣar Tafsīr Al-Qurṭubī*, vol. 4, 297.

117. Faḍlallah, *Min Waḥy al-Qur'ān*, vol. 20, 12–13.

118. Sayyid Quṭb, *Fī Ẓilāl al-Qur'ān*, vol. 5, 3070.

119. Fazlur Rahman, *Major Themes of the Qur'ān* (Minneapolis, Chicago: Bibliotheca Islamica, 1980), 138.

120. Ibid., 138–39.

and failure. Those reformers (*al-muṣliḥūn*) call out against corruption and remind people of virtuous action. This is shown in the following verse:

> If only there had been among the generations before you people possessing a remnant (of good sense) [*ʾūlū baqiyya*] to warn (their people) against corruption in the earth, as did a few of those whom We saved from them. And the unjust only pursued pleasures which corrupted their whole being, and so lost themselves in sinning. For, never would your Sustainer destroy towns unjustly while its people are reforming [*muṣliḥūn*]. (Qurʾān 11:116–17)

The premodern exegete At-Ṭabarī interprets *ʾūlū baqiyya*[121] as those who have understanding and use their intellect and take wisdom from God's guidance. God saved them because they fought corruption. God destroys towns whose people are unbelievers who insist on denying messengers and doing evil. At-Ṭabarī then presents another opinion, which he does not seem to endorse, that God does not destroy people who are unjust to him (by ascribing partners to God, Ar. *shirk*), only those who cause corruption on earth, irrespective of their belief.[122] However, al-Qurṭubī[123] supports the latter opinion, saying that God does not destroy people by disbelief only; rather he does when corruption becomes prevalent in society. He argues that committing injustice is evident to bring demise in this life, while *shirk*'s punishment is harder in the hereafter.

From the modern period, exegetes agree that corruption is the reason God destroys towns, rather than *shirk*.[124] Both Quṭb[125] and ʿAbduh

121. Al-Qurṭubī interprets them as people who submit to God and have intellect and vision in Al-Qurṭubī, *Mukhtaṣar Tafsīr Al-Qurṭubī*, vol. 2, 417.

122. At-Ṭabarī, *Jāmiʿ al-Bayān*, vol. 7, 180–83.

123. Al-Qurṭubī, *Mukhtaṣar Tafsīr Al-Qurṭubī*, vol. 2, 417.

124. ʿAbduh says that exegetes associated injustice with disbelief and ascribing partners to God (*shirk*) because of the Qurʾānic verse ". . . *lā tushrik billah ʾinna al-shirka la-ẓulmun ʿaẓīm*" ("Never ascribe anything as a partner to Allah; verily ascribing partners to Him is a tremendous injustice") (Qurʾān 31:13), Muhammad ʿAbduh and Muhammad Rashīd Riḍā, *Tafsīr al-Manār*, vol. 12, 192–93.

125. Sayyid Quṭb, *Fī Ẓilāl al-Qurʾān*, vol. 4, 1933.

say that God does not destroy those who associate partners with Him, as long as they are reforming their social life such that they do not usurp others' rights and are fair and just in their dealings. ʿAbduh supports this argument, saying: "nations can survive with disbelief, but they cannot survive with injustice."[126] ʿAbduh interprets *ʾulū baqiyya*[127] as the wise, good people who command good and forbid evil (*ʾāmirūna bil-maʿrūf, nāhūna ʿan al-munkar*), a Qurʾānic description that is discussed in more detail in the next chapter.[128] Fazlur Rahman makes a relevant point here by relating the previously discussed term *al-aḥzāb* with the *ummah*. Rahman says that the term *al-aḥzāb*, a Meccan term, disappears in Medina and is replaced by the term *ummah* or the collective term *ahl al-kitāb* ("people of the Book"). While each *ummah* is recognized with its own laws, the best *ummah* is the ideal or median *ummah* (*ummah wasaṭ*), which is distinguished by its act of commanding good and forbidding evil, referred to by ʿAbduh.[129] I think that Rahman is alluding to the point that continuous reform (through the means of commanding good and forbidding evil) is the only means to counteract the negative effect of splitting up the society into conflicting factions, which are represented by the word *al-aḥzāb*.

I think there is more emphasis in the modern period on fighting corruption rather than committing *shirk* (being the main cause of inviting destruction) because of the political conditions facing Muslims. Modern exegetes were witnessing the rise and success of secular nations that uphold law and implement justice, whereas Muslim nations were divided and exploited, despite their belief in one God, because of their passivity in fighting injustices. Therefore, modern exegetes emphasized the need for continuous reform in the *ummah*, showing that speaking up against corruption and reform are the only means to prevent an *ummah* from decline and to deter God's punishment.

---

126. Muhammad ʿAbduh and Muhammad Rashīd Riḍā, *Tafsīr al-Manār*, vol. 12, 192–93.

127. Faḍlallah interprets the term as people who follow a different path from their predecessors, again emphasizing the need for change in society, in Faḍlallah, *Min Waḥy al-Qurʾān*, vol. 12, 147.

128. Ibid., vol. 12, 190–91.

129. Fazlur Rahman, *Major Themes of the Qurʾān*, 144–45.

The verses discussed above are followed by verses that reveal the main purpose of creation: "And if your sustainer had willed, He could surely have made all humankind one single *ummah*, but [He willed it otherwise, and so] they continue to differ. Except those upon whom your sustainer has bestowed His mercy: and to this end he has created them all . . ." (Qur᾿ān 11:118–19).

The premodern exegesis were almost synonymous that people would have been one *ummah* if they followed one religion.[130] The modern exegetes, however, focused on the innate nature of human beings and their free will, which makes difference an inevitable fact. ʿAbduh suggests that God could have made people one *ummah* with one religion following their innate nature without choice or opinion, but he made them different in their choices, capabilities, and potential, and thus difference is God's law (*sunnat Allah*) manifested in creation.[131] Muhammad Asad presents ʿAbduh's idea and adds to it:

> The Qur᾿ān stresses once again that the unceasing differentiation in men's views and ideas is not incidental but represents God-willed, basic factor of human existence. If God had willed that all human beings should be of one persuasion, all intellectual progress would have been ruled out, and "they would have been similar in their social life to the bees and the ants,

130. Al-Qummī says that merciful people (*᾿ahl raḥma*) do not differ and disagree about religion, Al-Qummī, *Tafsīr al-Qummī*, vol. 1, 367. At-Ṭabarī presented a number of potential interpretations: first, conflict is the result of difference in religion and mercy is the result of abiding by one religion; second, those who differ are people of falsehood (*᾿ahl al-bāṭil*) and those who deserve God's mercy are people of truth (*᾿ahl al-ḥaqq*); third, God created two types of people: one group is bestowed with God's mercy so it does not differ, and another group is deprived of God's mercy so it differs, creating continuous conflict, At-Ṭabarī, *Jāmiʿ al-Bayān*, vol. 7, 183–86. Al-Qurṭubī also says that people would not have differed if they followed one religion in Al-Qurṭubī, *Mukhtaṣar Tafsīr Al-Qurṭubī*, vol. 2, 417.

131. Muhammad ʿAbduh and Muhammad Rashīd Riḍā, *Tafsīr al-Manār*, vol. 12, 193–94. The same argument is stated in Sayyid Quṭb, *Fī Ẓilāl al-Qur᾿ān*, vol. 4, 1933.

> while in their spiritual life they would have been like the angels, constrained by their nature always to believe in what is true and always to obey God"[132]—that is to say, devoid of that relative free will which enables man to choose between right and wrong and thus endows his life—in distinction from all other sentient beings—with a moral meaning and a unique spiritual potential.[133]

The verses show that this divinely planned difference is a "mercy" from God, which is the main reason behind all creation. The merciful purpose is the spiritual and intellectual growth of humanity, as Asad pointed out. Diversity was not made to create disharmony and conflict among different people, but as a means to uncover individuals' potential for growth or demise, and as a means to create better understanding among different people, as this verse shows: "O humankind! We have created you from a male and a female, and made you into nations and tribes, that you may know one another. Verily, the most honorable of you for Allah is the one who is most aware of his creator (*ʾatqākum*). Verily, Allah is All-Knowing, All-Aware" (Qurʾān 49:13). God consciousness (*taqwa*) is a unifying characteristic among all people, of different religions, ethnicities, and cultures. This characteristic shows in the Qurʾanic chapter of the Believers (*al-Muʾminiūn*): "And verily! This is your *ummah,* a single *ummah* (*ummah wāḥidah*) and I am your sustainer so be conscious of me (*ʾittaqūn*)" (Qurʾān 23:52). Thus, believers of all faith traditions across human history, similar to the prophets' *ummah*, belong to one *ummah* (*ummah wāḥidah*) that is unified by *taqwa* ("God consciousness").

Faḍlallah refers to the interpretation pointed out by ʿAbduh and Asad; however, he adds a different perspective. He argues that the context implies that difference has a negative connotation because it is based on transgression, while unity reflects God's mercy, which is a blessing. Those who deserve God's mercy are those who choose to follow his guidance. That is why the verse says people will still be different "except those upon

132. The quoted statement is a translation of ʿAbduh's words in Muhammad ʿAbduh and Muhammad Rashīd Riḍā, *Tafsīr al-Manār*, vol. 12, 193.

133. Muhammad Asad, *The Message of the Qurʾān*, 422.

whom your sustainer has bestowed his mercy."[134] Synthesizing the arguments presented by ʿAbduh, Asad, and Faḍlallah, we can deduce that while difference is a needed fact for human progress, it can become a threat unless people manage conflict by invoking God's mercy through believing in a merciful creator for all humanity.

While the premodern exegetes emphasized the unity aspect more, the modern exegetes focused on explaining how diversity is an unchangeable fact. It is clear that the political situation of Muslims in both periods has affected their outlook on life and hence their interpretation of the Qurʾānic verses. When Muslims were united under the banner of the Caliphate, exegetes focused on the merits of following one religion to invoke God's mercy and blessings. When Muslims became disunited under the modern system of secular nation-states, in addition to the supremacy of reason, modern exegetes emphasized the merits of difference by showing how it is a precursor for human growth.

Conclusion

This chapter showed how the same verses could be interpreted or seen through different perspectives based on the sociopolitical conditions of the exegetes' time. There is no doubt that this work follows the same premise. Nevertheless, this is precisely what makes the Qurʾān dynamic and engaging with a possibility of responding to developing needs across time through human reinterpretation.

The difference between premodern and modern exegesis was not constant throughout; there are many verses that were interpreted similarly irrespective of the time. However, there are other instances where the difference was noticeable. For example, there is a larger tendency among premodern exegetes to interpret the verses literally or use historical evidence from the Prophet's time, whereas the modern exegetes interpret the verses by reflecting on their contemporary conditions. While immigration was primarily regarded as important for the well-being of the individual for premodern exegetes, it became crucial for establishing a society based on Islamic ethics for the modern ones. Resisting imperialism, secular nationalism, or sectarianism encouraged modern exegetes to envision an

134. Faḍlallah, *Min Waḥy al-Qurʾān*, vol. 12, 151.

alternative society through adding another perspective to the understanding of Qur'ānic concepts.

Another noticeable difference is the tendency among premodern exegetes to be more exclusive, such as interpreting *ummah wāḥidah* as an *ummah* following one true religion, which is evidently Islam. The modern exegetes, on the other hand, witnessing the industrial revolution with its focus on the supremacy of reason, as well as globalization and intermixing of cultures and peoples, interpreted *ummah wāḥidah* as a universal concept. People are united by their *fiṭrah* (innate nature) rather than a religion. The modern interpretation places more emphasis on using reason to reach conviction before endorsing a specific religion. Compared with the premodern exegesis, the modern one is more critical of the past and embraces difference and diversity, which inspires religious tolerance. Difference became a divine means for human development and spiritual growth rather than a threat to the unity of the *ummah*.

Believing in one God (opposite of *shirk*) was regarded as the main criterion for the success and thriving of society for the premodern exegetes who witnessed the success of the Muslim caliphate across wide geographical areas. Corruption was regarded secondary to bring God's wrath. On the other hand, the modern exegetes witnessing the economic and political advancement of secular nation-states compared with modern Muslim nations regarded corruption as the primary cause for inviting God's wrath. ʿAbduh stated that "nations can survive with disbelief, but they cannot survive with injustice." The modern exegetes were examining the Qur'ān to understand what led the Muslim *ummah* to its current condition, so time and the different stages of development played a role in the modern exegesis compared with the premodern one.

On a parallel track, this chapter, utilizing the different Qur'ānic interpretations, also explored the many layers around the Qur'ānic term *ummah* and uncovered each layer to propose a more holistic understanding of the concept. The Qur'ānic Meccan manifestations of the term *ummah* challenge the orientalist understanding of *ummah* as a closed salvific community. A closer examination of the verses also refutes the common definition that defines *ummah* by religion. There is no mention of the word Muslim *ummah* or *sharīʿah* in all the Meccan verses, and the concept is mainly illustrated theoretically. The concept is demonstrated in relation to previous *umam* before the coming of Prophet Muhammad.

The only exception is the reference to the word *ummī*, which still relates to previous *umam* but also projects it to include the global *ummah* that includes Muslims.

The research conducted in this chapter shows that associating the term *ummah* with *ajal*, a purpose and direction, make it an active term that requires identification rather than endorsing a passive inherited identity. Thus, *ummah* cannot be defined as ethnic, religious, or linguistic groups of people. What is given does not determine membership in an *ummah*; instead, what is chosen is key. The Qurʾānic verses showed that religion (*al-Dīn*) could be taken as an inherited identity, hence it is not a defining feature of *ummah*. The *imām* is also an important attribute uniting *ummah*, yet is secondary to the Book. The Qurʾānic verses showed that individuals are judged according to their subjective choices (people are called by their *imām*, which is a personal choice), but the *ummah* is summoned to its book (*al-kitāb*). The book is more objective, as it represents a collection of individuals' subjective judgments. Thus, *ummah is an active community that is always seeking unity based on its book of guidance and thereby founds its leadership, so it is a collective effort of different individuals.*

A book serves not only to unify an *ummah*, but to provide specific ethics and an order to guide its members. The Qurʾān regards the book as a form of covenant (*mīthāq*), either between people and God (divine books) or between people (treaty). Making a covenant, which is an added attribute of the *ummah*, strengthens the awareness of responsibility associated with making choices, hence again reinforcing the connection between choice, responsibility, and the *ummah*. Unrelated individuals with common features such as a specific religion, language, ethnicity, or land can form a community (*qawm*), but not an *ummah*. On the other hand, *an ummah is a group of purposeful individuals covenanted to establish a particular way of life and maintain their unity and sovereignty as one ummah based on their agreed-upon book and covenant.* Thus, an *ummah* amounts to a deliberate collective effort of different individuals bound by a specific goal.

In a nation-state, integrating complex societies occurs through creating an imagined community through symbols and values that foster a national myth of supremacy. The process of creating a homogenous culture in one nation is sustained by renouncing the "foreign other," through minorities internally and neighboring nations externally; hence the need for military aggression outside national borders. In an *ummah*, there is no need to create a homogenous culture because the concept itself embraces diversity (not as a foreign other). While in the nation-state, multicultural societies are held together by a political culture, in an *ummah* diversity is celebrated by participation in politics as well as enjoying social and cultural rights publicly. This is practically sustained through establishing covenants internally (as well as externally outside borders). It was practically realized historically (as is discussed in chapter 3) through legal pluralism. Such a system shatters the binary concept of majority/minority inherent in modern nation-states. A global order based on nation-states is sustained by fear (tight security of borders), demonstration of power, and exploitation of the weak by the stronger nations. A global order based on *ummah* is sustained by constant interaction, interdependence based on covenants, porous borders, and tighter connection between the *umam* rather than within national borders.

The Qur᾿ān describes how in the evolution of human history, people were originally one *ummah* that eventually separated and differentiated into different groups. The Qur᾿ān shows that difference is an inherent nature of human beings and that unity is a desired value. Despite the vast diversity of human experiences, human beings can still form one *ummah* by seeking common values and establishing covenants. The shared covenant with the one God, that of the many different prophets sent throughout history evidences, is a model to the rest of humanity. In addition to the ideal unity desired, the Qur᾿ān tells that selfish desire and corruption will have ample manifestation on earth, and hence we see the introduction of new terms such as *al-aḥzāb* ("the confederates of evil") versus *al-muṣliḥūn* ("the reformers"). The Qur᾿ān points again to the choice of belonging to either confederate or reformer camp and stresses the value of continuous intentional action and reform, whose absence would lead to continuous conflict and chaos.

The Qur᾿ānic notion of the *ummah* challenges the common understanding of the *ummah* as a static salvific community. In a sociopolitical context, the later Medinan verses introduce the Qur᾿ānic vision of a shared *ummah* that is multireligious and pluralistic in its makeup, but unified in its goal and orientation. The unified *ummah* seeks to settle their differences through a common book that outlines mutual rights and obligations of its different members, thereby establishing justice for the whole *ummah*. By stressing the element of choice and its associated responsibility through covenant making, the Qur'ān frees the perception of the "human," whether the self or the other, from rigid static affiliations and provides much flexibility in establishing a global order. Yet this freedom is purposeful because it is channeled through establishing covenants to secure adherence to the common good of all, hence establishing peace and stability.

Chapter 2

Ummah in the Medinan Verses of the Qur'ān

This chapter discusses the evolution of the concept of the *ummah* in the Medinan verses of the Qur'ān and how it was articulated at that period. Most of what is written on the *ummah* in Islamic literature is focused on the Medinan verses because they are related to the Muslim *ummah*. In addition, the period in which these verses were revealed was concurrent with the establishment of the first political entity in Medina. The *ummah* of Medina, as shown in the Medina Constitution, started as a mixed society but later ended up as a Muslim society. In that regard, Muslim scholars focused only on the late period and associated the concept of the *ummah* with Muslims exclusively. That is why when the term *ummah* is used in Islamic literature, it usually refers to the Muslim *ummah* by default. Thus, how the concept evolved and what it represented in the early years of Medina as a historical realization and not only as a theoretical term is totally disregarded. It is true that the Medinan verses start addressing a Muslim *ummah*, however this *ummah* is addressed in the context of other *umam*. Even, the term Muslim *ummah* (*ummah muslimah*) is mentioned only once in the Medinan verses in relation to Prophet Abraham and not Prophet Muhammad. The characteristics of the emerging *ummah* that occur in the Medinan verses make the term much more inclusive than its common use, indicating solely Muslims. Instead, while it is specific, it is an active term with acquired characteristics that are accessible to any individual who is willing to endorse them.

While the description of the *ummah* in the Meccan verses was conceptual and general, the Medinan verses provide specific characterizations and attributes for different *umam*. Nonetheless, those attributes are usually acquired by specific actions rather than being inherited or culturally possessed. Therefore, the Medinan verses confirm the conceptual definition of the *ummah* established in the previous chapter, that it is a term referring to a collectivity based on choice and action.

The Notion of a Shared *Ummah*: Rights and Obligations

The first verse revealed in Medina that is related to the *ummah* is in *sūrat al-ʾAʿrāf*, a Meccan *sūra* except for a few verses revealed in Medina. The historical context of Medina is that it was composed of a multi-religious society, as reflected in the text of the Medina Constitution. Thus, the verses revealed there were dealing with the existent mixed society and showed the means by which different groups could coexist and positively interact with each other. This is exemplified through a conversation in the verse:

> And when an *ummah* from them said: "Why do you give advice to a people whom Allah is about to destroy or punish with a severe torment?" They replied: "To be free from blame before your sustainer, and perhaps they will become God conscious (*yattaqūn*)." (Qurʾān 7:164)

Both premodern and modern exegetes Al-Qummī[1], at-Ṭabarī,[2] ʿAbduh,[3] and Quṭb[4] say that there are three different groups referenced in the preceding verse; one is the group that disobeyed its Lord, went astray and deserves punishment; the second is a group of believers who obey the commands of their lord and admonish the first group, advising them to refrain from their wrongdoing; the third group consists of believers who obeyed the commands of their Lord, but who do not admonish the misbehavior of the first group and preferred to stay silent.

1. Al-Qummī, *Tafsīr al-Qummī*, vol. 1, 271.

2. At-Ṭabarī, *Jāmiʿ al-Bayān*, vol. 6, 124–31.

3. Muhammad ʿAbduh and Muhammad Rashīd Riḍā, *Tafsīr al-Manār*, vol. 9, 376–79.

4. Quṭb, *Fī Ẓilāl al-Qurʾān*, vol. 3, 1384–85.

The modern exegetes extend their interpretation to their vision of *ummah* in the modern period. Quṭb regards the three groups equivalent to three *umam*, and he defines the *ummah* as a group of people who share the same creed and vision and follow one leadership. He criticizes the modern depiction of the *ummah* as a group of people defined by borders and a state.[5] Quṭb's interpretation of this verse is affected by the Muslim Brotherhood's vision of the *ummah* as united under one caliphate rather than physical borders or one country.

Faḍlallah sees this verse as an invitation to reform in an *ummah* whose members share the same responsibility, irrespective of their views and inclinations. So he divides the people referred to in the verse into two groups. One group consists of people who are rebellious against God's commands and the second group consists of the believers, obedient to God's commands, who differ among themselves in how they wish to address the rebellious. Some of them did not see any hope in advising the rebellious as they have transgressed all bounds and refused to listen. Others did not give up hope in the human potential for change, no matter the extent of corruption and delusion. They do not despair of God's mercy and believe in the goodness of human nature and the ability to change. In addition, they feel a responsibility toward their Lord and openly declare their rejection of the deviant path for the sake of constructive change within the society.

Faḍlallah says that it is probable that the grammatical use of the word "your sustainer" rather than "our sustainer" in the believers' answer to their fellows who disagreed with them reflects the notion that the problem is not only the transgressors', but also that of those who share the same responsibility before their creator. Thus, the advising people are calling to action those who are refraining from advice by using the word "your sustainer" to remind them of their accountability by adopting a practical approach to the problem.[6] Faḍlallah thinks that the believers and the rebellious are members of a collective *ummah*, and they have responsibilities and duties toward each other. He was known for his endorsement of *al-Islām al-ḥarakī* ("active Islam"), which encourages continuous reform in society through education and establishing institutions.

---

5. Ibid., 1385.

6. Faḍlallah, *Min Waḥy al-Qur᾽ān*, vol. 10, 272–74.

I agree with Faḍlallah that the verse highlights the importance of discussion, interaction, and giving advice among different members of an *ummah*. It shows the significant need of keeping moral discussion alive that evokes the feeling of a "shared destiny." The latter is an important means by which different members or groups feel connected, feel a shared responsibility, and can live as an *ummah*. The action of giving advice is based on the premise of having one creator to whom everyone is accountable. With such a basis, there is no more debate of my God versus your God. Advice is exchanged freely, without expecting a personal return or attempting to impose religious belief. This removes the negative vibe of giving advice and creates a mediating atmosphere among the different parties that lessens conflict and pushes toward reconciliation. The verse actually sets the stage for the forthcoming verses where difference is established as a natural fact, isolation (closed community) is not a virtue but open communication is the desired aim; humans are not self-sufficient, but rather unity should be sought in an *ummah* through establishing a moral order. On the other hand, Quṭb's dividing the groups into three *umam*, each having a creed and a leadership seems a far-fetched interpretation reflecting a divided society on many levels. It appears to be a reflection of his own vision of how he regarded the Egyptian society during his time, where Islamists had their own leader who differed from the political leader of the nation state.

Prophet Abraham (*Ibrāhīm*) was an *Ummah*

Chronologically, the next Medinan verses that mention the word *ummah* are associated with Prophet Abraham (*Ibrāhīm*). In the Qur'ānic context, Prophet Abraham's life, character, and belief represent an exemplary model of the essence of Islamic belief. As such, the Medinan verses gradually reveal the character and attributes of the Muslim *ummah*. The first verse describes Abraham as an *ummah*;

> Verily, Ibrāhīm was an *ummah*[7] devoutly obeying God's will, *ḥanīfan*[8] and not being of those who ascribe divinity to others

---

7. Translated as "model" by Yusuf Ali; "nation" by Pickthal; "exemplar" by Shakir; "man who combined within himself all virtues" by Muhammad Asad.

8. Translated as "true in faith" by Yusuf Ali; "by nature upright" by Pickthal; "upright" by Shakir; "turning away from all that is false" by Muhammad Asad.

> beside God. [For he was always] grateful for the bounties of God who selected him and guided him to a straight path. (Qur'ān 16:120–21)

Premodern and modern exegetes interpret these verses similarly with minor variations. Al-Qummī interprets the word *ummah* as someone with a specific religion that nobody else was following and *ḥanīf* as Muslim.[9] At-Ṭabarī interprets the word *ummah* in this verse as the one who teaches people goodness. Thus, it is the *Imām* who leads people and people follow him (*yu'tamm bihi wayuqtada bihi*).[10] Similarly, Ibn Kathīr says an *ummah* in this case means an *Imām* or that he was a believer on his own and all people around him were disbelievers; hence he is described as an *ummah* by himself.[11] This is supported by a *ḥadīth* where Prophet Muhammad described one of his companions as an *ummah*: "Zayd will be resurrected on the day of judgment as an *ummah* by himself" (*yuḥshar [yubʿath] Zayd bin ʿAmrū ummatan waḥdahu*). The reason for describing Zayd as an *ummah* is clarified in another *ḥadīth* in al-Bukhārī which reports an encounter between Zayd bin ʿAmrū and his people (the pagans of Quraysh).[12] The *ḥadīth* shows that Zayd opposed the traditions of his people alone. They slaughtered their animals in one way, and he followed

9. Al-Qummī, *Tafsīr al-Qummī*, vol. 1, 423.

10. At-Ṭabarī, *Jāmiʿ al-Bayān*, vol. 8, 249–50.

11. Abīl-Fidāʿ Al-Ḥāfiẓ Ibn Kathīr, *Tafsīr Al-Qur'ān Al-ʿAẓīm*, vol. 2 (Beirut: Dār Al-Fikr, 1997), 615.

12. "Narrated ʿAbdullah bin ʿUmar: The Prophet met Zaid bin ʿAmr bin Nufayl in the bottom of (the valley of) baldah before any divine revelation came to the Prophet. A meal was presented to the Prophet but he refused to eat from it. (Then it was presented to Zaid) who said, "I do not eat anything which you slaughter in the name of your stone idols. I eat none but those things on which Allah's Name has been mentioned at the time of slaughtering." Zaid bin ʿAmr used to criticize the way Quraysh used to slaughter their animals, and used to say: "Allah has created the sheep and He has sent the water for it from the sky, and He has grown the grass for it from the earth; yet you slaughter it in other than the Name of Allah." He used to say so, for he rejected that practice and considered it as something abominable. . . ." Al-Bukhārī, *Al-Jāmiʿ as-Ṣaḥiḥ, Kitāb Manāqib Al-Ansār* (Beirut: Dār 'Iḥyā' at-Turāth al-ʿArabī, 1980) *ḥadīth* no. 24, vol. 3, 49.

another way. Thus, he represented an *ummah* by himself. Al-Qurṭubī claims that an *ummah* could represent one person if this person is an exemplary model of goodness for other people.[13]

From the modern period, Quṭb adds that because Abraham was an exemplary human model of guidance, obedience, and giving thanks to God, he was regarded as equivalent to a whole *ummah* (in terms of its goodness and obedience to God). Otherwise, he is considered the leader of the *ummah* such that he reaps the reward of every member of the *ummah* who follows his guidance and way. Then his reward is equivalent to that of an *ummah*.[14] Faḍlallah's interpretation is more philosophical, where he thinks that the character of Abraham brings together all characteristics of a human who lives the spirit of the *ummah* and through his character spreads the message. Thus, he lives the spirit of the community in the physical form of one individual. Faḍlallah says that this character, inspired by the essence of the divine message, is not based on seeking personal gain that boosts the ego and hinders its communication with other people. Instead, this open, accommodating character encompasses the whole *ummah* in such a way that breaks the barrier between the spirit of the individual and that of the community.[15]

The analysis conducted in the previous chapter could be used to clarify why Prophet Abraham is described as an *ummah*. The analysis deduced that choice and responsibility form the essence of the *ummah* concept. *Ummah* in the Qur'ān is represented as a concept opposed to unquestioned religion of the forefathers and against persons occupying illegitimate privileged positions in society. Prophet Abraham's life is a vivid application of what the term *ummah* means, for his life manifests itself as against all established and unquestioned values and concepts. As a child (Qur'ān 21:52–74), Prophet Abraham challenged the idol worshipping practice of his people and broke their idols. His people threw him in fire but God ordered the fire to be cool and not to harm him. Then he withdrew from his father because his father was following the wrong religion (Qur'ān 6:74–80 and 19:41–48). Prophet Abraham challenged King Nimrud's power and his illegitimate claim of appropriating himself

13. Al-Qurṭubī, *Mukhtaṣar Tafsīr Al-Qurṭubī*, vol. 1, 113.

14. Quṭb, *Fī Ẓilāl al-Qur'ān*, vol. 4, 2201.

15. Faḍlallah, *Min Waḥy al-Qur'ān*, vol. 13, 319.

as a god by invoking God's control of the sun's direction and the king's impotence in that regard (Qur᾽ān 2:258). Prophet Abraham, from among all prophets sent to humanity, asked God to show him how resurrection occurs, for he was seeking certainty in his heart (Qur᾽ān 2:260). Even the trial of Prophet Abraham was of a unique nature, for he was ordered to "willingly" slaughter his son, whom he was granted at a very old age (Qur᾽ān 37:99–111).

The Qur᾽ān describes Abraham's trial as the "clear or manifest trial" (*al-balā᾽ al-mubīn*). It is common that trials happen to prophets without their actively consenting to the process. On the other hand, the trial of Prophet Abraham was specifically that he had to "willingly choose" to slaughter his son following the will of God. Thus, the life of Prophet Abraham represents a sequence of choices that went against the normal course of people and events around him. All of his choices were repeatedly manifest as the surrendering of his will to the will of his creator and taking full responsibility for his choices. He was consciously and actively following a specific path, irrespective of the path others were following around him. This explains why Prophet Abraham is the only prophet in the Qur᾽ān to be characterized as an "*ummah*," for he was indeed and par excellence a devout *ummah*. In addition, the life of Abraham and his *ummah* character may explain his other attribute as *khalīl Allah* ("the intimate friend of God"). His standing alone as an *ummah* against the many obstacles in his life and in the absence of a community that would support his message leads one to conclude that God would be his closest friend.

Defining the Ideology and Outlook of the Muslim *Ummah* through Prophet Abraham

The distinguished character of Abraham and his sincere devotion to God shows through his profound care for not only his people, but also his progeny. Living the spirit of the *ummah*, as described by Faḍlallah in the previous section, becomes manifest through his prayers to God to raise an *ummah* from his progeny that is following the divine will (*ummah muslimah*). Thus, Prophet Abraham becomes the key source for clarifying the creed of this *ummah*, defining its attributes and situating it within the context of previous prophets and *umam*, as shown in the following Qur᾽ānic verses:

> And when *Ibrāhīm* and Ishmael (*Ismāʿīl*) were raising the foundations of the house [the *Kaʿba* in Mecca]; [they prayed] "O our Sustainer, Accept this (service) from us: for, verily, you are all-hearing, all-knowing. O our Sustainer, Make us submissive to your will (*muslimayn laka*), and of our progeny[16] an *ummah* submissive to your will (*ummah muslimah*), and show us our ways of worship (*manāsikanā*), and accept our repentance: for, verily, you are the acceptor of repentance, the merciful. O our Sustainer, and raise up in their midst a messenger[17] from among them, who shall convey unto them your messages, and instruct them in scripture (*al-kitāb*) and wisdom, and cause them to grow in purity: for, verily, you are almighty, truly wise." And who, unless he be weak of mind, would turn away from *Ibrāhīm*'s creed (*millat Ibrāhīm*), seeing that We have indeed chosen him in this world, and that, verily, in the hereafter he shall be among the righteous? When his Sustainer told him, "Surrender your will to Me (*ʾaslim*)"—he answered, "I have surrendered my will (*ʾaslamtu*) to the Sustainer of all the worlds." And this was the legacy *Ibrāhīm* bequeathed to his children, and [so did] Jacob: "O my children! Behold, God has chosen for you the religion (*ʾIsṭafa lakum ad-dīn*); therefore die not except as people who have surrendered (unto Him) (*Muslimūn*)." Or were you witnesses when death was approaching Jacob, he said to his sons: "Whom will you worship after I am gone?" They answered: "we will worship your God, the God of your forefathers *Ibrāhīm* and *Ismāʿīl* and *Isḥāq* ('Isaac'), the one God; and unto Him we surrender ourselves (*lahū Muslimūn*)." Now that *ummah* has passed away; they shall have what they earned and you shall have what you earn, and you will not be judged for what they used to do. (Qurʾān 2:127–34)

16. The expression "our progeny" indicates Abraham's progeny through his first-born son, Ishmael, and is an indirect reference to the Prophet Muhammad, who descended from the latter. Note by Muhammad Asad.

17. Reference to Prophet Muhammad.

Premodern exegetes such as Al-Qummī[18] and At-Ṭabarī[19] interpreted the verses literally. Al-Qurṭubī adds that Prophet Abraham was special because he was the only prophet who prayed not only for himself and his *ummah*, but also for the Muslim *ummah* who would come generations after him.[20]

From the modern period, ʿAbduh, as a champion of reason and being against slavish imitation of tradition, says that *ummah muslimah* does not imply that everyone born in it or accept its title becomes a Muslim. Rather, belonging to this *ummah* requires sincerity to constantly choose to follow God's will. Thus, Abraham asked God to raise an *ummah* whose approach to religion is like his. ʿAbduh asserts that only then through the strength of this *ummah* and the cooperation of the group can Islam, as an ideology and a way of life, thrive and continue.[21] Faḍlallah also distinguishes between a shallow conventional Islam and a responsible one (*al-Islām al-mas᾿ūl*). The picture portrayed in the verses about Prophet Abraham describes a responsible Islam that is not confined to personal interest but extends to embrace the interest and welfare of others, even the future generations. This spiritual outlook, Faḍlallah suggests, is an essential base for building institutions, specifically religious ones. In numerous cases religious institutions are established for the service of society, but when their founders are faced with its materialistic needs, they can neglect its original purpose. Instead the institution is transformed into a place of exercising personal power and fighting over personal interests. In this case, Faḍlallah continues, religious institutions pose a threat to religious ethics when their custodians use religious slogans to defend personal desires.[22] Faḍlallah founded several Islamic institutions (educational, religious, and medical) in Lebanon, so he was more critical of institutional authorities as reflected in his interpretation. Both ʿAbduh and Faḍlallah are critical of affiliation with Islam, without "acting" based on Islamic ethics. In addition,

18. Al-Qummī, *Tafsīr al-Qummī*, vol. 1, 87–90.

19. At-Ṭabarī, *Jāmiʿ al-Bayān*, vol. 1, 768–76.

20. Al-Qurṭubī, *Mukhtaṣar Tafsīr Al-Qurṭubī*, vol. 1, 113.

21. Muhammad ʿAbduh and Muhammad Rashīd Riḍā, *Tafsīr al-Manār*, vol. 1, 469–71.

22. Faḍlallah, *Min Waḥy al-Qur᾿ān*, vol. 3, 31–37.

they both see a relationship between the action of the individual and the collective character of the *ummah*.

The codependent relationship between the individual and the collective is specified; were it not to exist, there would be no need for prophet Abraham to ask for an *ummah muslimah*, and it would suffice for him and his son to be Muslims. It may be possible that the prayers of Prophet Abraham reflect his wish for an *ummah* that did not exist during his lifetime. His earlier description as an *ummah* by himself, and the dual adjective (*muslimayn*) used in the above verses describing both prophets Abraham and Ishmael, show that there were no other believers during their time, hence no believing community. In these verses, we see the word Muslim and its derivatives (in verb and noun formats) come out strongly and for the first and only time, there is a literal mention of the Muslim *ummah* (*ummah muslimah*). This seems to imply that the presence of an *ummah* with its own *manāsik* ("rituals") is an indispensable practical means for the continuity of the message. *While the ummah should not be the motive for an individual endorsing a certain belief, its presence is important for nurturing it.*

First, Prophets Abraham and Ishmael established the foundations of the house (*al-Kaʿba*), which will be critical in later verses showing the direction of prayer for Muslims. Establishing the foundation relates not only to the physical attributes of the house, but also to a spiritual and intellectual base upon which this Muslim *ummah* is to be founded. The Qur'ānic verses explain the meaning of Islam as submitting one's will to the will of the creator. Prophet Abraham's life reflects active submission, as described in the previous sections. His life is a testament to what it means to be a Muslim and what it takes to become a Muslim *ummah* at the individual level. His prayers to raise a prophet from among the people, a prophet who would instruct them in scripture and purify them, hint at the coming of Prophet Muhammad. In one aspect, this suggests that Prophet Muhammad and his establishing Islam was a divine plan already in the making; thus it is not a new religion. In another aspect, it shows the continuity and connection between all the prophets and how their message was passed along their progeny, from one prophet to another, from Prophet Abraham to Prophet Jacob and then to Prophet Jacob's children. This chain was necessary for the completion of the divine will to humanity and the coming of the last prophet, Muhammad, who would revive the monotheistic tradition of all preceding prophets. The support of the prophets to each other, as shown in the verses between Abraham, Ishmael, Isaac, Jacob, and their descendants, reflects the covenant between God and his prophets discussed in the previous chapter. Abraham's creed (*millat Ibrāhīm*), or submission to the creator, is the chosen creed as supported later by Prophet Jacob: "God has chosen for you the religion (*Isṭafa lakum ad-dīn*)."

The attribute "Muslim" is clear and definitive in the above verses; however, the reference is not exclusive to Muslims as understood today as followers of Prophet Muhammad. It is exclusive in the sense of defining its specific character and attributes but is not exclusive to a specific community in human history. The verses show that Muslim as an attribute appeared repeatedly in human history every time a prophet called for submission to the one creator. Prophet Abraham was an *'ummah 'qānitan lillah'* ("devoutly obeying God's will"), and prophets of his progeny were Muslims as well, shown in the repetitive use of the word *Muslimūn* (Muslims) in the verses. While "Muslims" existed since the beginning of time as an attribute and a character with a specific ideology (*when one chooses, willingly and peacefully, to surrender his will to the will of their creator and follow his rulings*), the Qur᾽ānic verses imply that the "Muslim *ummah*" appeared only later in history after the coming of the last prophet Muhammad. The difference between the "Muslim *ummah*" and "Muslim" is explored shortly.

While the "Muslim *ummah*" as a historical entity appeared with Prophet Muhammad, its creed and essence is embodied in the father Prophet Abraham, who represents pure monotheism. While describing the characteristic of this "Muslim *ummah*" and its relationship to other prophets and how the message was passed on from one prophet to another, the previous Qur᾽ānic verses conclude with "Now that *ummah* has passed away; they shall have what they earned and you shall have what you earn, and you will not be judged for what they used to do." Thus, while reinforcing the connection with earlier communities, spiritually and ideologically, the verses end with stressing individual responsibility. The creed of submission to the one creator is chosen by God as the best creed, and there is no concept of chosen people or chosen community.

Prophet Abraham was chosen because of his submission to God, that is, because of his action rather than his descent or affiliation. The same applied to other prophets where we see the concept applied to Prophet Jacob and his sons, as he asked them on his deathbed what religion they will choose to follow. It is indeed the same God of all Prophets and the same creed of submission to one creator, but each individual will be judged according to his own free will and choice, irrespective of others' choices.

Fred Donner also does not confine the term Muslim, as described in the Qur'ān, to the followers of Prophet Muhammad. He defines Muslim as "essentially, a committed monotheist, and Islam means committed monotheism in the sense of submitting oneself to God's will."[23] Donner thinks that the first *ummah* established in the early period of Islam was "confessionally open"[24] and had an ecumenical character as it enjoined people to the worshipping of one God and observing the law of God whether it is the Torah, Gospel, or Qur'ān. This early *ummah* cuts across the boundaries of confessional communities, inclusive by nature. Donner calls the first *ummah*, which is discussed in detail in the next chapter, the Believers' movement. The historical document of Medina also supports the latter notion and reflects a movement (as Donner calls it) open to monotheists of any confession. I call the first *ummah* established in Medina the "Islamic *ummah*," which is different from the "Muslim *ummah*," which is explained in the following paragraphs.

Donner argues that the inclusion of Jews in the early *ummah* of Medina makes one skeptical of accounts reported in traditional sources about the Prophet's conflict with specific Jewish tribes. He thinks that these stories could have been greatly exaggerated or even fabricated by later Muslim tradition to depict Muhammad as a strong character.[25] In response to scholars who regard Prophet Muhammad's preaching as anti-Jewish, Donner says: "in view of the inclusion of some Jews in the Believers' movement, we must conclude that the clashes with other Jews or groups of Jews were the result of particular attitudes or political actions on their part, such as refusal to accept Muhammad's leadership or Prophecy. They cannot be taken as evidence of a general hostility to Judaism in the Believers' movement, any more than the execution or punishment of certain of Muhammad's persecutors from Quraysh should lead us to conclude that he was anti-Quraysh."[26]

23. Fred M. Donner, *Muhammad and the Believers: At the Origins of Islam* (Cambridge: The Belknap Press of Harvard University Press, 2010), 71.

24. Ibid., 69.

25. Ibid., 69–75.

26. Ibid., 74.

Some Orientalists such as Montgomery Watt[27] understand the concept of the Muslim *ummah* as a closed community exclusive to Muslims who follow the *sharīʿah* of the Qur᾿ān practiced by Prophet Muhammad. According to Watt, membership in such a ritualistic community where members fulfill all their religious duties leads to salvation.[28] While I agree with Watt that the term "Muslim *ummah*" describes followers of Prophet Muhammad who adhere to Islamic *sharīʿah,* I disagree with him describing the Muslim *ummah* as a closed ritualistic community. The problem with such an understanding is that it transforms the terms Muslim and *ummah* into labels defined by affiliation to a particular prophet or cultural group, respectively. It usurps the term from conscious intent and meaningful action and transforms it into passive affiliation. This understanding contradicts the Qur᾿ānic perception of the term Muslim, as an attribute of people who surrender their will to the will of God, and following God's *sharīʿah*. Evidently God's *sharīʿah* changed across time where the *sharīʿah* of Moses differed from Jesus' *sharīʿah* and subsequently from Muhammad's. Concurrently, what signified the characteristic "Muslim" also changed across time. In essence, it represents a committed monotheist as Donner explains, yet in practice it manifested itself differently across history. For example, during the time of Prophet Abraham, being a Muslim meant being a committed monotheist who follows the Abrahamic *sharīʿah.* However, when God sends a new prophet, for example, Moses or Jesus, then being a Muslim requires the person to follow the *sharīʿah* of the last prophet during his or her time because that in itself manifests surrendering to God's will. So one cannot be considered a Muslim if he or she happens to exist during Prophet Jesus' time, yet reject him and his *sharīʿah* and insist on following the previous prophet, that is, Moses, exclusively. Thereby, the characteristic "Muslim," in addition to its essential meaning, has a practical manifestation that is cumulative in nature. By endorsing

27. W. Montgomery Watt, "The Conception of the Charismatic Community in Islam," *Numen* VII (1960), 77–90; "Conditions of Membership of the Islamic Community," *Studia Islamica* XXL (1964), 5–12.

28. Also according to Hava Lazarus-Yafeh, "Is There a Concept of Redemption in Islam?," ed. Werblowsky and Bleeker, *Types of Redemption* (Leiden: E.J. Brill, 1970), 168. Rudi Paret defines *Ummah* as "ethnical, linguistic or religious people who are objects of the divine plan of salvation," in *The Shorter Encyclopedia of Islam*, ed. H. A. R. Gibb Kramers (Leiden: E.J. Brill, 1954).

a new prophet, a Muslim does not reject the previous one(s), but rather confirms them and surrenders to God's will by accepting his last prophet and his *sharīʿah.* This acceptance reflects trusting in the divine wisdom and in any order it decrees, as was evident in Prophet Abraham's life. *The characteristic Muslim is an* active *term that has an essential meaning, yet is time contingent.* Based on this understanding, being a Muslim today necessitates believing in Prophet Muhammad as well as all previous prophets. This may explain why the "Muslim *ummah*" appeared later in time, after the coming of the last Prophet as it manifests a culmination of the experiences of previous prophets and *umam.* Nonetheless, the Muslim *ummah* embodies and rejuvenates the pure monotheism espoused by Abraham.

One may ponder, if Muslims existed much earlier in time, why the "Muslim *ummah*" did not appear then? It may be possible that humans did not have the maturity and knowledge to form a Muslim *ummah* before the last prophet who came to perfect and complete religion to humanity as the Qurʾān says: ". . . This day I have perfected for you your religion and completed My favor upon you and have approved for you Islam as religion . . ." (Qurʾān 5:3). Another reason is that the "Muslim *ummah*" has specific characteristics and it plays a unique role in human history, hence the right timing was critical for its realization. The remaining sections in this chapter will explore the characteristics and function of this Muslim *ummah.* Furthermore, because the Muslim *ummah* embodies the pure monotheism of Abraham, free from historical and cultural additions, and embraces the earlier prophets before Prophet Muhammad, it forms the nucleus for the wider inclusive Islamic *ummah.* The latter is the pluralistic *ummah* established in Medina that Donner describes as confessionally open. This pluralistic Islamic *ummah*, which embraced Jews and Christians, was unprecedented in earlier faith traditions and would not be realized without the teachings of the Islamic *sharīʿah* given to Prophet Muhammad. Thus, my usage of "Islamic *ummah*" denotes being influenced by general Islamic ethics irrespective of religious affiliation, whereas the term "Muslim *ummah*" denotes followers of Prophet Muhammad and adherents to Islamic *sharīʿah.*

From that perspective, Watt describing the Muslim *ummah* as a closed community is a grave limitation, as it is the Muslim *ummah* who embraces other religions under the umbrella of Islamic ethics. Besides, confining salvation to performing religious rituals reflects a superficial understanding of Islamic ideology. The Qurʾānic verses 2: 128–29, "O our Sustainer, Make us submissive to your will (*muslimayn laka*), and of our progeny an *ummah* submissive to your will (*ummah muslimah*), and show us our ways of worship (*manāsikanā*)," presents a sequence. The act of forming an *ummah* starts with an individual will (as shown with the grammatical usage of dual form '*muslimayn laka*' where prophets Abraham and Ishmael refer to themselves). Then it is followed by the formation of a group of willed individuals following the same intent "of our progeny (*ummah muslimah*)." Finally, rituals form the last stage in embellishing the character of the *ummah* but not its essence: "show us our ways of worship (*manāsikanā*)." Hence merely following ritualistic practices, though it implies an apparent membership to the *ummah*, does not automatically lead to salvation as Watt argues. Salvation is granted by the mercy of God and depends on intent and deeds rather than simply by community affiliation.

The Qur'ān shows that despite the hypocrites' association with the Muslim community and the Prophet, they were threatened with punishment rather than granted salvation. "And from among the Bedouins, who are around you, there are hypocrites, and so are some among the people of Medina; who persist in hypocrisy; you (O Muhammad) know them not, We know them. We shall punish them twice, and thereafter they shall be brought back to a great torment" (Qur'ān 9:101). This verse clearly shows that there are members who claim belonging to the Muslim community, who are not even known to the Prophet, but God exposes their hidden agenda and warns them of a severe torment.

A better explanation of the concept of salvation in Islamic thought is described by Frederick Denny. Though he describes the Muslim *ummah* as a "community of salvation"[29] and a "holy community,"[30] he does not mean by salvation what is commonly understood in Christianity concerning a savior and original sin. He means by salvation a "deliverance from hell and salvation to paradise"[31] which cannot be achieved unless a Muslim belongs to the *ummah*. Hence is the idea "community of salvation" whereby salvation is attained through membership to the community or

29. Federick Denny, "Community and Salvation: The Meaning of the Ummah in the Qur'ān" (PhD diss., University of Chicago, Illinois, 1974), 203.

30. Ibid., 26.

31. Ibid., 155.

the *ummah*. As such, the Muslim *ummah* is called *firqa nājiya* ("saved group").[32]

Denny then explains the nature of salvation through Qur'ānic concepts: *falāḥ* ("success in this world and the hereafter"), *al-fawz al-ʿaẓīm* ("great victory"), *thawāb* ("reward"), *dār as-salām* ("abode of peace"), and *al-janna* ("paradise").[33] In addition, He uses the Qur'ānic word *furqān* ("the criterion") that refers to the Qur'ān itself to describe salvation. Through the Qur'ān and the correct knowledge from the divine within it, believers are delivered from dangers and calamities and mainly from the deadly dangers of untruth.[34] Denny argues that "salvation in Islam requires every bit as much as 'becoming' as it promises 'receiving.' To receive the status of one who is saved is to become once again pure."[35] Denny refers to the statement "become once again pure" to the concept of *tazkiya* ("achieving purification from one's acquired sins through repentance, refraining from those sins in the future, and asking God for forgiveness"). Thus, the *ummah* defined as the Muslim community at any historical point is a very simple generalization. Denny thinks that the *ummah* doesn't simply refer to that practical definition, but "it is the community being the community in specific ways. There is a normal quality inherent in it as it is a holy community with a transcendent origin and purpose, enlivened and sustained by a transcendent power."[36]

While apparently Denny's description of the Muslim *ummah* as a "holy community" or "community of salvation" may seem deterministic as described by early Orientalists, his approach is actually different. "Holy community" implies inherent qualities which endow a community with divine favor irrespective of their worthiness. This idea goes against Qur'ānic teachings, which assert that human beings or communities attain a status through their deeds and action, which is blessed by God's mercy and bounty, rather than by God's favoritism. However, Denny emphasizes continuous action required by the members of the *ummah*, hence the

32. Ibid., 155–56.

33. Ibid., 173.

34. Ibid., 189.

35. Ibid., 167.

36. Ibid., 17–18.

terms "becoming," "being," and purification. He recognizes that not only nominal affirmation is required to be saved, but also right action and life. Yet for him, "the *ummah* is indispensable to salvation, for it is the nurturing environment for living the fullest possible Muslim life."[37] I agree with Denny that the *ummah* is critical as a nurturing environment for its members. It may be possible that Prophet Abraham and Zayd, who were both described as an *ummah* were given such a description, while they are single individuals, to show the importance of being part of an *ummah* to sustain a life of righteous belief and action.

The Best Religion (*Dīn*) is Following *Millat Ibrāhīm* "*al-Ḥanīf*"

Based on the above discussion, it is not surprising that the Qur᾿ān advocates the creed of Abraham as an ideal to be followed:

> And who could be of better religion (*᾿aḥsanu dīnan*) than he who surrenders his whole being to God (*᾿aslama wajhahū lillah*) and is a good-doer, and follows the creed of Abraham who turned away from all that is false (*ʿittabaʿa millata Ibrāhīm ḥanīfan*)—seeing that Allah took Abraham as an intimate friend. (Qur᾿ān 4:125)

The religion of Islam is defined through the Islam of Abraham, his submission to the creator. Before introducing the *sharīʿah* of the last prophet, the Qur᾿ān clarifies the basics of belief, the absence of which nullifies the meaning and practice of *sharīʿah*. The Qur᾿ān clearly stipulates:

> Then, We have inspired you, [O Muhammad, with this message:] "Follow the creed of Abraham (*millat Ibrāhīm*) *ḥanīfan* and he was not of those who ascribe divinity to anything beside the one God." (Qur᾿ān 16:123) The Qur᾿ān also rebukes those who turn away from the creed of Abraham: "And who, unless he be weak of mind, would turn away from Abraham's creed

37. Ibid., 250.

> (*millat Ibrāhīm*), seeing that We have indeed chosen him in this world, and that, verily, in the hereafter he shall be among the righteous? When his Sustainer told him, 'Surrender your will to Me (*ʾaslim*)'—he answered, 'I have surrendered my will (*ʾaslamtu*) to the Sustainer of all the worlds." (Qurʾān 2:129–30)

The word *ḥanīf* is intimately linked with Prophet Abraham in the Qurʾān, as evidenced by the fact that of the twelve times *ḥanīf* is mentioned, ten refer to Prophet Abraham. In many Qurʾānic verses, the term *ḥanīf* is contrasted with ascribing divinity to anything beside the one God (*mushrik*). Among the Arabs, in pre-Islamic times, *ḥanīf* had a monotheistic implication that described people who turn away from sin and doubtful beliefs, specifically idol worship. *Taḥannuf* denoted the zealous devotions, mainly consisting of long vigils and prayers, by the seekers of God in pre-Islamic times. The root of the word *ḥanīf* is *ḥanafa*, a verb that means to be inclined toward a right state or tendency. The noun *al-ḥanf* means to move away from the path of aberrance to the straight path.[38]

Premodern interpretations focused on the different meanings of the word *ḥanīf*.[39] The modern exegesis is more interpretive. ʿAbduh added that *ḥanīf* means to be inclined (*al-māʾil*) away from wrong beliefs toward the

---

38. Shams ad-Dīn Bin Ali Bin Ṭūlūn as-Ṣāliḥī, *Risāla fī Tafsīr Qawlihi Taʿāla: Inna Ibrāhīm Kāna Ummah*, ed. Muhammad Yūsuf (Beirut: Ibn Ḥazm Press, 1997), 17.

39. Al-Qummī defines the word *al-ḥanīfiya* as *at-tahāra*, meaning ritualistic physical cleanliness that Prophet Abraham came with, and it remains to be practiced until the Day of Judgment, in Al-Qummī, *Tafsīr al-Qummī*, vol. 1, 86–87. At-Ṭabarī mentioned different interpretations; one is *al-ḥāj* (the pilgrim) where the religion of Abraham is called *al-ḥanīfiya* because he is the first *imām* who instructed believers, during his time and all those who came after him until the Day of Judgment, to follow him in pilgrimage rituals and take him as their guide. Thus, everyone who goes to pilgrimage and performs the rituals of Abraham is following his *millah*. Another interpretation is genuine devotion to God (*mukhlis lillāh*). A third interpretation is *al-ʾIstiqāma*, meaning to follow a straight path or to follow the religion of Abraham straightforwardly, in At-Ṭabarī, *Jāmiʿ al-Bayān*, vol. 1, 785–87.

straight path. It referred specifically to Prophet Abraham because people during his time were following the way of disbelief, and he opposed them and followed the right path.[40] Al-Muṭahharī contrasts *al-ḥanīf* as meaning to be inclined toward the truth, with *al-janīf* meaning to be inclined towards excess and carelessness. Then he relates the noun *al-ḥanāfa* to being just and unbiased in affairs; hence the Muslim *ummah* is described as *wasaṭ*.[41] Faḍlallah says that Abraham's creed, *al-ḥanīfiya*, is a comprehensive *millah* that broadly defines the straight path of guidance. This path is not determined by personal or dogmatic desires, which can be transformed into sects and factions. Abraham's monotheistic message captures monotheism in creed, law, worship, and life. Afterward, God revealed to later prophets various details that suited the needs of different times. Despite the varying details, all messengers and messages meet at the path of monotheism endorsed by Prophet Abraham as "he was not of those who ascribe divinity to anything beside the one God (*wamā kāna minal-mushrikīn*) (Qur'ān 2:135)." Then Abraham's creed, *al*-ḥanīfiya, is defined as the pure faith in opposition to *al-shirk* (anything added to religion to divide people).[42] Through this inclusive definition, Faḍlallah historically situates prophet's Abraham creed by showing the relevance of his ideology and its connection to later prophets and thereby clarifies its critical importance for believers across time. While Prophet Abraham is considered the father of all monotheistic traditions, his life and belief also act as a criterion that demarcates truth from falsehood. This is shown in the following verses:

> And they say, "Be Jews or Christians and you shall be on the right path." Say: "No, but [ours is] the creed of Abraham who turned away from all that is false (*millat Ibrāhīm ḥanīfan*) and was not of those who ascribe divinity to anything beside the one God." Say: "We believe in Allah, and in that which has been revealed to us, and that which has been revealed to Abraham and Ishmael and Isaac and Jacob and their descendants, and that

40. Muhammad ʿAbduh and Muhammad Rashīd Riḍā, *Tafsīr al-Manār*, vol. 1, 480.

41. Murtaḍa al-Muṭahharī, *Ṭahārat al-Rūḥ*, trans. Khalīl Zāil al-ʿAṣāmī (Beirut: Mu'assasat at-Tārīkh al-ʿArabī, 2004), 33.

42. Faḍlallah, *Min Waḥy al-Qur'ān*, vol. 3, 52.

> which has been given to Moses and Jesus; and that which has been given to all the [other] prophets by their Sustainer: we make no distinction between any of them. And it is unto Him that we surrender ourselves (*naḥnu lahu muslimūn*)." (Qur'ān 2:135–36)

This verse reflects the cumulative nature of the characteristic "Muslim" explained in the previous section. Submitting one's will to the will of the creator means accepting the creator's decision when he decides to send a new prophet supporting earlier ones. Similar to the concept of the covenant between God and his prophets, discussed in the previous chapter, in which prophets pledge allegiance to support each other, believers should also believe in all God's prophets and avoid discriminating between any of them. Thus, followers of Moses submit by believing in Jesus as well. Then followers of Jesus submit by believing in Muhammad. Similarly, followers of Muhammad submit by believing in all preceding prophets. However, belief in God and not ascribing partners to anything beside him are central and prerequisite to believing in all his prophets without differentiation. That is why Prophet Abraham's life became a model that clarified the concept of submission, not only as a creed but also in relation to other prophets; he was the father whose legacy was bequeathed to all monotheistic prophets of his progeny.

I don't think that contrasting the creed of Abraham with that of the Christians and Jews in this verse is meant to emphasize the exclusivity of the Muslim *ummah* as Denny claims.[43] Rather, I think it is meant to show the inclusiveness of the Muslim *ummah* toward earlier prophets and their scripture. The Qur'ān upholds Jews and Christians as followers of prophets Moses and Jesus. However, it criticizes the unwillingness of Jews to accept prophets Jesus and Muhammad and the unwillingness of Christians to accept Prophet Muhammad. Thus, the verse clarifies to Christians and Jews using their own prophet, Prophet Abraham, the essence of believing in one God, surrendering to him, and—as a result—believing in all his prophets without distinction.

---

43. Federick Denny, "Community and Salvation: The Meaning of the Ummah in the Qur'ān" (PhD diss., University of Chicago, Illinois, 1974), 203.

I think that the chief implication of this verse is the concept of surrender to God rather than depicting competing ideologies of closed communities. The term *ḥanīf* is used to describe monotheists in general and thus it is perfect that it be used in this verse within a context of inclusivity. The premodern exegetes differed in their analysis of the verses. At-Ṭabarī interpreted *muslimūn* at the end of the verse as surrendering to God in obedience and submitting to Him in worship (*khāḍiʿūn lahu bi-l-ṭāʿa, madhʿunūn lahu bil-ʿubūdiyya*),[44] and not as an exclusive community of Muslims. However, al-Qurṭubī says that Abraham is called *ḥanīf* because he is inclined away from the despised religions to the religion of God which is Islam.[45]

Modern exegetes endorse the inclusive and unifying implication of the verses. ʿAbduh says that the verses elicit a rhetorical question to both Jewish and Christian communities, who are depicted as exclusive communities, about the religious identity of Prophet Abraham. If guidance were limited to being either a Jew or a Christian, and Prophet Abraham was neither a Jew nor a Christian; thus would that imply that Prophet Abraham was misguided? Thus, ʿAbduh concludes that the verses encourage believers to focus on unity and consensus, and call for the essence and the spirit of religion which does not provoke conflict.[46] By not restricting guidance to one specific community, Faḍlallah says that the verses demonstrate that God does not favor one people or nation over another; rather all people are equal before him. Prophet Abraham's creed represents the pure monotheism that encompasses all messages and embraces all messengers. The Qur᾽ān takes Prophet Abraham as a criterion that determines truth from falsehood. Those who follow the path taken by Prophet Abraham, because all agree that he is the father, are the guided and those who divert from his path and prefer to take the path of separation, division and exclusivity are the misguided. Faḍlallah adds that the Qur᾽ān presents us with a model for successful dialogue between different peoples who

44. At-Ṭabarī, *Jāmiʿ al-Bayān*, vol. 1, 788.

45. Al-Qurṭubī, *Mukhtaṣar Tafsīr Al-Qurṭubī*, vol. 1, 159.

46. Muhammad ʿAbduh and Muhammad Rashīd Riḍā, *Tafsīr al-Manār*, vol. 1, 480–83.

search for commonalities as a starting point.[47] Quṭb thinks that the unity implied in the verses forms the basis of Islamic thought which renders the Muslim *ummah* the inheritor of all previous divine messages. Besides, it makes the Islamic order cosmopolitan where all people can live in peace without fear of oppression or biases.[48]

The first verse referred to in this section states that the best religion (*dīn*) is surrendering one's will to the will of God and following the creed (*millah*) of Abraham "*ḥanīf*." The closest English translation of the Arabic word *dīn*[49] is religion. In a general sense, *dīn* means the sacred norm by which life in its totality is shaped. It is a way of life based on teachings that were revealed to a prophet.[50] At-Ṭabaṭabāʾī thinks that *dīn*, in Qurʾānic terms, is a term that describes morals and laws in general. Thus believers and atheists each have a specific *dīn*. His rationale is that each human being follows specific laws in life, whether these laws were derived from divine revelation, or conceived by a particular person or group as a followed ideology. Nevertheless, the best *dīn* described in the Qurʾān is that which is based on sound innate nature (*fiṭrah*) rather than desires, or individual and social inclinations and biases.[51] When *dīn* is based on sound innate nature, following a divine *sharīʿah* becomes peaceful and sincere without coercion. Shams ad-Dīn argues that there should be a distinction between religiosity, as a psychological state endorsed by individuals, and religion (*dīn*). *Dīn* is equivalent to certain laws and concepts endorsed by a society and used as a base to build a civilization. A civilization can create its own religion and, through it, define its values.[52]

---

47. Faḍlallah, *Min Waḥy al-Qurʾān*, vol. 3, 48–53.

48. Quṭb, *Fī Ẓilāl al-Qurʾān*, vol. 1, 118.

49. The word *dīn* is derived from the root *dāna*, which means to obey and submit. *Dīn* also means justice (*al-ḥisāb; al-jazāʾ*). In addition, *dīn* means the custom (*al-ʿāda*), in Ibn Manḍhūr, *Lisān al-ʿArab* (Beirut: Dār ʾIḥyāʾ at-Turāth al-ʿArabī, 1993), vol. 4, 460–61.

50. Seyyed Hossein Nasr, *The Essential Seyyed Hossein Nasr*, ed. William Chittick (Canada: World Wisdom Press, 2007), 53.

51. Muhammad Ḥusayn at-Ṭabaṭabāʾī, *Al-Qurʾān fil-Islām*, trans. Aḥmad al-Ḥusaynī (Tehran: Dār az-Zahrāʾ, 1973), 19.

52. Faraḥ Mūsa, *Ad-Dīn wad-Dawla wal-Ummah ʿand al-Imām Muhammad Mahdī Shams Ad-Dīn* (Beirut: Dār al-Hādī, 2001), 31.

Millah[53] is interpreted as a religion or denomination.[54] Half of the Qur'ānic verses (8 verses)[55] referring to *millah* associate it with Abraham and the word *ḥanīf*. Most of the remaining verses[56] mentioning the word *millah* refer to people who follow an opposite path to the one adopted by God's messengers. Thus, it seems that the *millah* of Prophet Abraham (*ḥanīf*) is contrasted with the *millah* of those who reject the path of submission and resort to other paths, usually a path of the forefathers or of the culture and ideas of a particular society.

I think that *millah* is the essence of *dīn* because people can subdue a particular *dīn* to their own *millah*. The Qur'ān clarifies that the essence of the best *dīn* is sincere submission to the will of the creator, which is exemplified in the Qur'ān through the *millah* of Abraham (al-*ḥanīf*). Any other *millah* deviant from the *millah* of *ḥanīf* will not be considered sincere, as it incorporates other guides such as society, culture, forefathers, and so forth. As a result, a deviant *millah* will affect the way *dīn* is practiced and understood. There is one verse in the Qur'ān that relates *millah* to personal desires and biases:

> For, never will the Jews nor yet the Christians be pleased with you (Muhammad), unless you follow their own *millah*. Say: "Behold, God's guidance is the only true guidance." And, indeed, if you were to follow their desires after what you have received of knowledge, you would have none to protect you from God, and none to support you. (Qur'ān 2:120)

It is worth noting that the verse mentioned *millah* instead of *dīn* and then related it to desires (*'ahwā'*). The *dīn* of Jews and Christians

---

53. In *Lisān al-ʿArab*, *millah* is defined as the followed way or path (*as-sunnah wal ṭarīqa*)—this meaning is based on its use in the Qur'ān—and it can also mean most of the *dīn* and the bulk of what messengers bring forth, in Ibn Manḍhūr, *Lisān al-ʿArab* (Beirut: Dār 'Iḥyā' at-Turāth al-ʿArabī, 1993), vol. 13, 188.

54. Check Denny's tracing of the word *millah* in the Qur'ān, its different interpretations and its Aramaic root in Federick Denny, "Community and Salvation: The Meaning of the Ummah in the Qur'ān" (PhD diss., University of Chicago, Illinois), 99–102.

55. Qur'ān (2:135); (3:95); (4:125); (6:161); (16:123) (*millat Ibrāhīm ḥanīfan*); and Qur'ān (2:130); (12:38); and (22:78) (*millat Ibrāhīm*).

56. Qur'ān (18:20); Qur'ān (7:88, 89); Qur'ān (14:13); Qur'ān (12:37).

is that brought forth by prophets Moses and Jesus, which is guidance from God similar to the *dīn* of Muhammad. However, the verse criticizes the *millah* of Jews and Christians that has deviated from the *millah* of Moses and Jesus (i.e., submission) because they started following their personal desires and inclinations. Thus, the *millah* is the critical element that defines and shapes the practice of religion (*dīn*), which is supported by its earlier definition (most of the *dīn*). That is why the first Qur'ānic verse mentioned in this section states that the best *dīn* is the one that follows *al-milla al-ḥanīfiya* of Abraham.

Al-Manāsik (the Rituals)

The term *ḥanīf* also incorporates a ritual dimension. "*Ḥanīf* is not an abstract concept, but one which in its very essence seems to reflect purposeful spiritual and ritual activity."[57] The Qur'ānic verse where rituals and submission are connected is mentioned in section i: ". . . Make us submissive to your will, and of our progeny an *ummah muslimah*, and show us our ways of worship (*manāsikanā*) . . ." (Qur'ān 2:128). However, what makes practicing the rituals a form of worship is their divine origin (Abraham said "show us our *manāsik*"). If the rituals originate in culture, they lose their significance; hence submission precedes and is prerequisite to performing rituals as the latter verse shows. Nevertheless, prescribed rituals are crucial for anchoring the concept of submission to the creator in practical life. After the latter verse, the concept of *manāsik* is associated with the concept of *ummah* twice in *sūrat al-Ḥaj* ("chapter of the pilgrimage"):

> For every *ummah*, we have appointed a holy rite (*mansakan*) that they may mention God's name over the sustenance he gave them from animals. Your God is the one God, so to him surrender (*'aslimū*) and give glad tidings to the humble (*mukhbitīn*). (Qur'ān 22:34)

> For every *ummah*, we have appointed a holy rite (*mansakan*) that they shall perform (or follow). Let them not therefore

---

57. Denny, "Community and Salvation: The Meaning of the Ummah in the Qur'ān," 98.

dispute with you [Muhammad] on the matter, and invite them to your Lord for you are surely on a right path. (Qur᾿ān 22:67)

It is worth noting that the first time the concept of *manāsik* and *ummah* are associated, is in the verse in which Abraham and Ishmael are raising the foundation of the house (*Ka῾ba*), whose location determines the direction of ritual prayers (*ṣalāt*) and is the center of pilgrimage for Muslims. The two concepts are associated again in the chapter of pilgrimage in the Qur᾿ān. The pilgrimage is the most intensified form of worship prescribed in Islam and relates to Prophet Abraham in its essence and form. I think relating the concept of *manāsik* to pilgrimage reorients the person back to the model of Prophet Abraham's submission and the essence of *ḥanīf.* The root of the word *mansak* is *nusuk* which means worship and every act that brings one closer to God.[58]

The first verse (22:34) implies the meaning of the animal sacrifice, and the second verse (22:67) implies other rituals prescribed by God for different *umam.* Premodern exegesis such as at-Ṭabarī[59] interpreted the verses literally, while Al-Qummī interpreted *mansak* as "*madhhaban yadhhabūna fīh*" which can be translated as a way or a sect they follow.[60] Modern exegesis went into more detail comparing the Muslim *ummah* with other *umam.* For example, Faḍlallah interprets the verses in an inclusive tone. He says that God has prescribed different ways or holy rituals for different *umam,* the rituals conforming to Islamic *sharī῾ah* in some points and differing with it in others because the particularity of place, time and culture.[61] Nonetheless, all divine rituals are representations of following God's commands and submitting to him. Hence verse 22:34 concludes by "Your God is the one God, so to him surrender (*᾿aslimū*) and give glad tidings to the humble (*mukhbitīn*)." Therefore, there is no need to create disputes that divide people into different sects resulting in conflicts and wars; rather, unity is encouraged by reminding people of the common source who prescribed the different rituals and the main reason behind practicing those rituals, which is submission to the divine will.

58. It also means sacrifice, and another meaning is whatever *sharī῾ah* commands in Ibn Manḍhūr, *Lisān al-῾Arab*, vol. 14, 127.

59. At-Ṭabarī, *Jāmi῾ al-Bayān*, vol. 10, 211–12, 259–60.

60. Al-Qummī, *Tafsīr al-Qummī*, vol. 2, 87.

61. Faḍlallah, *Min Waḥy al-Qur᾿ān*, vol. 16, 67.

While Faḍlallah stresses the commonalities, Quṭb highlights the differences. Quṭb distinguishes the Islamic ritual in comparison to other rituals by explaining how the practice reflects the human submission to the divine will. For example, while animal sacrifice is a ritual that is known for various *umam*, the Qur'ān rectifies its practice by clarifying its main purpose. Quṭb asserts that Islam unites feelings and actions all in the way of God, hence all life becomes fashioned by one's creed and the human self is not distracted by different yearnings. Consequently, mentioning God's name on the sacrificial animal becomes the clear purpose of conducting the practice, otherwise the sacrifice is nullified and becomes forbidden (*ḥarām*). In the Qur'ān, rituals are symbolic manifestations of one's creed. The purpose of the sacrificial animals is clarified in the following verse: "And the camels and cattle We have appointed for you as among *the symbols of Allah*; for you therein is much good. So mention the name of Allah upon them when lined up [for sacrifice]; and when they are [lifeless] on their sides, then eat from them and feed the needy and the beggar. *Thus We made them subservient to you that you may be grateful.* It is not the flesh and blood of your sacrifice that reaches (pleases) Allah. *What reaches (pleases) Allah is your piety (taqwa).* Thus, *He made them subservient to you that you may glorify Allah for that [to] which He has guided you*; and give good tidings to the doers of good" (Qur'ān 22:36–37).[62] The Qur'ān asserts that the mere fact of animals being made subservient to human beings is a sign from God which merits human's gratitude and humbleness. Hence, what merits the sacrificial act is not the technical part of it, but the intention behind doing it (it acts as a reminder to glorify the creator and thank him) and the way of conducting the sacrifice (i.e. how the animal is treated, hence the piety (*taqwa*) reaches God). The intention creates humility in the human self which manifests in the way the animal is treated and sacrificed. Therefore, the creed (intention) is critical for performing the act (the sacrifice) as Quṭb explains.

Submitting to the divine will is a continuous process of reorienting one's desire to the will of one's creator. That was clearly presented as the concept of "Islam" in Prophet Abraham's life. *His character "al-ḥanīf" was achieved by his persistent trusting in the divine wisdom over any personal inclination.* His sincere devotion inspired his actions of opposing falsehood in a dominant culture/religion, challenging corrupt political authority, and

62. Quṭb, *Fī Ẓilāl al-Qur'ān*, vol. 4, 2422–23.

even attempting to sacrifice his own son when God ordered it. We witness in his life a continuous divine training of the self, or the ego, resulting in a sincere devotion and trust in the divine wisdom. The order to physically sacrifice his son represents a symbolic culmination of a life full of different forms of sacrifice at various levels. Nevertheless, the end result (God sacrificed a lamb instead of the son, thereby marking a historic feast for generations to come) reflects the divine wisdom behind the essence of submission and the inevitable sacrifice it entails. It shows that submitting to the divine will is not about coercion and torture; rather it is a training of the self to raise it beyond its egoistic desires. Submission is a form of self-disciplining that leads to a sacred realm that purifies and nourishes an individual's holistic development. Developing a relationship of "trust" between the human being and his creator inevitably perfects the human self. *Submitting in peace (al-Islām) in that sense becomes a manifestation of one's trust in the divine wisdom rather than blind obedience to divine orders.* Now it is clear from Prophet Abraham's life that the multiple meanings of *nusuk*[63] ("ritual") are interconnected and represent different forms of submission. *The essence of any ritual or any command of sharīʿah is basically an act of submission to the creator. Such actions usually entail a sacrifice on behalf of one's ego resulting in prosperity and success in this life and the hereafter.*

The Middle *Ummah* (*al-Ummah al-Wasaṭ*) and the Witness (*Shahāda*)

After thoroughly clarifying the creed of the Muslim *ummah,* the Qur᾽ān describes the characteristic of this *ummah* and its function. The main exemplary model of the Muslim individual and *ummah* is the character and life of Prophet Abraham. In the same vein we find a connection between changing the direction of the *qibla* (direction of ritual *ṣalāt*) to Abraham's *qibla* (the *Kaʿba*), attributing to the *ummah* the characteristic of *wasaṭ* and as a result giving it the function of *shahāda* ("witness"). This connection will be explored in this section and is described in the following verses:

63. The word *nusuk* ("ritual") implies the meanings of worship, every act that brings one closer to God, the need for sacrifice, and whatever *sharīʿah* commands.

> "The fools among the people will say 'What has turned them from their *qibla* to which they used to face in prayer?' Say to Allah belongs the east and the west. He guides whom he wills to a straight path. And likewise we have made you *ummah wasaṭ*, so that you may bear witness [to the truth] before humankind and so that the messenger may bear witness [to it] before you and we appointed the *qibla* which you formerly observed only that We might know those who followed the Messenger from those who would turn on their heels (From the Faith). And indeed it was a hard test save those Allah has guided, But Allah would never make your faith (prayers) be lost for Allah is most merciful and compassionate." (Qur'ān 2:142–43)

Asma Afsaruddin discussed the Qur'ānic exegeses of the verses from the late first/seventh century to the modern time in an attempt to retrieve the Muslim understandings of *wasaṭ* through various times, thereby showing how different sociopolitical circumstances affect the understanding of Qur'ānic text.[64] Pre-modern exegetes from the earliest period such as Mujāhid b. Jabr (d. 104/722), Muqātil b. Sulaymān (d. 150/767) and ʿAbd al-Razzāq al-Sanʿānī (d. 211/827) interpret *wasaṭ* as just and temperate (*ʿadl*). After the late third/ninth century, starting with at-Ṭabarī, the interpretation expanded to mean "the best" (*al-khiyār*) and "most excellent" in comparison with other communities, such as Jews and Christians. Muslims are described as a moderate community because they avoid extremism in their practice of religion for they were neither too ascetic like Christians nor too legalistic like Jews. The late sixth/twelfth century al-Rāzī and late eighth/fourteenth century Ibn Kathīr relates the concept to Prophet Abraham's *qibla*, thereby drawing an analogy between God's choosing prophet Abraham in the world and his choosing the Muslim *ummah* to be the best *ummah*. Thus, Afsaruddin concludes that the pre-modern understanding of *wasaṭ* after the third/ninth century became increasingly confessional and exclusivist, signifying Muslims as God's select community.

By extending her research to the modern time, Afsaruddin presents a different interpretation that is more inclusive and universal, such as that

64. Asma Afsaruddin, "The Hermeneutics of Inter-faith Relations: Retrieving Moderation and Pluralism as Universal Principles in Qur'anic Exegesis," *Journal of Religious Ethics* 37, no. 2 (2009): 331–54.

which is endorsed by Muhammad ʿAbduh. The latter still interpreted *wasaṭ* as moderate and the best but does not confine those attributes to a closed Muslim community; rather he relates it to individual's actions that any human being can perform.[65] ʿAbduh adds that this just and middle attitude is represented by human perfection whereby rights are granted to each owner. Such a perfect human fulfills his duties towards his lord, towards himself, towards his physical body, towards his relatives and all human beings. This occurs by following the Prophet's *sunnah* and *sharīʿah*, as he represents the perfect model for this *wasaṭ* characteristic. This *ummah* will be a witness to other people by its path and its physical and spiritual merit.[66]

Faḍlallah interpreted (*ummah wasaṭ*) in terms of communal organization. Based on this moderate and balanced position of Islamic thought between spirit and matter, Faḍlallah describes a similar balanced position in community organization, which balances between two extreme positions: one is the extremist communal position which overstresses the rights of the community, thereby overlooking individual rights; the second is the extremist individualistic position which overstates the rights of individuals, thereby ignoring the role of community. When the *ummah* endorses this balanced position between spirit and matter, and in community organization, it becomes the reference point that the rest of the communities or people refer to; thereby the *ummah* becomes the witness. Similarly, the Prophet would be the witness to (and of) the *ummah* because he represents the most balanced and perfect model of that *ummah*. The Prophet also represents the focal point that all the members of the *ummah* refer to.

Next, Faḍlallah relates the concepts *wasaṭ* (middle), *shahāda* (witness), and *qibla* together. As ʿAbduh, he also relates the concept of *wasaṭ* to the best of something; thereby he deduces that the Muslim *ummah* has a leading role among nations. It should have the leading role in thinking, establishing justice, and guiding others, which in turn makes it a witness to (and of) other nations. Similarly, the Prophet was the model and the guide to humanity as well as the witness to them. As for changing the direction to the *qibla*, this was a critical test to determine the sincerity of believers' belief. Those who hold a critical position should be required to pass the hardest tests in order to deserve such a place and to sustain the

65. Ibid., 332–50.

66. Muhammad ʿAbduh and Muhammad Rashīd Riḍā, *Tafsīr al-Manār*, vol. 2, 4–5.

responsibility associated with it. Hence, changing the direction of prayers is relevant to the context of the verse in which the *ummah* is described as a middle *ummah* and a witness to (and of) other nations.[67] Quṭb goes at length to describe how the *ummah* holds a middle or moderate position among other *umam* which merits it to the unique attribute of being the best and the leader. Similar to ʿAbduh's and Faḍlallah's interpretation, he adds that the Muslim *ummah* is *wasaṭ* in its location on earth as it located in the center between East and West. It is also central in time for it mates between the spiritual heritage of divine messages and progressive rational thought in a balanced way which keeps it developing. Nonetheless, Quṭb thinks that the Muslim *ummah* has lost its leading role because it abandoned the path that God has chosen for it and instead imitated paths of other nations.[68]

The modern exegete at-Ṭabaṭabāʾī does not abide by the interpretation of middle between the extremes, whether in terms of religious practice or understanding. Instead, he says the *ummah* is *wasaṭ* because it acts as a medium between the Prophet and the people (*takhalulihā bayna al-rasūl wan-nās*). He supports his point through the Qurʾānic verse that makes the condition *wasaṭ* prerequisite to the position of witnessing, as shown in the verse by the use of 'so that': "we have made you a *wasaṭ ummah*, so that you may bear witness [to the truth] before humankind and so that the messenger may bear witness [to it] before you."[69] We find a similar kind of interpretation of the *ummah* as a mediator in al-Qummī's interpretation, but he interprets middle *ummah* as middle *aʾimma*, i.e. justly guided *aʾimma*, and mediators between the Prophet and people. The just *aʾimma* will in turn be witnesses to (and of) people.[70]

Shams ad-Dīn also addresses the concept of the witness in relationship to *wasaṭ*. He finds it incumbent upon the Muslim *ummah* to be open and interactive with other people to warrant holding the position of the witness. The description of the Muslim *ummah* as a middle *ummah* and a witness to (and of) other *umam* defines it in relation to other

67. Faḍlallah, *Min Waḥy al-Qurʾān*, vol. 3, 73–84.

68. Quṭb, *Fī Ẓilāl al-Qurʾān*, vol. 1, 130–32.

69. Muhammad Ḥusayn at-Ṭabaṭibāʾī, *Al-Mīzān fī Tafsīr al-Qurʾān* (Beirut: Muʾasassat al-ʾAʿlamī lil-Maṭbūʿāt, 1983), vol. 1, 322–23.

70. Al-Qummī, *Tafsīr al-Qummī*, vol. 1, 91.

umam. The witness has to be separate and distinguished from the one witnessed to. At the same time, the witness has to be open and maintain constant communication with the witnessed. It would be impossible to be a witness to something from which one is totally isolated. Witnessing necessitates knowledge and constant interaction with the other.[71] This is a closer interpretation to that of At-Ṭabaṭabā'ī, as they both imply that the *ummah* holds the position of a witness because of its presence among other people and its way of interacting with them. Denny also describes *ummah wasaṭ* as a forgiving community that allows for mediation between human beings, thereby reflecting God's forgiveness.[72] He adds that the *ummah*, by its obedience to God expressed through rituals, becomes the bearer of the Prophetic message to humankind.[73] Thus, the *ummah* acts as a mediator between Prophet Muhammad and humankind. Then Denny seemingly contradicts himself by saying that there is no easy friendship between the *ummah* and others because the *ummah* is a closed group always seeking unity and self-sufficiency and is not interested in having open relationships with others.[74]

In the coming paragraphs, I combine the latter differing interpretations in relation to what has been discussed earlier in this chapter and in relation to the meanings of the Qur'ānic terms in the Arabic lexicon.[75] In the science of logic, it means the reason for the meeting of the extremities, and it also means the proof (*ad-dalīl*).[76] *Al-shahīd* (witness) is the one who is present (*al-ḥāḍir*) and the one who tells what he has seen or

71. Muhammad Mahdī Shams ad-Dīn, *Fil-Ijtimā' as-Siyāsī al-Islāmī* (Beirut: Al-Mu'asassa al-Jāmi'iya lil-Dirāsāt wal-Nashr, 1992), 101–2.

72. Denny, "Community and Salvation: The Meaning of the Ummah in the Qur'ān," 226.

73. Ibid., 61–62.

74. Ibid., 226–39.

75. In Lisān al-'Arab, the term wasaṭ is used to describe the middle of a thing or what is between the extremes. What is in the middle implies balance, hence it is just ('adl) and thus the best (Al-khiyār) compared to the extremes. Wasaṭ also means among or between when used to describe someone living among his people (wasaṭ al-qawm [baynahum]) in Ibn Manḍhūr, Lisān al-'Arab, vol. 15, 293–96.

76. Jīrār Jihāmī and Samīḥ Daghīm, Al-Mawsū'a al-Jāmi'a li-Muṣṭalaḥāt al-Fikr al-'Arabī wal-'Islāmī (Beirut: Maktabat Lubnān Nāshirūn, 2006), vol. 2, 3052–53.

witnessed. It also means the one who delivers the message and clarifies it (*muballigh* wa-*mubayyin*) when the term is used to describe prophets. *Shahāda* ("witnessing") is a function attributed to the best, then the best of the *ummah*, so Prophet Muhammad is the first *shahīd*.[77] In the science of logic, *shahāda* acts as a medium between the accuser and the accused (*wasaṭ bayna al-mudda ʿī wal-mudda ʿī ʿalayh*), so a witness can be a friend, foe, or neutral party.[78]

The Muslim *ummah* has been associated specifically with Prophet Abraham as a character and religion, and the discussed verses (Qurʾān 2:142–43) urge the Muslims to follow the direction of Prophet Abraham in their prayers. The verses show that changing the direction of prayer was a difficult test for the believers, which, when followed, manifest the essence of peaceful submission to God, as previously discussed. Only those who passed that test understood the meaning of submission and trusted the wisdom of their creator, thereby following his orders willingly and peacefully. Similar to the character of Prophet Abraham, who was constantly tested in his submission, the *ummah* was also tested in its submission to the creator. Furthermore, when Prophet Abraham passed his tests, he was rewarded by being chosen in this world and among the righteous in the hereafter,[79] and his religion is acknowledged to be the best religion.[80] Similarly, when the *ummah* passed its test, it was rewarded by being granted the attribute of *wasaṭ* and chosen to be the witness to (and of) other nations.

---

77. Ibn Manḍhūr, *Lisān al-ʿArab*, vol. 7, 222–25.

78. Jīrār Jihāmī and Samīḥ Daghīm, *Al-Mawsūʿa al-Jāmiʿah li-Muṣṭalaḥāt al-Fikr al-ʾArabī wal-ʿIslāmī*, vol. 1, 1535.

79. This has been discussed in the earlier sections and shown in the Qurʾanic verse "And who, unless he be weak of mind, would turn away from Abraham's creed (*millat Ibrāhīm*), seeing that We have indeed chosen him in this world, and that, verily, in the hereafter he shall be among the righteous? When his Sustainer told him, 'Surrender your will to Me (*ʾaslim*)'—he answered, 'I have surrendered my will (*ʾaslamtu*) to the Sustainer of all the worlds' " (Qurʾān 2:129–30).

80. This was discussed in the Qurʾanic verse "And who could be of better religion (*ʾaḥsanu dīnan*) than he who surrenders his whole being to God (*ʾaslama wajhahu lillah*) and is a good-doer, and follows the creed of Ibrahim who turned away from all that is false (*ʾittabaʿa millata Ibrāhīm ḥanifan*)—seeing that God took Ibrāhīm as an intimate friend" (Qurʾān 4:125).

Those who have gained the attribute of *wasaṭ* by continuously reorienting their direction toward the *Kaʿba* (*qibla* can be metaphorically used to denote one's orientation in life, whether it is submitting to God or to false desires, and not only as a prayer direction) are those who are chosen to witness to the truth before people. As defined in the dictionary, *wasaṭ* as a characteristic implies justice and the best of something, a definition that is supported by the latter attribute of *shahīd*, which is a function granted to the best of the *ummah*. The first *shahīd* is Prophet Muhammad, who bears witness to the truth before Muslims because he is present among them (*ḥāḍir*), whether physically or figuratively, and their leader and model. Likewise, those who chose to follow the Prophet and who are consequently the best of the Muslim community form a *wasaṭ ummah* who bear witness to the truth before all people (including Muslims and others). This interpretation does not equate *ummah wasaṭ* with the denominational community of Muslims, but rather to those who chose to follow the *qibla* of Prophet Abraham, the father whose legacy stands as a witness and a criterion, to determine those who follow God's will from those who do not. It is exclusive in the sense that Prophet Abraham is the guide to be followed to join that *ummah*, but it is inclusive in the sense that it is open to anyone interested in joining it.

Ummah from *Ahl Al-Kitāb* (Jews and Christians)

Attributing specific characteristics to other *umam* belonging to different religious communities is a common trend in the Qur'ān. For example, the Jews and Christians who are described as the people of the book (*Ahl Al-Kitāb*) also had a righteous contingency of people described as an *ummah* with specific characteristics, as shown in the following verses.

> They are not all alike, from the people of the book there is an *ummah qā'ima* reciting the verses of Allah at night while prostrating in prayer. They believe in Allah and the Day of Judgment and they enjoin righteousness and deter wrongness and they hasten (in emulation) in (all) good works and these are among the righteous. And whatever good they do, they shall not be denied it for Allah is aware of those conscious of Him. (Qur'ān 3:113–15)

Premodern exegetes such as At-Ṭabarī reported different interpretations for *ummah qā'ima*. Two interpretations restrict this *ummah* to the people of the book who have accepted Islam.[81] Another interpretation is based on a *ḥadīth* reported by *Imām* Ahmad in which Prophet Muhammad arrived in the mosque when it was dark and found his companions waiting for the last prayer (*'ishā'*). He told them that there are no religious groups who performs that prayer except the Muslims. However, the Qur'ānic verses (3:113–15) of inclusion were revealed in response to what the Prophet said.[82] This interpretation obviously does not restrict *ummah qā'ima* to those who have accepted Prophet Muhammad.

Modern exegetes such as 'Abduh and Faḍlallah focused more on the inclusive nature of the verses by not restricting this *ummah* to those who accepted Islam. 'Abduh honestly says that most interpreters found it hard to accept the idea that there are righteous people among Christians and Jews, people who are believers and do good deeds. Hence these verses descended to clarify divine justice and remove that misconception among Muslims. In addition, this is a clear statement that God's religion is one with the same message sent by all prophets. Anyone who takes the message seriously and honestly, such that he or she commands what is right and forbids the wrong, is considered among the righteous. 'Abduh emphasizes that these verses prove to the people of the book that the Qur'ān is divine because God does not equally judge them and polytheists, hence recognizing their merit as believers. It also forbids people to discriminate between different *umam* and religious groups, only because of disagreement on minor details. 'Abduh adds that the Qur'ān's description of some of the people of the book as upholding the truth in their religion does not nullify other verses in the Qur'ān that rebuke and identify another

81. One of them is a group of Jewish people who believed in Prophet Muhammad and accepted Islam. This is why the verse started with "they are not the same" to indicate that some of the people of the book were believers and others disbelievers in the prophethood of Muhammad. Another interpretation is a group loyal to the truth (*jama'a thābita 'ala al-ḥaqq*). It is also interpreted as being just (*'ādila*) or obedient to God (*muṭī'a*). In summary, it is a group that is upholding God's book and following his guidance, which came through his prophet. Thereby, all interpretations are restricted to those who have accepted Islam. In At-Ṭabarī, *Jāmi' al-Bayān*, vol. 3, 70–75.

82. Ibid., vol. 3, 70–75.

group from the people of the book, described as disbelievers, who have distorted the message of their holy books for worldly desires. He defends his argument by saying that also among Muslims, some strictly adhere to the Prophet's *sunnah* without knowing that some *'aḥadīth* ("prophetic sayings") are weak or fabricated (*ḍa'īf aw mawḍū'*). These people are still regarded as those who sincerely follow the practice of the Prophet, even though they are ignorant of the fact that some practices were added later by those who wanted to support their opinion or sect. The same argument applies to Jews and Christians who sincerely follow what they were told as the truth, even if parts of it are not authentic.[83] Faḍlallah says the uniqueness of this group from the general people of the book is their spiritual closeness to God (represented by their prayers and prostration during the night), a closeness that urges them to do good deeds, and hence they are associated with the righteous.[84] These interpretations support the notion suggested in this book that the concept of the *ummah* is associated with specific actions rather than denominational labels. Nonetheless, other modern interpreters are exclusivist, such as Quṭb, who restricts this *ummah* to those who joined the Muslim *ummah* and realized its characteristics by commanding righteousness and deterring evil.[85]

The second time *Ahl Al-Kitāb* is described as an *ummah* appears in the following verse:

> If they [the people of the book] had acted according to the Torah, the Gospel and what was sent down to them from their Lord [the Qur'ān], they would have been given abundance from above and from below; some of them constitute an *ummah muqtaṣida* but many of them are prone to wrong doing. (Qur'ān 5:66)

Afsaruddin compares the term *ummah muqtaṣida*, which describes the people of the book in the latter verse, with *ummah wasaṭ*, which describes Muslims in the earlier verse, by similarly discussing its premodern

---

83. Muhammad 'Abduh and Muhammad Rashīd Riḍā, *Tafsīr al-Manār*, vol. 4, 71–72.

84. Faḍlallah, *Min Waḥy al-Qur'ān*, vol. 6, 229–30.

85. Quṭb, *Fī Ẓilāl al-Qur'ān*, vol. 1, 450.

and modern Qur᾽ānic exegesis. The earliest premodern exegetes understood *ummah muqtaṣida* as a group of Jews and Christians who displayed righteous conduct as represented by being moderate and fair. These inclusive views, endorsed by exegetes such as al-Rāzī and al-Qurṭubī, based their interpretation on reports of the Companions attributed to the first two centuries of Islam.

The later medieval period witnessed exegetes such as al-Zamak̲šarī endorsing exclusive views that limited the interpretation of *ummah muqtaṣida* to Jews and Christians who have accepted Prophet Muhammad. From the modern period, Muhammad ʿAbduh finds a relationship between *ummah muqtaṣida* and *ummah wasaṭ* where he argues that there has never been a community that did not have a righteous group striving to better their *ummah*. Therefore, similar to how Muslims are described as *wasaṭ* because they uphold the ethical values of their scripture, people of the book are also described as *muqtaṣida* because they live up to the morals of their own scripture. ʿAbduh thereby concludes that religious affiliation as a name or cultural ascription is not the determining factor in earning the designation of being moderate or just; rather it is one's actions.[86] Afsaruddin thinks that "such a perspective offers the possibility of formulating universal principles of ethical and moral conduct, which may contribute to the formation of a genuinely pluralist global society today."[87] On a similar note, Faḍlallah says the beginning of the verse "If they had upheld the Torah and the Gospel and what was sent down to them from their Lord" suggests that the essence of these divine messages (Torah, Gospel, and Qur᾽ān) are equivalent, sharing common values.

The next part of the verse, "they would have been given abundance from above and from below," states the common goal of all divine messages, which is to establish justice and thereby create abundance on earth, allowing all people to live in peace and harmony. Thus the messages of the Torah and Gospel do not differ from the last message of the Qur᾽ān in their general concepts; rather there are differences in the details because of the variability of time and place. This is established by the Qur᾽ānic verses that speak of the Gospel confirming that which preceded it: "And

---

86. Asma Afsaruddin, "The Hermeneutics of Inter-faith Relations: Retrieving Moderation and Pluralism as Universal Principles in Qur᾽anic Exegesis," *Journal of Religious Ethics* 37, no. 2 (2009): 339–50.

87. Ibid., 331.

in their footsteps We sent Jesus the son of Mary, confirming the Torah that had come before him, and We gave him the Gospel in which was guidance and light and confirmation (*muṣaddiqan*) of the Torah that had come before it, a guidance and an admonition for the God-conscious" (Qur'ān 5:46). Then the Qur'ān speaks of itself as confirming both scriptures before it: "It is He Who has sent down the Book [the Qur'ān] to you [Muhammad] with truth, confirming what came before it. And he sent down the Torah and the Gospel" (Qur'ān 3:3). The latter verses are usually understood by Muslim scholars to imply supersession (*naskh*), where the newer message nullifies the earlier one. Faḍlallah argues that supersession addresses the specificities of each message that are confined to the time and place in which the message was revealed, but that does not tackle essential concepts about life and belief, which are common to all divine messages and indeed mutually confirmed. He adds that people usually have a tendency to judge communities based on the performance of the majority, but this verse warns against spreading misconceptions and being unfair to the minorities at the expense of the majority. Instead, one should be cautious about judging others in order to give each his due right.[88]

Two exclusivist views from both premodern and modern periods are Al-Qummī and Quṭb respectively. Al-Qummī interpreted "from above" meaning the rain and "from below" meaning the vegetation. He interpreted *ummah muqtaṣida* as Jewish people who have accepted Islam, so God called them *muqtaṣida.*[89] Quṭb thinks that the only condition for receiving this abundance is establishing God's law, which is not confined to the people of the book. The verse guarantees abundance, peace, and security as well as bliss in the hereafter for those who believe and establish God's law in all their affairs. On the other hand, the people of the book would receive this abundance only if they become Muslims and establish the laws of the Qur'ān.[90]

Yet what if Islam, as the final religion sent to humanity through Prophet Muhammad, has not reached a specific community or reached them as a distorted message through the misbehavior of some of its

88. Faḍlallah, *Min Waḥy al-Qur'ān*, vol. 8, 257–59.

89. Al-Qummī, *Tafsīr al-Qummī*, vol. 1, 198–99.

90. Quṭb, *Fī Ẓilāl al-Qur'ān*, vol. 2, 935–36.

followers? I think the verses address such a community. In that regard, I do not think there is a contradiction between inclusive and exclusive interpretations, but rather they become complementary. Inclusive interpretations, such as ʿAbduh's, suggest that God judges people by what they know as He sees directly through their hearts and intentions. It is possible that the knowledge that reached them is not complete, yet to the best of their knowledge they think it is complete and accordingly they are judged. This does not mean, however, that one should favor ignorance and undermine furthering their knowledge. Rather, this interpretation shows God's perfect justice as well as immense mercy in judging people. Besides, it emphasizes the most critical element in human behavior, which is sincerity in belief and action, and warns against ulterior motivations such as lies, hypocrisy, or rejecting the truth. Exclusive interpretations, such as Quṭb's, would then explain the situation of people only after receiving the message of Islam through legitimate sources.

Nonetheless, several commentaries from both the premodern and modern period confirm my conclusion in chapter 1 that the *ummah* does not describe a religious group of people labeled by a specific name or following specific cultural practices. Rather, the term has been used in the Qurʾān to denote a group of people from a community who act in a specific way such that they earn the designation of a characteristic *ummah*. Thus, choice and action are fundamental for the concept of the *ummah*. In addition, it refutes Orientalists' claims as well as those of Muslim exclusivists that the Muslim *ummah* is a closed community that is not open to anyone who wishes to be part of it. The above verses break barriers between different confessional communities and open them to each other by reminding them of the common moral values they share and by stressing that righteousness is one and the same for all, attained through sincere worship and as a result acting morally.

The Best *Ummah* (*Khayr Ummah*) Ever Raised Up for Humankind

The latter idea becomes further developed in this section, where we find a call to establish an *ummah*, practicing righteous deeds and constantly inviting its members and others to goodness (*khayr*); thereby this *ummah* earns the attribute "*khayr ummah*."

> Let there be from among you (*minkum*) an *ummah* inviting to goodness (*khayr*) and enjoining righteousness and deterring wrongness (*ya'murūna bil-ma'rūf wa yanhawna 'an al-munkar*) and those are the successful. (Qur'ān 3:104)

> You were (*kuntum*) the best (*khayr*) *ummah* ever raised up for humankind for you enjoin righteousness and deter wrongness and believe in Allah, and if the people of the book were to believe it would have been better for them, among them are believers but most of them are transgressors. (Qur'ān 3:110)

Premodern exegesis focused on who is given the designation "*khayr ummah* where both Shī'ī and Sunnī scholars confine it to a select group. Al-Qummī interprets the *ummah* that enjoins righteousness and deters wrongness as the family of Prophet Muhammad and whoever followed them. Al-Qummī then, based on a question asked to an *Imām*,[91] confines the designation "best *ummah*" to only those who "enjoin righteousness and deter wrongness and believe in Allah."[92] Similarly, At-Ṭabarī says that the verse implies a condition (*sharṭ*), where only Muslims who fulfill the latter three conditions are merited being the best *ummah*. Another interpretation discusses the grammatical use of *kuntum* (you were) instead of *'antum* (you are), which implies that only a select group of people are designated as the best *ummah* rather than describing all Muslims. At-Ṭabarī also proposes another interpretation through a narration that confines the best *ummah* to those who migrated with Prophet Muhammad from Mecca to Medina, specifically his companions (*as-ṣaḥāba*). As for the people of the book, At-Ṭabarī restricts the believers among them to those who have accepted the prophethood of Muhammad, and the rest are those who rejected him.[93]

Modern exegetes took a different trajectory in interpreting the verses where the focus shifts to a sociopolitical function given to this *ummah* for its members to excel as well as taking a leading position in relation to

91. Al-Qummī reports a tradition in which one of the *a'imma* (pl. of *imām*) asked a rhetorical question: how could the best *Ummah* kill *Imām* Ali and the grandsons of Prophet Muhammad, al-Ḥasan and al-Ḥusayn?

92. Al-Qummī, *Tafsīr al-Qummī*, vol. 1, 136–37.

93. At-Ṭabarī, *Jāmi' al-Bayān*, vol. 4, 59–63.

other *umam*. ʿAbduh suggests that *khayr* in the first verse means Islam. Then he argues that there must exist a bond that unifies the members of the *ummah* "whose likeness is like the body, if one organ gets sick, the rest of body becomes sick and tired." "Enjoining righteousness and deterring wrongness" is that bond that will preserve the unity of the *ummah* by preventing discord and separation. Next he mentions two interpretations for "Let there be from among you" (*minkum*). The first, endorsed by ʿAbduh, suggests only a select group who carry out those duties, such as scholars who have knowledge of *sharīʿah* and its wisdom, whose main job is guiding people. The second interpretation refers to all Muslims, the knowledgeable and the ignorant, who advise each other based on their individual levels of knowledge.

Combining the two interpretations, ʿAbduh suggests that the verse "Let there be from among you an *ummah* . . ." addresses all Muslims, as they are obliged to choose from among themselves an *ummah* to carry out the duty of enjoining righteousness and deterring wrongness. The chosen should be the best of them, hence the usage of *minkum* ("from you"). Nevertheless, every member of the Muslim community should work toward meriting inclusion within that *ummah*, helping to establish it, and monitoring its performance such that if it goes astray, it can be rectified. ʿAbduh concludes that the concept of the *ummah* is more specific than the concept of a group (*ʿakhaṣṣ min al-jamāʿa*) because *ummah* necessitates the presence of a bond that connects its members and unifies them. Then he speaks at length of the different kinds of knowledge this select *ummah* should be equipped with. He added that this *ummah* should be strong enough to be able to deter injustice in society, fight corruption, and introduce change. In addition, this *ummah* should have a leader to maintain its organization and stability. ʿAbduh concludes that the backward condition of Muslims in the present is the result of Muslims ignoring their duty to advise each other, the effect being that they become enslaved to their selfish desires rather than empowered to improve themselves and their *ummah*.[94]

Similarly, Quṭb makes the description "*khayr ummah*" conditional upon taking on the responsibility and duty of fighting corruption on earth; otherwise this title is invalidated. A position of leadership according to

94. Muhammad ʿAbduh and Muhammad Rashīd Riḍā, *Tafsīr al-Manār*, vol. 4, 26–47.

Quṭb requires two main conditions. First, the best *ummah* should be a pioneer in every field (spiritual, scientific, educational, etc.). It leads through its contributions by always giving other *umam* the right knowledge, wisdom, vision, and system. The second condition is political power (*sulṭān* or *sulṭa*), where Quṭb thinks it is not possible to "command and forbid" without a coercive political power. This "*jamāʿa Muslima*" is based on belief in God and brotherly love and bases its affairs on God's *sharīʿah*, a basic order through which it can command righteousness and deter evil. However, a big danger that faces the Muslim *ummah* is separation and dissension. Quṭb warns the Muslim *ummah* from the plague that destroyed the people before them (when the people of the book disunited, God took away from them the leading position and gave it to the brotherly Muslim *ummah*). Therefore, unity, cooperation, and brotherly love are all indispensable for the Muslim *ummah* to stay in its leading position, similar to the first Muslim *jamāʿa* established in Medina by Prophet Mohammad.[95]

For Faḍlallah, a leading *ummah* who leads the world to good and reformation should be open and not self-enclosed. The latter would ensure its vitality, renewal, and relevance. Faḍlallah agrees with ʿAbduh that calling people to goodness is the responsibility of each Muslim. However, the *ummah* that fulfills that duty can either be a small group or enlarged to include all Muslims, depending on the extent of need for reform. Thus, depending on the circumstances of the time and the society, Muslims should address their needs.[96] Faḍlallah speaks of a belief that has practical benefits in life and that introduces change and reform in societies, calling it *al-Islām al-ḥarakī* ("dynamic Islam"). He adds that the worth of any *ummah* relative to other *umam* is determined according to its moral values and the extent to which they play a role in people's lives. Thus, when God gave the Muslim *ummah* the best characteristic over other *umam*, it was due to their active role in society to change corruption by all possible means. It was not due to specific characteristics inherent in Muslims, such as the belief of Jews who believe themselves to be God's chosen people. Consequently, the *ummah* acquires its leading role by continuous work, which, if abandoned, will automatically lead to the *ummah*'s failure to maintain its position of best. In very explicit terms, ʿAbduh asserts the same idea and rejects the notion of being best simply through

95. Quṭb, *Fī Ẓilāl al-Qur'ān*, vol. 1, 444–47.

96. Faḍlallah, *Min Waḥy al-Qur'ān*, vol. 6, 202–5.

religious affiliation. He reiterates: "even those who pray, pay *zakāt*, fast *Ramaḍān*, perform pilgrimage, abide by *ḥalāl* and refrain from *ḥarām* in sincere devotion to God would not deserve this rank unless they enjoin righteousness and deter wrongness."[97] This confirms the earlier discussed notion of the *ummah* and refutes the Orientalists' idea that an *ummah* is a closed community of Muslims granted salvation by practicing *sharīʿah* prescribed rituals.

Along the same lines, the Qurʾān addresses the people of the book: "if the people of the book were to believe it would have been better for them, among them are believers but most of them are transgressors." ʿAbduh wonders: if there are believers among the people of the book, why would the Qurʾān invite them to believe, as shown in the latter verse? He argues that the verse shows their belief as incomplete because they have abandoned the duty of reform in society and limited belief to personal practice and rituals. Hence the verse, by referring to the people of the book as an example, also speaks to Muslims. Thus, it urges everyone to uphold their duty by showing that real belief is the one in which inner belief is accompanied by practical implementation in society.[98] Those who follow and implement that kind of belief are those merited to comprise the best *ummah*. *Proper belief should blossom right action in society; otherwise the belief is deficient.* Faḍlallah agrees with ʿAbduh and adds that current Muslims, like the people of the book, have confined their religion to rituals and general ethics that barely influence practical life. Thereby, the Muslim *ummah* has lost its leading role among other *umam* because it has alienated itself from its true identity and genuine path.[99] ʿAbduh finds a historical justification of the current bad condition of the Muslim *ummah*. He thinks the *ummah* did not abstain from its duty willingly; rather, it was forced by the tyranny of its kings and leaders from the Umayyad dynasty and those who followed their oppressive strategy afterward. That oppression continued to increase with time until it usurped the *ummah* of its best privilege.[100]

97. Muhammad ʿAbduh and Muhammad Rashīd Riḍā, *Tafsīr al-Manār*, vol. 4, 58.

98. Ibid., 63–64.

99. Faḍlallah, *Min Waḥy al-Qurʾān*, vol. 6, 212–20.

100. Muhammad ʿAbduh and Muhammad Rashīd Riḍā, *Tafsīr al-Manār*, vol. 4, 60.

Echoing modern exegesis, Western political scientists, such as Jonathon Moses, argue that the Islamic *ummah* maintained its religious component over time yet lost its political one. The Muslim *ummah* sustained its religious component through the Islamic rituals and even expanded in the form of a transnational Islamic religious community. However, it lacks a common political identity, and henceforth contemporary Muslim states are in a continuous state of conflict. He thinks that, similar to modern democracies, the only way to sustain a well-functioning *ummah* is for it to have a strong, just, and legitimate political authority. He references the famous historian Ibn Khaldun, who noted that the political *ummah* deteriorated when the caliphate lost its identity and was replaced with a pure royal authority at the end of the Umayyad period.[101] Moses advocates the idea of having a political hegemon for the *ummah*'s survival, similar to the ideas propagated by ʿAbduh and Quṭb. He thinks that modern democracies sustain their peace because of the presence of a political hegemon, represented by the United States currently. "While public support for the ideal and institutions of democracy may remain strong, the absence of a strong and legitimate political authority can weaken—even bring to an end—*Pax Democratica*."[102] Likewise, he argues that the demise of *Pax Islamica* was a result of the weakening of the political leadership of the *ummah* despite its strong religious community. The next chapter addresses how the Prophet established an *ummah* through a political treaty. The following chapter addresses the political function of the *ummah*, which is regretfully missing in Islamic scholarship and is the main purpose of writing this book.

The Qur'ānic duty required of the best *ummah* resonates with earlier verses speaking of the *ummah*'s obligation to continuous reform and advice, which warrants the *ummah*'s characterization as the middle one and the witness. Truthful witnessing requires a just, honest, and noble character that necessitates a continuous appeal for justice. At the same time, the foundation of this action should be a belief in one creator for all humankind; otherwise it becomes a proselytizing process intended to achieve superiority and boost a false ego of supremacy over other people. This has been shown in exclusivist interpretations of *khayr ummah* and

101. Jonathon W. Moses, "The *Ummah* of Democracy," *Security Dialogue* 37, no. 4 (2006): 500–4.

102. Ibid., 505.

also by Denny, who argues that the verses imply that Muslims are more righteous than those before them (in the absolute); hence the Qur᾽ān refers to them as the best *ummah*.[103] I disagree with that absolute claim based on the Qur᾽ānic verses (3:113–15)[104] previously discussed, which gave the very same description of the people of the book. "They believe in Allah and the Day of Judgment and they enjoin righteousness and deter wrongness and they hasten (in emulation) in (all) good works and these are among the righteous." Are not these the same conditions required for Muslims to become *khayr ummah*? So achieving the status of best *ummah* is conditional upon fulfilling those duties and not an absolute value given to Muslims.

From this perspective, I do not find validation for some traditional Muslim scholars who separate between Muslims and non-Muslims with the abstract notions of *dār as-salām* ("abode of peace") and *dār al-ḥarb* ("abode of war"). Their arguments draw an image of a peaceful area under Muslim rule against another area governed by non-Muslim rule and thereby ruled by war and conflict. It could be possible that Muslim jurists proposed this classification because it reflected reality at a specific time; for example, when the Muslim *ummah* was prospering in the medieval period, Europe was in the dark ages. While historical circumstances always affected scholarly interpretation, it should not be taken as an unquestioned Islamic norm. Jonathon Moses, in his article comparing nations ruled by democracy with the Islamic *ummah*, argues that jurists proposed this dichotomy, the abode of peace versus the abode of war, to create a strong sense of community among Muslims as they unite against the external threat outside the *ummah*. The dichotomy would keep peace among members of the *ummah*, yet create an aggressive attitude toward

---

103. Denny, "Community and Salvation: The Meaning of the Ummah in the Qur᾽ān," 238.

104. "They are not all alike, of the people of the book there is an *Ummah qā᾽ima* reciting the verses of God at night while prostrating in prayer. They believe in Allah and the Day of Judgment and they enjoin righteousness and deter wrongness and they hasten (in emulation) in (all) good works and these are among the righteous. And whatever good they do, they shall not be denied it for God is aware of the God-conscious" (Qur᾽ān 3:113–15).

the outside world.[105] I think this understanding reads the *ummah* through the lens of modern liberal democracies, which define the nation and keeps their unity through demonizing the different other outside their borders. First, there is no need to create an outside enemy to forge unity among members of a Muslim *ummah*. As previously discussed in this chapter, unity is maintained through belief, performing rituals, as well as continuous reform in society (enjoining righteousness and deterring wrongness). The need to create an outside enemy to maintain unity and cohesion in a modern nation-state is born out of a necessity: modern multicultural nations have lost common bonds that were sustained historically, such as religion, culture, or ethnicity. As individualism and secularism became the contemporary norm, alternative bonds need to be created to maintain national unity. Second, the characteristics of this Muslim *ummah* in the Qur᾿ān analyzed and described in this chapter show an *ummah* that is just, interactive, reforming, a witness to other people, and an intermediary as well as a leading *ummah* giving and contributing to prosper humanity, as discussed by several scholars, despite their different intellectual orientations. The Qur᾿ānic description does not portray a closed society that maintains an aggressive or hostile attitude toward other nations. Third, the following section lays out a general framework that organizes how the Muslim *ummah* deals with other *umam* through the book; that is, through covenants and treaties. Chapter 1 of this book concluded that the "book" forms the backbone of the *ummah* as a concept. This idea will materialize in the Medinan verses, as is described in the following section. The notion of establishing covenants with other nations is actually espoused by Shāfiʿī jurists who acknowledged a third abode that determines relations between the Muslim *ummah* and non-Muslim *umam*. That is the abode of covenant (*dār al-ʿahd*) or the abode of reconciliation (*dār al-ṣulḥ*).[106] The next chapter, which describes the prophetic practice in establishing the first *ummah* in Medina, shows that establishing covenants and peaceful treaties is not only a means of dealing with others outside the *ummah* but

---

105. Jonathon W. Moses, "The *Ummah* of Democracy," *Security Dialogue* 37, no. 4 (2006): 499.

106. Majid Khadduri, "Translator's introduction," in *The Islamic Law of Nations: Shaybānī's Siyar* (Baltimore, MD: John Hopkins University Press), 12.

is evidently an internal practice as well. The Prophet established peaceful covenants in Medina itself to unite the fighting tribes into one *ummah* (*ummah wāḥidah*).

Ummah of the Book and Governance

> People were one *ummah* (*ummah wāḥidah*) so Allah sent Prophets as bearers of good news and as warners, and with them he sent the Book (*al-kitāb*) in truth to judge between people in matters wherein they differed; and none but the very people who were given it differed about it, after clear proofs (*al-bayyināt*) had come to them, through selfish contumacy. Then Allah, by his grace, guided the believers to the truth concerning that wherein they differed. And Allah guides whom He wills to a straight path. (Qur'ān 2:213)

Premodern exegesis such as At-Ṭabarī says the one *ummah* refers to those who were following one religion. He interpreted the book in this verse to mean the Torah. Those who differed among themselves are the Jews. Those who were guided are the Muslims.[107] Modern exegesis employs a rational understanding of the verse. ʿAbduh interprets one *ummah* as people guided by their *fiṭrah* (innate nature), that is, guidance derived of reason (*hidāyat al-ʿaql*). However, when people are left to their own discretion without divine guidance, each starts following his personal motives, and thereby dissent and conflict occur. Hence, there was a need for prophets who came to guide people and organize their life according to an unbiased divine book. Faḍlallah also refers to a similar understanding of *ummah wāḥidah*.[108] Another interpretation is that the human being is civil (*madanī*) by nature because people cannot live without depending on each other. Thus, divine mercy sent prophets with books of law and guidance to show people how to organize their life through one system that can fulfill their needs and resolve their conflicts.[109]

---

107. At-Ṭabarī, *Jāmiʿ al-Bayān*, vol. 2, 455–61.

108. Faḍlallah, *Min Waḥy al-Qur'ān*, vol. 4, 142–44.

109. Muhammad ʿAbduh and Muhammad Rashīd Riḍā, *Tafsīr al-Manār*, vol. 2, 278–95.

The clear proofs (*al-bayyināt*) mentioned in the verse refer to the evidence in divine books that explain that divine wisdom cannot be attained by understanding only part of a book while ignoring the other parts. To understand the divine message in its totality, scholars need to understand all parts of the divine book concurrently. Only then can scholars reach the full truth of the divine book, which is spreading harmony and peace among people. However, some people who know this truth have chosen to hide it purposefully and instead focus on separate verses to suit their selfish desires and achieve their worldly goals. This is how divergent sectarian groups arise and are nurtured. Nonetheless, the verse ends by saying that the "believers" are the only ones guided to the truth, about which others have differed and therein separated. This true belief (*al-īmān as-ṣaḥiḥ*) is a belief that does not neglect rationality, but rather uses it to understand religion.

A sincere believer does not abide by any advice without thinking deeply upon it, looking for evidence and clear proof. Thus, one needs to make use of his intellect and channel it to the right direction, which is divine guidance. ʿAbduh then touches upon the different stages of human development, another implication alluded to in the verse. In the first stage, human beings are controlled by their innate nature; thereby they have divergent views because of natural self-interest. In the second stage, prophets are sent with glad tidings and warnings and basic beliefs about life and divine justice. The latter part of this second stage is a preparation phase for the third stage that is the book and its divine laws. ʿAbduh argues that people have to be educated and mentally prepared before accepting laws and implementing them. The third stage is the introduction of *sharīʿah* with its laws and regulations. The fourth stage is the highest level of divine guidance: following the straight path or the truth.[110] Only those who possess sincere belief and who understand the divine wisdom behind divine laws such that they implement them knowingly and peacefully attain this last stage. Such persons have a complete understanding of stages two and three, the mind and religious law. However, there are people who use religion to promote their personal gain; thereby they revert back to stage one. The latter deprive themselves of the opportunity of divine guidance and instead focus on self-interest, hatred, and conflict.

110. Muhammad ʿAbduh and Muhammad Rashīd Riḍā, *Tafsīr al-Manār*, vol. 2, 278–95.

Quṭb argues that the "book" was not sent by God to erase diversity among people because it is embedded in human nature to differ. The latter serves a high wisdom in the appointment of the human race as a caliph (trustee) on earth. This human stewardship requires various functions and diverse capabilities for worldly life to be complemented and fully integrated. Instead, the Book was sent to serve as a foundation for people to invoke and use as a criterion and judge when they differ among themselves. Therefore, what people choose, based on personal inclinations and desires, does not represent the truthful criterion. The Book was sent with the Truth to guide different people, as it is not based on personal interests or desires.[111]

The previous verse explains the function of "the book" in general. While At-Ṭabarī interpreted it as the Torah, all the remaining exegetes interpret it as a divine book generally, and focused rather on the function. The following verse specifically addresses Prophet Muhammad and the Qur᾿ān, thereby explaining the latter's function with respect to the other divine books and *umam.*

> And to you (Muhammad), We revealed the Book (*al-kitāb*) in truth, confirming the book (*al-kitāb*) that came before it and a guardian (*muhaymin*) over it (old Scriptures). So judge between them by what Allah has revealed, and follow not their vain desires, diverging away from the truth that has come to you. To each among you, We have prescribed a law and a clear way (*shir῾atan wa minhājan*). If Allah willed, He would have made you one *ummah*, but that (He) may test you in what He has given you; so strive as in a race in all virtues. The return of you (all) is to Allah; then He will inform you about that in which you used to differ. (Qur᾿ān 5:48)

Both premodern and modern exegetes agree that what is meant by the "the Book" (*al-kitāb*) in the beginning of this verse is the Qur᾿ān. At-Ṭabarī explains *Muhaymin* as a witness over other scriptures (the second book mentioned in the verse), and *amīn* (safeguarding books before the Qur᾿ān).[112] ῾Abduh adds that the Qur᾿ān is *raqīb* ("watchful over the

111. Quṭb, *Fī Ẓilāl al-Qur᾿ān*, vol. 1, 215–18.

112. At-Ṭabarī, *Jāmi῾ al-Bayān*, vol. 4, 360.

divine books that came before it"), watchful in that it judges truth from falsehood in the preceding divine books.[113] Faḍlallah says that the entire book, referring to the Qur᾿ān, may indicate its inclusiveness toward all books sent to prophets before it. Its teachings reflect the legal aspect of Torah and the spiritual and ethical aspect of the Gospel; thereby it confirms previous books in their intellectual essence and practical outlook. Thus, the Qur᾿ān is *muhaymin*, meaning a trustworthy witness to divine scriptures before it, as well as protecting such scriptures.[114]

At-Ṭabarī[115] and ῾Abduh[116] refer to a saying by Qatāda wherein he says that religion (*dīn*) is one, but *sharī῾ah* varies. Each of the holy books, Torah, Gospel, and Qur᾿ān, has its own *sharī῾ah*. But religion represents the fixed fundamentals that do not change across time and different prophets. *Sharī῾ah* represents practical laws that depend on the needs of the time in which the message was revealed. ῾Abduh argues that the difference in *sharī῾ah* across human history is related to human progress. It was necessary that each phase in human existence would have its own regulations that are suitable for its needs. For example, the Jews were immersed in materialism because of their early history of enslavement, so the *sharī῾ah* of the Torah was strict in its laws to educate an *ummah* that was accustomed to enslavement and had lost its independence. On the other hand, the *sharī῾ah* of the Gospel was focused on the spiritual aspect of humanity. Finally, the Qur᾿ānic *sharī῾ah*, being the last revealed law to humanity and thereby addressing the highest stage of human development, is based on the intellectual side of humans and their independence (*qā᾿ima ῾ala ᾿asās al-῾aql wal-᾿istiqlāl*). Thereby, the Qur᾿ānic *sharī῾ah* combined both material and spiritual sides of humanity; hence those abiding by its ethics are worthy of the attributes *ummah wasaṭ* and *khayr ummah* raised up for humankind. Quṭb[117] adds that the Torah and Gospel were both sent to a specific community, the Jews and Christians respectively; however, the

113. Muhammad ῾Abduh and Muhammad Rashīd Riḍā, *Tafsīr al-Manār*, vol. 6, 411.

114. Faḍlallah, *Min Waḥy al-Qur᾿ān*, vol. 8, 197.

115. At-Ṭabarī, *Jāmi῾ al-Bayān*, vol. 4, 362–69.

116. Muhammad ῾Abduh and Muhammad Rashīd Riḍā, *Tafsīr al-Manār*, vol. 6, 413–20.

117. Quṭb, *Fī Ẓilāl al-Qur᾿ān*, vol. 2, 900–1.

Qur'ān, as the final message, was sent to all humankind. In that regard, the Qur'ān is a guardian over previous messages and is considered the final reference.

By relating the verse (5:48) to the earlier verse discussed in this section (2:213), ʿAbduh argues that when different *umam* had different levels of mental and spiritual maturity, it was unavoidable and logical that an advanced *ummah* would lead the preceding one. Thus, we see that leadership represented in the verse (5:48) in that the role of judging between the different *umam* is assigned to the Prophet and the last message, the Qur'ān; "So judge between them by what Allah has revealed, and follow not their vain desires, diverging away from the truth that has come to you." This idea is discussed in the next chapter, which analyzes the *ummah* of Medina, established by the Prophet, and the role the Prophet assumed as a judge in that pluralistic *ummah*. This verse also addresses the Muslim *ummah* and clarifies its role with respect to other *umam*. Following the footsteps of Prophet Muhammad, the Muslim *ummah* is also asked to use its book as a guide to judge for itself as well as other people. Yet the verse speaks of legal pluralism (To each among you, We have prescribed a law and a clear way), so the Muslim *ummah* should not enforce its *sharīʿah* on other *umam*, that is, it is not a theocracy. Rather, the Muslim *ummah*, as a leading *ummah*, should allow each *ummah* to follow its own *sharīʿah* (book) based on the Qur'ānic injunction and the prophetic practice. Practically, as discussed in the next chapter, this was established internally by the Prophet through a treaty, that is, through a covenant. I propose that the same strategy could be used externally with other non-Muslim sovereign *umam* through covenants as well; the idea was introduced in the Meccan verses and described in detail in chapter 1.

Nonetheless, the verse (5:48) continues to say that if God had willed, he would have made humanity one *ummah* following one *sharīʿah*, but he did not do so in order to give human beings the freedom of choice. The presence of different divine laws is meant to test people in their faith. Faḍlallah comments that this is the way God knows the sincere believers from the fanatic, obstinate people who only adhere to the details of the message at the expense of the essence in order to create conflict and hatred among people. Thus, the verse reminds all believers of the essence of divine messages, which is the betterment of their communities, urging them to "so strive as in a race in all virtues." The successful, who will receive the bounties and pleasure of God and reach the highest level of human development, are those who focus on the essence in applying their prescribed *sharīʿah*, and who thereby implement God's law to good action in society rather than exploiting it for division and conflict. The verse concludes that all will return to God who will settle their differences.[118] Therefore, we find a consistent theme of encouraging recognition of the commonalities and seeking unity, accepting differences and not considering them a threat. However, Quṭb interprets this verse by urging Muslims to stick to the details of the last prescribed message, and not modifying any Qur'ānic law to appeal to others (from different sects or religions) for the sake of unity. He asserts that the Qur'ānic message implies the implausibility of uniting all humankind under one law. People will continue to differ, so the Qur'ān urges each community to follow its own law and compete with each other in that regard.[119] While both Faḍlallah and Quṭb agree on the intrinsic diversity of humans, and that people are being tested in their faith by following their respective laws, their conclusions may first appear conflicting. Faḍlallah focuses on the core of all divine messages, which is the betterment of humans and their communities, encouraging unity and detesting division and conflict created by focusing on details. Quṭb, on the other hand, argues that details should not be sacrificed for the sake of unity, and no minute modification should be undertaken to appease people at the expense of *sharīʿah*. On closer inspection, Faḍlallah focuses more on verse 5:48, and Quṭb focuses on the following verse (5:49).[120] In that regard, the two interpretations are complementary. In addition, the social and political context of both authors affected their interpretation emphasis. Faḍlallah's background is war-torn sectarian Lebanon; hence focusing on common grounds was his goal and his message after witnessing the bad effects of exploiting politicized sectarianism. Quṭb had a long struggle with political power, which he criticized as un-Islamic and was unyielding to any compromise

118. Faḍlallah, *Min Waḥy al-Qur'ān*, vol. 8, 201–2.

119. Quṭb, *Fī Ẓilāl al-Qur'ān*, vol. 2, 902–3.

120. "And judge, [O Muhammad], between them by what Allah has revealed and do not follow their inclinations and beware of them, lest they tempt you away from some of what Allah has revealed to you. And if they turn away—then know that Allah only intends to afflict them with some of their [own] sins. And indeed, many among the people are defiantly disobedient" (Qur'ān 5:49).

that would hinder the establishment of an Islamic government, and that is reflected in his interpretation.

Conclusion

Modern exegetes, in comparison with premodern exegetes, are more rational in their understanding of *ummah* in the Medinan verses. They place more emphasis on the individual responsibility whose success will directly affect the success of the *ummah* as a whole. There is less emphasis on the idea of cultural Islam or passive affiliation to the *ummah*. Premodern exegetes interpreted *khayr ummah* as a select group from the family of Prophet Muhammad or his companions. However, modern exegetes attributed that characteristic to those who choose to excel and lead. Therefore, modern exegesis gave the Muslim *ummah* a sociopolitical function and stress that achieving the status of the best *ummah* is conditional rather than an intrinsic quality. In addition to requiring the Muslim *ummah* to continuously engage in reform and establishing justice, modern exegetes such as ʿAbduh and Quṭb advocated the necessity of having strong political leadership. While the *ummah* is described through its religious rituals (*al-manāsik*), modern exegetes assert that an *ummah* adhering only to religion, as a set of rituals, and abandoning sociopolitical reform in society will lead to its backwardness. Modern exegetes as well as Western scholars use the current condition of Muslims, as divided and conflicting states, to support their claim. Jonathan Moses argue that the failure of the Muslim *ummah*, despite its strong religious component, is attributed to the weakness of its political component. The research conducted in this book supports this argument and aims at uncovering the nature of the political function of the *ummah*, which is analyzed in the last chapter.

While the Muslim *ummah* is customarily defined by its adherence to religious rituals in Islamic literature as well as by Orientalists, modern Qurʾānic exegesis challenges this definition not only for political reasons but also for religious ones. As explained in this chapter, the Qurʾān criticizes belief that is not translated into fruitful action and reform in society. There is no doubt that modern exegetes are affected by the post-colonial condition of Muslims; however, we cannot consider this political circumstance as the main reason inspiring their thinking. This is evident in the prophetic practice, where the first *ummah* was established through a socio-political treaty and not through religious affiliation only.

The first chapter showed that the Meccan verses presented *ummah* as a general theoretical concept with specific attributes: intent, covenant, book, and leadership. The Medinan verses, on the other hand, deal with diverse *umam*, their attributes and functions. The term "*Muslim ummah*" is introduced as well as an *ummah* from "*ahl al-kitāb*." In addition, the verses in Medina describe the attributes of the best *ummah*, the conditions to be part of it, how it relates to other *umam*, and how this system, of shared rights and obligations could be realized practically. Thus the Medinan verses describe actual *umam* that existed historically and lay the foundation for the Islamic *ummah* to be established by Prophet Muhammad in the seventh century.

The core of the Islamic *ummah* is the Muslim *ummah*. I mean by Islamic *ummah* the *ummah* that includes Muslims, Jews, Christians, and others yet is founded based on Islamic ethics. The Islamic *ummah* is multi-religious and is legally pluralistic. The Muslim *ummah*, on the other hand, represents the *ummah* united by one book and follows one *sharī῾ah*, that of the Qur᾿ān. The Muslim *ummah* forms the nucleus from which the Islamic *ummah* grows, which is inclusive and pluralistic in character and has a global potential (this is described in detail in the next chapter).

The Medinan verses, in which Muslim *ummah* is mentioned, were focused on Prophet Abraham. His character and life represent the embodiment of what a Muslim means. His character "*al-ḥanīf*" was achieved by his persistent trusting in the divine wisdom over any personal inclination. Through the exemplary model of Abraham, the Qur᾿ān describes the attributes of a Muslim, which are key to the formation of the Muslim *ummah* and consequently the pluralistic Islamic *ummah*. The Abrahamic model represents an Islam that is mindful, active, and interactive rather than a mere submission to divine law. Submitting in peace (*al-Islām*) in that sense becomes a manifestation of one's trust in the divine wisdom, based on experience, rather than blind obedience to divine orders. This cognitive and experiential Islam frees the concept from historical and social determinisms: a prominent Qur᾿ānic theme in the Meccan verses discussed in the previous chapter. That is why Islam (as an ideology and ethical framework) existed since the beginning of time, though manifested through different laws that suit the different periods in history. Hence the

Qur᾽ān speaks of all prophets previous to Prophet Muhammad as being Muslims (having the foundational ethics that are unchanging), yet were given different *sharī῾ah* according to the time (changing[121]). As such, it is not surprising when the Qur᾽ān states that each *ummah* has a *mansak* (religious ritual) and should follow its *sharī῾ah*. This ideological framework of a "Muslim" has many implications. First, the characteristic Muslim is not reduced to merely following specific *manāsik* ("religious rituals"), which is the norm in defining Muslim today. Rather, Muslim is associated with endorsing a specific attitude and possessing a specific spiritual and intellectual outlook on the divine and the world, rather than indicating belonging to a particular culture in history. Muslim is an active term that has an essential meaning, yet is time contingent. Second, the latter ideological framework forms the essence of the last "Muslim *ummah*," which appeared after the coming of Prophet Muhammad. While Muslims existed since the beginning of time, the Muslim *ummah* is a historical entity that first appeared in the seventh century. The characteristics and function of the Muslim *ummah* necessitated its being the last *ummah* sent to humankind because it is embracing of previous religions and accepts the different other as a divinely ordained reality. Its later appearance in history was inevitable when members of this *ummah* would have reached a level of mental and spiritual maturity (hence the perfection of religion mentioned in the Qur᾽ān) to embrace and lead the preceding *umam*. The Muslim *ummah* in addition to sustaining itself is asked to establish the wider pluralistic Islamic *ummah*.

Along the same framework, the Qur᾽ānic verses describe the characteristics of each *ummah*, whether Muslim or *ahl al-Kitāb*, by virtue of their actions and not their denominational affiliation. The Muslim *ummah* is described by two attributes, *wasaṭ* and *shahīd*, in relation to other *umam*. Subsequently, the Qur᾽ān describes the function of this *ummah*, a function that will make it worthy of deserving the attribute of the best (*khayr ummah*). Enjoining righteousness and deterring wrongness while believing in the one God is the meritorious action. Hence the Qur᾽ān alludes to the idea that

121. Changing based on the divine decree and not based on people's opinions. I am not implying that people have the right to change the *sharī῾ah* once it is divinely decreed for a specific period. For example, because the Qur᾽ān states that Prophet Muhamad is the last prophet until the end of time, that translates into his *sharī῾ah* being followed until the end of time.

society should be able to reap the benefits of belief through a continuous process of active reform invigorated by the members of the *ummah.*

The Qur᾿ānic attributes describing the Muslim *ummah* and its function require the *ummah* to be open and interactive with people and other communities. Rather than being a closed ritualistic community, membership in the *ummah* becomes accessible to anyone who is willing to perform the proper actions and endorse the proper beliefs. This is evident from similar Qur᾿ānic descriptions of some members of *ahl al-kitāb*, such as *ummah qā᾿ima* and *ummah muqtaṣida*. Moreover, the Qur᾿ānic verses have always implied a selection of people from among many, which is evident from the usage of the preposition "from" (*min*).[122] The latter confirms the conclusion reached in chapter 1 that the term *ummah* does not merely represent a community but rather a group of purposeful individuals joined by a specific goal or action. Finally, there is a reference to the book of the Islamic *ummah*, the Qur᾿ān, which is the embracing element that recognizes all in their merit.

Because the Qur᾿ān is *muhaymin* (a guardian and witness over earlier scriptures) and inclusive, like Prophet Abraham the common father and the criterion, it was given the authority to be the judge. The Muslim *ummah* is instructed to organize its affairs and judge itself by the teachings of the book, the Qur᾿ān. The last Qur᾿ānic verse discussed in this chapter (5:48) refers to sociopolitical leadership and alludes to the idea of an Islamic *ummah* as well as the Muslim one. The Muslim *ummah* abides by Qur᾿ānic *sharī῾ah* and assumes the leadership of the Islamic *ummah*, which comprises other *umam* who abide by their own *sharī῾ah*. Evidently, this leadership is incumbent upon the *ummah*'s maintaining its active role in society and upholding inclusive Qur᾿ānic ethics of pluralism and interaction. Thus, the *ummah* cannot exercise its leading role by reverting to a closed society and confining the teachings of its book merely to prescribed rituals. A prototypical example for this Islamic *ummah* described in the Qur᾿ān will be manifest through the *ummah* of Medina established by Prophet Muhammad in 622 CE, which is analyzed in the next chapter.

---

122. The preposition was used frequently in the Qur᾿anic verses discussed in this chapter: Qur᾿ān [. . . *min dhuriyyatanā Ummah Muslimah* . . .] (2:128); [*min alhl al-kitāb Ummah qā᾿ima* . . .] (3:113); [. . . *minhum Ummah muqtaṣida* . . .] (5:66), and [*wal-takun minkum Ummah ya᾿murūna bil-ma῾rūf wa yanhawna ᾿an al-munkar* . . .] (3:104).

Chapter 3

Ummah in the Medina Constitution

The aim of this chapter is to analyze the Medina Constitution[1] based on the Qur'ānic description of the *ummah* in the previous two chapters.

1. The Medina Constitution was drafted by Prophet Muhammad in 622 CE between the conflicting tribes of Yathrib (previous name of Medina) and the Muslim immigrants from Mecca. Yathrib was a city that had been worn out by more than a century of feudal wars and tribal conflicts between its different groups: the two major Arab tribes *al-'Aws* and *al-Khazaraj* and Jewish tribes. Therefore, the city was in desperate need for peace and an outside impartial arbitrator who is trustworthy and of noble character. All these factors culminated in the preparation of that land and its people to invite Prophet Muhammad and his followers to migrate to it and choose him as their judge and leader. Before drafting the constitution in Medina, Prophet Muhammad was delivering the message of Islam in Mecca for thirteen years in a hostile environment. The prophet endured maltreatment and ordered his followers to endure persecution with patience by not fighting back or engaging in violence. Some Muslims were killed, some migrated to Abyssinia, and others hid their faith or practiced secretly. During those thirteen years, the news of the prophet and his message and the abuse of his followers spread all over the region. The number of Muslims increased, but they were scattered. After that time, the main supporter of the prophet, his uncle, died, and his life became in serious danger. Concurrently, a good number of pagan pilgrims from Yathrib embraced Islam. They were leaders from different tribes in Yathrib who swore an oath of allegiance, called *Bay'at al-'Aqaba,* to the prophet to protect him and his followers with their lives. Thereafter, Prophet Muhammad migrated with his persecuted followers to Medina and drafted the Medina Constitution for the mixed society of Medina: the new Muslims of

The Medina Constitution (MC) represents a prophetic practical model manifesting Qur'ānic ethics. We will check if the Medina Constitution validates the conclusion reached thus far. The word *ummah* is mentioned only twice in the MC in decrees 2 and 25. It is mentioned in the context of defining what constitutes the *ummah* of Medina and defining its common unifying attributes. The common unifying attributes, which are discussed in the first chapter, are a goal, a book that reflects that goal and accordingly establishes a covenant between its members, a leader, and possibly land (or geographical space).

This document, in addition to other documents drafted by Prophet Muhammad, was mentioned by premodern Muslim scholars since the first century of Islam. Scholars such as ʿAbdulla ibn ʿAbbas, Al-Zuhrī, Ibn Isḥāq, Al-Wāqidī, and others mentioned the Medina document in their books.[2] However, most of this early scholarship is not available in our time, either because it was lost or is available in antique manuscripts that haven't been discovered yet. What is known to us came through books of *sīra* and history such as *Kitāb al-Kharāj*, *Sīrat ibn Hishām*, *Kitāb al-Ṭabaqāt*, and *Kitāb al-Amwāl*.[3] Those who mentioned the *ummah* in Medina did not define it; rather it was mentioned as the Medina Constitution describes it. For example, Ibn Hishām stated that Prophet Muhammad drafted a book with the Muslim immigrants and Muslims of Medina (*al-Anṣār*), and he made a treaty with the Jews. The treaty acknowledged the Jews their religion and their money, and he made conditions for them, and made it conditional upon them that they are one *ummah* apart from the people.[4] However, Abū ʿUbayd al-Qāsim associated the term *ummah* with Muslims exclusively. He argues that the statement "one *ummah* apart from the people" is the major/foundational statement (*Al-ʿibāra al-ʾumm*) that

---

Medina (*al-anṣār*) and the Muslim immigrants considered the prophet a religious and political leader, while the other groups, the pagans and the Jews, regarded him as a respected leader and impartial outsider. The Prophet established the first *ummah* in Medina through a constitution that resolved the enduring hostilities of the conflicting tribes.

2. Ibn an-Nadīm, *Al-Fahrast*, trans. Ayman Sayyid (London: Muʿassasat Al-Furqāan lil-Turāth, 2009) V.1 (2), 315–23.

3. Muhammad, Ḥamīdulla, *Majmūʿat al-Wathāʾiq as-Siyāsiyya* (Cairo: Lajnat at-Taʾlīf wat-Tarjama wal-Nashr, 1941).

4. Abou Mohammad Abd al-Malek Ibn Hisham, *Al-Sīra Al-Nabawiyya,* ed. Suhail Zakkar (Beirut: Dār al-Fikr, 1992).

gave all the Muslims the attribute (*al-ummah*) such that Muslims became known as "*ummat al-Islam.*"[5] Abū ʿUbayd shares with the Orientalists the opinion that *ummah* is exclusive to Muslims only. Ibn Hishām does not seem to endorse this opinion. To decipher whether *ummah* in the Medina is exclusive or not, this chapter analyzes the concept *ummah* in the MC in light of the first two exegetical chapters and by engaging with modern scholarship on the constitution.

The MC starts with the following decrees:[6]

1- This is a book (*kitāb*) from Muhammad the Prophet (the messenger of God) between the believers and Muslims of Quraysh and the people of Yathrib and those who follow them, join them, and strive along with them.

2- They are one *ummah* (*ummah wāḥidah*) apart from the people.

The first decree defines the members of the Medina *ummah* and begins by referencing itself, the MC, as a book upon which the *ummah* is to be established. The book, through its decrees, clarifies the goal of the *ummah*, the covenants established, their common leader, and land. The first decree starts by identifying the members belonging to that one *ummah*; hence the term is an active term that reflects a source of identification rather than an established identity. Nevertheless, the *ummah* of Medina comprises people of different established identities as shown in the first decree: believers, Muslims from Quraysh, people of Yathrib, and those who chose to follow them. This diversity directly reflects the element of choice associated with the concept and also shows that the term *ummah* does not depict a closed society. Rather, it is an open community for whoever wishes to join and abide by its goals and covenant. Religion (*dīn*) is not the common element among the members of the *ummah*, which is further clarified in decree 25:

25- The Jews of Banī ʿAwf, together with[7] the believers, constitute an *ummah*,[8] the Jews having their religion/law (*dīn*) and the Muslims having

5. Abū ʿUbayd Ibn Sallām, *Kitāb al-Amwāl*, ed. M. Khalīl Harrās (Cairo: Maktabat al-Kullīyāt al-Azharīyah, 1968), 290–97.

6. Appendix A lists the original Arabic version of the Medina Constitution.

7. A different reading, "The Jews are an *ummah* (from) the believers," in Abū ʿUbayd Ibn sallām, *Kitāb al-Amwāl*, ed. M. Khalīl Harās (Cairo, 1968), 147. Also Ibn Kathīr, *Al-Bidāya wal-Nihāya* (Cairo, 1932), I, 43.

8. A bizarre reading is argued by Michael Lecker where he replaced *ummah* with *amina* (secure) based on an Indian edition that was remarked by later editors

their religion/law (*dīn*). This includes both their *mawla* and themselves personally. But whoever performs an unjust action or commits a crime shall harm solely himself and the people of his house.

The Jews and believers form a common *ummah*, despite each possessing their own religion (*dīn*). Denny argues that the Jews were an *ummah* "alongside" the Muslims such that the term *ummah* represents a closed community defined by common religion.[9] Denny supports his claim proposing a theory of rupture: establishing a new community in Medina necessitated a prior break with the old ways of Christians, Jews, and pagans; hence there was a continuous rupture with earlier traditions to establish the new order.[10] I disagree with Denny for several reasons.

First, it is worth noting that the terms "Jews" and "Muslims," not Jewish *ummah* and Muslim *ummah*, are used to refer to religious differences—"The Jews having their religion/law (*dīn*) and the Muslims having their religion/law (*dīn*)." However, *ummah* is the term used for describing both communities under one banner. Such inclusive phrasing is seen in decree 25, "The Jews of Banī ʿAwf, together with the believers constitute an *ummah*," and in the beginning of the constitution through use of the term *ummah wāḥidah*. *Ummah wāḥidah* is a Qurʾānic term used to reflect unity before God; hence the goal of this *ummah* in Medina was to unite the different groups. This strongly suggests that the term *ummah* does not refer to a group of people following a specific *dīn*; rather, it has broader implications, as has been already shown. If the Prophet was not sent to a universal *ummah* and if the Qurʾānic ideology was exclusive, it would have been impossible to establish that united *ummah* in Medina given its significant ethnic, religious, and cultural diversity. Politically, Shams ad-Dīn thinks that decree 25 reflects a political community that unites two communities following two different creeds. Its public order is based

---

to be inaccurate. However, Lecker still supported the reading (*amina*). I totally dismiss Lecker's argument for a simple grammatical reason, because if *amina* (in a verb or a noun form) was used, it has to be conjugated in the plural form to match the noun (the Jews). The reading argued by Lecker is in singular form, which is grammatically impossible. In Michael Lecker, *The "Constitution of Medina" Muhammad's First Legal Document* (Princeton, NJ: The Darwin Press, 2004), 139.

9. Denny, "Community and Salvation: The Meaning of the Ummah in the Qurʾān," 214.

10. Ibid., 246.

on Islamic values and led by Prophet Muhammad. Shams ad-Din calls it a "diverse contractual society," which maintains diversity while simultaneously establishing unity. The statement "The Jews together with the believers constitute an *ummah*" conveys that, while both the Jews and the believers are distinct communities having their own religion and law, neither forms a separate political community on its own.[11]

Second, the inclusion of Jews and their law in the *ummah* and in the constitution reflects a desire to communicate with earlier traditions rather than form a closed community breaking with them. The Prophet is described as the *ummī* prophet, foretold of in earlier scriptures,[12] whose message confirms those earlier scriptures and who acts as a guardian and witness to those earlier communities.[13] Thus, the Qur'ānic message represents a continuation with earlier divine traditions, and Prophet Muhammad, whose Qur'ānic model is Prophet Ibrahim, functions as the father who embraces and unites all of them. Arjomand considers that the constitutional recognition of the Jewish religion represents the foundation of religious pluralism in Islam.[14] Besides, the Qur'ān endorses legal pluralism where religious communities possess the divine right to follow and implement their prescribed *sharīʿah*, as was discussed in verse (5:48): ". . . To each among you, we have prescribed a law and a clear way. . . ." Common ethical values, which form the essence of any divine revelation, represented through the Qur'ānic concept of *taṣdīq* (later revelation confirms previous ones) make possible the introduction of a common law to organize a pluralistic society, which nevertheless is inspired by divine scripture.

Third, in terms of conflict resolution, emphasizing that the conflicting tribes of Medina represent *Ummah wāḥidah* ("One *Ummah*") shifts the focus from the individual tribes to the central community. Thereby, the Islamic approach to mediation portrays conflict as a communal issue rather than an individual matter. "The charter does not address individuals; rather it addresses communities and tribes, calling not for individual reparations

11. Muhammad Mahdī Shams al-Dīn, *Fil-Ijtimāʿ as-Siyāsī al-Islāmī* (Beirut: Al-Muʾassasa al-Jāmiʿiyalil-Dirāsātwal-Nashr, 1992), 293–95.

12. See Qurʾanic verse 7:157 discussed in detail in chapter 1.

13. See Qurʾanic verse 5:48 discussed in detail in chapter 2.

14. Said Amir Arjomand, "The Constitution of Medina," *International Journal of Middle East Studies* 41 (2009): 560.

or settlements, but for the creation of a new community."[15] Nonetheless, the new community simultaneously acknowledges independent identities, and that is another effective means of reconciling differences: "by recognizing that we can be loyal to our principles without insisting that our opponents be disloyal to theirs."[16] Instead of the theory of rupture proposed by Denny, the aim of identifying the tribes by their religion is to realign their focus from being militaristic tribes into allied followers of their own religions. This process is called "realignment" whereby hostilities can be dissolved through destressing the old alliances so that the tribes view their new alliances through their own religion. By shifting their focus to religion, the Medina Constitution allowed the tribes to uphold their independent identities while simultaneously forsaking tribal enmity.[17]

The process of realignment through religion to resolve the conflict is evident in the way the constitution is structured. The first decrees (3–23) address the believers (*al-mu'minīn*). The following decrees (24–36) specifically address the Jews (*al-yahūd*), and the remaining decrees (37–47) address the people of the document (*ahl al-ṣaḥifa*). There is one decree that addresses polytheists (20B). The term Muslims is mentioned only three times, twice to differentiate from Jews (25 and 37) and once in the beginning of the document. Despite that each tribe is mentioned by name in the MC, the general makeup of the constitution is organized around religious lines initially, the believers and the Jews, and toward the end through an inclusive terminology that transcends religious differences (the people of the document). The other inclusive term used is obviously the *Ummah* used in decrees 2 and 25. The remaining decrees of the book/MC discuss the ideas and governing relations between the members of the *ummah*. It describes the *ummah*'s rights and obligations, thereby clarifying how its members will be judged and how to organize their life together.

15. Yetkin Yildrim, "The Medina Charter: A Historical Case of Conflict Resolution," *Islam and Christian-Muslim Relations* 20, no. 4 (2010), 444.

16. R. Fisher, "Fractioning Conflict," in *Conflict Resolution: Contributions of the Behavioral Sciences*, ed. C. G. Smith (Notre Dame, IN: University of Notre Dame Press, 1971), 162.

17. Yetkin Yildrim, "The Medina Charter: A Historical Case of Conflict Resolution," 445.

Al-Mu᾿minūn ("The Believers")

Serjeant translates *mu᾿min* as someone who is secure or granted security (*amān*), a definition related to the linguistic root (*᾿amn*). Then he argues that the Jews formed a separate *ummah* parallel to the believers, and he therefore endorses the reading: *yahūd Banī ʿAwf ummatun maʿa al-mu᾿minīn* ("The Jews of *Banī ʿAwf* are an *ummah with* the believers").[18] Denny does not agree with this translation because the constitution addresses all parties involved equally; it would be unlikely that only one party would be granted security and not others. He favors the translation "believers" (instead of those granted security).[19]

Rubin also translates *mu᾿minīn* as believers and endorses the second reading: *yahūd Banī ʿAwf ummatun mina al-mu᾿minīn* ("the Jews form an *ummah* of [a part of] the believers"). He supports his argument by noting that the preposition *min* typically follows *ummah* in the Qur᾿ān, for example, *ummatan mina an-nās, umamin mina l-jinni wal-insi*, and so forth. He adds that this reading better explains the use of the term *ummah wāḥidah* in the beginning of the document (second decree), diction that implies uniting all the different parties under one *ummah*. Thus Jews are regarded as monotheistic believers distinguished from other monotheistic believers (e.g., Muslims who follow Prophet Muhammad). Rubin thinks that being recognized as believers in the MC granted them the privilege to practice their own *dīn*.[20] Arjomand combined the latter interpretations and translated *mu᾿minīn* as "faithful covenanters," referring to those who enjoy the security and protection of God through the covenant of Medina, and he considers the MC as "the Covenant of Unity."[21]

---

18. R. B. Serjeant, "The Sunnah Jami'ah, Pacts with the Yathrib Jews and the Tahrim of Yathrib: Analysis and Translation of the Documents Comprised in the So-Called 'Constitution of Medina,'" *Bulletin of the School of Oriental and African Studies, University of London* 41, no. 1 (1978): 12–14.

19. Frederick Denny, "Ummah in the Constitution of Medina," *Journal of Near Eastern Studies* 36, no. 1 (January 1977): 43.

20. Uri Rubin, "'The Constitution of Medina' Some Notes," *Studia Islamica*, no. 62 (1985): 13–16.

21. Said Amir Arjomand, "The Constitution of Medina," 562–64.

I endorse the first reading of decree 25 that the Jews form an *ummah* with the believers (*yahūd Banī ʿAwf ummatun maʿa al-muʾminīn*) for several reasons. First, it is more suitable to the context of this constitution whose main goal is to unite the different groups and establish peace in Medina. Saying that the Jews are an *ummah* of believers has no political or unitary connotations, but saying that they form an *ummah* with the believers imply sociopolitical unity. Second, there are other decrees (24, 38, 45) that distinguish between Jews and believers. Decrees 24 and 38 use the preposition "with" (*maʿa*), stating that "Jews along with the believers shall bear (their own) war expenses during war." In addition, the first decrees (1–23) address the believers, then decrees 23–36 address the Jews of the same tribes being addressed in decrees 1–23. If the Jews are considered from the believers, there is no point of addressing them separately in different decrees, especially considering that the same tribes are being addressed (in both the believers and the Jews decrees).

Third, the previous chapter explained the Qurʾānic description of believers and Muslims. People of the Book, Jews and Christians, are recognized by the Qurʾān as believers in God and the Day of Judgment, some are privileged with good attributes such as *ummah muqtaṣida and ummah qāʾima*, and others are described as prone to wrongdoing for their rejection of later prophets and distorting the message of their divine books. Later in time, in comparing the Muslim *ummah* with the people of the book, the Qurʾānic verse 3:110,[22] explained in the previous chapter, introduces the idea of complete belief as total acceptance of all prophets of God as well as manifesting that through action in society. Then, while the Jews are believers, they did not fully believe for rejecting the prophecy of Muhammad. Jews accepted Prophet Muhammad as a judge and a political leader, not as a religious authority. Hence, the constitution distinguishes between the Jews and the believers. The believers in Medina, that is, the Muslims, not only acknowledged the prophecy of Muhammad but also supported him politically and materially (with arms). For example, decree 45 requires of the believers to support the Prophet in wars over religious causes yet does not require that of the Jews. However, in case of defending Medina against any attack (no religious reason here),

22. "You were (*kuntum*) the best (*khayr*) *ummah* ever raised up for humankind for you enjoin righteousness and deter wrongness and believe in Allah, and if the people of the book were to believe it would have been better for them, among them are believers but most of them are transgressors" (Qurʾān 3:110).

decree 37 requires both the Jews and the Muslims to defend the people designated by the constitution. Thus, there is a distinction made between support for religious causes and general support to defend their common land, and accordingly both groups are addressed.

In addition to the first decree, Muslims are mentioned twice in decrees 25 and 37: the first to distinguish between the Jewish and Islamic religion, and the second to separate between the Jewish and Muslim expenses during war, considering that the Jews will not participate in all wars as described above. Other than those three decrees, it is noticeable that the term "believers" is used mainly to describe the Muslims. The word believers (*al-muʾminīn*) or its singular form (*muʾmin*) is mentioned thirty-two times in the MC, while the word Muslims is mentioned only three times. The word Jews (*yahūd*) is mentioned twenty-one times. One would wonder why Muslims, instead of believers, is not the terminology used throughout. It is be possible that the Prophet wants to emphasize the commonalities between the different tribes who were waging wars for decades to enforce the idea of inclusivity and unity within one *ummah*. So the prophet used the term "believers" more than he used "Muslims" because both Jews and Muslims are believers in one God. The Arabic term *muʾmin* also implies security, as suggested by Serjeant and Arjomand and stated in the last decree (. . . Whoever goes out shall have security (*Āmin*) and whoever remains in Medina shall also have security . . .). However, the constitution is still distinguishing between Jews and believers, evident in using both terms together in many decrees to distinguish between their roles. I think that while the differences are obvious and known, the Prophet wants to invite the Jews to Islam by highlighting the common core value, which is belief in one God and the securing of peace resulting from that belief. The Qurʾānic narrative emphasizes the commonalities before introducing the differences:

> Say: "O People of the Book! Come to common terms between us and you: that we worship none but Allah; that we associate no partners with him; and that none of us shall take others as lords beside Allah." But if they turn away, say: "Bear witness that we are Muslims (accepted peacefully Allah's will)." (Qurʾān 3:64)

If Muslims were used more often, the Jews may feel that they are leaving behind their identity and acquiring a new one, following the theory of rupture suggested by Denny; in other words, they will feel disconnected. However, using believers more frequently is more prone to make it evident for them to see Prophet Muhammad and Islam as an addition or a continuation of their own belief, rather than breaking grounds with an old belief and replacing it with a new one. It could be more likely, knowing that Jews take pride in their ethnic origin as descending from Banī Israel. This is more in line with the makeup of the constitution, inspired by Qur'ānic ethics, which acknowledges the difference without undermining it. The constitution mentions each tribe by its name in a separate decree, an acknowledgement of ethnic and cultural diversity in which Arabs take pride.

Using believers frequently could also bring another message. The unifying religious component in the MC is not equivalent to exclusive religious law (*dīn* or *sharī'ah*) applied to followers of a specific prophet and a divine book. This is confirmed in decree 25, in which each group is instructed to follow its own religious law. Rather, the unifying religious foundation of the MC is inspired by Qur'ānic ethics. Belief represents the essence of its foundation. Believers form the founding unit or the building block for the embracing *ummah wāḥidah*. This is reflected in the terminology used in the MC (believers is mentioned thirty-two times). I would argue that this is meant not only to strengthen the relationships between Muslims and Jews and others, but also to emphasize another crucial point for everyone, Muslims included: Belonging to the *ummah* requires choice and responsibility, not cultural, religious, or ethnic affiliation. This critical point is related to the core concept of the *ummah* discussed in the previous chapters and actually implemented in the MC. As discussed in chapter 1, religion can be reduced to a set of rituals and practices, thereby losing its vigor. It is not surprising that the word *ummah* became associated with a closed community performing specific religious rituals over time! In order not to succumb to the problem of transforming belief into a cultural identity, the word "believers" was emphasized. This is better explained in the Qur'ānic verse:

> The desert Arabs (Bedouins) say, "We believe (*āmannā*)." Say (to them, O Muhammad), "You did not believe; but rather say, 'we have surrendered' (*aslamnā*), for faith has not yet entered your hearts. Yet if you obey Allah and His Messenger, He will not belittle any of your deeds: for Allah is forgiving, most

> merciful." *Indeed the believers are only those who have believed in Allah and his messenger and have never since doubted, and have striven with their wealth and their selves in the way of Allah, such are the truthful ones.* (Qur'ān 49:14–15)

The verse addresses the problem of following a religion superficially by confessing adherence to it or merely endorsing its public manifestation. Belief on the other hand necessitates taking action by "striving with the wealth and the self," as shown in the latter verse. The same idea is stipulated in the first decree of the constitution that describes the members covenanted to establish the *ummah*: ". . . those who follow them, join them and strive along with them." Thus, it is evident that establishing an *ummah* requires a choice and ongoing responsibility to adhere to that choice.

Ali Bulac interprets the word believers, in the first decree, as the emigrants from Mecca to Medina.[23] Bulac refers to the believers who emigrated with the Prophet from Mecca, leaving behind family and homes, and who harnessed their wealth to support the nascent Muslim *ummah* in Medina. Their action reflects a sincere devotion to God and his messenger; hence they are described as believers. These believers are distinguished from the general Muslims who accepted the Prophetic call but who did not equally strive or sacrifice to support it. This interpretation may also explain the frequent use of "believers" instead of "Muslims" throughout the constitution.

In the previous chapter, I concluded that the Muslim *ummah* forms the nucleus from which the Islamic *ummah* grows, which is inclusive and pluralistic in character and has a global potential. The Medina constitution reflects this idea through historical practice. The constitution starts with the basic unit of the *ummah* represented by the believers/Muslims, and then expands the *ummah* to include Jews, though they are distinguished as following their own religion. Moreover, the *ummah* expands to include the respective communities' allies (*mawālī*) and protected persons (*jār*), privileging the latter identified members as well. Finally, the constitution begins to address its entire people (*ahl al-ṣaḥifa*). This cumulative addition, represented in changing the addressee terminology, shows that the *ummah wāḥidah*, in essence, is open to include whoever wills to be a member of

23. Ali Bulac, "The Medina Document," in Charles Kurzman, *Liberal Islam* (New York: Oxford University Press, 1998), 171.

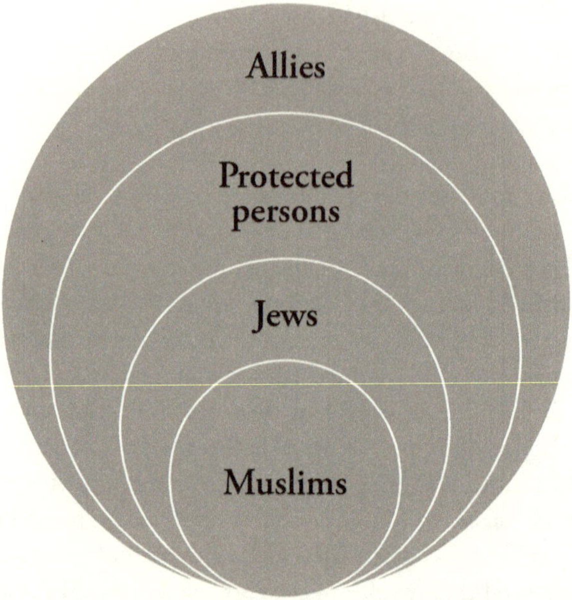

Figure 3.1. The embracing united *Ummah* (*ummah wāḥida*): The *Islamic Ummah.*

it (shown in figure 3.1). It is not a closed society, as Orientalists, as well as some early Muslim scholars (e.g., Abū ʿUbayd), claim, and it does not merely represent a political confederation.[24] While it is indeed a unifying political treaty, its core founding principles are based on Qurʾānic ethics, which stress the unity of humankind before God, connectedness between different prophets and divine messages, and common belief in one creator for all people.

Decrees Addressing the Believers

Decrees 3–23 address the believers and clarify their duties and rights in the MC. We analyze the decrees and their significance in light of the Qurʾānic description of the *ummah* discussed in the previous two chapters.

3- The *muhājirūn* (migrants) of Quraysh are in charge of the management of their affairs, they shall defray the cost of bloodshed among

24. Ibid., 12. Uri Rubin presents a survey of different scholars, such as Wellhausen, Wensinck, Watt, Serjeant, and Gil, confining the *ummah* of Medina to a mere political confederation.

themselves, and shall join in ransoming their war prisoners according to *ma*ʿ*rūf* and equity (justice) among the believers.

4- The Banī ʿAwf are in charge of the management of their affairs, they shall continue to pay the costs of their bloodshed among themselves as has been the custom, and each group shall ransom its war prisoner according to *ma*ʿ*rūf* and equity (justice) among the believers.

The same conditions are repeated in the following seven decrees, while changing the name of the tribe only. 5- The Banūl- Ḥārith (. . .), 6- The Banū Sāʿida (. . .), 7- The Banū Jashm (. . .), 8- The Banū-Najjār (. . .), 9- The Banū ʿAmrū bin ʿAwf (. . .), 10- The Banū- Nabīt (. . .), 11- The Banūl- ʾAws (. . .).

Decrees 3–11 address each tribe by its name. Watt says that this organization shows that everything in the *ummah* is interpreted in terms of the kinship group.[25] Denny refutes Watt's claim and argues that the *ummah* is only arranged along kinship lines because the kinship system was the only means to describe and differentiate between the elements of the Arabian society.[26] I agree with Denny and disagree with Watt because by looking at the structure of the latter decrees, one will notice that each decree starts by addressing the specific name of a tribe and ends with common rules binding all believers: "according to *ma*ʿ*rūf* and justice among the believers" (*bil-ma*ʿ*rūf wal-qisṭ bayna al-mu*ʾ*minīn*)." Therefore, while using the tribe as a unit for organizing the pluralistic structure of the *ummah*, the MC did not judge each tribe by its own tribal rules, but rather by the common rules binding all of them equally before the constitution. That is why each decree ends with the same binding statement, which identifies new regulations based on *ma*ʿ*rūf* and justice between the believers.

*Ma*ʿ*rūf* is a Qurʾānic concept describing the action of the best *ummah* to be raised for humankind, an *ummah* that commands righteousness and deters wrongness while believing in God. The Qurʾānic verses[27] mentioning this term, discussed in the previous chapter, relate

25. Watt, *Muhammad at Medina*, 242.

26. Denny, "Community and Salvation: The Meaning of the Ummah in the Qurʾān," 216.

27. See chapter 2 for the discussion of the related verses: "Let there be from among you (*minkum*) an *ummah* inviting to the good (*khayr*) and enjoining righteousness and deterring wrongness (*ya*ʾ*murūna bil-ma*ʿ*rūf wa yanhawna* ʾ*an al-munkar*) and those are the successful" (Qurʾān 3:104); "You were (*kuntum*) the

ma ͑rūf to belief in God. *Ma ͑rūf*[28] is translated as "customary" by some scholars who argue that the Medinan *ummah* did not offer anything new to the Arabian society and was rather just maintaining Arab tradition.[29] I do not think that the latter claim is valid because the remaining decrees addressing the believers (12–23) explain what signifies "*ma ͑rūf* and equity." Obviously, some decrees contradict established Arabian customs preceding the coming of Prophet Muhammad. For example, decree 13 altered the pre-Islamic Arabian understanding of crime from a tribal responsibility to an individual one. Decree 13 states: "All God conscious believers shall be against the person who intends to commit an aggressive and unjust act among them, or who aims to infringe one's rights or to cause turmoil among believers. And even if this person is the offspring of one of them, they shall all raise their hands against him." In this case, kinship and tribal rules do not apply anymore; on the contrary, they are forfeited for the sake of establishing peace and equity among the believers, regardless of tribal affiliations. However, the custom of pre-Islamic Arabia associates the guilt of offense to the whole tribe, not to the individual criminal, as explained by Serjeant:

> To expiate the guilt of offence, the guilty *tribe* must execute one of its own members, not necessarily the actual murderer, or else the other tribes will unite and attack it, remaining at war until they have exacted proper atonement in the way of killings adequate to the heinous crime of violating the sanctity of the sacred enclave.[30]

The concept of the sacred enclave (*ḥaram*) is addressed later in more detail. This quote is presented to show how the concept of *ma ͑rūf* in

---

best (*khayr*) *ummah* ever raised up for humankind for you enjoin righteousness and deter wrongness and believe in God, and if the people of the book were to believe it would have been better for them, among them are believers but most of them are transgressors" (Qur ͗ān 3:110).

28. Translated as "customary" by R. B. Serjeant and Arjomand; "uprightness" by Denny; "proper" by Bulac.

29. R. B. Serjeant, "Haram and Hawtah, the Sacred Enclave in Arabia," Melanges Taha Hussein, ed. Abdurrahman Badawi (Cairo: Dār al-Ma ͑ārif, 1962), 41–58.

30. Ibid., 47. Emphasis added.

the MC is not equivalent to pre-Islamic Arabian practice. In addition, arranging the Medinan *ummah* along tribal lines did not mean a loss of individual responsibility at the expense of the tribe. This idea is implied in Arjomand's analysis where he claimed that "the *ummah* was organized as a community of clans, not individuals."[31] I disagree with Arjomand because I see an amalgam of rights and responsibilities associated with both the tribe as a community unit within the *ummah*, and the individuals as affiliated *ummah* members. This idea is discussed by Faḍlallah[32] in his interpretation and explanation of the concept of *ummah wasaṭ*, which offers a middle position in community organization, and which does not overstress the rights of community at the expense of the individual and vice versa.

Shams ad-Dīn also addresses this point by saying that the decrees that refer to the different tribes and their functions reveal a considerable internal independence of each tribe in managing its internal affairs. However, this privacy and independence are partial for the sake of a united *ummah* into which different communities merge. Thus, the tribes were not destroyed as a social unit, but were kept and even used to strengthen the spirit of internal collaboration between the different parties.[33] The pluralistic structure did not threaten the unity of the *ummah*. This unity will be confirmed through studying the subsequent decrees (12–24), specifically decrees 12, 15, 17, 19, 22, and 23. In decrees 15 and 17, the word "*wāḥidah*" appears again, emphasizing a united *ummah*.

12- The believers shall not leave a *mufraḥ*[34] (one under financial burden) among them without giving him what is (established by) custom for ransom or blood-wit.

12B- No believer shall oppose the *mawla* (client/ally) of another believer. (According to another reading: No believer may enter into an agreement with the *mawla* of another believer, so as to harm the latter.)

This decree with its subsection reflects the mutual duties of believers. It may also reflect the concept of brotherhood (*mu'ākhā*) established by Prophet Muhammad between the Muslim natives of Medina and the

31. Said Amir Arjomand, "The Constitution of Medina," 565.

32. See chapter 2.

33. Muhammad Mahdī Shams al-Dīn, *Fil-Ijtimā' as-Siyāsī al-Islāmī* (Beirut: Al-Mu'asassa al-Jāmi'iyalil-Dirāsātwal-Nashr, 1992), 293.

34. In another reading, *mufraj* (one turned Muslim among a people to whom he does not belong).

Muslim immigrants. The institution of brotherhood was a critical step toward the final realization of the *ummah*. It facilitated reconciliation between the believers and increased their cohesion. The tribe and kinship were no longer the bonding link, and faith became the everlasting bond, as shown in Qurʾānic verses referring to brotherhood in religion (*ʾikhwānukum fid-dīn*).[35] The institution of *muʾākhāh* was part of the development process from the tribe to the *ummah*.[36]

13- All God-conscious believers shall be against the person who intends to commit an aggressive and unjust act among them, or who aims to infringe one's rights or to cause turmoil among believers. And even if this person is the offspring of one of them, they shall all raise their hands against him.

This decree has already been discussed as reflecting a new understanding of justice different from pre-Islamic Arab practice, which used to hold the offender's whole tribe responsible for his or her crime. Thereby, the decree opposes the inherited practices of forefathers that failed to establish unbiased justice. In chapter 1, such justice was discussed as one of the basic elements in understanding the concept of the *ummah*; the Qurʾānic verses 43:21–24 challenge those who blindly follow the traditions of their forefathers by presenting them with better guidance.[37] The better guidance is represented in this decree. Other than individual responsibility, the decree urges for collective responsibility to hold the offender responsible for his or her offensive act. The Meccan verses explored in chapter 1 introduced the idea of the believers carrying out continuous reform (*ʾiṣlāḥ*). Then the Medinan verses in chapter 2 practically elaborated on the idea by stressing the need for interaction, discussion, and mutual advice among different people of the *ummah* because all members share the same destiny. The Medinan verses culminated with the notion of the best *ummah*, the successful one, whose belief will urge it to invite people for the good by enjoining righteousness and deterring wrongness (*yaʾmurūna bil-maʿrūf wa yanhawna ʾan al-munkar*). *The notion of being best instills in the ummah a culture of social and political obligations that are*

35. Qurʾān (9:11); also Qurʾān (49:10): "The believers are but brethren, therefore make peace between your brethren and be careful of (your duty to) Allah that you may have his mercy."

36. Elias Giannakis, "The Concept of Ummah," *Graeco-Arabica* 2 (1983), 103–4.

37. See detailed discussion in chapter 1.

not dependent on a central power for implementation. This active *ummah* and its dynamic culture are inspired by a Qur᾽ānic ideology that considers belief deficient if it does not blossom right action and virtue in society.

Decrees 13 and 37 represent a practical realization of the Qur᾽ānic concepts discussed thus far. An active *ummah* by default puts limitations on the central power. In other words, the believers are required to deter injustice by acting collectively against an aggressor before resorting to the central authority, that is, the Prophet in this case. This form of deterring wrongness gives the *ummah* members direct political agency. Nevertheless, we may witness here a middle position best fit to politically realize the *ummah wasaṭ*, where central power and *ummah* members assume different responsibilities without either negating the other. Shams ad-Dīn considers the *ummah* in this case to be equivalent to the political community. The *ummah* is responsible for maintaining its integrity and deterring evil and injustice irrespective of tribal or even kinship affiliations.[38]

14- No believer shall kill another believer for the sake of an infidel or shall assist an infidel at the expense of a believer.

15- The security (*dhimma*) of Allah (for life and property) is the same for everyone; this protection (acknowledged by the least important of the believers) applies to them all. And some of the believers are allies of others who are apart from the rest of the people.

Decree 14 emphasizes collaboration of the believers to protect and defend each other as a united *ummah* against any threat. This condition reflects the common goal of maintaining peace and security inside Medina after a long period of strife and war. Similarly, the persecuted believers who emigrated from Mecca to Medina with the Prophet were mainly concerned with practicing their religion in a secure environment without fearing loss of life or oppression. Decree 15 confirms decree 14 by representing the concept of security as a covenant with God. The covenant represents one of the constitutive principles in the *ummah*. In Lisān al-ʿArab, *dhimma* means covenant, security, assurance, inviolability, and right (*al-ʿahd wal-᾽amān wal-ḍamān wal-ḥurma wal-ḥaq*).[39] This decree reflects the Qur᾽ānic verses 16:92–93,[40] which emphasize the critical importance of upholding

38. Muhammad Mahdī Shams ad-Dīn, *Fil-Ijtimāʿ as-Siyāsī al-Islāmī*, 295.

39. Ibn Manḍhūr, *Lisān al-ʿArab*, vol. 5, 59–60.

40. Discussed in detail in chapter 1.

covenants "equally" between weak and strong *umam*. The Qur᾿ān supports its argument using metaphorical imagery comparing the established covenants with the threads forming a piece of yarn: the loss of one thread will lead to the destruction of the whole piece. Similarly, decree 15 states that protection by God is equally bestowed upon the lowliest of believers (in terms of prestige and material status) as it is for the most privileged. God does not discriminate based on societal statuses; rather all are equal before Him. In one respect, associating security with a covenantal status and religious inviolability maintains security for the Medinan *ummah*. Arjomand considers that the indivisible protection of God over the community and its members strengthened the covenantal solidarity by providing it with a new dimension.[41]

Shams ad-Dīn translates the second part of decree 15 as "the believers are guardians of each other apart from the rest of the people." The verse reflects the equality of all people, irrespective of the statuses created by human societies. All members have the same rights, including the right of giving protection to others. This right, which only the most privileged in pre-Islamic Arabia possessed, became the right of the least privileged as well in Medina. All believers should acknowledge that right, honor it, and endorse it because security of God is the same for all believers. Shams ad-Dīn concludes that the guardianship of believers (*wilāya*) toward each other shows the responsibility of the *ummah* toward itself politically and reinforces the concept of *shūra* practiced among the believers.[42]

Thus, while keeping the basic structural unit of the society, the tribe, the MC introduced new modes of interaction based on Qur᾿ānic ethics, which fosters a novel understanding of *ummah wāḥidah*. This unifying sociopolitical structure does not differentiate between its members based on kinship (decree 13), privileged status (decree 15), or religious difference (decrees 16, 25–35). Rather, the *ummah wāḥidah* establishes its unifying order based on common principles of impartial justice and equity.

16- Among Jews, those who join (follow) us shall receive our assistance and equal treatment; they shall not be oppressed, nor shall we give assistance to their enemies.

I think that this decree is a clause of decree 15 whereby Jews who choose to join the *ummah* are also granted the indivisible protection of

41. Said Amir Arjomand, "The Constitution of Medina," 566.

42. Muhammad Mahdī Shams ad-Dīn, *Fil-Ijtimā῾ as-Siyāsī al-Islāmī*, 296–97.

God under the common covenantal security of the MC. Hence the members or tribes of the MC should equally support them and do not befriend their enemies; thus this implies that the enemies of the Jews become the enemies of the believers.[43] Shams ad-Dīn says that equality extends to all parties involved in the sociopolitical contract. It is not only equality to believers of different status in society, but also to those of different religious background. The Jews here are granted support and equal treatment as long as they support the Muslims living with them in Medina and do not betray them or give assistance to their enemies.

17- Peace is one among believers. No believer, in a war fought in the path of God, may agree to a peace accord by excluding other believers. This peace shall only be made among them (believers) according to the principles of equity and justice/fair dealing between them.

Shams ad-Dīn thinks that this decree is a continuation of decree 15. This decree deals with peace treaties as a means to end war. It shows that being at peace or at war is a decision that cannot be taken by individuals. It is rather a collective decision of the whole *ummah* that results from *shūra* and must "accord to the principles of equity and justice/fair dealing between them."[44] While decree 15 addresses individuals and their right to be supported by the whole *ummah* (Any individual can give protection to another person, such as a polytheist, and the rest of the *ummah* should accept this protection), decree 17 requires an obligation of the individual to maintain the unity of the *ummah* by not making any peace agreement separately. Therefore, decree 15 gives individuals rights, and decree 17 places on individuals obligations; thereby a balance is created between the rights of individuals and that of the whole *ummah* (*ummah wasaṭ*).

While decrees 12–16 organized individual, internal relationships between Medina members, the decrees 17–22 will organize their dealings with each other as one coherent group fighting external enemies.

---

43. R. B. Serjeant reports an incident mentioned in Ibn Isḥāq/Ibn Hishām (Guillaume, 263): "In a quarrel, Abu Bakr struck Finḥāṣ the Jew, adding that but for the pact (*ʾahd*) between them, he would have cut off his head. Finḥāṣ went to redress Muhammad as head of the *Muhājirūn* and Muhammad rebuked Abu-Bakr." In R. B. Serjeant, "The Sunnah Jami'ah, Pacts with the Yathrib Jews and the Tahrim of Yathrib: Analysis and Translation of the Documents Comprised in the So-Called 'Constitution of Medina,'" 22.

44. Muhammad Mahdī Shams ad-Dīn, *Fil-Ijtimāʿ as-Siyāsī al-Islāmī*, 297–98.

18- Each raiding party that raids along with us—one shall succeed another.

19- Believers shall execute retribution on behalf of one another with respect to their bloodshed in the path of God.

20- Surely, God-conscious believers follow the best and straightest path (*ʿala aḥsan hudā*).

20B- No polytheist [affiliated with the community] may protect the life and property of a person affiliated with Quraysh or intervene with a believer in this matter.

Decrees 17–20 establish an internal cohesion between the members of the *ummah* in cases of war against them, and ends by stating that this represents better guidance than that which was followed in pre-Islamic Arabia. The statement "*ʿala ʾaḥsan hudā*" (following best guidance) in decree 20 reflects the Qurʾānic promise of bringing better guidance than that of the forefathers: "*Qul a-wa-law jiʾtukum bi-ahdā mimma wajadtum ʿalayhi ābāʾukum*?" (Qurʾān 43:23).[45] The terms *hudā* and *ahdā* have the same root and imply the same meaning. Decree 20B shows that there are polytheists who are recognized as affiliate members of the *ummah*, but this is the only decree that mentions a polytheist and his obligation toward the *ummah*. It seems that polytheists were not recognized as an organized community in Medina like the Jews or the believers, which explains why they do not show up in the remaining decrees of the MC. This decree may reflect a protected person or client by any member or tribe of the Medina *ummah* who happens to be a polytheist.

Because the context of decrees 17–22 is related to war situations, it is conceivable that Quraysh and its affiliated members will be addressed in the MC. Quraysh represents the main enemy of Prophet Muhammad and his followers not only for its persecution of the believers and its expelling them outside Mecca, but also because of its ideology. The word *mushrik* (polytheist), which represents the creed of Quraysh, opposes the word *muʾmin* (believer), representing belief in God. The sociopolitical conditions of strife and war in the pre-Islamic tribal society reflect the state of *shirk* (polytheism) endorsed by the pagan society. That state is contrasted with the peaceful state of the believers and the covenanted members of the one *ummah*, a state resulting from a unity inspired by belief in one common God and enacted through a treaty based on Qurʾānic universal

45. Discussed in detail in chapter 1.

ethics. The Qur'ānic inference of "monotheistic belief versus *shirk*" and its sociopolitical consequences will be addressed in detail in decree 39. Decree 20B shows that polytheist confederates are part of the *ummah* through abiding by the decrees of the confederation. This decree shows again that religion does not form one of the constitutive principles of the *ummah*; rather it is the covenant that relates and unites the members of the *ummah*.

21- If it is proven with certainty that one person has killed a believer (unjustly without a reason that necessitates killing), then it is his own responsibility unless the guardian of the victim grants him a pardon; and all believers shall be against him. And it is not permissible for the believers to fight for him.

22- It is not lawful for any believer approving the contents of this sheet (document) and believing in God and the Day of Judgment to support or shelter an aggressor; whoever supports or shelters him shall receive the curse and wrath of God on the Day of Judgment, when financial compensation or sacrifice shall no longer be accepted.

Decree 21 shows the individual's responsibility for a crime, rather than the individual's tribe or people. Simultaneously, it stresses the importance of the collective responsibility of the *ummah* in maintaining this norm instead of tribal norms and ensuring implementation: "All believers shall be against him" confirming the ideas in decrees 13, 15, and 17. In addition, decree 21 highlights the responsibility of the *ummah* to implement law as the *ummah* has guardianship over itself (*wilāyat al-ummah ʿala nafsihā*).[46]

Both decrees link individual responsibility to the collective's, whereby individuals cannot fulfill their obligations without the *ummah*'s commitment to establish a norm in society. At the same time, a community cannot maintain its norms and order without the contribution of each constituent member. Therefore, the success of the *ummah* is a direct result of fulfilling both obligations: the individual and the collective. It is the direct interaction between the two that creates a healthy balance in society and ensures the maintenance of order with the least need for intervention from a central power. Then it becomes possible to genuinely understand the meaning of "the *ummah*'s guardianship over itself," which is endorsed by Shams ad-Dīn.

46. Muhammad Mahdī Shams ad-Dīn, *Fil-Ijtimāʿ as-Siyāsī al-Islāmī*, 300.

The collective obligation of the members of the *ummah* to fight an aggressor among them and hold him the "only" one responsible for his crime is emphasized only in the decrees addressing the believers. It is worth noting that this collective attitude is not present in the decrees addressing the Jews. The believers could not have implemented that constitutional norm if they were not educated accordingly, especially as it directly opposes established tribal norms. Hence we find the link in decree 22 between implementing decree 21 and believing in God, the Day of Judgment, and fearing his wrath. This direct relationship reflects the Qur'ānic education of the believers for a period of thirteen years before they immigrated to Medina to establish the *ummah*.

The Medinan verses addressing the collective commitment of the members of the *ummah* toward each other in enjoining the right conduct and fighting aggression are directly implemented in decrees 21 and 22.[47] These constitutional decrees represent a cultivation of the new Islamic values and norms taught by the Prophet in the pre-*hijra* period. Thus, there was a process of socialization before institutionalization. It is obvious from the Medina Constitution that the concept of socialization of norms is rendered seriously for the *ummah*'s establishment and continuation. That is why there is a stress on the collective obligation of the believers in this transitional period.

The Jews as a collective body are addressed differently (it is discussed later) in the decrees related to them. I assume that this difference pertains to the different ways in which Islamic and Jewish law deal with aggression in society. Of note, the Jews of Medina were not socialized in Islamic values, as were the Muslim immigrants who had been taught these concepts for a period of thirteen years before immigration. However, because any divine message in its essence represents the same values, the Prophet expected the Jews to be more aligned with Islamic ideals than Pagan Arabs. The common decree explicitly addressing both Jews and believers demands loyalty to the constitutional act. Decree 22 requires it specifically of the believers, and there will be other decrees requiring it of the Jews and whoever is affiliated with the *ummah* of Medina.

Decree 22 invokes the concept of "choice" before requiring loyalty to the covenant between the affiliated members by saying "any believer

47. Refer to Qur'anic verses discussed in chapter 2, which discuss the concept of enjoining righteousness and deterring wrongness.

approving the contents of this document." This statement shows that the MC came about through the agreement and consensus of its members, and explicitly states that they have willingly chosen to be part of the covenanted *ummah*. Consequently, they are obliged to assume the responsibility associated with their choice by upholding their covenant with each other. Strengthening their covenant is realized by equating their covenant with each other to taking a covenant with God (as discussed in chapter 1). Hence, decree 22 associates between revoking the covenant and provoking God's wrath and punishment.

23- In whatever thing you are at variance, its reference back (*maradd*) is to Allah and to Muhammad.

Decree 23 comes directly after the decree requiring constitutional loyalty, which reflects that the judicial authority of Prophet Muhammad is also part of the covenant chosen and enacted by the covenanted members of the *ummah*. Thus, abiding by Prophet Muhammad's leadership in settling disputes is another form of upholding the agreed-upon covenant. Prophet Muhammad's leadership is not above the constitution, and therefore it does not make sense to consider his authority a real theocracy, as Denny claims.[48]

Decrees Addressing the Jews

24- Jews along with the believers shall bear (their own) war expenses as long as they are fighting.

This decree is repeated in decrees 37 and 38. Shams ad-Dīn regards this decree to be representative of a "political community." The responsibility of defending Medina is a shared responsibility for all its residents because the beneficiary of the sovereignty and safety is the whole political community.[49] Arjomand thinks that obligating the Jews to pay the war levy is the Prophet's condition in return for their protection by the law and assuring them religious tolerance.[50] I do not think that the war levy was imposed on the Jews, as Arjomand argues, because the same condition

48. Denny claims that "Medina developed into a real theocracy" in Frederick Denny, "Ummah in the Constitution of Medina," *Journal of Near Eastern Studies*, 47.

49. Muhammad Mahdī Shams ad-Dīn, *Fil-Ijtimāʿ as-Siyāsī al-Islāmī*, 301.

50. Said Amir Arjomand, "The Constitution of Medina," 567.

applies for the believers. It appears to be a shared duty of both communities in the *ummah* rather than a tax imposed on one community in return for granting equal rights.

In addition, the decree specifies that the Jews will pay the war levy "as long as they are fighting with the believers." Decree 45, for example, distinguishes between a war for common defense, which is the duty of all affiliated members of the *ummah*, and a war for religious reasons, which would be carried out by one group without involving the other members of the *ummah*. Therefore, if the Jews are not fighting alongside the believers in a war carried out for religious reasons, they do not have to pay the war levy because the decree explicitly states "as long as they are fighting." I conclude that the decree is not an imposition by the Prophet; rather it is assuring that every group is equally and "fairly" responsible for upholding their duties toward the one *ummah*.

25- The Jews of Banī 'Awf, together with the believers, constitute an *ummah*; the Jews having their religion/law (*dīn*) and the Muslims having their religion/law (*dīn*). This includes both their *mawla* and themselves personally. But whoever performs an unjust action or commits a crime shall harm solely himself and the people of his house.

26- The Jews of Banī Najjār shall have the same (rights) as the Jews of Banī ʿAwf.

27- The Jews of Banīl-Ḥārith shall have the same (rights) as the Jews of Banī ʿAwf.

28- The Jews of Banī Sāʿida shall have the same (rights) as the Jews of Banī ʿAwf.

29- The Jews of Bin Jashm shall have the same (rights) as the Jews of Banī ʿAwf.

30- The Jews of Banīl-Aws shall have the same (rights) as the Jews of Banī ʿAwf.

31- The Jews of Banī Thaʿlaba shall have the same (rights) as the Jews of Banī ʿAwf. But whoever performs an unjust action or commits a crime shall harm solely himself and the people of his house.

32- The Jafna (family) is a branch of the Thaʿlaba [tribe] and because of this they shall be considered as the Thaʿlaba.

33- Banī Shuṭayba shall have the same rights as the Jews of Banī ʿAwf. Observation of one's undertakings eliminates treachery/breaking of treaties.

34- The clients/allies of Thaʿlaba shall be considered as Thaʿlaba themselves.

35- Those associated with Jews (by alliance and bonds of mutual protection) shall be considered as Jews themselves.

36- Among them (Jews) none may go (on a military campaign with the Muslims) without the permission of Muhammad.

36B It shall not be forbidden to take revenge of a wound. Surely if a person happens to kill another, both he and his family shall be responsible as a consequence, except if he kills one who acts wrongfully (*ẓalama*). God is with those who best obey this document.

Decree 25 has been discussed earlier in this chapter in detail. The following decrees (26–35) basically mention each tribe by name to guarantee all of them the same rights as the tribe of Banī ʿAwf mentioned in decree 25. As has been discussed, the decrees reflect religious as well as ethnic and cultural pluralism in Islam; Jews with believers constitute one *ummah*. Decrees that govern interactions of the members of both communities seem to be based on the religious law of each community. For example, we have already shown that the governing ideology of the decrees addressing the believers is the Qurʾān, as referenced in decrees 13, 15, 17, 21, and 22. The decrees that address Muslims are identifiable from the use of specific expressions such as "according to the principles of justice and equity among the believers," "God conscious believers," or "*ḥalāl*." These decrees invoke in the believers a sense of collective responsibility by enjoining right conduct in society and forbidding wrongness, both directives based on a belief in God and the Day of Judgment. We do not see similar decrees aimed at fostering communal action in the decrees addressing the Jews. This could be due to the difference between the teachings of Islamic and Jewish law. We notice that decree 25 explicitly states that the Jews have their own religion/law, which implies that the Jews are free in organizing their internal affairs based on Jewish law. However, there needed to be a way to ensure stability in the *ummah* as a whole and prevent aggression between its different members.

Because Islamic values are specified as nonbinding on the Jews, a different approach is used to preserve order and justice for the Jews. For example, in decrees 25 and 31: ". . . But whoever performs an unjust action or commits a crime shall harm solely himself and the people of his house." If a Muslim commits an act of injustice, all Muslims are against the offender based on the Qurʾānic teaching of enjoining goodness and deterring wrongness; for a Jewish offender, the social pressure is exerted by the people of his house. In Jewish law, the Torah states: "And he that kills any man shall surely be put to death . . . Breach for breach, eye for eye, tooth for tooth: as he has caused a blemish in a man, so shall it be done to him again" (Leviticus 24:17–20). The Jewish law allows for personal retaliation for a wound or harm, but there is no equivalent for the social pressure exerted by the community fostered in Islamic law. So I would argue that citing "the people of his house" as responsible for sharing blame[51] is a means to foster positive community relations among the Jews, hindering unjust acts and maintaining peace and justice. For Muslims, the means of deterrence comes from the *ummah*, whereas for Jews the means of deterrence comes from the people of their house.

Another instance that shows the difference between Jewish and Islamic law is decree 36B, which allows personal retaliation for a wound. This decree seems to contradict decree 21, which addresses the believers, stating that "if a person kills a believer (unjustly), then it is his own responsibility unless the guardian of the victim grants him pardon; and all believers shall be against him . . ." The question to be raised here is: why can the killer of a believer be granted a pardon from the believer's guardian, but for one who wounds a Jew, retaliation should be enacted? The answer can be traced back to the difference between Islamic and Jewish law. At-Ṭabarī says that retribution for a murdered or wounded person was obligatory on Banī Isrāʾīl, that is, there is no *diyya* (blood wit) as compensation for a murder or wound in Jewish law. However, God relieved the community of Muhammad by allowing them the option of paying blood money in cases of murder and injury if the family of the victim agreed to it.[52] Therefore, the difference between the decrees addressing the believers and those addressing the Jews in the case of murder and injury can be explained by referring to the difference between Islamic and Jewish law. The latter confirms that fact that the legal structure of the *ummah* is pluralistic and supports the Qurʾānic principle of legal pluralism (Qurʾān 5:48) where each religious group abides by its *sharīʿah*.

37- In the case of war, Jews bear their expenses and the Muslims theirs. Surely they shall cooperate among themselves in opposing those who wage war against the people designated on this sheet (document).

51. R. B. Serjeant, "The Sunnah Jami'ah, Pacts with the Yathrib Jews and the Tahrim of Yathrib: Analysis and Translation of the Documents Comprised in the So-Called 'Constitution of Medina,'" 31.

52. Ibid., 31.

There shall be good counsel and advice between them. Observation of one's undertakings eliminates treachery/breaking of treaties.

37B- No one may commit a crime against his ally; surely the oppressed shall receive help.

Decree 37 is very similar, conceptually, to decree 25, in which independence is granted to both communities while simultaneously creating their political unity. Decree 25 specifies the religious independence of both communities, while decree 37 specifies financial independence. Nevertheless, this independence does not stand in the way of uniting both communities as one *ummah* sharing a common constitution, land, leader, and responsibility to defend their existence against any threat (external or internal). Decree 37 shows that each community should spend from its own financial resources to defend the *ummah* against any external power that threatens the stability and peace of the people designated in the constitution.

Starting with decree 37, the addressee changes into "*ahl as-ṣaḥīfa*" (the people of the constitution) to reinforce the feeling of sociopolitical unity. The decree also declares that both communities should interact with each other in good counsel and mutual advice, which implies deterring any internal threat from among them that could cause chaos and mischief between the two communities. The notion of providing mutual advice is necessary for members sharing one *ummah*. This idea was discussed in chapter 2, in which good counsel was shown to be both a right and an obligation. Then decree 37 ends with a general unifying statement that defends the oppressed rights, irrespective of his or her affiliation. At the same time, it stresses the individual responsibility of an aggressor, stating that a human being cannot be accused of a sin committed by his ally. Despite the fact that allies have the same rights as the members of the community, responsibility for an act of aggression by an ally would not be shared by other members as well (following the same logic of rights). Instead, the aggressor must carry sole responsibility of his or her crime, and justice will prevail in favor of the oppressed.

38- Jews along with Muslims shall bear the expenses of wars fought together.

Decree 38 is the same as decree 24. Shams ad-Din considers it to be a copying mistake of those who transmitted the constitution.[53] I do not

53. Muhammad Mahdī Shams ad-Dīn, *Fil-Ijtimāʿ as-Siyāsī al-Islāmī*, 305.

agree with this assumption. First, there is a possibility that we have two separate documents, one specifically addressing the Muslims and the other addressing the Jews. Second, decree 38 may similarly seem to be redundant after decree 37. However, I do not think this is the case either because decree 37 describes general threats (which include internal ones, and that is why there is the specific mention of allies), while decree 38 specifies external threats. Decree 38 is directly followed by specifying the sanctity of the land, which means that war cannot be conducted inside Yathrib (the previous name of Medina). Thus, decree 38 specifically addresses cases of war against external threats, which should be conducted outside the borders of Medina. Thus, there is no repetition; rather it is clearly emphasizing the specific duties and obligations. I think that decrees 38 and 39 could be joined together as one verdict.

DECREES ADDRESSING *AHL AS-ṢAḤĪFAH* (THE PEOPLE OF THE CONSTITUTION)

39- On behalf of the people designated by this document (constitution), the Yathrib (*jawf*) constitutes a protected territory (*ḥaram*).

Sacred Land (*ḥaram*)

Decree 39 defines the borders of the land that contain the people addressed by the constitution. The concept of the *ummah*, in this case, embraced the concept of the land within it. It not only defines the borders of the land, but also considers the land as sacred (*ḥaram*). This is interpreted that inside Medina, no wars are to be conducted, and this eliminated the struggle that existed for more than a century among Yathrib's different tribes. However, I think that the idea of a "sacred land" for the *ummah* has a deeper significance than what was stated. In traditional Arabia, the concept of *ḥaram* or *ḥawṭah* signified a secure location established by a holy person or family in agreement with diverse neighboring tribes. The agreement allows different tribes to safely come together in this location and conduct business or resolve disagreements, and so forth, while all the affected parties pledge to preserve its sanctity and neutrality. Murder is one of the biggest offenses within the *ḥaram*.[54] Thus, the central point is securing a safe common area

54. R. B. Serjeant, "Haram and Hawtah, the Sacred Enclave in Arabia," 45–47.

where different tribes, who do not have defined common rules regulating their dealing with each other, can meet and interact based on common agreement. While there is a great emphasis on safety or security, there is also a need to provide a common, legitimate ground by which differences can be settled and negotiated. That is why a "holy" person or family establishes the *ḥaram*, because trust and legitimacy play a critical role in preserving the sanctity of the place and upholding the trust of the diverse tribes.

In the Qur᾽ānic context, the *ḥaram* represents the center of peace and safety and is directly related to belief. The symbolism of peace and safety that is associated with the territorial piece of land is a direct result of belief and worship. The Qur᾽ānic verse "Do they not see that We have set up a secure sanctuary[55] (*ḥaram ᾽āmin*), while people are ravaged[56] all around them? Will they, then, [continue] to believe in falsehood and deny God's blessings?" (Qur᾽ān 29:67) defines the word *ḥaram* as a state and contrasts it with its opposite state, that of fear, anxiety, and disorder. The Qur᾽ān invokes the spiritual dimension of the word (*ḥaram*) by highlighting the contrast between safety, associated with belief, and fear, associated with remoteness from belief or God.

The relationship between the security of the land and the belief in the one God is traced back historically to the prayer of Prophet Abraham:

> And, lo, Abraham prayed: "O my Sustainer! Make this a land secure (*baladan ᾽āminan*), and grant its people fruitful sustenance—such of them who believe in Allah and the Last Day.' [Allah] answered: 'and whoever shall deny the truth, I will let him enjoy himself for a short while—but in the end I shall drive him to suffering through fire: and how vile a journey's end" (Qur᾽ān 2:126).

The verse shows that the state of spiritual belief and peace will result in the betterment of the *ummah*'s physical life by bring sustenance in

55. In another translation, a sanctuary immune from violence (Pickthall).

56. In another translation, people swept away by fear and despair. Muhammad Asad relates the secure sanctuary to belief and spiritual fulfillment: "In contrast to the "sanctuary secure," the inner peace and sense of spiritual fulfillment which God bestows on those who truly believe in Him, the atheist or agnostic is more often than not exposed to fear of the unknown and a despair born of the uncertainty as to what will happen to him after death."

abundance; hence the word *balad* is used, which refers to a physical piece of land or country. Thus, there is a direct relationship between belief in God and receiving His sustenance and security, while those who reject belief are drawn to fear and anxiety (verse 29:67) and hell as a final abode (verse 2:126).

In another Qur'ānic verse, Abraham's prayer is accepted, and again the theme of security and asylum is stressed in the context of the Kaʿba (first house on earth erected for the worship of God): "And (remember) when We made the House (the Kaʿba at Mecca) a place of resort for humankind and a place of safety. And take then, the place whereon Abraham once stood as your place of prayer . . ." (Qur'ān 2:125). The Kaʿba is described in another verse as "*al-bayta al-ḥarām*," the sacred house, whereby the connotation of the word "*ḥarām*" is more clarified:

> Allah made the Kaʿba, the Sacred House (*al-bayta al-ḥarām*), *qiyāman*[57] for the people, and so too the sacred months, the offerings and the sacrificial animals with garlands; that you may know that God is aware of all that is in the heavens and all that is on earth, and that God has full knowledge of everything. (Qur'ān 5:97)

The word "*qiyāman*" has been translated differently by exegetes because it has no counterpart in the English language. However, the interpretation of this word is critical for exploring the word "*ḥaram*." *Qiyām* is translated by al-Qurṭubī as both 1) maintaining a livelihood by establishing *sharīʿah* (law), and 2) as meaning a basis and support.[58] At-Ṭabarī said that the *qiwām* of a thing is the means by which it is rectified. For example, the great king is the *qiwām* of his people because, through him, people's affairs are managed, their enemies are pushed away, and oppressors are withheld from those potentially oppressed.[59]

The king's rules could be equivalent to constitutional laws in modern times. We can combine the meanings as "establishing founding principles

57. Translated as "asylum of security" by Yusuf Ali, "standard" by Pickthall, "maintenance" by Shakir, and "symbol" by Asad.

58. Al-Qurṭubī, *al-Jāmiʿ li-'Aḥkām al-Qur'ān*, vol. 6, 325.

59. At-Ṭabarī, *Jāmiʿ al-Bayān*, vol. 5, 104.

that support and maintain a peaceful and righteous livelihood." The Kaʿba is described as *ḥarām* and *qiyām,* so the Kaʿba represents a sacred symbol because of its function of being a *qiyām* for the people. The sanctity of the Kaʿba is a derivative of its symbolic function in maintaining a peaceful livelihood for the people through establishing an ethical base governing their interaction with each other. The same argument goes for the sacred months and rituals. Here we find a direct relationship between the concept of *ḥarām* ("sacred") and living peacefully among the people, a means by which people attain righteousness and by which their affairs are set right.

Along similar lines, Faḍlallah says God made the Kaʿba the sacred meeting place for pilgrims from all over the globe so that *hajj* would be a peaceful time during which pilgrims' lives are preserved in an atmosphere of peace and security. The main point of rituals, as the rest of the Qurʾānic verse declares, "that you may know that God is aware of all that is in the heavens and all that is on earth, and that God has full knowledge of everything," is that people realize that God knows what makes human beings happy. So when people observe the sacred months and experience peace and security, they become at peace with God's law and order. Then people can trust divine legislation in solving problems of humanity and reap benefits in this world.[60] Ṭabātabāʿī summarizes the latter ideas: the sacred (*ḥaram*) place, rituals, or months are "*Qiyām yaqūmu bihā ṣulb ḥayātihim*"[61] ("the foundation or basis that constitutes the essence or core of life").

I think it is significant that the word "*jawf*"[62] is used in the MC to describe the inside of Medina in decree 39: "the Yathrib *jawf* constitutes a *ḥaram*." I think that the word *jawf* in the constitution not only is used to describe a physical area of land, but also has metaphorical significance. The *jawf* of Medina is described as sacred to again stress the connotation of sacredness of the core or essence, the center of the *ummah* of Medina. The

60. Faḍlallah, *Min Waḥy al-Qurʾān*, vol. 8, 349–50.

61. At-Ṭabaṭabāʾī, *Al-Mīzān fī Tafsīr al-Qurʾān,* vol. 6, 142.

62. *Jawf* is defined in *Lisān al-ʿArab* as the interior or core of something. The *jawf* of a human being is his or her interior, and mainly refers to the abdomen. The *jawf* of a land is the portion of the land that is most stable (*mā ʾittasaʿa wa-ṭmaʾanna faṣara kal-jawf*) and covers an area broader and deeper than a single valley. *Jawf* also describes the center. In Ibn Manḍhūr, *Lisān al-ʿArab*, vol. 2, 421–23.

basis of unity for this new community is not territory, as Rubin claims,[63] and is not merely a political confederation, as previously discussed, but it is a unity based on making the sacred represent its essence and core. This sacredness is manifest physically in the land where no bloodshed or oppression is allowed. It is also manifest in the unprejudiced rules governing people's interaction with each other, and manifest in its legitimate leadership.

Declaring the inside of Medina as "*ḥarām*" means establishing Medina as a secure and peaceful place for the different tribes. It is a reminder of what constitutes the essence of their life. The sanctity of the place is a symbol for the sacredness of human life, whether physical or spiritual. This sacredness is related to the holiness of the creator; life becomes sacred when it is associated with a sacred being who provides it with its provision and sustenance and is solely in charge of its existence. When human beings are constantly reminded of the source of their sustenance and their existence through an awareness of their sustainer, their appreciation of the sacredness of their life and others' lives becomes more prevalent. So when the sacred represents the center and essence of one's life (as a belief or as manifest in rituals and orderliness of living), the result is virtue, peace, and security. This explains the relationship between the sacred (*ḥaram*) and peaceful coexistence and preservation of one's life and property.

The idea of the sacred being the center and its critical importance in preventing or dealing with conflict is shown in decrees 23 and 42. Decree 23 addresses the believers: "in whatever thing you are at variance, it should be referred to Allah and to Muhammad." Decree 42 addresses all the people of the constitution: "whatsoever aggression/misdemeanor or quarrel that occurs between the people designated on this sheet, which is feared to cause dissension, will be referred to Allah and his messenger Muhammad . . ." In both decrees, the centrality of God and his messenger as the arbiter for resolving conflict enforces the connection between peace and the sacred. It also shows the interconnection between the different decrees in the constitution and the consistency in its formation. At the same time, it reflects that the constitution is not a compilation of different unrelated parts at different periods of time.

---

63. Uri Rubin, "The 'Constitution of Medina' Some Notes," *Studia Islamica*, no. 62 (1985): 10.

For example, Serjeant[64] divided the constitution into no fewer than eight arbitrary separate documents. He suggests that the declaration of Medina as a *ḥaram* occurred after the failure of the Prophet's enemies to seize Medina at the battle of al-Khandaq, which is much later in time. Serjeant based his assumption on another historical reference that is traced back to the tradition of al-Bukhārī, in which the Prophet mentioned Medina to be *ḥaram*. However, no chronological conclusion can be drawn from these readings.[65] Another tradition by Al-Wāqidī[66] states that the *taḥrim* of Medina ("making Medina a *ḥaram*") occurred much earlier, when the Prophet was on his way to the battle of Badr. This assumption dates the *taḥrim* much earlier than the time dated by Serjeant; however, it is still at a time later than the date the constitution was established. Thus, this assumption still assumes that the constitution was not crafted as a complete document.

Rubin supports the Wāqidī dating because he relates the *taḥrim* of Medina to the *taḥrim* of Mecca. Rubin said it was a step taken by the Prophet before the battle of Badr to make Medina equivalent to Mecca in its sanctity so that its inhabitants would be devoted to it and defend it exactly as the Meccans were devoted to Mecca.[67] A similar argument was adopted by Arjomand, who added that *taḥrim* of Medina is a sign of incorporating pagan religion into Islam.[68] Rubin's claim is not plausible simply because the battle of Badr was conducted outside the borders of Medina in a place called Badr (hence the name of the battle), and Muslims (which historical record numbered as 313 followers of the Prophet) were the only participants in the war. Jews and the rest of the tribes inhabiting Medina did not participate in this war. On the other hand, decree 39 clearly states, "*On behalf of the people designated by this document*, the Yathrib (*jawf*) constitutes a *ḥaram*." Thus, the decree clearly addressed all

---

64. R. B. Serjeant, "The Constitution of Medina," *The Islamic Quarterly*, 111 (1964): 3–16.

65. Uri Rubin, "The 'Constitution of Medina' Some Notes," *Studia Islamica*, no. 62 (1985): 10–11.

66. Al-Wāqidī, *Kitāb al-Maghāzī*, ed. J. M. B. Jones (London: Oxford University Press, 1966), 22.

67. Uri Rubin, "The 'Constitution of Medina' Some Notes," 11.

68. Said Amir Arjomand, "The Constitution of Medina," 569.

the tribes inhabiting Medina and sharing its constitution. It would be a gross reduction of the concept of *ḥaram* to be significant only for war situations. The reason behind this superficial reading is that the interpreters did not try to understand the word *ḥaram* in its Qurʾānic context in order to deduce its significance in a sociopolitical context. The latter explains Arjomand's conception of *ḥaram* that is shaped by pre-Islamic Arabia.

40- The protected person is like (one's) self, he shall not be oppressed nor shall he commit any crime.

41- A woman shall not be accorded protection except by permission of her people.

Decrees 40 and 41 extended the protection enjoyed by the Medina members to one's neighbors based on the custom of *ʾijāra* (making one a neighbor). However, the MC requires conditions in return for protection; first, that a protected person should not commit a crime, and second, that women should have the permission of their family beforehand.

Decree 39, which specifies borders, is directly followed by clarifying the neighboring borders in decrees 40 and 41. Defining who belongs to the *ummah* is not achieved by alienating the other, which is considered the same as the self. The latter represents a critical difference between the concept of the *ummah* and the nation-state, which establishes itself by demeaning or alienating the different other. "The process of othering is a facet of the collective identity building that is related to a specific territory and refers to the building of the figure of the foreigner, the neighbor, the other."[69] Bordering territories to create a nation-state is obsessed with state sovereignty as well as security from external aggression. Randy Widdis defines the borderland as "a physical, ideological, and geographical construct, a region of intersection that is sensitive to internal and external forces that both integrate and differentiate communities and eras on both sides of the boundary lines."[70] The *ummah* is not invested in creating boundaries, for example, ideological with respect to differentiating its members from outside members who represent a threat. By contrast, diversity is part of the internal structure of the *ummah*, resulting in accepting diversity from outside its borders as well. That is why the neighbor is framed as a friend deserving protection rather than as an enemy suspect of aggression. The physical boundary of the *ummah* is used as a symbol of peace and the

69. Daniel Meier, "Bordering the Middle East," *Geopolitics* 23 (2018): 500–1.

70. Ibid., 500.

sacred to unify members of the *ummah* and prevent them from aggression against each other. Aggression is not regarded differently outside or inside the borders; it is one and the same. Aggression against any human being, whether a member of the *ummah* or not, is equally despised in the eyes of God. These ideas are the opposite of what some traditional Muslim jurists refer to as of *dār as-salām* ("abode of peace"), describing those who live under Islamic rule, versus *dār al-ḥarb* ("abode of war"), describing the external world outside the borders of the *ummah*, hence prone to war and aggression. The *ummah* is open to whoever would like to abide by its ethics; hence its borders are porous and welcoming ideologically and physically. As shown in this chapter, the concept of the *ummah* kept expanding by including more diverse members. In early Islamic history, the boundaries were expanded whereby more nations, ethnicities, and religious groups became part of the *ummah*. In this process of expansion, boundaries that separate people from each other were destroyed. In the early caliphate system, the *ummah* is the sovereign and not the state (or political power), contrary to the modern nation-state.

The next decree confirms that the *ummah* is invested with evading aggression among its members more than outside aggression. 42- Whatsoever aggression/misdemeanor or quarrel that occurs between the people designated on this sheet, which is feared may cause dissension, will be referred to Allah and his messenger Muhammad. Allah is (surety) for the truest and most righteous observance of what is in this document.

This decree reaffirms decrees 23 and 36 that assign judiciary authority to Prophet Muhammad; however, the addressee in this decree is not only the believers or the Jews, but rather the united *ummah* of the constitution (*ahl as-ṣaḥīfa*). This decree reflects the Qur᾽ānic verse 5:48,[71] which assigns the governance of the *ummah* to its book and judgment to the one

71. "And to you We revealed *al-kitāb* in truth, confirming the Scripture that came before it and a guardian (*muhaymin*) over it (old Scriptures). So judge between them by what Allah has revealed, and follow not their vain desires, diverging away from the truth that has come to you. To each among you, We have prescribed a law and a clear way (*shir῾atan wa minhājan*). If Allah willed, He would have made you one *ummah*, but that (He) may test you in what He has given you; so strive as in a race in all virtues. The return of you (all) is to Allah; then He will inform you about that in which you used to differ" (Qur᾽ān 5:48) (discussed in detail in chapter 2).

knowledgeable of its book. The book (*al-kitāb*) precedes the function of the judge and legitimizes the judge in the latter part of the verse. Hence the decree started by addressing the people of the constitution before assigning the Prophet the role of judge and ended with emphasizing that the people should follow its rules to ensure God's surety. Emphasizing God before the prophet is critical because it makes the law objective, not subjective and biased to serve the elite or the privileged. In the same regard, if the law is objective in regards to aggression in general, there should be no difference between aggressive acts inside or outside the borders.

43- Neither Quraysh nor those assisting them shall receive protection.

44- There shall be cooperation among them (Muslims and Jews) against those who invade Yathrib.

45- If they (the Jews) are invited (by the Muslims) to make and adopt a peace agreement, they shall make that agreement and adopt it; and if they (the Jews) suggest the same thing (to the Muslims), they shall have the same rights from the Muslims, except in cases of war over religious issues.

45B- Each group is responsible for the area belonging to it (with regard to defense and other needs.)

Decrees 43–45 address the defense of Medina by calling for mutual participation of its members in war and peace, and single out a common enemy. Quraysh represents the main opponent of Muslims, as it drove the Prophet and his followers out of their hometown, besides its persecution of Muslims. It is important to note that this is a "specific" case in which part of the *ummah* had an existing conflict with a tribe, rather than defining outsiders in general as a potential threat. Nevertheless, Quraysh did not represent a threat to the people of Medina until Prophet Muhammad and his followers entered the city. In order to solve this problem, the Prophet adopted two strategies. First, it was expected that Quraysh would attack the Muslims in their new land (Medina), so the Prophet cited Quraysh as an enemy to the general defense of Medina, a space that is declared sacred (*ḥaram*) for all its inhabitants. Second, to ensure equality for all affiliated members of the MC, the Prophet obligated both communities, Muslims and Jews, to respect and support each other in peacemaking and in war.

Therefore, the Jews did not need to feel obligated to consider Quraysh as an enemy for the sake of the Muslim members in Medina without expecting reciprocal support from the Muslims. However, decree 45 singles out religious war as a potential point of contention, which is understandable because the two communities have different religious affiliations. Serjeant interprets this decree as a deterrent from one of the parties entering into a peace agreement to preserve their own interests at the expense of the others.[72] In both cases, the decrees ensure the rights of both communities while maintaining unity by constantly reminding them of their common goals. Decree 45B is a continuation of decree 45, as it makes each community responsible for defending the area within its domain.

46- The Jews of al-ʾAws, their *mawla* and themselves, shall have the same rights agreed upon on this sheet (document), with sincere/complete observation from the people designated on this sheet. Observation of one's undertakings eliminates treachery/breaking of treaties. He who commits a breach (of this treaty) commits it against himself alone. God is with those who best and truly observe the rules described on this sheet.

With a cursory reading, this decree may seem to imply an addition of a new Jewish tribe and its allies to the affiliated members of the constitution. However, the Jews of Banī ʾAws are already mentioned in decree 30. Maybe this decree is meant to specifically emphasize the rights of the allies of Aws. The rest of the decree reemphasizes that committing a crime is a personal responsibility rather than a tribal one. It ends by stating that the covenant between the members of Medina is equivalent to a covenant with God, hence the ending statement, "God is with those who best and truly observe the rules described on this sheet."

Decree 47 represents a summary of the major points iterated in the whole constitution. 47- This book (*al-kitāb*) shall not protect the perpetrator of an unjust act or crime from punishment. Whoever goes out shall have security, and whoever remains in Medina shall also have security; except one who commits an unjust act or a crime. Allah protects the person who observes undertakings and keeps free of dishonorable acts and offenses, and Muhammad the messenger of Allah, Allah bless and honor him.

Conclusion

The last decree (47) reiterates what has already been said in the constitution by summarizing it and emphasizing the main bonding ele-

72. R. B. Serjeant, "The Sunnah Jami'ah, Pacts with the Yathrib Jews and the Tahrim of Yathrib: Analysis and Translation of the Documents Comprised in the So-Called "Constitution of Medina," 38.

ments unifying the *ummah* of Medina. First is the book (*al-kitāb*), which forms the backbone of the *ummah*, organizing the relationships between its members, clarifying their goals, establishing a covenant, and preserving their rights while defining their obligations. The first decree defines the constitution as a book from the Prophet to guide relationships between its different members, and the last decree specified that this book does not protect an aggressor. The strong relationship between the first and last decree suggests that this constitution is one coherent document.[73]

The Medina Constitution describes an inclusive *ummah* receptive to any human being who is willing to be affiliated with its inclusive values. That inclusive *ummah* does not eliminate religious, cultural, or political diversity but acknowledges them as respected choices with meriting consequences. The constitution, with its principles and values, represents the foundation that unites the diverse communities of the *ummah* into one shared body, *ummah wāḥidah*. The decrees reflect different kinds of pluralism. Religious pluralism is manifested by inclusion of Muslims and Jews within the *ummah*, each community following its own religion and law. Cultural pluralism appears through the mentioning of each tribe by its own name, thereby reinforcing the connection between the private and public spheres. Political pluralism is evident from the way the constitution details reciprocal rights and obligations for its diverse communities.

73. Serjeant dismantled the constitution into eight distinct documents in "The Sunnah Jami'ah, Pacts with the Yathrib Jews and the Tahrim of Yathrib: Analysis and Translation of the Documents Comprised in the So-Called 'Constitution of Medina,'" *Bulletin of the School of Oriental and African Studies, University of London* 41, no. 1 (1978): 1–42. Serjeant's work was criticized by many scholars: Gil disapproved Serjeant's theory in Gil, "The Medinan Opposition to the Prophet," *JSAI* 10 (1987): 65; Rubin argued that Serjeant's work was done in "a highly arbitrary manner"; Lecker regards Serjeant's argument to be inconsistent in Lecker, *The "Constitution of Medina" Muhammad's First Legal Document,* 189; Simonsen considered Serjeant's work to be "methodically doubtful" in J. B. Simonsen, *Studies in the Genesis and Early Development of the Caliphal Taxation System* (Copenhagen: Akademisk Forlag, 1988), 41; Tibawi also criticized Serjeant in A. L. Tibawi, "Second Critique of English-Speaking Orientalists and Their Approach to Islam and the Arabs," *Islamic Quarterly* 23 (1979): 17–18; Hoyland calls Serjeant's division "excessive" in R. Hoyland, "Sebeos, the Jews and the Rise of Islam," in *Medieval and Modern Perspectives on Muslim-Jewish Relations*, ed. R. L. Nettler (Oxford: Publisher, 1995), 100.

Different decrees urge the members of the *ummah* to actively oppose an aggressor among them, even if a member of their kin. Thereby it portrays an active *ummah* assuming the responsibility of maintaining and implementing justice between its members and not confining the responsibility to the central power. In addition, mutual advice and consultation are urged between the various religious communities. The decrees of the constitution put into practice the Qurʾānic verses that describe the function of the best *ummah*, being one that enjoins goodness and forbids wrongness in society discussed in the previous chapter.

Another noticeable feature of the Medina Constitution is its incorporation of religious and ethnic diversity in public through the constitution as a law document and through legal pluralism. Religion, as in *sharīʿah*, is not a unifying element in the formation of the *ummah* in Medina because each group was given independence in practicing its own religion. In addition, the decrees addressing each group were relevant to their respective religious laws. Yet in matters that affect the mutual dealings between the religious communities and ethnic groups, as well as defense of the common territory, the law becomes common. Similarly, maintaining peace and stability is a joint venture of all affiliate members, and they are urged to stand collectively against external aggression and spend of their resources to defend the land.

The *ummah* expanded from the Muslim community (along with its ethnic diversity) to incorporating the Jewish diverse community, then enlarged to include allies or individuals; hence the addressee at the end of the charter became *Ahl al-Ṣaḥīfah* ("the people of the constitution"). Associated with the latter term, a new concept is introduced, *ḥaram* (sacred land). This term implies peace, security, and trust, which represent desired goals for the flourishing of the *ummah*. Contrary to the nation-state, the bordering is not created to alienate the neighboring other and protect its members from outside aggression. Rather, the *ḥaram* represents a symbol of peace for the *ummah* members that is aimed at constant expansion by welcoming more members to the *ummah,* thereby destroying boundaries that separate people from each other.

Chapter 4

The *Ummah* and Political Governance—Comparative

Islamic philosophy considers man to be a special kind of being because of his ability to reason, an ability that grants him the capability to know himself and his surrounding world. The human being is the central concern of both philosophy and divine law. Philosophers postulate that philosophy urges man to understand the world through his reason, while divine law requires faithful obedience to the laws of God.[1] Muslim philosophers argue that divine law calls for free inquiry, and hence they subject ancestral opinion to scrutiny. The difference between divine law, legal tradition, and philosophy is best expressed in the following words:

> The divine law sets forth the principles that govern the beliefs and the actions of the Islamic community; the legal determination of what the community must believe and do is entrusted to those who are best equipped to make legal inference, namely, the jurists; the interpretation of the theoretical writings in the divine law, on the other hand, should be entrusted to those members of the community who, in turn, are best equipped to perform this function, namely, the philosophers.[2]

1. Muhsin S. Mahdi, *Al-Farabi and the Foundation of Islamic Political Philosophy* (Chicago: University of Chicago Press, 2001), 16–18.

2. Ibid., 45–46.

This chapter does not fall under the general field of philosophy but rather under political philosophy in particular. Political philosophy is a practical field that is not concerned with validating a specific theology or focused on legislating laws for a specific religious community. Political philosophy focuses on understanding the foundations upon which a community is based in order to improve and help the community develop to its highest potential. Thus, while preserving the good of a community, political philosophy aims at reforming it to achieve a higher good.[3] Arabic and Islamic political philosophy are influenced by Greek philosophy, especially that of Plato and Aristotle. The Islamic religious tradition and Greek philosophy exhibited mutual influence in the works of Muslim political philosophers such as Abu Nasr Muhammad al-Fārābī (d. 339/ 950), who is the pioneer of political philosophy in the Islamic tradition. Just as the Islamic religious tradition assisted Muslim philosophers in understanding Greek philosophy, so too did the latter facilitate the effort of Muslim philosophers to comprehend the Islamic vision of a good political life.[4] Islamic theology urges the human being to continually use his reason to understand himself and the surrounding world and examine previous civilizations to benefit from their wisdom as well as learn from their mistakes. This intellectual outlook provided the Muslim philosopher with a good foundation to examine and understand Greek philosophy.

The core of Al-Fārābī's political philosophy, for example, is concerned with the social and political success of the community at large rather than personal salvation of the individual. Philosophy usually focuses on the private salvation of the individual and is often articulated among an elite class of philosophers. On the other hand, political philosophy addresses every citizen to improve the quality of his or her public communal life. In addition, theology and jurisprudence cannot substitute for political philosophy because the former lack the necessary freedom required to understanding and tackling new radical conditions. For example, theologians and jurists are typically preoccupied with resolving the issue of the community's leadership and other questions of public law. However, political philosophy seeks to broaden the community's horizon by introducing

3. Ibid., 46.

4. Ibid., 37.

and encouraging public discourse on alternative forms of government and various means to reform.[5]

John Walbridge contends that the Farabian political philosophy of religion failed in the Muslim world because it did not appeal to serious Muslims. Walbridge cites the underlying premises constituting the Farabian philosophical treatise that subordinated religion to philosophy. All the tenets of religion were subject to rational analysis; the Prophet was regarded as a philosopher, and Qur'ānic beliefs that could not be rationalized were interpreted by resorting to symbolism. Hence, Walbridge argues that such a portrayal of religion lacked spiritual vitality and transcendence, the result being incompatibility with the Islamic understanding of God, religion, prophethood, and revelation.[6]

While there is some validity to Walbridge's argument, I do not intend to copy the Farabian philosophical style. I am rather interested in teasing out a political philosophy based on the Qur'ān and *Sunnah*, the most important primary sources for developing Islamic political philosophy. In that regard, my research precisely addresses what Walbridge claims Farabi did not do sufficiently.

However, historical factors and human interpretation play a critical role in tackling the text of the Qur'ān. Both factors are at play in the form of Qur'āṇic exegesis. All Qur'ānic exegetical works interpret the Qur'ān within its historical context in addition to the historical context of the exegetes' time. At-Ṭabarī and al-Qummī's exegetical works provide us with some of the closest interpretations in time to the time in which the Qur'ān was revealed, whereas ʿAbduh's and Faḍlallah's interpretations are more reflective of the modern period. Both earlier and modern interpretations tackle the historical context of the Qur'ān, but their analysis and understanding of that historical context differ.

For example, the next section discusses the purpose of the human being in the Qur'ān, which is articulated in the form of a story describing other non-human creatures, named angels and Jinn (Satan belongs to this category). Both earlier and modern Qur'ānic exegeses mention the

5. Ibid., 60–62.

6. John Walbridge, *God and Logic in Islam: The Caliphate of Reason* (Cambridge: Cambridge University Press, 2011), 82–85.

prophetic sayings describing a physical creation of different creatures at one point in time. However, modern exegetes will add that those creatures may represent spiritual forces inside the conscience of the human being, or could be symbolic of good and evil thoughts. Thus, it is clear that the modern rational discourse affects Qur᾽ānic exegesis even among traditional theologians.

From the perspective of this book, whether angels and Jinn are actual creatures or symbols is beyond the point of discussion. By presenting different exegetical ideas, I am interested in deciphering the Qur᾽ānic view of the nature and purpose of a human being in order to understand an individual's political role in the context of an *ummah*. In order to do so, I am analyzing the Qur᾽ānic text, not in isolation or as a timeless document, but through the lens of historical exegetical works that reflect Qur᾽ānic historicity as well the ideas of their own time simultaneously.

In the field of Western political philosophy/theory, ideas are discussed across time with considerable flexibility unparalleled in the field of religious studies. For example, a concept like "democracy" would be discussed as a theoretical concept with different practical applications starting from Plato until the modern period with little reference to underlying assumptions. The main challenge in this interdisciplinary work is crossing the boundaries of traditional methodologies between the disciplines. Therefore, I would like to reiterate that the main goal of this chapter is discussing and comparing the idea of community involvement in the political sphere.

Choosing Aristotle and communitarian thinking for comparison with the idea of the Qur᾽ānic *ummah* is not arbitrary. First, Aristotle, in contrast to Plato, does not define the city or the polis by a priestly class or philosopher king. The hierarchical organization characteristic of Plato's thought is replaced by equal participation in a shared constitution in Aristotle's polis. The concept of the Qur᾽ānic *ummah* and its historical realization in the prophetic Medina discussed in this book do not reflect a hierarchical, platonic makeup. Instead, the Aristotelian polis is closer to the Qur᾽ānic structure of the *ummah*.

Second, many communitarians draw heavily upon Aristotelian ideas, as they advocate morally virtuous politics. The latter idea necessitates an understanding of the culture specific to a community instead of the theoretical abstraction proposed by the liberal John Rawls. For example, Alasdair MacIntyre argues that a "moral philosophy . . . characteristically presupposes a sociology." In other words, it should be aware of how philosophical concepts "are embodied or at least can be in the real social world."[7] Similarly, this research started by apprehending the *ummah* in hermeneutic and historical terms in the preceding chapters. In this chapter, I study the *ummah* philosophically through Aristotle, who provides us with the theoretical framework of inquiry. The outcome of this comparison is situated within Islamic discourse on Islamic political governance by comparing it with ideas of major contributors to the field, such as al-Fārābī (d. 339/950), Ibn Khaldūn (d. 808/ 1406), Abd al-Raḥmān al-Kawākibī (d.1320/1902), Rashīd Riḍa (d. 1353/ 1935), Abd al-Rāziq (d. 1385/1966), Quṭb (d. 1385/1966), Mālik Bin Nabiy (d. 1393/1973), Mawdūdī (d. 1400/1979), Shams ad-Dīn (d. 1421/2001), Mohammad ʿImāra (born 1350/1931), Ḥasan Ḥanafī (born 1353/1935), and Mohammad Shaḥrūr (born 1357 /1938). Simultaneously, the role of diverse communities in the modern liberal state is addressed in light of contemporary debates between liberals and communitarians.

The *Ummah* and the Aristotelian Polis

KHALĪFA AND POLITICAL ANIMAL

Aristotle's *Politics* is very relevant to this research because it outlines some basic notions about the role of politics in human societies. According to Aristotle's theory, the political community (polis) is a "natural" institution. Aristotle's view of nature is that it is not a random process that exists without deliberation; rather it reflects an inner principle of change. "For what each thing is when fully developed, we call its nature, whether we are speaking of a man, a horse or a family."[8] Thus, the nature of something does not refer to its constituent matter but rather to what it tends to be when it reaches its full culmination. However, something growing to its full potential does not describe its final state; rather it describes what the thing was designed *for*. This Aristotle refers to as the

7. Alasdair C. MacIntyre, *After Virtue: A Study in Moral Theory,* 2nd ed. (London: Duckworth, 1985), 23.

8. Aristotle, *Politics* (1252b 33–35).

telos. The *telos* represents the purpose of any creation or institution, which is indispensable to understanding the nature of something.

The *telos* of the polis is to allow its members to achieve the best life of which they are naturally capable. Thus the polis is a natural institution because it is explained by reference to the nature of its members, the human beings. Aristotle says: "Hence it is evident that the state is a creation of nature, and that man is by nature a political animal."[9] The polis is prior to the individual, not in time, but in purpose because men have a social instinct by nature. A human being cannot achieve the best life in isolation. "The individual, when isolated, is not self-sufficing; and therefore he is like a part in relation to the whole. But he who is unable to live in society, or who has no need because he is sufficient for himself, must be either a beast or a god: he is no part of a state."[10]

Aristotle explains man's need for political association by referring to his peculiar nature because man is the only being given the gift of language. The purpose of language is to declare what is good versus what is evil and thus what is just and what is unjust.[11] "It is characteristic of man that he alone has any sense of good and evil, of just and unjust, and the like, and the association of living beings who have this sense makes a family and a state."[12] Thus, Aristotle explains the intrinsic need for a political community by analyzing the innate characteristics of human beings. The purpose, *telos*, forms the essence and the building block of his theory, and it recurs throughout his work. For Aristotle, the *telos* of the human being is not mere life but the perfect life, which is based on deliberate choice and action: "But a state exists for the sake of a good life, and not for the sake of life only: if life only were the object, slaves and brute animals might form a state, but they cannot, for they have no share in happiness or in a life based on choice."[13]

Al-Fārābī thinks that human association is an innate need for human beings because they cannot reach perfection, and thereby attain happiness,

---

9. Aristotle, *Politics* (1253a 2–3).

10. Aristotle, *Politics* (1253a 26–30).

11. David Minar and Scott Greer, *The Concept of Community; Readings with Interpretations* (Chicago: Aldine Publishing Company, 1969), 191.

12. Aristotle, *Politics* (1253a 16–18).

13. Aristotle, *Politics* (1280a 32–35).

except through the help of other fellow humans. Because of a human incapacity to satisfy all his needs by himself, he needs others to fulfill this role. Therefore, a human being cannot attain perfection, for which he was created for, except by human associations whereby each association fulfills one of the human needs for the whole society to prosper.[14] The smallest form of a complete human association is that represented by a city in Al-Fārābī's thought. By "complete" association, Fārābī meant one that was self-contained, unlike a household or a village, which is too small to fulfill that purpose. The virtuous city (*Al-Madīna Al-Fāḍila*) is one whose people cooperate for the things by which true felicity can be attained. The structure of the virtuous city is like that of the sound, healthy body whose different limbs and organs cooperate to make its life perfect and preserve it in that state.[15] Through this analogy, Fārābī implies that a single person cannot reach perfection and attain happiness without mutual cooperation within an organized community. Similar to the moral life of individuals, the fashioning of the virtuous city is not involuntary but dependent on whether will and choice are directed toward the true good.

Therefore, Al-Fārābī agrees with Aristotle that the *telos* or purpose of the polis (city in al-Fārābī's case) is the perfection and happiness of the human beings who form its basic elements. Similarly, in order to understand the *telos* of the *ummah*, we first have to find out the *telos* of the human being described in the Qur᾿ān. By revealing the story of the creation of the first human being, the Qur᾿ān presents the purpose of that creation and what the human being is destined for, that is, the *telos* according to Aristotle. The story sheds light on different aspects of the human experience.

Khalīfa

The Qur᾿ān describes the human being as a "*khalīfa*" whose essence is clarified by analyzing the following verses:

14. Abū Naṣr Muhammad Al-Fārābī, *Arā᾿ Ahl Al-Madīna Al-Fāḍila*, ed. Albert Naṣrī Nādir (Beirut: Maṭbaʿat Al-Kāthūlīkiyya, 1959), 96.

15. Ibid., 97–99.

> Behold, your Lord said to the angels: "I will render a (*khalīfa*)[16] on earth." They said: "Will you place therein one who will make mischief in it and shed blood?—whereas we do celebrate your praises and hallow your name?" He said: "Verily, I know what you do not know." And He taught Adam all the names; then He brought them within the ken of the angels and said: "Tell me the names of these, if what you say is true." They replied: "Limitless is your glory! No knowledge have we save that which you taught us. Verily, you alone are all knowing, truly wise." He said: "O Adam! convey unto them the names of these." And when he had informed them of their names, He said: Did I not tell you that I know the hidden reality of the heavens and the earth? And I know that which you disclose and which you hide. And when We told the angels, "Prostrate yourselves before Adam!"—they all prostrated themselves, save *Iblīs*, who refused and was arrogant: and thus he became one of those who deny the truth. (Qur'ān 2:30–34)

These verses reveal three kinds of beings, two of whom were created before the first human being, Adam. There are the angels and another kind of creature made from fire, as described in the Qur'ān,[17] which belongs to a category called *Jinn*. *Iblīs*, who will later be called *Shayṭān* ("Satan") after being exiled from paradise, belongs to the latter kind. The verses show that God's decision to render a *khalīfa* on earth triggered questions, concerns, and even rebellion among the previous creatures. The angels were concerned about why God would make a creature that would cause corruption and bloodshed on earth, whereas they (the angels) never disobey God's will and always glorify him. *Iblīs* directly rebelled against God's order, thereby declaring himself the enemy of human beings, aiming to divert them from fulfilling their role on earth as *khalīfa*. Thus, it is implied that this role of *khilāfa*[18] given to the human being is a critical and elevated position sought by other creatures.

---

16. Translated by Muhammad Asad as "establish upon earth one who shall inherit it (a successor)."

17. Qur'ān (15:27) and (55:15).

18. *Khilāfa* is the function and the status given to the *khalīfa*. It is usually translated as "caliphate."

Khalīfa in Early, Classical, and Modern Exegesis

There are three significant points raised in the above verses: first, what is the role of this new creature (humans) that is signified in the Qurʾān by the word *khalīfa*? Second, what is the intrinsic quality that this human possesses that makes him different from other creation that is signified by teaching Adam the names? Third, what is the relationship between this new human creation and previous creatures signified in the Qurʾān by angels and Jinn? Exploring these questions can help us realize the purpose (*telos*) of the human creation as a *khalīfa*.

Early and classical exegesis focused on the first question: the role of *khalīfa*. First, exegetes wondered how the angels knew that the human being would cause bloodshed and corruption on earth before he was sent to earth. Al-Qummī answered this question through a saying attributed to the Prophet's grandson Al-Hussein, who said that the angels raised the question based on the first experience of the Jinn as a *khalīfa* on earth.[19] Thus, *khalīfa* means a successor on earth to Al-Qummī.[20] The first human being, Adam, was a successor to the previous creatures inhabiting the earth, the Jinn. Another interpretation for *khalīfa* mentioned by Al-Qummī is "God's evidence on earth before his creatures" (*ḥujja lī fil-ʾarḍ ʿala khalqī*). From Adam's progeny will be prophets, messengers, virtuous people, and guiding *aʾimma* (plural of *Imām*) whom God will appoint as *khulafāʾ* (plural of *khalīfa*) on earth to guide people to righteousness and deter them from evil. The best of Adam's progeny will be God's proof for his creatures (*ḥujja lī ʿalayhim*); hence God answered the angels "Verily, I know what you do not know."[21] The second interpretation is selective, where only some people, the most righteous, will be appointed as *khalīfa*. This interpretation, which implies selection and appointment, is also endorsed

19. Al-Hussein said that God initially created the Jinn to establish life on earth and make it flourish. However, the Jinn spread corruption and spilled blood on earth, which incurred God's wrath on them. God sent his angels to fight them, and *Iblīs*, who was a ruler on earth, was taken by the angels to heaven, as he was a good worshiper of God. Thus, when God decided to create a new creature, Adam, the angels were perplexed and wondered why God would create another creature that would cause mischief on earth, Al-Qummī, *Tafsīr al-Qummī*, vol. 1, 65–70.

20. Al-Qummī, *Tafsīr al-Qummī*, vol. 1, 65–70.

21. Ibid., 66.

by At-Ṭabarī, though he adds the political dimension to it, as shown later.

Wadād Al-Qāḍī surveyed the term *khalīfa* in the early exegetical Sunnī literature before At-Ṭabarī through *Tafsīr Muqātil b. Sulaymān* (d. 150/767), *Tafsīr Mujāhid* (21/641-103/721), and *Tafsīr Sufyān al-Thawrī* (95/713-161/777). The exegetical works cited five meanings for *khalīfa*: the main meaning is based on the root *kh.l.f.*, to succeed or to follow. The following two are derived from the first: one is to replace or substitute, and the other is to take the place of another being after that being is gone. The fourth meaning is to dwell, cultivate (*sakana, ʿammara*), and the last meaning is related to governing and ruling based on the Qurʾānic verse "O David, We have appointed you a *khalīfa* on earth, so judge between people by the Truth (justice, Ar. *ḥaq*)" (Qurʾān 38:26). Al-Qāḍī concluded her study that the early exegetes were puzzled by the term because of the different meanings of the root mentioned and hence derived various conclusions about it. Yet they identified the term mainly with humankind, who, based on *israʾīliyyāt* material, would succeed/replace the angels or jinn on earth. She added that no early exegete endorsed the meaning of "God's *khalīfa*" except At-Ṭabarī. Al-Qāḍī thinks that the last two meanings, "to cultivate, to rule," were derived from the verses Q 2:30–34, which distinguish the human being from the angels and jinn by *khalīfa*. There is nothing unique about succeeding/replacing another creature, yet the verses imply that the new creature (human) is given the specific function "*khalīfa*." Besides, she argues that historical change, manifested by urbanization of Muslims under the Umayyads, inspired the last two meanings, as Islamic societies were getting more complex. However, despite the fact that the Umayyad Caliphs called themselves "*khalīfat Allah*," the early exegetes did not correlate between the Qurʾānic *khalīfa* and the ruling Caliphs.[22]

Han Liew extended Al-Qāḍī's work by surveying later exegetes starting with At-Ṭabarī (d. 310/923) through Ibn Kathīr (d. 774/1373). Liew argues that At-Ṭabarī politicized the interpretation of *khalīfa* where he "goes beyond the notion of "succession" and "replacement," portray-

22. Wadād Al-Qāḍī, "The Term "Khalīfa" in Early Exegetical Literature," *Die Welt des Islams*, New Series, Bd. 28. No. ¼ (1988), 392–411.

ing Adam as a political ruler and vicegerent of God in governing God's creation."[23] At-Ṭabarī considered the supreme ruler (*as-sulṭān al-aʿẓam*) a *khalīfa* because he succeeds and replaces the one before him. He cites a report by Ibn Abbas: *khalīfa* is a vicegerent from God who would rule his people in his name (*khalīfa minnī yakhlufnī fil-ḥukm bayna khalqī*). That *khalīfa* is Adam, and whoever follows him by obeying God and judging justly between God's creations.[24] Later exegetes followed suit; for example, al-Thaʿlabī (d. 427/1035) used the Qurʾānic verses to validate the Sunnī orthodox view of the four Rightly-Guided Caliphs. Liew's study suggested that political discourse affected scriptural interpretation in the medieval Islamic period. Interpreting *khalīfa* as deputy of God (*Khalīfat Allah*) in the *tafsīr* of al-Zamak̲šarī, Ibn al-Jawzī, and al-Qurṭubī, among others, supports his claim. However, despite interpreting *khalīfa* as more of a ruler position over time, Liew notices that this semantic shift did not proceed linearly throughout history, nor did it reflect a collective support of the exegetes for or against the historical caliphate.[25]

The fact that the term "*khalīfat Allah*" was not correlated with the historical caliphs in most premodern exegetical works shows that what the exegetes meant by *khalīfat Allah* is not limited to political ruling. Rather, it is a term that describes following/obeying God and thereby judging with Truth, which (despite being practiced by people in power) is at the disposal of every human being. Hence, I do not agree that At-Ṭabarī completely politicized the term; rather, I would say he added its political component, which is implied clearly in verse 38:26. Nonetheless, what is striking in premodern exegesis is the general focus on cultivate/rule/righteous judgment as being the distinctive feature of this *khalīfa*, compared with their predecessors (the angels and jinn), without analyzing *khalīfa*'s relationship to the "names." I think that modern exegesis will do a better job in uncovering the secret and uniqueness of the *khalīfa*, which is essentially related to the names as well as the previous creatures.

---

23. Han Hsien Liew, "The Caliphate of Adam: Theological Politics of the Qur'ānic Term *H̲alīfa*," *Arabica* 63 (2016): 8.

24. At-Ṭabarī, *Jāmiʿ al-Bayān*, vol. 1, 289.

25. Han Hsien Liew, "The Caliphate of Adam: Theological Politics of the Qur'ānic Term *H̲alīfa*," 12–28.

Addressing the second question, "The names which God taught to Adam," is interpreted in premodern exegesis of both al-Qummī[26] and at-Ṭabarī[27] to represent the names of animate and inanimate things such as the names of animals, plants, mountains, seas, and all God's creations. God taught Adam the names of each and every thing, without limitation. Modern exegetes employed a more philosophical interpretation of the names. ʿAbduh interpreted "names" as the image of what is known in the mind such that we believe in the things' existence and ascribe to it their characteristics. Thus names are the means by which we know about things. The words ascribed to things differ according to different languages, but the meaning does not change. ʿAbduh thinks that the main reason for the human to acquire the position of *khalīfa* is his knowledge, which is superior to the knowledge of the angels. The human is "*khalīfa bil-ʿilm*" ("successor by knowledge").[28]

According to Faḍlallah, based on the at-Ṭabāṭabāʾī exegesis,[29] teaching Adam the names is not merely a linguistic matter but conveys his knowing the essence of things, and beings, and their characteristics. This knowledge and the means of acquiring it enable the human being to manage his affairs on earth and practice the role of *khalīfa*. Faḍlallah thinks that teaching Adam the names is not an automatic process, but it represents endowing the human race with the progressive ability to learn. Faḍlallah distinguishes between two kinds of *khilāfa*: the first is a general kind for all human beings that allows them to channel their endowed capabilities for the goodness of humanity; the second one is more specific and involves direct political ruling and power over others as reflected in the Qurʾān verse 38:26.[30] In both cases, it is *khilāfa ʿan Allah* ("*khalīfa* on behalf

26. Al-Qummī, *Tafsīr al-Qummī*, vol. 1, 74.

27. At-Ṭabarī, *Jāmiʿ al-Bayān*, vol. 1, 309.

28. Muhammad ʿAbduh and Muhammad Rashīd Riḍā, *Tafsīr al-Manār*, vol. 1, 261–62.

29. At-Ṭabāṭabāʾī, *Al-Mīzān fī Tafsīr al-Qurʾān*, vol. 1, 118–19.

30. "O David, We have appointed you a *khalīfa* on earth, so judge between people by the Truth (justice, Ar. *ḥaq*), and do no follow whimsical desires for they will mislead you from the path of Allah. Indeed, those who go astray from the way of Allah will have a severe punishment for having forgotten the Day of reckoning" (Qurʾān 38:26).

of God"), that is, management of life on earth by following the will of God.[31]

I think that what the verse refers to is the ability of humans to convey meanings to each other through language, which is directly connected to the mind and rationality. ʿAbduh then addresses the third question where he interprets the angels and Satan as representatives of good and evil thoughts, respectively. Each human being possesses conflicting thoughts representing good and evil until one wins and the other recedes. We usually attribute to these thoughts power (*quwwa*) and call that power thought (*fikr*). ʿAbduh argues that it could be possible that God calls "good thoughts" an angel (or makes an angel the cause of good thoughts) whereas Satan is the representative or the cause of evil thoughts. Whether angels and demons are creatures or spiritual forces that affect human beings, they were both ordered to prostrate before Adam, that is, human beings. ʿAbduh does not interpret prostration as worship because only God is worshiped; rather, it signifies their compliance and submission (*khuḍūʿ*) to human beings.[32] Thus, these creatures or forces were created for the service of human beings, and as such humans possess agency in deciding which way to follow. Faḍlallah also says that the prostrating act reflects the elevated status of the human being with respect to the world (seen and unseen) around him. It shows that the human being is endowed with the capability to subdue external and internal forces to control the world around him, if he so chooses. The magnanimous role of *khilāfa*, bestowed on him by his creator, provides him with a power that withstands all challenges.[33]

Faḍlallah emphasizes the role of the mind and knowledge as a basic feature of the human race. He thinks that *khalīfa* is a creature that possesses reason (*al-ʿaql*), will, freedom of action, and possibilities of creativity and production to organize life on earth and make successful communities. These abilities make humans on earth similar to angels in heaven, with the intrinsic difference that the human being is a free creature while angels are innately obedient. However, the angels' question concerning humans' destructive potential illustrates another side of human beings who

31. Faḍlallah, *Min Waḥy al-Qurʾān*, vol. 1, 220–36.

32. Ibid., vol. 1, 265–69.

33. Faḍlallah, *Min Waḥy al-Qurʾān*, vol. 1, 220–36.

experience a conflict between rationality and selfish desires, driving them to destroy and corrupt. Here God answers that the angels are judging matters by their appearance, without knowing their hidden benefit (this would be the *telos* according to Aristotle), hence He knows what they do not know. *Iblīs* represents the selfish desire potential in a human being. His refusal to prostrate before Adam is mentioned in another verse: "What prevented you from prostrating as I ordered you to do so? (*Iblīs*) said I am better than him as you created me from fire and created him from mud" (Qurʾān 7:12). Al-Qummī relates *Imām* As-Ṣadiq's comment on the latter verse, who said that *istikbār* ("arrogance") is the first sin by which God was disobeyed, and the first creature who did so was *Iblīs*. Arrogance was the sin that incurred God's wrath on *Iblīs* and cursed him out of paradise.[34]

Moḥammad Shaḥrūr makes an interesting argument that relates the process of acquiring knowledge to the Satanic and Angelic functions. The Qurʾān makes the basis of human knowledge to be the constant separation between truth and falsehood, which are interlinked by dialectic contradictions. The function of knowledge is separating the truth from the illusionary. Shaḥrūr goes at length to describe the semantic meanings of *shayṭān* ("Satan") in the Qurʾān, showing how the term signifies the illusionary part in the human thinking process. By contrast, the term *raḥmān* (one of the names of Allah, the merciful) represents the objective reality in the human intellect. This objective reality is conveyed to the human being in two ways: first, God conveys it through his laws of the material world whereby humans can control the material world to their own benefit. Second, God bestowed on humans the ability to legislate through God's breath, as shown in the verses "And when your Lord said to the angels, "I will create a mortal (*bashar*) out of pure mud-molded clay. And when I have proportioned him and breathed into him of My spirit, then fall down to him in prostration" (Qurʾān 15:28–29). This divine breath specifically gifted to humans is the unifying and un-contradictory part, which allows the human being to become God's *khalīfa* on earth by being in charge of the material world (all physical sciences) and legislation for the sociopolitical existence (social sciences).[35] The angels take the function

34. Al-Qummī, *Tafsīr al-Qummī*, vol. 1, 65–70.

35. Moḥammad Shaḥrūr, *Al-Kitāb wal-Qurʾān: Qirāʾa Muʿāṣira* (Damascus: Al-Ahālī lil-Ṭibāʿa wal-Nashr wal-Tawzīʿ, 1990), 251–62.

of inspiring the humans with the Godly unifying objective reality, while Satan assumes the role of falsifying the reality in the human intellect. Through this constant dialectic of oppositions, humans acquire knowledge by confirmation (*taṣdīq*) of truth whereby the intellectual idea is consistent with the outside material world or made to be so through the human will and rejection of falsehood/illusions when contradictions persist and are not resolved.[36] Along similar lines, Jeffrey Lang regards Satan as critical for the moral and spiritual development of humans whereby his "tempting function" becomes a catalyst for human's ethical decision-making process.[37]

It is true that there may be some negative repercussions in the cosmos to the existence of humans, but the innate benefits emanating from this experience are more important, influential, and productive, such that the disadvantages are outweighed by the positive benefits.[38] As a result, Faḍlallah argues that *khilāfa* does not represent a new creature succeeding an old one, that is, humans succeeding Jinn, as reported by premodern exegesis. Instead, the concept of *khilāfa* reflects the duty and role of this new race that could not be performed by any other creature. While angels are innately made to only perform good deeds, and thereby gain no merit for their actions, human beings are invited to subdue the forces within their reach and use their capabilities for the sake of goodness rather than evil, which make their actions more merited than the angels'.

The latter interpretation shows God's wisdom in creating the human being and the purpose (or *telos* according to Aristotle) for which he is destined, to be *khalīfa*. Yet this discussion cannot be complete without referring to the following two verses in the Qur'ān in which God specifically states the purpose of the human creation and what is expected of them:

> I have not created jinn and humankind except to worship Me. I desire of them no provision; neither do I desire that they should feed Me. Indeed, it is Allah who is the [continual] provider, the firm possessor of strength. (Qur'ān 51:56–58)

---

36. Ibid., 252–53.

37. Jeffrey Lang, *Even Angels Ask: A Journey to Islam in America* (Beltsville, MD: Amana Publications, 2014), 41.

38. Ibid., vol. 1, 215–16.

> And if your Lord had willed, He could have made people one *ummah*; yet they will not cease to differ. Except those on whom your Lord has bestowed His Mercy and to that purpose he created them . . . (Qur'ān 11:118–19)

At first glance, the verses may seem contradictory where the concept of worship may imply an obligation placed upon humans or an act of vanity that would then contradict the idea that the human creation is an act of mercy from God. In addition, what is the relationship between worshiping God and acting as a *khalīfa*? This apparent contradiction stems from the common misconception of worship to be confined to prescribed rituals. Lang reports a *ḥadīth* in which Prophet Muhammad was asked about the greatest acts of worship, and among his answers were taking care of aging parents, a mother giving birth to a child, confronting a tyrant, and struggling to establish justice.[39] Scholars also interpreted worship as knowledge, that is, knowing the creator. In simple terms, how can you experience mercy if you do not know the merciful creator? The succeeding verses (I desire of them no provision . . .) eliminate the idea that God needs human worship or that it is an obligation required of them that would bring Him any benefit.[40] Scholars said that knowing the merciful creator includes knowledge of his creation (i.e., understanding how the world functions in order to build prosperous life on earth) and understanding oneself. Thus, knowledge not only helps humans in their spiritual evolution but also in their intellectual and physical thriving on earth, that is, being a *khalīfa*. In this case, worship is not merely performing rituals but any act that includes bettering the human life on earth. This process of being, working, and achieving is designed by a merciful creator who loves his creation to thrive and be content. Thus all the benefit of knowing, worshiping, and working returns solely to the human being, and that is pure mercy. Then it becomes clear how intending for the human being to worship through becoming *khalīfa* on earth is actually an act of mercy toward humans. On a deeper level, Jeffrey Lang says:

---

39. Jeffrey Lang, *Even Angels Ask: A Journey to Islam in America*, 67.

40. The same idea is reflected in this verse "O people, you are the ones in need of God; He is the all-sufficient, the praiseworthy" (Qur'ān 35:15).

> It seems that God, in accordance with His attributes, intends to make a creature that can experience His being (His mercy, compassion, love, kindness, beauty, etc.) in an intensely personal way and at a level higher than the other beings known to humankind. The intellect and will than man has been giving, together with the strife and struggle that he will surely face on earth, somehow contribute to the development of these individuals, this subset of humanity that will be bound to God by love.[41]

Lang goes on at length to explain how a human being has the capacity to experience God through His names, which Adam was taught and the angels did not recognize, at a completely different level. One of God's names in the Qur᾽ān is *al-wadūd* (the loving), and this is one of the seeds implanted in the human soul by virtue of God's divine breath. So people experience this loving attribute toward each other and other creatures, yet not at the same intensity. For example, feelings of love and connection toward one's child are more intense than toward a pet because of the different natures of each being (in terms of intellectual and spiritual growth). When people experience this divine name (the loving) toward others, they draw closer to God by experiencing his divine name at a fuller capacity than other creatures.

After demonstrating the exegetical references, I would like to compare the latter Qur᾽ānic ideas with Aristotelian understanding of the political animal. It is clear from the reactions of both the angels and the Jinn toward the creation of the human being that neither creature understood the *telos* or the purpose of creating the human being. Satan, representing the Jinn, looked at the constituent matter of Adam, thereby comparing himself to Adam according to physical strength. Satan saw himself more worthy of being a *khalīfa* because he is physically stronger or purer than the human being, as he argued, "I am better than him as you created me from fire and created him from mud."

Aristotle can help us understand this comparison by saying that the constituent matter does not represent the nature of something or the *telos* of its creation. Similarly, the angels compared themselves with Adam by

41. Jeffrey Lang, *Even Angels Ask: A Journey to Islam in America*, 33–34.

their immediate actions; they praise God's name constantly while Adam will cause corruption on earth. God answers, "I know what you do not know." Aristotle would probably say that God was referring to the *telos* of the human being, what he would become when he achieves his full potential. One cannot understand something until we see the final end to which it matures. ***For the human being to achieve his full potential (i.e., become khalīfa), God taught him the names, that is, the ability to communicate with other beings by means of language, the knowledge described by ʿAbduh, the reason described by Faḍlallah, or meanings described by Lang.*** These tools by which a human being can differentiate between good and evil, just and unjust, enable him to fulfill his role as a *khalīfa*. Thus, instead of weighing his merit according to his humble source of physical creation (the mud), or his lack of being molded to worship all the time (such as the angels), his ability to choose and reason and communicate in more complex ways elevated the human being to the position of *khalīfa*. Faḍlallah said that angels are innately obedient; hence, according to Aristotle, they are incapable of forming a political community because they don't possess the ability for deliberate choice and action where the Qurʾānic verses imply that they do not have the ability to make evil choices. By default, choice necessitates the presence of both good and evil, which ʿAbduh describes as the two basic features of our thinking process (*al-fikr*).

However, it seems that not all human beings will utilize the tools innate in them to develop to their full potential as a *khalīfa*. This would explain the puzzling question of the angels: that humans will cause corruption on earth. While all humans by the fact of their creation are endowed with all the capacities to become a *khalīfa*, humans will utilize their capacities differently. Some will master these tools and become a *khalīfa*, while others will lead a life based on whimsical desires, hence taking the path of corruption. This is best explained in the Qurʾānic verse addressing Prophet David's function as a *khalīfa*, "O David, We have appointed you a *khalīfa* on earth, so judge between people by the Truth (justice, Ar. *ḥaq*), and do no follow whimsical desires for they will mislead you from the path of Allah. Indeed, those who go astray from the way of Allah will have a severe punishment for having forgotten the Day of reckoning" (Qurʾān 38:26). For a human to judge/rule by truth and justice, he/she needs the knowledge, ability to make the right decision, intellect to decipher truth from falsehood, proper communication, ability to master one's evil desires, and so forth, which sum up all the previous descriptions of a *khalīfa*. Therefore, all humankind are endowed with these potentials and are eligible to become *khalīfa*. An aspect of this *khalīfa* is political ruling, exemplified through Prophet David. This does not make the term absolutely political nor apolitical, but rather it denotes that humankind are sociopolitical beings by nature. By conveying this discourse between God, the angels, and *Iblīs*, the purpose of the creation of the human being is clarified. The *telos* of his creation is to experience God's mercy and discover His attributes through the active role of *khalīfa* on earth, a role that reveals the human need for social and political association as well as spiritual evolution; hence his being taught the names. The discourse uncovers the peculiarity of the *khalīfa* by contrasting it with the roles undertaken by the other creatures (angels and Jinn).

The *telos* of the Aristotelian political animal is different from the Qurʾānic *khalīfa*. First, while Aristotle reduced the human being to a political animal, the Qurʾān addressed the human as a whole, that is, with different facets and potentials. The need for social and political association is connected to the human's need for spiritual growth. Social and political association become a means to a higher end: experiencing the attributes of the merciful and bettering oneself and life on earth. The telos of the political animal is the perfect life based on choice and action, which should lead to happiness. However, the telos of *khalīfa* is using choice and action to enhance the life experience for oneself and other humans and all creation. While the Aristotelian human seems to be mainly concerned with his own happiness as an end goal, the Qurʾānic *khalīfa* is endowed with a responsibility and a duty whereby his own happiness cannot be realized without ensuring the happiness of others. Experiencing the mercy of the divine is reflected by experiencing mercy toward the rest of his creation. This is a recurring feature in Islamic ideology that is based on *tawḥīd* ("unifying"), not only in the perception of who is the God, but also in the different facets that form the essence of a human being as well as how the *khalīfa* relates to and unifies with the universe.

Khilāfa in Islamic Literature

In Islamic literature, *khilāfa* has been often correlated with political leadership. For example, Abul Ala Mawdūdī, a Muslim revivalist, political activist, and the founder of Jamāʿat-i-Islāmī (the Islamic revivalist party), understood *khalīfa* as a representative of God. The human *khilāfa* is realized by his exercising God-given authority according to the precepts and confines of God's law. The *khalīfa* bears resemblance to an administrator of the real owner of an estate. The administrator follows the instructions of the real owner and exercises authority based on the latter. The administrator does not act upon his own will because the actual ownership is not vested in him.

Mawdūdī then asserts that the God-given caliphate bestowed upon every individual imparts a characteristic of equality necessary for democratic rule. The difference between an Islamic democracy and a Western democracy is that sovereignty belongs to people in the latter, whereas in the former, sovereignty belongs to God, who delegates people as his representatives or *khulafāʾ*. In a Western democracy, people fulfill their will by making their own laws, whereas in an Islamic democracy, people fulfill the will of God by following divine law (*sharīʿah*). Hence, Mawdūdī concludes that the Western concept of democracy represents an absolute authority where power is exercised in a free and uncontrolled way, but Islamic democracy is compliant to the divine law and is controlled by it.[42] Along similar lines, Ibn Khaldūn regards *khilāfa* as an authority bestowed upon people to act according to religious obligations for their interests in both this world and the hereafter. The religious law is a substitute for the lawgiver, Muhammad, as it serves to protect the religion and to exercise political leadership in light of divine rules. However, a political authority that causes people to act based on rational insight to advance their worldly interests lacks the divine light, which consequently makes it reprehensible.[43]

Interpreting the *khalīfa* as an administrator who does not act upon his own will is problematic. A more precise interpretation would be an administrator who does not act upon his whimsical desires rather than will. Negating the will of the human being implies blind obedience or coercion. The Qurʾānic verse describing the creation of the human being does not indicate blind coercion because even the angels, who are by nature prone to following God's will, inquired about the creation of the *khalīfa*. Then, God taught Adam the names and answered the angels'

42. Sayyid Abul ʿAlāʾ Mawdūdī, *The Islamic Way of Life*, ed. Khurshid Ahmad and Khurram Murad (United Kingdom: The Islamic Foundation, 1986), 30–31.

43. Ibn Khaldūn, *The Muqaddimah: An Introduction to History*, trans. Franz Rosenthal (Princeton, NJ: Princeton University Press, 1967), 388–90.

question by revealing their ignorance about the new creation. Therefore, submitting to God's order did not negate their quest for knowledge and understanding or negate their will. Their will was revealed through their curiosity and questioning, whereas the will of Satan was revealed through his rebellion. Both the angels and Satan exercised their will. The angels chose to follow God's will while Satan chose to follow his desires. Hence, the angels' fulfilling God's order was not blind submission, rather it was a peaceful submission based on their trust in the divine wisdom. This idea was explained in detail in chapter 2 through the Qur᾽ānic perception of the term "Muslim."

The suggestion that the concept of *khilāfa* implies coercion has led some scholars to renounce its political aspect altogether. For example, Ali Abd al-Rāziq, a jurist and scholar at al-Azhar, is an advocate of the idea that Islam is purely a religion in which Prophet Muhammad is like all other prophets who came to proclaim what has been revealed by God, that he was not a king who came to establish a kingdom. Al-Rāziq thinks that dominance, *al-ghalaba*, was always the pillar of *khilāfa* throughout history. Any kind of kingship in every nation is based on dominance and coercion because reign encompasses all worldly goods and desires and force is needed to conquer competing powers.[44] Abd al-Rāziq thinks that the Prophet indeed exercised some kind of leadership and authority that granted him good standing among the people and facilitated the acceptance of his *daʿwa* ("proclamation") and the spread of God's message. However, his sovereignty was a spiritual one, whereas the political authority exercised by traditional rulers is a secular one. Thus, for Abd al-Rāziq, religion and politics should not be mixed.[45] He accepts the fact that any organized *ummah* should have a government to regulate its affairs and order it so that anarchy is averted. However, he thinks that this government does not have to be restricted to a specific religion or a definite type of ruling. He adds that scholars who advocate *khilāfa* as the ideal government for Muslims have a weak argument.

For Abd al-Rāziq, a *khilāfa* was never needed to manage religious or secular matters, and it has always brought misfortune for Islam and Muslims. He understood *khilāfa* in a historical context by referring to preexisting caliphates throughout Islamic history, such as the Umayyad

---

44. Ali ʿAbd al-Rāziq, *al-Islām wa Uṣūl al-Ḥukm* (Cairo: Misr Press, 1925), 25–26.

45. Ibid., 65–69.

and Abbasid caliphates.[46] Abd al-Rāziq regards the main problem of these caliphates to be the caliph's abuse of power. Muslim scholars (*ʿulamāʾ*) granted the caliph total guardianship, absolute obedience, and interminable tenure. Everyone has to obey because the caliph's obedience stems from obedience to God. He has the absolute right to make all decisions and has no partner in his reign. All others are working under his authority and are his representatives. He retains absolute right to appoint or isolate whomever he wishes. His only limitations are those related to establishing *sharīʿah*, which should hinder him from going astray.[47]

Rashīd Riḍa, a strong opponent of Abd al-Rāziq, is an advocate of a *khilāfa* definition inclusive of both religion and government (*dīn wa dawla*) and regards Islam as offering "a spiritual guidance and a civil social policy."[48] Riḍa opposes Abd al-Rāziq's arguments that *khilāfa* entails merely a spiritual authority and that political leadership should be vested in a separate venue. *Khilāfa* loses its true essence, and the contract between the *ummah* and the *khalīfa* will be abolished if the two kinds of leadership are separated from each other or if *khilāfa* is restricted to either one of them. The concept of *khilāfa* does not allow for the presence of two leaderships simultaneously. That is because one of the essential features of the religion is the unity of the Islamic *ummah* and its safeguarding the shared interests of the Muslims of different nations who are regarded as one body with one heart that nourishes the rest of the organs. Therefore it is necessary to have one leader or *khalīfa* in both spiritual and political respects.[49]

Nonetheless, Riḍa agrees with Abd al-Rāziq that the subservience of the *ʿulamāʾ* to the rulers distorted the Caliphate "from its ideal form under the Rāshidūn into an apparatus serving the basest interests of the despots and dynasts, thus making tyranny the normal form of government in Islamic history. Hence the very people who are charged with the task of preserving the justness of the system prove to be the mainstay of its abuses. The vicious circle is complete—freedom from injustice is not

46. Ibid., 33–38.

47. Ibid., 3–6.

48. Rashīd Riḍa, *al-Khilāfa wal Imāma al-Uẓma* (Cairo: Manār Press, 1923), 4.

49. Rashīd Riḍa, "Bayān Ḥaqiqat al-Khilāfa wa Shurūṭ al-Khalīfa fil-Islām," *al-Manār*, 27, i. 3 (1926): 226.

possible without the *ʿulamāʾ* taking the lead, but the *ʿulamāʾ* themselves perpetuate injustice by giving it an air of divine providence."[50] Riḍa attributes the latter problem to the absence of legislation based on *ijtihād* ("exercising intellectual reasoning to interpret *sharīʿah* in order to answer contemporary questions and concerns that were not pertinent during the time of Prophet Muhammad"). This is due to the fact, Riḍa argues, that many Islamic scholars and jurists have lost the distinction between the essential and nonessential in Islamic law. Riḍa contends that few of them knew it, but they were silenced by their fear of the government. "Thus there crept into Islam that disease to which [Riḍa] refers sometimes as congealment (*jumūd*) and sometimes as blind imitation (*taqlīd*). In the sphere of law this takes the form of slavish obedience to one or other of the four recognized legal schools."[51]

Riḍa thinks that the solution resides in creating new laws that match the needs of the age because Muslim societies are facing a new civilization different from that which existed at the time of Qurʾānic revelation. There is a need for an "Islamic progressive party" that has the independence of mind necessary to understand the Islamic laws and the essence of modern civilization at the same time. Then they can reconcile change with the moral principles of Islam. This party needs to be strong and unified to accomplish its purpose.

In order to be unified, these reformers need to develop a new and unified system by modifying the four existing traditional schools, which can be achieved by performing *ijtihād* to integrate them according to the needs of the age. He also adds that unity is more easily attained in the modern world because of the ease of communication, such that *Ijmāʿ* ("consensus") is much more feasible because all *ʿulamāʾ* of the age can be gathered in one place and time.[52] Mawdūdī advocates transforming laws of the secular state into Islamic ones. However, he does not confine this job to the *ʿulamāʾ*; rather, he advocated the creation of an "academy of law" run by legal minds knowledgeable about religious sciences and acquainted

---

50. Hamid Enayat, *Modern Islamic Political Thought* (London: Macmillan, 1982), 73.

51. Albert Hourani, *Arabic Thought in the Liberal Age* (London: Oxford University, 1962), 235.

52. Ibid., 236–43.

with modernity. Mawdūdī thinks that the classical form of *sharīʿah* does not tackle the issues of governance for a modern state. Therefore, *sharīʿah* should be reinterpreted and developed to suit the needs of the state in the modern time.[53]

I think that the main conflict arising between advocates of a political *khilāfa* and the advocates for a religious one is a result of associating the political experience with the fundamentals of religion. In other words, when *ʿulamāʾ* are in charge of sanctifying and legitimizing political rule according to religious law, going against their ideas implies going against the law of God. But there needs to be some room for voicing concerns and disagreement, allowing for differences of opinion and multiple options for keeping those in power under scrutiny. In order for this to happen, a clear-cut dichotomy has to be established between what is essential and unchangeable in religion and what is changeable and can be modified or interpreted differently according to the needs of the time. This practice would allow political theorists considerable flexibility to propose theories and discuss new means to enhance systems of governance. Islamic ethics and morals would provide the foundation; nonetheless, the Islamic foundation does not imply making the system normative or cause rebelling against it to be a sin.

I do not think that Abd al-Rāziq's suggestion to dismiss any involvement of religion in politics would be acceptable to Muslim societies where we witnessed in the late modern period that marginalization of Islamist groups led to the rise of extremism, fanaticism, and sometimes violence. At the same time, I do not think that Riḍa's suggestion for lawmaking to be confined in the political sphere to the *ʿulamāʾ* will be a viable option in the modern world unless the *ʿulamāʾ* traditional learning system is expanded to include practical social sciences, not merely religious studies. In that regard, Mawdūdī's suggestion seems to offer a more practical alternative. Nonetheless, besides the executive field of law, studies in political theory need to be established in Islamic culture to nurture and sustain the making and remaking of practical laws for society. The last section of this chapter discusses how the religious and political spheres interact within an *ummah*.

---

53. Seyyed Vali Reza Nasr, *Mawdudi and the Making of Islamic Revivalism* (Oxford: Oxford University Press, 1996), 96–97.

Aristotelian *Polis* and Qur'anic *Ummah*

Aristotle clarifies the *telos* of the polis, which I would like to compare with the *telos* of the Qur'ānic *ummah*. The *telos* of the political community, according to Aristotle, is to build the good life by promoting moral virtue for the perfection of the human being and his flourishing. Individuals' harnessing their natural capabilities, such as reason and speech, can build the good life.[54] The political community makes the good life possible in two ways: first, it is a provider of laws, and second, by living in a political community, one has to exercise those laws by developing relationships and exchanges with others, which in return perfects the human being. Thus, the political community helps the human being acquire virtue by putting the laws into action, that is, education through repeated performance.

By showing the *telos* of the polis, Aristotle differentiates it from any other political community that does not contribute to human perfection. The polis exists for the sake of human flourishing and not vice versa; consequently the polis becomes a means to an end beyond itself. In addition, the *telos* of the polis is not a mere association of human beings sharing a common land or even living apart, and the *telos* of law is not only a convention assuring reciprocal justice. Instead, the *telos* of the political community is achieving excellence, and the *telos* of law is making citizens good and just.[55] Thus, Aristotle's conclusion is:

> Political society exists for the sake of noble actions, and not of living together. Hence they who contribute most to such a society have a greater share in it than those who have the same or a greater freedom of nobility of birth but are inferior to them in political excellence; or than those who exceed them in wealth but are surpassed by them in excellence.[56]

---

54. Bernard Yack, *The Problems of a Political Animal: Community, Justice and Conflict in Aristotelian Political Thought* (Berkeley: University of California Press, 1993), 2–3.

55. Aristotle, *Politics* (1280 b).

56. Aristotle, *Politics* (1281a 3–8).

Bernard Yack makes a relevant point by saying that the community of the polis does not represent a communion whereby individual identity is lost at the expense of collective identity. Rather, the polis represents the participation of free and equal individuals who may share important elements of their identities without forsaking their distinction.[57] The polis embodies "different individual *actors* expressing a *general will*."[58]

Justice serves as the communal bond between citizens of a polis. Justice comes about as a result of our capacity for reasoned speech that allows us to publicly communicate with each other about mutual and shared rights, obligations, and specific actions. The concept of justice in the Aristotelian polis, which is discussed later in detail, is directly tied to speech and public deliberation, the hallmark of humankind.[59] Thus, the goal of creating a polis is the security and self-sufficiency resulting from mutual accountability and concern shared by a relatively heterogeneous group of individuals with different goods and skills.

A variety of interests will oblige individuals to propose competing conceptions of justice for public approval. This process of refining and redefining justice in a polis, which is discussed later, makes it possible for people to develop virtues and perfect themselves. However, some social conflict and distrust also result from individuals arguing about political justice. *Therefore, social heterogeneity and social conflict resulting from the presence of diversity are characteristic features of the Aristotelian polis.* Elimination of social heterogeneity by suppressing public argument about justice threatens the existence of a political community.[60] That is why nonpolitical, homogeneous communities are less likely to experience the social conflict characteristic of political communities. *When one conception of justice is enforced, people are discouraged from participating in the political sphere because of implicit suppression of their freedom to bring forward their own conception of justice for public approval. The result is a superficial social unity, signified by the absence of an active citizenship and the death of a political community. This constraining of people from using and developing*

57. Bernard Yack, *The Problems of a Political Animal*, 30–33.

58. Ibid., 31. Emphasis added.

59. Ibid., 56–57.

60. Ibid., 65–71.

their natural powers of deliberation and speech in nonpolitical communities hinders the development of *human beings into fully civilized adults.*

Nonetheless, while conflict is unavoidable in a political community, Aristotle argues that a disposition to lawfulness among its members will tend to lessen conflict and contribute to a relatively more stable order. Aristotle supports society's fostering a "law-abiding character" for three reasons. First, the most critical role of law is to adapt citizens to specific standards of justice; second, the moral education of individuals is better accomplished under a rather stable legal order; third, citizens following general rules will abide by the regular rotation in power that establishes a political community (for Aristotle, the rule of law means taking turns in ruling and being ruled).[61] This way, Aristotle seems to counteract the aforementioned problem characteristic of a political community that is conflict resulting from competing conceptions of justice.

While the city is associated with "laws," the *ummah* is associated with "ways of life" in al-Farabi's thought. "Particular *Ummahs* may establish human language and literary tradition, while particular cities bind their inhabitants with laws."[62] Al-Farabi considers language a distinctive mark of any *ummah*: "language gradually establishes itself in the soul and emerges as the driving force behind the growth and particularity of the *ummah*."[63] Then he relates language to law through the formation of cultural conventions. Al-Farabi distinguishes an *ummah* by two traits: natural traits caused by climate and nutrition and the conventional trait of language, which is dynamic and more important in shaping an *ummah*. The more complex a language becomes, the more civilized an *ummah* is, where al-Farabi relates the giver of utterances (*wāḍiʿ al-alfāẓ*) to the giver of laws (*wāḍiʿ ash-sharīʿah*) as both establishing conventions. Development of the language allows its speakers to be more established in the linguistic customs that have been standardized by earlier generations and passed down to the

61. Bernard Yack, *The Problems of a Political Animal*, 203–4.

62. Alexander Orwin, *Redefining the Muslim Community: Ethnicity, Religion and Politics in the Thought of Alfarabi* (Philadelphia: University of Pennsylvania Press, 2017), 32–33.

63. Ibid., 47.

next ones. Through these customs, members of an *ummah* cultivate *adāb*[64] (manners), which are critical for the political and religious education of both rulers and citizens.[65]

Al-Farabi brings up an important distinction of the *ummah* compared to the city in Greek thought. An *ummah* is based on language and ways of life that developed over many generations, which cannot be reproduced by a mere legislator.[66] The first and foremost function of the polis is that it is a provider of laws that are required to create good citizens. In that regard, the nation in Aristotle's thought is subordinate to the city's laws, and by extension the nation is subordinate to the state in the modern period. However, the *ummah* is neither a provider of laws nor subordinate to a legislator's/ruler's laws. Then, what is the *telos* of the *ummah*, and what is the difference between the Farabian "ways of life" and "laws"? In order to explore these questions, one cannot evade two distinctions. First, a distinction need to be clarified between *ummah* in general and the virtuous *ummah* in particular. Second, a distinction needs to be made between the concept of law and *sharīʿah*, which is discussed consequently.

Al-Farabi differentiates between the ethnic and religious *ummah*. The latter comprises two fundamentally distinct origins: one based on divine religion and *sharīʿah*, whereas the other is a merely human phenomenon rooted in philosophy.[67] Al-Farabi contends that the Islamic *ummah* develops in addition to the older ethnic *umam* where both should coexist.[68] He then introduces the "virtuous *ummah*" (*khayr ummah*), which is the term given to the Muslim *ummah* in the Qurʾān described in chapter 2. While the ethnic *ummah* is united by language or natural character, the virtuous *ummah* is held together "by customary dispositions and voluntary traits, which induce its parts to act in tandem . . . the oneness of its actions and parts approximates the oneness of the first principle of the world, as well as the oneness of the world itself, brought about by the governance of that

64. "Translated as "upbringing" by Charles Butterworth and "formation of character" by Muhsin Mahdi" in Alexander Orwin, *Redefining the Muslim Community: Ethnicity, Religion and Politics in the Thought of Alfarabi*, 52.

65. Ibid., 47–53.

66. Ibid., 34.

67. Ibid., 99.

68. Ibid., 113–15.

first principle: 'the Ummah and Ummahs become like a single (*wāḥid*) thing performing a single action by which a single purpose is obtained.' "[69] The activity of the virtuous *ummah* brings happiness not only to itself but also to other *umam* and cities of the world. Alexander Orwin rightly deduces that al-Farabi is talking about the best *ummah* that came about for humankind that commands good and forbids evil, and while al-Farabi hints at the uniqueness of this *ummah*, it is not entirely clear how its parts act in tandem. Orwin poses an interesting question: "why does religion establish itself in an *ummah* and not some other kind of community?"[70]

In order to know the telos of the *ummah*, there needs to be a discussion of the best *ummah* in the Qur᾿ān because the telos describes the purpose of something and what it tends to be when it develops to its full potential. Therefore, understanding the best *ummah* will highlight the telos of the *ummah*. The uniqueness of the virtuous *ummah* is based on its "voluntary" activities and the unity of its actions, which is further explored in the following sections.

POLIS AND *UMMAH*: MEDIUM WHEREBY CITIZENS EXERCISE VIRTUOUS ACTIVITY

Aristotle thinks that virtue is acquired through action. Repeated training or habituation makes living virtuously pleasant; it becomes an innate disposition. External forces such as educators, parents, and lawgivers typically inculcate virtuous habits in others through continuous moral training. Thus we see that the training of virtuous dispositions requires both an internal and external, or compulsive force. Aristotle associates this compulsive aspect with law, and he regards it as a more palatable form of compulsion than direct, personal coercion by individuals. That law (ideally) affects all members of a community indiscriminately, and individuals typically find abiding by the law fair and acceptable. Thus, when a virtuous disposition is not natural and innate but acquired from external factors, the polis and its laws intervene and make it possible for human beings to develop those virtues.[71] This is what makes the polis "the

69. Ibid., 115.

70. Ibid., 104.

71. Bernard Yack, *The Problems of a Political Animal*, 96–99.

cause of the greatest of goods"[72] and makes the polis essential for human beings, because "just as man is the best of animals when completed, so he is the worst of all when separated from law and adjudication."[73]

Human beings need justice to develop their natural capabilities and elevate themselves to the level of *khalīfa*, which is the best creation. The virtuous *ummah* "You were the best (*khayr*) *ummah* ever raised up for humankind for you enjoin righteousness and deter wrongness and believe in Allah . . ." (Qurʾān 3:110) provides its members with the environment for continuous moral training (reflected in the grammatical usage of present continuous for the verbs *yaʾmurūna* [enjoining] and *yanhawna* [deterring]). This moral training is realized by *ummah* members acting according to *maʿrūf* and prohibiting *munkar*. The terms *maʿrūf* and *munkar* describe the law accepted and practiced by people, not merely codified law, the dry subject of legislators. I think that using those specific terms has two implications: first, law is "practiced"; thereby it becomes a habit or a norm accepted or rejected by people; second, by becoming an accepted and common norm, it becomes less burdensome for people to practice it than if it were enforced by higher authorities, a critical point that Aristotle discussed earlier. Thus, within an *ummah* setting, people can attain success (*falāḥ*) by the practice of enjoining *maʿrūf* and deterring *munkar*.

Aristotle does not consider moral or civic virtue an inborn characteristic but one that is acquired through repeated performance of virtuous actions in society. "In all the things that come to us by nature we first acquire the potentiality and later exhibit the activity."[74] In the Qurʾān, this potentiality is not acquired but is instilled in the human self: "By the self, and Him who perfected it. So, He instilled in it the potentiality to do wrong and to refrain from it (*fa-ʾalhamahā fujūrahā wa-taqwāhā*). He is indeed successful who purifies it (*zakkāhā*), and he will indeed fail who corrupts it." (Qurʾān 91:7–10) The verses indicate that we are born with an innate potential to either do wrong or refrain from doing wrong; nonetheless it is the human responsibility/choice to develop either potentiality through action that cannot be performed in

72. Aristotle, *Politics* (1253a30).

73. Ibid. (1253a31).

74. Aristotle, *NE* (1103a25).

isolation. The act of purifying one's self to attain success happens in an *ummah* setting. Notably, the same root, success, is used in a verb format (*ʾaflaḥa*) in verse 91:9 and as an adjective (*mufliḥūn*) in verse 3:104. Those described as *mufliḥūn* are constantly engaging in the acts of enjoining virtue and deterring wrongness, whereby they attain *tazkiya* (purification of their souls) that leads to success. *Tazkiya* is a virtuous disposition that can be attained by practicing virtuous activity[75] in the *ummah*. Therefore, the *ummah* becomes a means for human beings to purify their souls and reach perfection, as well as fulfill their *telos* as a *khalīfa*.

Another major implication of the Qurʾānic verse 3:110, which highlights the difference between a polis and *ummah* as being the medium by which individuals develop virtues, is the adding of "belief in one God" to the practice of enjoining *maʿrūf* and deterring *munkar*. Qurʾānic exegesis of the latter verse in the second chapter showed that belief is deficient if it does not blossom right action in the *ummah*, that is, if the believers do not practice virtue by acting righteously in society. Thus, belief (ethical sphere) and sociopolitical action are inseparable in a thriving *ummah*. Adding this belief component makes the moral action in society voluntary rather than compulsive, and this is probably what al-Farabi meant by the "voluntary traits" of the virtuous *ummah*, rather than "natural character" of the ethnic *ummah*. In addition, it points to the difference between "ways of life" and "laws," which invites a discussion of the Qurʾānic and Aristotelian understanding of law.

Difference between Law and *Sharīʿah*

Aristotle regards law as externally imposed on individuals by whoever has the power to make, interpret, and enforce his understanding of law in society.[76] Thus, law for Aristotle is externally enforced by moral educators so that they may internalize in people a disposition to lawfulness.

75. Virtuous activity is not normative for all societies. There is no theoretical prescription about what a virtuous activity entails for human societies. Each human community is unique and should reach an understanding about what constitutes their common good through thoughtful deliberation. Aristotle, *NE* (1140a25–1140b4).

76. Bernard Yack, *The Problems of a Political Animal*, 177.

With repeated performance, laws become familiar and no longer painful. Through habituation, laws become part of our character rather than merely being something we are asked to do.[77]

From an Islamic perspective, religious law (*sharīʿah*) is not externally imposed but originates inside individuals as a result of personal conviction. Thus persons implement the law themselves, specifically with respect to the rituals (*manāsik*) discussed in the second chapter. It was shown that through the repetitive acts of performing the rituals a person attains purification; nonetheless, the rituals do not produce the desired effect on human beings without their possessing belief or conviction beforehand. Even the part of *sharīʿah* that requires enforcement by external powers also requires consent by the people involved. This explains why the Medina Constitution provided freedom for each religious group (Muslims and Jews) to practice their own religion and law. In addition, other decrees did not carry a direct religious bearing but were more political and required the approval of the people involved, such as stipulated in decree 22.[78]

Ibn Khaldūn in his *Muqaddimah* discusses the difference between externally imposed laws, such as technical instruction or scientific education, and internally motivated adherence to religious law. Law from formal, secular education, encountered since childhood, develops in persons a sense of fear and docility according to Ibn Khaldūn. As a result, persons will grow up with a character trait of submissiveness to law, which decreases fortitude and power of resistance, both needed for action and change. This is due to the fact that educators or figures of authority, that is, external restraining influences, constantly apply these laws. However, when religious law is received orally, where the principles of religion are observed as a result of a deep-rooted conviction in the truth of the articles of faith, will not develop a submissive character. This is because discipline caused by religious law is motivated by an inner self-restraining influence and not by external authority. As a result, human character will be improved in terms of courage, fortitude, self-reliance, and freedom to resist and act. However, Ibn Khaldūn notes that when religious law is transformed into an acquired craft and a branch of learning instructed by education,

77. Ibid., 204.

78. 22- "It is not lawful for any believer ***approving the contents of this sheet*** (document) and believing in God and the Day of Judgment, to support or shelter an aggressor."

it becomes equivalent to other laws imposed externally and thereby loses its advantage.[79]

Therefore, when the law is endorsed as a personal conviction and imposed by the self, then exercised in society as a norm to develop a "way of life," not only do human beings develop to their full potential as a *khalīfa,* but there also is unity between the different parts that constitute an *ummah.* This may explain what al-Farabi meant by "the oneness of its actions and parts approximates the oneness of the first principle of the world," which I think alludes to the concept of *tawḥīd.* In the virtuous *ummah*, which people seek and aspire to establish, there is harmony between the human inner potential for growth with the laws that organize society and the universe. Compulsion should be the exception rather than the norm. *Sharīʿah* conforms with human needs and is fully espoused based on believing in its efficacy and benefit rather than its being imposed by an external educator/legislator.

Modern Islamists grant the "Islamic state" the duty of reforming its citizens and making them virtuous. For example, Mawdūdī thinks that the purpose of the state is the development of virtues and the abolition of evils: "The state in Islam is not intended for political administration only nor for the fulfillment through it of the collective will of any particular set of people. Rather, Islam places a high ideal before the state for the achievement of which it must use all the means at its disposal. The aim is to encourage the qualities of purity, beauty, goodness, virtue, success and prosperity which God wants to flourish in the life of his people and to suppress all kinds of exploitation and injustice."[80] Mawdūdī thinks that the state can achieve its purpose because it represents a coercive power needed to organize society and instill in people the aforementioned virtues: "Human history and the knowledge of human nature show that the establishment of civic life is essentially dependent on a coercive power."[81]

On the other hand, Wael Hallaq discusses in his book *The Impossible State* the inherent contradiction in the concept of a modern Islamic state that is based on modernity's moral predicament. One of the main

79. Ibn Khaldūn, *Al-Muqaddimah*, 95–97.

80. Mawdūdī, *The Islamic Way of Life*, 32.

81. Glenn E. Perry, "The Islamic World: Egypt and Iran," in *Politics and Religion in the Modern World*, ed. George Moyser (London: Routledge, 1991), 110.

reasons for the impossibility of an Islamic state is the critical difference between the sovereign will (where law is enforced coercively by a state apparatus in modern times) and the rule of law in Islam (*sharīʿah*). The latter is not the product of a state apparatus or political power but the product of the legal experts in the *ummah*. The political power (i.e., the state in modernity) was transient and changing, termed in Arabic (*dawla*), while the *ummah* and its organic ties to *sharīʿah* were fixed. This stability of the *ummah* and its *sharīʿah*, in comparison to the changing dynastic powers, made the *ummah* the main custodian of *sharīʿah*, not political power. Therefore, the inherent contradiction of the term "Islamic state" is based on the fundamental difference between the Islamic concept of law, *sharīʿah,* as a constitution and a practice, and the modern concept of law and practice as well as its custodianship.[82] Ibn-Khaldūn would agree with Hallaq's analysis because he argued that when religious law and virtue become the coercive function of a state apparatus, law loses its educational role and instead becomes a tool of suppression. When the role of the *ummah* and *sharīʿah* are both reduced to the role of a coercive state apparatus, the role of a human being as a *khalīfa* is usurped by the state, which in turn becomes an obstacle impeding the development of human virtue rather than serving as a means to sustain it.

The Qurʾānic *ummah* provide an opposite model to what some Islamists propose. Practicing law and attaining virtue is an individual effort within an *ummah*, which then affects political power, and not vice versa. Personal conviction and character developed in private life automatically contribute to the political realm of the *ummah*, which is manifest in public; hence *there is a direct relation between moral and civic virtue. Performing the rituals (personal implementation of sacred law) internalizes in the people a disposition to lawfulness such that they become more prone to follow and implement law publicly in the ummah.* The latter idea is represented in decree 13 in the MC,[83] discussed in chapter 3, which makes law a collective duty of every member in the *ummah*. Decree 13 represents a practical

82. Wael B. Hallaq, *The Impossible State* (New York: Columbia University Press, 2013), xi–xiii, 63–65.

83. 13- "All God conscious believers shall be against the person who intends to commit an aggressive and unjust act among them, or who aims to infringe one's rights or to cause turmoil among believers. And even if this person is the offspring of one of them, they shall all raise their hands against him."

example of "enjoining *maʿrūf* and deterring *munkar*" in the *ummah*. As discussed in chapter 3, Shams ad-Din argued that decree 13 makes the *ummah* equivalent to the political community.

Rule of Law (Polis and *Ummah*)

Aristotle says, "For political justice, as we saw, depends on law and applies to people who are naturally subject to law, and those are people who have an equal share in ruling and being ruled."[84] Yack interprets the latter phrase by saying that those who alternate positions of political power are only those who are disposed to follow rules because "taking turns in ruling and being ruled" is already law.[85] The absence of rule of law means the absence of the political community according to Aristotle. Yack calls the rule of law an "enabling constraint" that enables people to perform specific actions by constraining them from engaging in others. Thus, a disposition to lawfulness will put a limit on our use of power. "The freedom to exercise political power is, from this point of view, bound up with constraints on its exercise."[86]

Then the rule of law and political power can be seen as complementary rather than negating each other. From an Islamic perspective, the rule of law is not restricted to taking turns in ruling and being ruled; rather it is activated within the whole society in the form of *sharīʿah* interpreted earlier by Ibn Khaldūn. In other words, law becomes a social norm rather than a reciprocal form of power rotation by political elite (this is explained in more detail in a later section). Decree 13 in the MC exemplifies how law is activated by society. First, concerning the actors themselves, members of the *ummah* are allowed by law to act against an aggressor (or to exercise political power); nonetheless they are to abstain from acts of aggression and/or sever kinship and tribal connections for the sake of justice. The latter two acts are limitations undertaken by the members, which, nonetheless, allow them to exercise political power. Second, as discussed in chapter 3, an active *ummah* would automatically place limitations on political

84. Aristotle, *NE* (1134b13).

85. Bernard Yack, *The Problems of a Political Animal*, 206.

86. Ibid., 207.

power without, however, negating it.[87] Decree 13 specifically granted the collective members of the *ummah* the political right to directly oppose an aggressor before resorting to the central political power.

In the *ummah* of Medina, first, education of its members preceded the establishment of the *ummah* and its constitution. Second, the constitution granted the citizens the right to directly implement its rules. Thereby law was activated by allowing its members to implement rules rather than a coercive law being exercised on them in an authoritarian fashion. A reciprocal relationship was established whereby citizens share political ruling rather than being subjects of a political power. Consequently, this explains how every human being assumes the Qur᾿ānic role of a *khalīfa*. Therefore, the Medinan Qur᾿ānic *ummah* does not agree with the ideas proposed by some Islamists who ascribe to a coercive state instilling virtue by enforcing religious law. Besides, Islamic understanding and practice of law, or *sharī*ʿ*ah*, differ from the Aristotelian one. Taking turns in ruling and being ruled is not restricted to the political elite or a rotational system of governing but is embedded in societal norms and stated as a right in constitutional terms. By this means, it is not only circulated among the political elite but practiced by all members constituting the *ummah*.

Resolving Conflict by Invoking Competing Virtues in Aristotle and the Qur'ān

Aristotle constantly reminds us that the polis has no *telos* by itself, but is a means to realize a higher purpose that is the good of the human being. The disciplines of politics and ethics are inseparable in Aristotle's thought—the good life is the life of human flourishing (*eudaimonia*), which represents the "activity of the soul in accordance with complete virtue."[88] The latter idea was also presented in the Qur᾿ān: the function of the human being on earth is to undertake the role of *khalīfa*, which translates human virtue (the ultimate manifestation of sincere worship to God) into justice in society. By this means, members of an *ummah* are not merely bonded by common values, a community, or even a common good, but their bond is actually the realization that their personal virtue is constantly shaped and affected by their public interaction. This is eloquently

87. Chapter 3, decree 13.

88. Aristotle, *NE* (1102a5).

put in the Qurʾānic verse ". . . To each among you, We have prescribed a *sharīʿah* and a clear way (*shirʿatan wa minhājan*). If Allah willed, He would have made you one *ummah*, but that (He) may test you in what He has given you; *so strive as in a race in all virtues.* The return of you (all) is to Allah; then He will inform you about that in which you used to differ" (Qurʾān 5:48).[89] The verse clearly shows that the ultimate goal is not the *sharīʿah* itself; otherwise God would have made all humanity as one *ummah* sharing one *sharīʿah*; rather it is the virtue resulting from practicing the *sharīʿah*. The overarching, critical goal is "to strive as in a race in all virtues." Interestingly, Aristotle shares with the Qurʾān the latter understanding; Yack articulates it as:

> In the political community, Aristotle insists, we share the most important interest that human beings possess: concern about developing the ethical characteristics that make a flourishing human life possible. Nevertheless, no matter how high this interest reaches, it is still a shared interest that brings individuals together into the political community. That is why Aristotle treats the polis as community of shared interest throughout his writings even while insisting that the polis exists for the sake of the good life. What we share in the polis, according to Aristotle, is an interest in making the good life possible, not the good life itself.[90]

Aristotle argues that people engage in communities for some common advantage, usually some kind of external good, such as material things, honors, and pleasures. Conflict arises when people compete for these external goods, and thereby injustice arises due to the greed of some who exceed their fair share in acquiring those external goods. The only way to solve this problem, according to Aristotle, is to compete for goods and activities that do not decrease in the sharing.[91] For example, friendship (instead of honor) is an activity that does not diminish in the sharing but equally satisfies and nurtures people. Therefore, if people in a community were to compete for noble and beautiful actions rather

89. Discussed in chapter 2.

90. Bernard Yack, *The Problems of a Political Animal*, 102. Emphasis is mine.

91. Aristotle, *Politics* (1323b10–29)

than external goods, then "all the needs of the community would be met and each individual would have the greatest of goods, since that is what virtue is."[92] When people reorient their interest to engage in more virtuous activities rather than to acquire external goods, citizens will not only flourish and reform their political life but will also be eager to preserve their community. Their incentive to share a community together is oriented to what is lovable and mutually shared. "In sum, citizens in such a regime have an incentive to act justly toward one another, because actions guarantee the relationships that make possible the striving for common advantage."[93] According to Aristotle, the best polis is the one that contributes most to the flourishing of human lives rather than a specific kind of justice. *Only in the best polis will the good man and the good citizen have exactly the same virtues.*[94]

When the community's goal is aimed at the collective flourishing of its members and when its citizens are aware of this fact, justice will prevail, and the community will thrive. This positive outcome occurs when the common good that is sought by the members of a community is virtuous activity rather than external, finite goods. *Law is a means in such a community, and justice is a result, rather than an end unto itself.* This is what Aristotle means by people sharing an interest in developing the ethical characteristics that make a good life possible and are not simply focused on the good life itself. The good life is the natural result of ethical commitment. Similarly, the Qur᾿ān enjoins each community to follow its own divine *sharīʿah* (Qur᾿ān 5:48) and to strive in a contest of virtue. The striving in virtue (and not law) is what actually unites the diverse communities. Their mutual interest in the activity of striving in virtue is the mutual advantage gained by the diverse communities and is their main incentive to forming a shared *ummah*. Aristotle's ethics is an ethics of being rather than of possessing. "The cause of this is that being is a choice worthy and lovable to all. We all exist in activity for [we exist] by living and doing. Now in a way, the work is the maker

---

92. Aristotle, *Nicomachean Ethics* (1169a11).

93. Thomas W. Smith, "Aristotle on the Conditions for and Limits of the Common Good," *The American Political Science Review* 93, no. 3 (September 1999): 630–31.

94. Aristotle, *The Politics and the Constitution of Athens*, ed. Stephen Everson, 59. Emphasis added.

in act. So [the benefactor] loves the work [i.e., the recipient] since he loves being. And that is natural, for that which is potentially the work discloses in activity."[95]

The concept of the *ummah* examined in the previous chapters also encourages action and becoming, or the community "being" in Denny's words or the *ummah* still in a state of becoming.[96] However, the Qurʾānic *ummah* provides a more practical solution that can hold large diverse populations together. While Aristotle's ideas of virtue are sound, they are functional only within the city and are not suitable for larger associations. What would be the incentive of people to compete in beautiful actions instead of acquiring external goods, unless these beautiful actions such as "friendship" are directly impacting their lives? The Qurʾānic *ummah* provides an incentive for diverse populations to each follow their own *sharīʿah*, then compete with each other in virtues. *Sharīʿah*, unlike law, provides its followers with "personal" supreme incentives not only in this life but also in the hereafter; this is owing to the difference between *sharīʿah* and law discussed earlier. Second, living in a diverse population motivates people more to excel and realize their self-worth compared to others. Bonds such as natural traits, customs, language, ethnicity, or kinship tend to weaken as communities expand. However, the bond of an *ummah* that is based on enduring qualities shared by large numbers of people rather than on inherited traits or instant acquaintance is more capable of holding larger communities together.[97] While the best political cooperation is realized best in the polis for Aristotle, al-Farabi does not consider the small size to be the most perfect: "the perfection realized in each of these associations differs from the other in degree: the association arising in a city is beneath the association arising in an *ummah,* and the latter is beneath the association comprising all humanity."[98] The research conducted in this book with the concept of the expanding *Ummah* confirms this conclusion,

95. Aristotle, *NE* (1168a5–9).

96. Riḍwān As-Sayyid, *Al-Ummah wal-Jamāʿa was-Sulṭa* (Beirut: Dār Iqraʾ, 1984), 50–52.

97. Alexander Orwin, *Redefining the Muslim Community: Ethnicity, Religion and Politics in the Thought of Alfarabi,* 176–77.

98. Naṣīf Naṣṣār, *Mafhūm al-Ummah bayna ad-Dīn wal-Tārīkh* (Beirut: Dār at-Talīʿa, 1978), 37.

as shown in chapter 3. The *ummah* as an overarching concept is more feasible for organizing societies within a global framework.

Alexander Orwin deduces that al-Farabi would not consider national self-determination, which is based on a shared memory and a will to live together, effective in limiting conflict and creating a political bond. He adds: "religious and national solidarity both require a rewriting of the bloody events that gave rise to them."[99] Orwin thinks that diversity and tolerance are the most feasible means to limit conflict according to al-Farabi.

Apart from their differences, both the Aristotelean polis and the Qurʾānic *ummah* have a basis that is different from modern liberal societies. In the liberal society, the chief concern is equality because people are constantly overreaching for external goods, that is, some kind of material advantage. Hence, individuals portray equality as the ideal goal to protect their interests, thereby transforming human relationships into business interactions based on narrow self-interest.[100] The liberal society is a community whose members are constantly competing to acquire individual rights and to evade the threats of domination and exploitation. The idea presented by Aristotle that the doer of action receives more pleasure than the one receiving the action fosters a sense of giving and sharing rather than taking and keeping for oneself. The latter represents the dominant feature of contemporary economy in which human beings are transformed into mere consumers with endless desire to possess external goods. The following section is devoted to an analysis of how modern societies address conflict as well as the role of the community and the state.

Community and State in Contemporary Political Theory

Dealing with conflict is a major concern of contemporary political theorists in modern pluralistic societies. John Rawls says that the diversity of comprehensive religious, philosophical, and moral doctrines is an inherent feature of modern democratic societies. However, Rawls fears comprehensive doctrines that comprise ideals and values about personal

99. Alexander Orwin, *Redefining the Muslim Community: Ethnicity, Religion and Politics in the Thought of Alfarabi,* 190.

100. Thomas W. Smith, "Aristotle on the Conditions for and Limits of the Common Good," 629–30.

virtue and character in a human life and thereby define the nonpolitical conduct of human beings. He sees it as a general fact that "only the oppressive use of state power can maintain a continuing common affirmation of one comprehensive, religious, philosophical or moral doctrine."[101] In order to avoid the oppressive use of state power to maintain one comprehensive doctrine, Rawls suggests that there should arise a special domain of a "political conception of justice" that does not presume adhering to any specific comprehensive doctrine. This special domain of the political should provide an "overlapping consensus": "a consensus in which a diversity of conflicting comprehensive doctrines endorse the same political conception."[102] This liberal political conception should provide a reasonable framework of principles for diverse citizens, who are free and equal as well as reasonable and rational, to resolve conflicting issues and share a common life. Therefore, the main aim of Rawlsian liberal regime is social unity and how *to maintain the stability and durability of the political regime and insure the allegiance of a diversity of citizens (holding different comprehensive doctrines) to its well-being.*[103]

Rawls thinks that the political domain is "moral" but not "comprehensive" in the sense that it does not provide a complete set of ethical values about how a human being should lead a life. The political is a special domain with its own values separate from the nonpolitical domain in which citizens endorse their own particular values. How do citizens relate the two domains? Rawls says: "It is left to the citizens individually, *as part of their liberty of conscience,* to settle how they think the *'great values of the political domain'* relate to *other values* within their comprehensive doctrine."[104] The way Rawls describes the "great" values of the political domain relative to "other" values makes it seem that he is proposing a set of alternative values versus others. This idea has been noted by others such as MacIntyre, who says that the liberal order merely represents another tradition among many.[105] Moreover, while Rawls rejects

101. John Rawls, "The Domain of the Political and Overlapping Consensus," *New York University Law Review* 64, no. 2 (May 1989): 235.

102. Ibid., 246.

103. Ibid., 240–47. Emphasis added.

104. Ibid., 245. Emphasis added.

105. Alasdair MacIntyre, *Whose Justice? Which Rationality?* (Notre Dame, IN:

the idea of a comprehensive doctrine because its implementation requires oppressive state power, he supports coercive power to keep the stability of his liberal political regime; he just names it differently.

For Rawls, "political power is the coercive power of free and equal citizens as a corporate body, this power should be exercised, when Constitutional essentials are at stake, only in ways that all citizens can *reasonably be expected* to endorse publicly in the light of their own common human reason."[106] Rawls puts his high hopes on the "reasonable" means and values that will unite citizens from different backgrounds and provide a satisfying basis for public justification and sharing. Meanwhile, Rawls admits that conflict does not necessarily arise only from individuals' selfish narrow interests or prejudice but also from reasonable disagreement between reasonable persons, which he refers to as the burdens of reason.[107]

Charles Taylor thinks that the primacy of "instrumental reason" is one of the main problems facing liberal societies. The institutions and structures of industrial and technological societies greatly limit people's choices by forcing them to give more weight to instrumental reason instead of serious moral deliberation. Highly centralized and bureaucratic institutions shaped by market-state relations create self-centered individuals who only care about self-fulfillment and satisfaction of the private life as long as the government supplies and property distribute the means to attaining satisfaction. As a result, these self-centered individuals are impartial toward what constitutes a good life and are unaware of greater problems that transcend the self. The ultimate result is alienation from the public sphere and the loss of a vigorous political culture and political control in the face of a highly centralized and bureaucratic political world. Taylor calls it the "soft despotism" of contemporary liberal societies.[108]

Amitai Etzioni thinks that the absence of shared values leads to a spiritual vacuum and moral and social anarchy that in turn leads to political corruption. The absence of shared values is a result of a lack of interest in the common good in liberal societies. The independent allegiance to

University of Notre Dame Press, 1988), 326–69.

106. John Rawls, "The Domain of the Political and Overlapping Consensus," 244. Emphasis added.

107. Ibid., 235–36.

108. Charles Taylor, *The Ethics of Authenticity* (Cambridge: Harvard University Press, 1992), 2–17.

the political conception and the need for an overlapping consensus, proposed by Rawls, allows for a contract by which rational individuals protect their rights rather than allowing for reaching an agreement about shared values or attainment of common good. Those who are willing to live cooperatively with others and accept reasonable differences in religious and philosophical views will be able to approve of the same basic principles of constitutional order in light of common human reason.[109] In order for people to live peacefully together, they should establish a state neutral to the common good, that is, a state committed to multiple conceptions of the common good that nonetheless should remain private. In the public realm, Rawls suggests that individuals interact with each other "behind a veil of ignorance" to avoid conflict resulting from their personal doctrines.

MacIntyre thinks that this method of demarcation between the political public and the private life of individuals has undervalued the importance of community to the identity formation and integrity of the human being. Hence, liberalism fails to see the direct connection between the presence of a community and the moral life of an individual.[110] Etzioni analyzes the problem in greater depth by saying that the fading of traditional values that used to sustain communities was not replaced by solid confirmation of new values. This lack led to moral confusion and social anarchy.[111] Etzioni argues that "the social and political system should reflect and support the moral values the society is educated with."[112] In addition, Etzioni emphasizes that when the public discussion is focused on the rights of specific parties or individuals, the debate is automatically polarized, depriving the discussion of sensibility or moderation. As a result, people adopt a defensive position and lose the sense of mutual obligation toward each other, greatly suppressing moral discussion and consensus building.[113]

On similar lines, other communitarians criticize Rawlsian liberalism because it produces "asocial individuals," that is, selfish individuals who

109. John Rawls, *Political Liberalism* (New York: Columbia University Press, 1993), 140–41.

110. Stephen Mulhall and Adam Swift, *Liberals and Communitarians* (Cambridge: Blackwell Publishers, 1996), 71.

111. Amitai Etzioni, *The Spirit of Community: Rights, Responsibilities, and the Communitarian Agenda* (New York: Crown Publishers, 1993), 24.

112. Ibid., 30.

113. Ibid., 6–9.

are not interested in common issues of the society (Aristotelian common good). Embedded in generalized tolerance, there is a certain measure of indifference. "Not hating the other often derives from simply not caring about what he or she thinks or does."[114] This results in social exclusion of some communities such as ethnic minorities and disabled people because, despite their legitimate status as legal citizens, they frequently have little recognition or respect. ***Thus state neutrality with respect to the common good does not necessarily lead to the practical recognition of diverse communities.*** The Rawlsian method of tolerance that is based on the "method of avoidance" falls short of accounting for the realities of modern diverse communities. This is due to the fact that in our modern, deeply interdependent world, diverse communities depend on each other for survival. This necessitates positive engagement with the different other, rather than just mere recognition, in order to attain general solidarity in the society.[115]

While liberals proposed a system to protect the political sphere from the conflict associated with the competing private moral doctrines of individuals, Aristotle warns that the absence of conflict in the political sphere is a sign of a nonpolitical community with forced homogeneity and superficial unity. Rawls is afraid of the control and oppression of one comprehensive doctrine; however, he proposes a liberal system whose "great political values" supposedly provide the best alternative to any other doctrine and the best means to maintain unity and stability. By analyzing contemporary liberal societies, communitarians have shown that the liberal political conception has created "less political" and less interested individuals. A highly centralized system and a political culture based on prioritizing individual rights have discouraged citizens from participating in public discourse about common issues that affect them as one community. Communitarians have hinted that the absence of a common good has shattered the idea of a shared community, thereby affecting the moral integrity of human beings.

Aristotle, who is not a liberal or a communitarian, grants new insight into this debate as he shows how the private and public lives of individuals are deeply intertwined and reflective of each other. Aristotle argued

114. G. P. Fletcher, "The Case for Tolerance," *Social Philosophy and Policy* 13, no. 1 (1996): 231.

115. D. Hollenbach, "Virtue, the Common Good and Democracy," in *New Communitarian Thinking: Persons, Virtues, Institutions and Communities*, ed. A. Etzioni (London: University Press of Virginia, 1995), 149–50.

that public deliberation in the political life is necessary for the moral development of human beings in private life. Similarly, communitarians have witnessed the moral decline of individuals in liberal societies resulting from the absence of shared values required for public deliberation in a shared community. On the other hand, while communitarians are closer to Aristotle as they advocate a more active and engaged citizenry, the communitarian critique of liberalism is mainly concerned with the ills befalling liberal societies, such as the absence of shared values and norms, a fragmented society sundered by competing private interests, and excessive state encroachment. Hence, communitarians respond to these ills by advocating the empowerment of different communities and voluntary associations in society. In this way, individuals articulate their moral voice and establish social relationships, substituting for the lack thereof in the liberal state.[116] These communities or associations are meant to provide an empowering system for individuals to counteract the authoritarianism of the neutral liberal state.

Communitarianism is criticized for engendering societal oppression by majoritarian communities. Communitarians respond by acknowledging the tension between the "centripetal forces of community and the centrifugal forces of autonomy"[117] and advocate a balance between the two forces to relieve that tension. It occurs to me that communitarian members are torn between the fear of being enveloped by the wishes of the majority in a community and the fear of state nonrecognition and usurpation of their rights. It also strikes me that both the community and the state seem to assume an alien position before the citizen who is constantly trying to evade their dangers. I think that this resulting dilemma is due to the fact that communitarianism came about as a reaction against liberalism rather than as a coherent ideology of its own. *Both theories, liberalism and communitarianism, dismiss the telos of the citizen, the human being, by subjecting him to the conflicts of competing systems whereby he ends up serving those systems rather than being served by them!*

The historical *ummah* of Medina analyzed in chapter 3 illustrates a practical example of not only dealing with comprehensive doctrines but

116. Amitai Etzioni, "Communitarianism," *Encyclopedia of Sociology*, 2nd ed., vol. 1 (New York: Macmillan Reference USA, 2001), 358–59.

117. Amitai Etzioni, "The Attack on Community: The Grooved Debate," *Society* 32, no. 5 (July/August 1995): 13.

also addressing many issues raised by contemporary political theories. Public deliberation, espoused by Aristotle, is not merely a public discussion of problems or undertaken by voluntary associations as communitarians suggest. Public deliberation about mutual rights and obligations of distinct ethnic and religious groups in Medina was reiterated in the form of a legal binding document that ensures the results of that deliberation and secures the rights of all. The direct connection between the public political and private life espoused by MacIntyre and Etzioni was reflected in how the constitution dealt with comprehensive doctrines. The constitution politically endorsed that each *ummah*, the Muslim and the Jewish, practice its own religion and *sharīʿah*, not only as a private belief and ritual but also as a legal tradition. Therefore, the public mirrored the private, and there was no need to endorse a separate allegiance to the political sphere. This practice of public recognition and political endorsing of ethnic and religious differences paved the way for the different groups to reach a consensus about the common good of this diverse *ummah*.

The latter practice resolves a persistent challenge in liberal societies, which is the difference between the requirements of justice and those of citizenship. Justice requires a member to simply not break the law and render legal duties required of him without identifying with the political system, contributing to its welfare or participating politically.[118] The latter requirements represent citizenship requirements, which minorities usually do not enjoy. Hence, they are often designated as a resident alien or "alienated citizen" who "receives whatever protection the state provides and lives everyday with his fellows in the shadow of that protection. But he does not participate at all in political life; *he chooses not to participate. He thinks of the state as an alien* though not necessarily a hostile force, and he wants to live in peace under its jurisdiction."[119] Based on this definition, Andrew March claims that: "A doctrine of resident alienage—political quietism mixed with alienation from the community and its political system—is precisely what political liberalism seeks to avoid through its philosophy

118. Andrew March, "Liberal Citizenship and the Search for an Overlapping Consensus: The Case of Muslim Minorities," *Philosophy and Public Affairs* 34, no. 4 (2006): 382–83.

119. Michael Walzer, *Obligations: Essays on Disobedience, War and Citizenship* (Cambridge, MA: Harvard University Press, 1970), 226–27. Emphasis added.

of public justification."[120] His book *Islam and Liberal Citizenship: The Search for an Overlapping Consensus* is an engaging and thorough work that addresses the problem of resident alienage, specifically for Muslims living in liberal democracies. The book explores Islam's classical tradition to find common reconciliation points between Islamic political ethics, as a comprehensive doctrine, and political liberalism. Thereby, March tries to show how the Islamic tradition provides Muslim citizens with moral reasons to be politically active in liberal societies. He is interested in "residence in a society to which one can *belong*."[121] Following the Rawlsian method, one has to be motivated through his own tradition/comprehensive doctrine to endorse the liberal political conception. While March discusses a real challenge that faces minorities in liberal democracies, and he pins down the root cause of the problem (absence of a sense of belonging), he misses some critical points. First, the term "resident alien" is a title/status given by the liberal state to legal immigrants that changes after naturalization (usually this takes several years). Thus, citizens "do not choose" to be alienated citizens; rather the liberal state "defines" them as alien and imposes limitations on their political activity. After living as resident aliens for a good duration of time, it becomes quite hard to change the inner perception of the person even when he becomes a full citizen. This perception/culture is then passed down to later generations who are born citizens. Therefore, the liberal state needs to change its symbolic terminology and its perception of the people whom it wishes to become its own citizens. The state cannot expect active participation of its minority citizens when it perceives them initially as aliens.

Second, while I applaud March's work on engaging the two traditions (quite needed in today's world), and though he admits that his work may change how we conceive of liberal citizenship, his work is still defined by the liberal perspective, which he nonetheless does not deny. "Liberal political theorists cannot perform exegesis of Islamic texts for Muslim citizens, but they can say that given arguments derived from such exegesis are insufficiently principled from the standpoint of political liberalism . . . and they can suggest . . . what types of formulations *would* be reasonable from a

120. Andrew March, "Liberal Citizenship and the Search for an Overlapping Consensus: The Case of Muslim Minorities," 383.

121. Ibid., 386.

liberal standpoint while preserving the language and fundamental concerns of the comprehensive doctrine."[122] This book engages in exegesis of Islamic texts as well as historical practice to shed light on the Islamic perspective of these pressing concerns. In that regard, this book is complementary to March's work; nonetheless it addresses the concept of diversity in general. If political liberalism were to benefit from the Islamic perspective on dealing with diversity, several points will be raised. Looking at the Medina Constitution, the concept of "minority" based on numerical numbers is not considered an important factor in Islamic political governance. Rather, what is highlighted is the public recognition of diversity through: 1. a public legal document, "the constitution," mentioning diverse ethnic and religious affiliations; 2. coupling law with diverse religious groups (legal pluralism); and 3. assigning duties and obligations to the diverse groups. From the onset, the diverse groups (whether they are a smaller percentage of the whole or not) feel the sense of belonging by being recognized as well as being assigned political roles. In that regard, there is no difference between the requirements of justice and those of citizenship. Having a pluralistic legal system evades the problem of being alienated by the law of the majority that does not cater to one's needs or ideology. Assigning different political roles to the diverse groups triggers the incentive to identify with the political system and contribute to its welfare, hence maintaining stability and security. In the Islamic paradigm, requirements of justice and citizenship are intertwined. Acceptance and public endorsement of difference respect the choices of a human being without imposition or coercion. This foundation creates a peaceful atmosphere for negotiation and makes it easier to reach a "binding legitimate" consensus, rather than an imposed coercive system with its own values.

The case of Copts in modern Egypt's Muslim majority, discussed by Sherman Jackson, provides a practical illustration of the difference between the Islamic and the modern nation-state paradigms. Upon receiving a high number of petitions from divorced Coptic Christians, the Egyptian government issued an order to the Coptic Church to allow the divorcees to remarry by issuing them marriage licenses from the Church. The court in the modern nation-state of Egypt asserted that their order is based on legal provisions equally enforced on all citizens of Egypt. Hence the state

---

122. Ibid., 379–80.

claims its neutrality to the Coptic faith regulations. However, the Coptic Church regarded that by forcing it to issue marriage licenses, the state was challenging the Church religious authority, violating religious freedom and the integrity of the Coptic community. The Church objected to the state order based on biblical law, which confines divorce to specific conditions; otherwise it is forbidden. Besides, the Church did not deny Coptic Christians to seek civil marriage, yet it denied them readmission to the Church in case they chose the civil path, as it is not recognized by the Church.[123] This practical case shows that state neutrality toward the Christian faith, as a comprehensive doctrine, and its attempt to homogenize a legal order on all its citizens forfeited the Christians of their right to implement their faith as they deem right according to the Bible. Hence, as mentioned earlier, the secularization claim that state neutrality toward the common good allows the practical acknowledgement of diverse communities is futile. In order to resolve their dilemma with the state, Pope Shanoudah and Church officials resorted to Islamic *sharīʿah*, which acknowledges religious groups their right to not only practice their faith but also legally implement it in public. Pope Shanoudah stated in a public official newspaper: "We simply ask the judges, if they want to reconcile with the Church, to apply the Islamic *sharīʿah*."[124] The Islamic practice of legal pluralism, evident in the prophetic example in Medina, and later upheld historically before the rise of the modern nation-state, protected human choice and freedom from the monopoly of the majority or a state that enforces its own liberal values (practically legal monism) under the thin disguise of neutrality. Contrary to the liberal claim that a comprehensive doctrine, and its understanding of the common good, should be banned from the political sphere out of fear of imposing its own conception of the good on the different other, the Coptic example in Egypt proves the opposite. Jackson asserts: "Clearly, for the Coptic Church, it was neither Islam nor *sharīʿah* that were calling upon them to forfeit their commitment to their sacred texts and tradition but the basic, homogenizing structure of the modern Egyptian state."[125]

---

123. Sherman Jackson, "Islamic Reform between Law and the Nation-State," in *The Oxford Handbook of Islam and Politics*, ed. John Esposito and Emad El-Din Shahin (Oxford: Oxford University Press, 2013), 46–47.

124. Ibid., 48.

125. Ibid., 47.

Polis and Constitution versus *Ummah* and *al-Kitāb*

While the elements comprising the polis are its citizens, Aristotle does not identify the polis by its constituent elements, but rather by its form and structure. Each citizen is part of the whole, and the polis is, as a unique whole, the most perfect association. The best form for a political community according to Aristotle is one that best helps people realize the ideal life. Aristotle thinks that the true form of government is the kind in which the one, or the few, or the many govern by the common good and not by private interest. However, Aristotle argues that the judgment of the many is better than a single judgment, and the nature of the state is plurality of men, which is tending toward a greater unity, a unity and interdependence of men that will make them self-sufficient. Thus, the best form of political community is the one in which the many administer the state for the common interest, and the generic name of this government is a constitution; "the constitution is in fact the government."[126]

Therefore, Aristotle identifies the polis by its constitution because the polis is a partnership of citizens in a constitution that allows them to be "true" citizens as they participate in its advantages.[127] The polis with constitutional rule is an association of "freemen and equals."[128] Aristotle emphasizes the role of the constitution in defining the polis because he believes that there is no regime, hence no political community, where laws do not rule.[129] Laws rule in a political community in which members, including the legislators and adjudicators, have a disposition to follow rules. It is not a community that merely respects general constitutional rules; rather it is one whose members follow and apply those rules.

On the other hand, Al-Fārābī identifies the virtuous city with the virtuous ruler where his presence leads to the establishment of the virtuous city and its different parts. In addition, the ruler is not elected by the people; instead he is the direct cause of the founding of the members of the city and their acquiring virtuous qualities. The ruler is the main pillar

126. Aristotle, *Politics* (1278b11).

127. Ibid. (1279a 15–1279b 5).

128. Ibid. (1255b 21).

129. Ibid. (1292a32).

that maintains the balance and stability of the city and its different parts.[130] This ruler acts as the teacher and the guide who possesses all knowledge to guide others and is able to allocate to others the duties suitable to them, thereby directing them toward happiness. According to Al-Fārābī, he is either a prophet or a philosopher. The supreme ruler has a fully developed rational faculty and is naturally endowed with the capability to rule and guide others. Thus, the ruler "does not need to be ruled by a human in anything at all."[131] This absolute authority granted by Al-Fārābī, reminiscent of Plato's philosopher king, does not match an association of equal men before law in an Aristotelian polis. Similarly, placing the ruler above the law is neither characteristic of the *ummah* discussed so far nor reflective of the Medinan *ummah* established by Prophet Muhammad. Al-Fārābī's emphasis on the absolute authority of the supreme ruler explains his earlier support of an authoritarian regime that instills virtue in its citizens.

INTRODUCING REFORMS THROUGH THE CONSTITUTION

Introducing new laws in the Medina Constitution required two conditions: first, a predisposition by the members to follow rules, and second, the consent of the involved parties, which was demonstrated through the terminology used, for example, "*approving what is in this document* . . ." in decree 22. In addition, the different decrees that stipulated reciprocity in obligations and rights between its different tribes (16, 25–35, 37, 44–46), reflecting the Qur'ānic concept of a shared *ummah*,[132] also reveal a deliberative process that required consent and consensus by the tribes. Furthermore, it was important that the Prophet introduced changes that are reasonable for all the involved tribes; otherwise the whole project would immediately collapse. Aristotle says:

> One should not consider only what is best, but also what is possible and similarly what is easier and more attainable by

130. Ibrāhīm Al-ʿAtī, *Al-Insān fī Falsafat Al-Fārābī* (Beirut: Dār al-Nubūgh, 1998), 235–36.

131. Al-Farābī, *Kitāb as-Siyāsa al-Madaniyya al-Mulaqqab bi-Mabādiʾ al-Mawjūdāt*, ed. Fawzi al-Najjar (Beirut: Maṭbaʿat Al-Kāthūlīkiya, 1964), 78.

132. Discussed in detail in chapter 2.

> all . . . But what should be done is to introduce the sort of organization that people will be easily persuaded to accept and be able to participate in, given what they already have, as it is no less a task to reform a constitution than to establish one initially, just as it is no less a task to correct what we have learned than to learn it in the first place.[133]

Aristotelian statesmen should not be perfectionist but practical such that they are devoted to implementing political ideals while taking into consideration the prevalent circumstances. Fred Miller describes the Aristotelian statesman as "approximist" and the best constitution as the one that serves as a "regulative ideal" aiming at "reforming the existing system so that it approximates this ideal as closely as is feasible."[134] The Medina Constitution introduced new ideas to the tribal society, which were willingly adopted by diverse parties. While the constitution confirmed some existing norms, it opposed other norms that would harm the common good of the *ummah*. For example, while it was a usual practice for a tribe to make peace or fight another tribe for its own personal interest, the constitution banned such practices without consulting all the involved tribes in the *ummah*. Decree 17 states that peace is one among believers and no person can go to war or make peace while excluding the others; peace should be made among them according to principles of justice and equity. Many other decrees introduced new laws to the tribal society present then (e.g., decrees 13, 15–20, 21).

Examining the content of the MC, the Prophet did not disrupt the tribe as a social unit, but rather organized the *ummah* along tribal lines as it was the only social structure feasible for Arabs at that time. Nevertheless, he modified some tribal practices by introducing new laws. By working with what is available and by introducing sustainable reforms, it is easier to maintain a more just and stable order. Second, the events preceding the establishment of the *ummah* in Medina also show how the Prophet dealt with the existing historical conditions before drafting the

133. Aristotle, *Politics* (1288b37–1289a6).

134. Fred D. Miller Jr., "Aristotelian Statecraft and Modern Politics," in *Aristotle's Politics Today*, ed. Lenn E. Goodman and Robert Talisse (Albany: State University of New York Press, 2007), 18.

ummah's constitution. The first condition, aforementioned, for introducing reform is a predisposed lawful character, which was a characteristic of the inhabitants of Medina and its immigrants. That character was a prerequisite to forming the political community of Medina. The Prophet could not have established the *ummah* in his hometown of Mecca, which was composed of competing tribes who did not follow common laws but depended on aggression and force for their survival. Accordingly, it was no surprise that Mecca staunchly fought against new Islamic principles brought by the Prophet.

Medina was more suitable for establishing the *ummah* for two reasons. First, a good percentage of its population were Jews and Christians, whom the Qur᾿ān refers to as "People of the Book" (*ahl al-kitāb*). As the Qur᾿ānic name implies, Jews and Christians already abide by their books or scriptures; that is, they are already disposed to follow rules. As a result, they were more prepared than the Meccan tribes to either accept the message of Islam or understand its essence in order to participate in the making of the *ummah*. Historically, this is precisely what happened, as some of the inhabitants of Medina were convinced with the Islamic message and endorsed it (those were included as believers in the first half of the MC) and others kept their own religion but welcomed the establishment of a constitution that would grant them equal rights and means to resolve their conflicts with other tribes (those were the Jews mentioned in the second half of the MC). Second, concerning the Muslim immigrants from Mecca who were not followers of earlier scriptures, they were educated by the Prophet for thirteen years prior to immigration.

During that initial period of thirteen years, the Qur᾿ān was being revealed to the Prophet and his followers and addressing their intellect and shaping their worldview. The guidance during that period was addressing them as individuals, not as an *ummah* with common laws. It was a kind of contemplative guidance focusing on the moral education of individuals. That initial period was necessary as a preparation phase for Muslims to be able to participate in the formation of the political community in Medina. From an Aristotelian perspective, the immigrant Muslims had to be predisposed to law to form a political community. ʿAbduh and Riḍa also addressed the need for this preparation phase, which is depicted in the Qur᾿ānic verse (2:213) and discussed in chapter 2. The verse illustrated that God sends prophets with basic teachings about life and justice as a preparation stage before sending laws and regulations (*sharīʿah*). ʿAbduh and Riḍa argued that people have to be educated and mentally prepared before accepting laws and implementing them.

In the historical case of Medina, after immigration and the formation of the *ummah* and its constitution, the Qur'ānic teachings began addressing an *ummah* and subsequently established the Islamic rules of *sharī'ah* dealing with public law, legislation, punishment, and so forth needed for the thriving of individuals as an *ummah*. The Qur'ānic teachings that were revealed over a period of twenty-three years (thirteen years before immigration and ten afterward) were constantly dealing with the education and moral development of the people, initially as distinct individuals and later as members of one *ummah*. Nonetheless, that the establishment of the *ummah* and the institution of public legislation happened in the later stage of the prophetic mission confirms Aristotle's idea that the political community is needed for the moral perfection of the human being and the full development of his faculties. Meanwhile, it also confirms the Qur'ānic message, previously discussed, which states that the human's full potential is attained through performing his duties as a *khalīfa*.

The Characters of Constitution and the Citizen Mirror Each Other

Moreover, the subsequent change in the Qur'ānic teachings following the formation of the *ummah* reveals the critical need for continuous education succeeding the formation of the constitution for the advancement of human beings and the preservation of their community. In that regard, Aristotle says:

> No one will doubt that the legislator should direct his attention above all to the education of youth; for neglect of education does harm the constitution. The citizen should be molded to suit the form of government under which he lives. For each government has a peculiar character which originally formed and which continues to preserve it. The character of democracy creates democracy, and the character of oligarchy creates oligarchy; and always the better the character, the better the government.[135]

135. Aristotle, *Politics* (1337a10–16).

There is an inherent correlation between the character of the individual and the character of the government he or she lives in. This strong relationship is realized by Aristotle, who regards the polis as a means to pursue the human good, a state that cannot be achieved in isolation but only through public deliberation with a community committed to the common good. Similarly, *the Qurʾān links human development to public action within the ummah; personal good is simultaneously achieved in the act of fostering public good.* Ultimately, the human being not only shapes the character of his or her government but also, in return, is shaped by it. It is a reciprocal relationship, as Aristotle clarified in the abovementioned quote.

If we try to analyze the relationship between the citizen and the modern liberal state, we find an incongruous relationship. The liberal state claims to allow its citizens to pursue individual ends whereby its *telos* is to prevent any obstacles from hindering the achievement of their aims. However, the liberal state claims neutrality toward a "common good," so individuals pursue their ends without connecting or associating with others for the public good. Essentially, that relationship represents "the supreme irony of the liberal state: individuals are free to do nearly everything, but only because nothing any of them could do is deemed really to matter. It is just because everyone's choices are personal choices that no choice has real significance."[136] If an individual has to preserve the liberal state because it allows him to pursue his aims, while the state is indifferent to his aims, he ends up pursuing two contradicting objectives. "While striving for my ends, I must also strive to preserve a system where those ends do not matter."[137] This is why MacIntyre sees that moral and political cultures are in a state of confusion. The moral views of society members are essentially incommensurable. There is no common framework to justify one position against another; hence there is no rational means to reach a widely agreed consensus to serious questions affecting the society as a whole.[138]

In Aristotle's words, the character of indifference creates indifference. Nietzsche recognized that on a personal level, dissatisfaction in modern societies is a result of conflicting trajectories in one's life, for how could

136. Edward Halper, "Aristotle and the Liberal State," in *Aristotle's Politics Today*, ed. Lenn E. Goodman and Robert Talisse (Albany: State University of New York Press, 2007), 39.

137. Ibid., 40.

138. Stephen Mulhall and Adam Swift, *Liberals and Communitarians*, 71–72.

an individual pursue his aim knowing that it is merely his aim (not a collective's), that it does not hinder others to act, and at the same time it has no significance on a larger scale?[139] Accordingly, the problem of a state neutral to the common good is precisely the absence of what Aristotle argues to be the main *telos* of a polis: human good and perfection. While the liberal state claims to be helping human beings pursue their aims, it is indirectly working against them by alienating them from fulfilling their goals. The absence of a common good and its being replaced by individual competing interests means the absence of a public deliberation about conceptions of justice. Hence the liberal state does not satisfy the requirements of a political community specifically because of its claim to neutrality concerning the common good.

The character of the *ummah* of Medina was reflected in its constitution. The society of Medina was a mixed society described as "*akhlāṭ*" by Wāqidī.[140] The Medina Constitution reflected the social and religious makeup of its inhabitants as discussed thoroughly in the previous chapter. A mixed constitution is more just and stable if it combines features representing different political values.[141] This is demonstrated in the MC allowing each religious group to be judged according to its own *dīn* (law) in internal matters pertaining to their respective *ummah* while not affecting the comprehensive constitutional *ummah*. For example, decrees 3–11 address the Muslim *ummah* to ransom their war prisoners according to "*maʿrūf* and justice between believers" whereas the equivalent decrees addressing the Jews (25–34) do not mention the same criteria for dealing with war prisoners but left it to their discretion by saying "the Jews having their own *dīn*." Because each religious group will have its own conception of justice based on its revealed book, the constitution allowed each group to deal with its internal affairs based on its own conception of justice. However, in matters dealing with the whole constitutional *ummah* comprising both groups, the constitution clearly specified their mutual

139. Friedrich Nietzsche, *Beyond Good and Evil: Prelude to a Philosophy of the Future*, trans. R. J. Hollingdale (Harmondsworth, United Kingdom: Penguin, 1974), 166.

140. Muhammad b. ʿUmar al-Wāqidī, *Kitāb al-Maghāzī*, ed. Marseden Jones (London: Oxford University Press, 1966), vol. 1, 184.

141. Fred D. Miller Jr., "Aristotelian Statecraft and Modern Politics," in *Aristotle's Politics Today*, 30.

obligation and rights. In that case, the MC reflected a high level of reciprocity between both communities, as evident in decrees 12, 13, 15, 17, 22, 23, 37, 39, 44, and 45.

Aristotle says, "The salvation of the community is the common business of them all. This community is the constitution; the excellence of the citizen must therefore be relative to the constitution of which he is a member."[142] Hence, when the constitution specified both communities' rights and obligations toward each other, it assigned them (its different members or citizens) the responsibility of caring for and sustaining their common *ummah* and held them accountable for its success or failure. Therefore, the success of the *ummah* is not based on the genius of a specific political theory or a specific coercive state apparatus. Rather, the success of the *ummah* is based on the success of every single member comprising it, in other words, according to every member fulfilling his or her role as a *khalīfa*.

CONSTITUTIONAL LAW TRANSFORMED INTO COMMUNITY NORM

Law, according to Aristotle, does not merely represent constitutional and statutory rules but also customary and conventional norms. By means of law, members of a polis develop and impose standards of mutual obligation toward each other.[143] *Nomos* is a general term Aristotle uses to describe the way a community behaves and the general rules it follows. *Nomoi* are "legislated or customary, written or unwritten, sanctioned or unsanctioned, enforced by shame or punishment."[144] What makes law important for Aristotle is not its adjudicative ideal but its ability to shape people's moral dispositions through habituation, which represents the *telos* of the polis. For that reason, Aristotle considers unwritten laws more supreme than written laws, for they deal with the most important goal, the moral education of individuals. The common unwritten laws (*koinon*) are more familiar to the individual than written laws and thereby more easily shape human behavior and develop general norms.[145]

---

142. Aristotle, *Politics* (1276b 29–32).

143. Bernard Yack, *The Problems of a Political Animal*, 198–200.

144. Ibid., 179.

145. Ibid., 180–81.

Chapter 1 showed that the covenantal "book" defines the *ummah*. This was confirmed through analyzing the Medina Constitution in chapter 3, where the constitution defined the *ummah* of Medina to be a pluralistic *ummah* and stipulated the reciprocal rules governing the tribes' interaction with each other. Madigan's analysis of the term "book" in the Qur'ān showed that it does not represent a codified set of rules but has a dynamic and engaging role of continuous guidance. Madigan supports his argument with the historical fact that the Qur'ān, as a book, descended over a period of twenty-three years in the form of teachings that were continuously engaging with the needs of the believers and their virtuous development. Thus, Muslims did not regard the book as a fixed set of regulations but rather as a source of continuous guidance. Madigan's analysis can help us understand the nature of law from a Qur'ānic perspective; guidance is the emphasis rather than strict obedience to rules. Likewise, Aristotle does not regard the tenets of law to be an end unto themselves but a means to a higher end that is to mold the moral character of human beings.

Looking at the decrees of the MC, we find an interplay between written rules and established norms. *Maʿrūf* would be the Qur'ānic equivalent of *Nomoi* described earlier. For example, decrees 3–11 all end with the statement "according to *maʿrūf* and justice among the believers." The decrees do not specify what is meant by *maʿrūf* in ransoming the war prisoners, but nonetheless it is clear that the term refers to a common practice that is known to the involved tribes. Similarly, decree 25 mentions that each group (Muslims and Jews) follows its own *dīn* (religion/law) but it doesn't articulate the tenets of those religions or laws. Thus, the decrees of the constitution refer to both written laws governing the interaction between the *ummah* members, and unwritten laws representing the common practice or norms that are specific to a religious group or a particular situation.

The constitution empowered the political community to enforce its norms as shown in decrees 13, 21, and 44. By allowing the citizens to act publicly against injustices and specifying practical implementations for enjoining *maʿrūf* and deterring *munkar*, the constitution enables citizens to assume greater responsibility and self-sufficiency. In return, this will lead to a more stable society whereby maintaining order is not merely the responsibility of the central power or a specific state apparatus but the responsibility of every citizen constituting the *ummah*.

The *ummah* preserved its norms not only though the medium of law, the constitution, but also by publicly implementing the law (the norms/convention). Here, we find a practical case whereby written law is transformed into a public common practice, in other words a community "norm" through people's practice. That is exceptionally relevant to situations where reform is introduced and new institutions are to be established. Aristotle warned of the dangers associated with political change, as it weakens established institutions and threatens habits of obedience. In Medina, major changes were introduced by Prophet Muhammad against prevalent tribal practices. The introduction of new ethics pertaining to all human beings irrespective of race, religion, or kinship was destabilizing to the norms and social order of the tribal society at that time. People had to prioritize their commitment to the common good of all above other personal loyalties, obviously a difficult endeavor. In order to accomplish that, newly introduced laws were publicly implemented through *citizens, endorsing and supportive of these laws, who activated them.* Such reflects the role of education, which represents the starting phase and is completed by public implementation. *In that sense, the ummah becomes the means by which sharīʿah (legislation) is transformed into maʿrūf and munkar (community norm).*

Similarly, Wael Hallaq contends that neither the Islamic state nor the ruler legislate *sharīʿah* rules in premodern Muslim societies. Rather, "the community, the common social world, *organically* produced its own legal experts, persons who were qualified to fulfill a variety of legal functions that, in totality, made up the Islamic legal system."[146] He adds that there was no difference between the "social order" and the "legal order" because *sharīʿah* values were embodied in the moral fabric of society. "It *lived* legal ethics and legal morality, for these constituted the religious foundations and the codes of social praxis."[147] Hence, there was no need for professional mediation between the people and the law, that is, the lawyers. People knew the law because it was a living tradition. There was a mutual sustainable relationship between legal norms and social morality. This model stands opposite to the modern legal system, which alienates society by making the legal system a "profession" known only to a few elite who master and manipulate it.[148]

146. Hallaq, *The Impossible State*, 52.

147. Ibid., 55–56.

148. For a detailed comparison between the Islamic and modern legislative system, see Hallaq, "Separation of Powers: Rule of Law or Rule of the State?," in *The Impossible State*, 37–73.

Alexander Orwin claims that Al-Farabi does not answer the question "Do convention and *sharīʿah* cohere as firmly as nature?"[149] However, al-Farabi realizes that the governor of the *ummah* and the first ruler need the help of convention to fulfill their goals.[150] This unclear position of al-Farabi seems to be influenced by Greek philosophy. For Aristotle, the polis is a provider of laws as well as a provider of educators who train citizens to exercise those laws in public. The citizens assume the role of implementing the rules given to them by the political elite and the educators. However, the *ummah* does not provide laws/*sharīʿah*; neither do the legal experts or the rulers. Rather, the *ummah* embodies *sharīʿah* by actively and publicly engaging in enjoining *maʿrūf* and deterring *munkar*. The legal experts, organically produced by the *ummah*, as Hallaq explained, interpret *sharīʿah*, and the rulers ensure its implementation. In this system, there is no place for a "first ruler" in the sense of an authority that legislates as well as ensures order and implementation. The ruler's role in an *ummah* is limited to the executive realm. Figure 4.1 clarifies how the different parts of an *ummah* interact with and relate to each other. The following sections explain the relationship between the different entities constituting an *Ummah*.

Polis and Justice versus *Ummah* and *Wasaṭiyyah*

Justice as a "Mean" and the Concept of "*Wasaṭ*"

While Aristotle defines the polis by its constitution, he identifies the chief virtue of the polis to be justice. The polis is instrumental for the moral education and training of individuals to be just. Justice, according to Aristotle, is similar to other moral virtues that require education and continuous training to be acquired.[151] Moral training in the polis makes individuals "disposed to act justly." Justice is a virtue manifested in "lawfulness" and "fairness": "The just, then, is the lawful and the equal, the unjust

149. Alexander Orwin, *Redefining the Muslim Community: Ethnicity, Religion and Politics in the Thought of Alfarabi,* 118.

150. Ibid., 119.

151. Aristotle, *NE* (1103b).

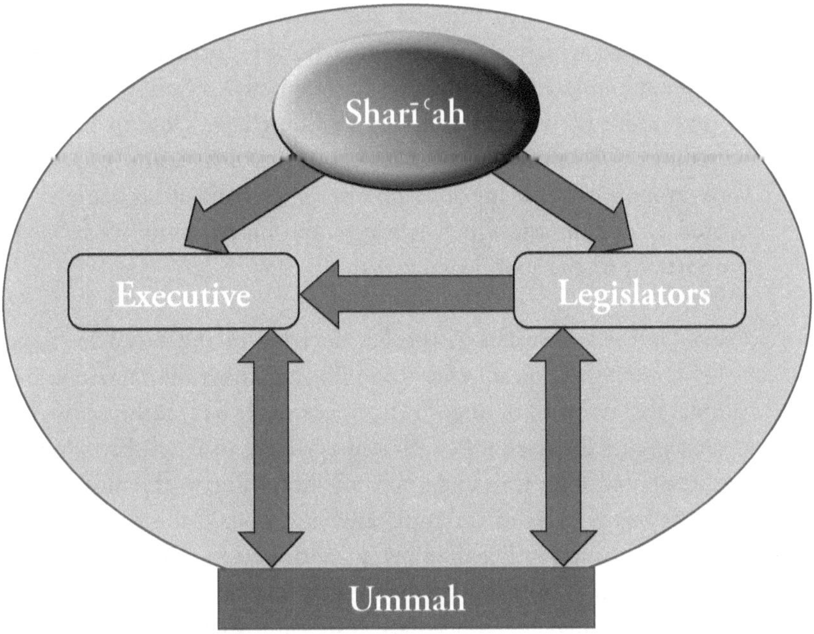

Figure 4.1. Different parts of an *Ummah*.

The one-headed arrow indicates a one-way influence, while the double-headed arrow indicates a mutual influence/relationship. The act of enjoining *maʿrūf* and deterring *munkar* is mutually undertaken and represented by the double-headed arrows.

the unlawful and the unequal."[152] Equality is the basis of law because law is natural only among equal freemen who take turns in ruling and being ruled. Fairness is a proportionate reciprocity between individuals sharing a community.[153] Aristotle characterizes this reciprocity as a tendency toward achieving equilibrium, or "hitting a mean." Each virtue for Aristotle is found in the mean.

> Justice is a kind of ***mean***, but not in the same ways as the other excellences, but because it relates to an intermediate amount, while injustice relates to the extremes. And justice

152. Ibid. (1129a1–2).

153. Susan D. Collins, *Aristotle and the Rediscovery of Citizenship* (Cambridge: Cambridge University Press, 2009), 74.

> is that virtue of which the just man is said to be a doer, by choice, of that which is just, and one who will distribute either between himself and another or between two others not as to give more of what is desirable to himself and less to his neighbor . . . , but so as to give what is equal in accordance with proportion. . . . Injustice on the other hand is similarly related to the unjust, which is excess and defect, contrary to proportion, of the useful or hurtful.[154]

Paula Gottlieb identifies Aristotle's doctrine of the mean by three aspects. First, hitting the mean reflects equilibrium rather than moderation. For example, the emotion of anger is not necessarily bad; rather Aristotle thinks one is poorly disposed if he feels anger fiercely and foolishly, whereas one is well disposed if he feels anger meanly (according to the mean). The latter suggests being angry at the right moment, toward the right people, and in the right manner rather than being continuously, moderately angry. The virtuous person is properly balanced such that he will react correctly to any situation, similar to an accurate scale that reacts correctly to any weight placed on it. Thus, one becomes virtuous by avoiding the extremes to reach equilibrium, which is self-sustaining.

Virtue is analogous to health where both excess and deficiency in food and drink would ruin one's health, but a balanced quantity would not only make a person healthy but also preserve his health. The second aspect of the mean doctrine is its being "relative to us." Considering the health example, the proportionate amount of food and drink to keep one's health is different for a professional athlete and a non-athlete. However, it is not always simple, and sometimes other factors are at stake. After surveying different opinions concerning relativity, Gottlieb concludes that ethical decisions are affected by circumstances of the agent, as well as conditions of others partaken in the agent's actions. Thus the mean is "relative to us as human beings" and "relative to the agent." The third aspect of his doctrine is that each virtue is a mean between two vices: one related to excess and the other to deficiency.[155] Aristotle says, "the people at the extremes push out the intermediate person, and the coward calls the brave

154. Aristotle, *NE* (1133b32–1134a8). Emphasis added.

155. Paula Gottlieb, *The Virtue of Aristotle's Ethics* (Cambridge: Cambridge University Press, 2009), 19–36.

person rash and the rash calls him a coward, and analogously with the rest."[156] Al-Farabi also argues that sound political judgment depends on finding the mean, which he thinks is not fixed but shifts based on external variables such as the size and character of the community.[157]

Man is perfected when he is equipped with justice and law, and he becomes the worst of animals when separated from law "since armed injustice is the more dangerous, and he is equipped at birth with arms, meant to be used by intelligence and excellence, which he may use for the worst ends. That is why, if he has not excellence, he is the most unholy and the most savage of animals and the most full of lust and gluttony."[158] Aristotle's statement recalls the angels' description of the negative side of human beings in the Qurʾān (shedding blood and causing corruption). The administration of justice is the principle of order in the polis and is essential for enabling the human beings to lead the best life and secure their happiness. Similarly, the Qurʾān intended for the human being to be *khalīfa* by implementing justice on earth, as stated in the previously discussed verse: "O David, we have appointed you a *khalīfa* on earth, so judge between people by the Truth (justice, Ar. *ḥaqq*)" (Qurʾān 38:26).

I think that the Aristotelian concept of the mean resembles the Qurʾānic term "*wasaṭ*" discussed in chapter 2. The previously discussed Qurʾānic interpretations related the characteristic *wasaṭ*, meaning the middle or balanced position between extremes, to justice (*ʿadl*) and the quality of being best (*al-khiyār*) in describing the *ummah*. ʿAbduh attributed perfection of human beings, in an *ummah wasaṭ*, to realizing a balanced position whereby rights are granted to each owner. Such a perfect human fulfills his duties toward God, toward himself, toward his physical body, and toward all human beings.

Faḍlallah interpreted *ummah wasaṭ* in terms of communal organization. As Islamic thought balances between spirit and matter, the *ummah wasaṭ* balances two extreme positions (in Aristotle's terms, it hits the mean between two vices). The first extreme in communal organization is represented by a communion whereby individual rights are underestimated at the

156. Aristotle, *EN* (1108b 23–26).

157. Alexander Orwin, *Redefining the Muslim Community: Ethnicity, Religion and Politics in the Thought of Alfarabi*, 155.

158. Aristotle, *Politics* (1253a 33–37).

expense of a majority's, whereas the second extreme position is represented by extreme individualism in which individuals' rights are emphasized at the expense of a common good in a liberal society. Faḍlallah continues that when the *ummah* achieves that balanced position, *wasaṭ*, it becomes the reference point for others, and it thereby becomes the witness to other nations.

Faḍlallah here is trying to find a connection in the Qur'ānic correlation between the *ummah* being *wasaṭ* and a witness to people. The Qur'ān (2:142–43)[159] makes an analogy between making the *ummah wasaṭ* a witness before humankind and the Prophet a witness to the *ummah*. Faḍlallah says the Prophet would be the witness to the *ummah* because he represents the most balanced and perfect model of that *ummah*; likewise the *ummah wasaṭ* is a witness before humankind because it represents the most balanced and perfect model of a community. Aristotle can actually help us better interpret the correlation between the *ummah* achieving the *wasaṭ* position and its being assigned the status of a "witness" before humankind.

As discussed earlier in this section, Aristotle argued that justice is a virtue and the virtuous person is correctly balanced such that he will react properly (in the right manner and time to the right people, etc.) to any situation facing him. People who have achieved the mean avoid extremes and are self-sustaining. Truthful witness necessitates a virtuous and balanced character. Hence, achieving that balance and virtue through the *wasaṭ* was a prerequisite for the *ummah* to be a witness before humankind. Nevertheless, if the *ummah wasaṭ* is self-sustaining and self-sufficient because of its balanced, virtuous character, it remains open and communicative with other people to serve as a witness. For the *ummah* to keep its balance and cancel out the extreme vices, it has to have a focal, reference point—which the Qur'ān determines to be the *qibla* of Prophet Ibrahim. A reorientation toward Prophet Ibrahim's life and character was discussed thoroughly in chapter 2.

Aristotle considers justice to be the "greatest of excellences" because the one who possesses it exercises excellence not only internally, but also toward others, which is not an easy task. Justice is related to others, as its execution entails what is beneficial to the other, whether a ruler or a

---

159. The Qur'anic verse is discussed in chapter 2: ". . . And likewise we have made you a *wasaṭ ummah*, so that you may bear witness [to the truth] before humankind and so that the messenger may bear witness [to it] before you . . ."

partner. Aristotle affirms a saying, "rule will show the man," because only through ruling and thereby dealing with other society members will one's character reveal itself.[160] Therefore, Aristotle argues that the polis allows for the development of either virtue or vice in a human being.[161] In the Qur'ān, a human being is rendered a *khalīfa* on earth because only through acquiring that status would a human's potential be realized. In order to become a *khalīfa,* a person needs to assume responsibility with respect to others, whether it is political power or any kind of power exercised within society.

Understanding "Prophet Abraham Was an *Ummah*" through Aristotle's "Unity of Virtues"

The Aristotelian "unity of virtues" theory can help us understand the Qur'ānic description of Prophet Abraham (discussed in chapter 2) as an *ummah.*[162] At-Ṭabarī interpreted the relevant verse that Prophet Abraham was an *Imām* who taught people virtue. Ibn Kathīr added that the verse describes the person who diverted from polytheism to pure unity (*tawḥīd*).[163] Al-Qurṭubī regarded Prophet Abraham to be the human model uniting all virtues (*jāmi'an li-khiṣāl al-khayr*).[164] Prophet Abraham resembles the Aristotelian man who is of perfect integrity, has all the virtues or complete virtue, such that he does not need the presence of other individuals to understand the whole. In Aristotelian terms, he is self-sufficient and consequently the best. However, from the Qur'ānic perspective, Prophet Abraham is described as an *ummah* specifically because of

160. Aristotle, *NE* (1129b28–1130a5).

161. Paula Gottlieb, *The Virtue of Aristotle's Ethics*, 194.

162. "Verily, Ibrāhīm was an *ummah* devoutly obeying God's will, *ḥanīfan* and not being of those who ascribe divinity to others beside God. [For he was always] grateful for the bounties of God who selected him and guided him to a straight path" (Qur'ān 16:120–21).

163. Ibn Kathīr ad-Dimashqī, *Tafsīr al-Qur'ān al-'Aẓīm* (Beirut: Dār al-Fikr, 1997), vol. 2, 615.

164. Al-Qurṭubī, *Mukhtaṣar Tafsīr al-Qurṭubī* (Beirut: Dār al-Kitāb al-'Arabī, 1987), vol. 3, 104.

devoutly following God's will. Self-sufficiency, according to the Qur᾽ān, cannot be realized based on one's self solely. Humans are in constant need for divine guidance; the human being is a *khalīfa*, that is, he represents Godly attributes. So the ideal human being from a Qur᾽ānic perspective is not the one who sees himself as completely independent but the one who gains self-sufficiency (from people) through constantly seeking guidance from God. In that regard, people achieve freedom from being needy before others and those who possess powerful positions in society through absolute and complete dependency on the sustainer and ultimate provider (God). In the Qur᾽ān, self-sufficiency with regard to creation is "only" achieved through complete dependency on the source of everything (God), in other words *tawḥīd*.

While other human beings need the presence of a deliberating *ummah* to attain the best judgment, Prophet Abraham achieved that status through his sincere devotion to God and complete dependency on Him: "verily, Abraham was an *ummah* devoutly obeying God's will, *ḥanīfan* and not being of those who ascribe divinity to others beside Allah." Because humans are not infallible like prophets and are more prone to error, they need each other's minds to come closer to a just status. Hence, what the prophet could achieve solely would be achieved collectively by the *ummah*. Prophet Abraham was described as an *ummah* and his creed as the best: "And who could be of better religion than he who surrenders his whole being to Allah and is a good-doer, and follows the creed of Abraham who turned away from all that is false (*ʿittabaʿa millata Abraham ḥanīfan*)—seeing that Allah took Abraham as an intimate friend" (Qur᾽ān 4:125). The Muslim *ummah* is asked to follow the creed of Abraham and take him as a model whereby the *ummah* members can hit the mean (*wasaṭ*) and as a result attain complete virtue (*khayr*). This may explain why the Qur᾽ānic term *wasaṭ* associates the Muslim *ummah* with the *qibla* of Abraham.

Ummah Attains Justice through *Shūra* (Collective Judgment of *Khulafāʿ*)

The *ummah* is encouraged to conduct its affairs through *shūra* because together they are closer to the truth, as the *ḥadīth* shows: "Allah does not unite my *ummah* upon error and the hand of Allah is with the assembly (*᾽inna Allāh lā yajmaʿ ᾽ummahtī ʿala ḍalāla wa-yadu Allāh ʿala* *al-jamāʿa . . .*)."[165] Similarly, Aristotle argues that the judgment of many individuals is better than the judgment of a single person. When different individuals assemble to figure out a solution for a common concern, the extreme opinions are balanced out and they are closer to approaching a just resolution (in Aristotelian words, hit the mean; in Qurʾānic terms, *wasaṭ*). The process through which this equilibrium is achieved is referred to in the Qurʾān as *shūra* (translated as mutual or reciprocal consultation).

The concept shows in the Qurʾānic verse: "and those who answer the call of their Lord, and establish regular prayer, and who (conduct) their affairs by *shūra*, and who spend of what We have bestowed on them" (Qurʾān 42:38). At-Ṭabarī reports a saying that restricts the practice of *shūra* to the *ummah* in the case that the Prophet is not present among them.[166] Faḍlallah argues that *shūra* is a practical means by which people mutually consult each other to reach the truth when evaluating different matters in life. He continues that a ruler should not oppress his people with his own opinion; rather he should consult wise and experienced people to reach a decision in order to reduce the error associated with deciding solely. Thus, *shūra* represents the Islamic basis upon which Muslims are to conduct their affairs.[167] Faḍlallah refers to a saying by *Imām* Ali that says: "He who has a despotic opinion will perish and he who consults men shares with them their minds (*man ʾistbadda bi-raʾyihi halaka wa-man shāwara al-rijāl shārakahā fi ʿuqūlihā*)."[168]

165. At-Tirmithī, *Sunan at-Tirmithī* (*Al-Jāmiʿ as-Ṣaḥīḥ*), *Kitāb al-Fitan, Bāb: Mā jāʾa fi luzūm al-jamāʿa*, 2167 (Beirut: Dār al-Kitāb al-ʿArabī, 2005), 620. It is worth noting that many scholars did not associate this *ḥadīth* with the concept of a "majority" (as a numerical percentage) being closer to the truth compared to a minority. The latter opinion is based on many verses in the Qurʾān that condemn the majority, for example, "And most of humankind will not believe even if you desire it eagerly" (Qurʾān 12:103), "And if you obey most of those in the earth, they will lead you astray from Allah's way; they follow nothing but conjecture and they are not but falsifying" (Qurʾān 6:116).

166. At-Ṭabarī, *Jāmiʿ al-Bayān*, V.13, 48.

167. Faḍlallah, *Min Waḥy al-Qurʾān*, vol. 20, 191–92.

168. Ali Bin Abī Ṭālib, *Nahju-l-Balāgha*, Sermon 161, ed. Muhammad ʿAbduh (Beirut: Muʾassasat al-ʾAʿlamī lil-Maṭbūʿāt, 2003), 500.

Shams ad-Dīn argues that the latter verse not only describes characteristics of believers but also proposes a legal order to organize believers' lives as an *ummah*. However, the fact that *shūra* is presented with worshipping rituals such as establishing prayers and giving charity indicates that it is equivalent to worship. Similar to the fact that establishing prayer is an obligation, establishing a sociopolitical order based on *shūra* is a parallel obligation for the *ummah*. Thus, the *ummah* has to establish *shūra* or it will forfeit its faith—the exact result as giving up prayers, charity, or not answering the call of their lord.[169] Shams ad-Dīn argues that the *ummah* should elect its leader by means of *shūra*. In return, the leader is also addressed in the Qur'ān to practice *shūra* with his people as shown in the verse ". . . And consult them in all matters of public concern (*shāwirhum fil-'amr*) . . ." (Qur'ān 3:159). Therefore, a reciprocal relationship of consultation and deliberation is a means of interaction not only between members of an *ummah* but also between the members and their leader. The latter implies that the leader is on equal footing as the rest of the *ummah* and is not above the law as the Farabian supreme ruler. The preceding verse was revealed in the context of a battle[170] in which the Prophet (as the leader) was directed to conduct *shūra* before making a decision that would affect the *ummah* as a whole. Despite the fact that the decision (reached after mutual consultation between the *ummah* and

---

169. The same idea is discussed by Muhammad Shaḥrūr, who adds that rejecting *shūra* is similar to rejecting prayers and *zakāt*; hence *shūra* forms part of a Muslim's creed and religious behavior (*ʿibādāt*) in Moḥammad Shaḥrūr, *Dirāsāt Islāmiyya Muʿāṣira fi al-Dawla wal-Mujtamaʿ* (Damascus: Al-Ahālī lil-Ṭibāʿa wal-Nashr wal-Tawzīʿ, 1994), 150.

170. This verse was revealed after the battle of Uḥud, where Muslims were defeated despite the consultation process that occurred between the prophet and his companions before the battle. The prophet and a few companions had the opinion of conducting the battle inside Medina, while the majority of the companions wanted to fight outside the borders of Medina. The latter opinion was endorsed as a result of *shūra*. The Muslims ended up being defeated in the battle. The defeat was not a result of conducting *shūra*, but because certain Muslims disobeyed one of their leader's orders during the battle. A group abandoned their post as they rushed to collect booty; thereby they focused on their private gain and ignored the common good of the *ummah*, which consequently led to the defeat of the Muslims. Nevertheless, the revelation that descended after the Muslims' defeat ordered the prophet to still consult them in their affairs.

their leader) was ignored during the battle and led to the Muslims' defeat, the Qur'ānic injunction still ordered the Prophet to consult the *ummah*:

> And it was by Allah's mercy that you [Prophet] were lenient with them (the believers), for if you had been harsh and hard of heart, they would have indeed broken away from you. So pardon them, and pray that they be forgiven and consult them in all matters of public concern (*shāwirhum fil-'amr*); then, when you had decided upon a course of action, put your trust in Allah: for, verily, Allah loves those who trust in Him. (Qur'ān 3:159)

Thus, this was established as a sociopolitical order for both the *ummah* and its leader whereby a reciprocal relationship was to be sustained. *Shūra* became the constitutional principle upon which the *ummah* was and is to conduct its public affairs. Shams ad-Dīn contends that this was a new norm that went against the prevalent political practice of tyranny and authoritarianism, practices in which the community's opinion had no value. Political power had been wielded by elite tribes or families who conducted public affairs based on their private interest without involving the *ummah* in public matters. Shams ad-Dīn indicates that *shūra* is conducted within the limits of *sharī'ah,* so the consultation process would not result in a decision that contradicts an established legal order in *sharī'ah*. Other than that, all matters related to society and governance are liable to consultation, and the resulting decisions are binding.[171]

At-Ṭabarī says that the Prophet had no need for his people's consultation; however, God wanted him to be a representative model to the Muslims, teaching them how a leader should deal with his *ummah*. He adds that when people consult each other while aiming for truth, God will guide them and make them successful as their hearts and desires unite toward righteousness.[172] 'Abduh considers *shūra* to be the basis for the *ummah*'s governance in circumstances of peace and war, and he also thinks that the *ummah* (as a collaboration of different individuals) is less susceptible to error than the sole individual. Nonetheless, he argues that *shūra* should be conducted for worldly affairs and not for basic religious ethics

171. Muhammad Mahdī Shams ad-Dīn, *Fil-Ijtimā' as-Siyāsī al-Islāmī*, 108–9.

172. At-Ṭabarī, *Jāmi' al-Bayān*, vol. 3, 203–4.

(such as beliefs, rituals, or what is allowed and prohibited).[173] Faḍlallah also agrees with ʿAbduh as he differentiates between what was a divine order (*taklīf ʾilāhī sharʿī*) and the Prophet's personal opinion (related to his humanness rather than to his being a prophet). In the domain of the latter, the *ummah* can practice *shūra* but not in the former. Accordingly, Faḍlallah says that the practice of *shūra* in the above verse addresses the relationship between a leader and his *ummah* rather than the relationship between a prophet and his people, hence agreeing with at-Ṭabarī.

The positions of Shams ad-Din, ʿAbduh, and Faḍlallah concerning the limits of *shūra*, that people cannot practice *shūra* in matters already defined by *sharīʿah*, resonate with Aristotle's earlier argument that people are not supposed to deliberate about legislative matters that are determined by the law. Aristotle also limited deliberation to matters about which the law is silent. Aristotle's rationale for defining a limit to deliberation was that law (defined by the constitution) should filter out the vices resulting from deliberation, and hence keep it within the right discourse. I think that in both cases, Aristotelian and Qurʾānic, law or *sharīʿah* provides the foundation upon which people deliberate and provides a focal point for unity in case of excessive conflict. "The constitution provides the basic framework and the law regulates the practice within this framework."[174] Constitutional law or *sharīʿah*[175] provides the basic guidelines for a specific community, while the details are left to the discretion of the people, based on the circumstances of time and place. In other words, there must be

173. Muhammad ʿAbduh and Muhammad Rashīd Riḍā, *Tafsīr al-Manār*, vol. 4, 198–200.

174. Moḥammad Shaḥrūr, *Dirāsāt Islāmiyya Muʿāṣira fi al-Dawla wal-Mujtamaʿ* (Damascus: Al-Ahālī lil-Ṭibāʿa wal-Nashr wal-Tawzīʿ, 1994), 142.

175. The common view is that constitutional law and *sharīʿah* are incompatible. However, the historical example of the Medina Constitution shows that a pluralistic constitution can be established based on *sharīʿah* and ethical principles without obligating non-Muslims to adhere to laws that are specific to Muslims. *Sharīʿah* could be divided into general ethical principles (upon which a common constitution could be drafted) and laws that are aimed at organizing a Muslim society (such as penal laws, laws of inheritance, etc.). Any constitution requires a set of ethical principles as a foundation for its drafting. In that specific regard, *sharīʿah* and constitutional law are similar.

common ground from which people can begin the deliberation process in the first place; otherwise deliberation is futile.

Faḍlallah thinks that the practice of *shūra* has two training goals: first on the individual level by training individuals to consult and discuss with others in order to analyze the different options before making a critical decision in one's life (following that consultation process, an individual would carry on with the reached decision more firmly and effectively); second is the collective level by training the *ummah* to think with its leadership about its plans and goals as well as about the means to achieving those goals. Thereby, the *ummah* can engage with its leader's decisions from the outset in order to monitor its leadership and guard it from deviation or betrayal. Thus, the *ummah* becomes capable of replacing those in power when the need arises. At the same time, an *ummah* that "thinks" and is involved in its leadership decisions is an *ummah* that follows and obeys its leadership due to conviction. This differs from an *ummah* that obeys and follows unconsciously and blindly. Faḍlallah reports the answer of the Prophet's companions when he consulted them about the battle of Badr: "Oh prophet of God, if you asked us to cross the sea, we would cross it with you . . . and we would not tell you as the people of Moses told him 'go, you and your lord, fight we are here sitting,' but we will say 'go, as we are with you and in front of you and on your right and on your left fighting.' "[176] The latter answer reflects how the practice of *shūra* strengthens the bond between the people and their leader and unites their outlook and goal. That healthy relationship between the *ummah* and its leadership is indispensable for a successful *ummah*.

JUSTICE IS MANIFESTED IN THE "COMMON GOOD" RESULTING FROM COLLECTIVE JUDGMENT

The Qur'ānic concept of practicing *shūra* in an *ummah* creates a community engaged in the implementation of common good for all, resulting in shared justice. Aristotle understands justice in general as the chosen acts that promote the common good of the society, as opposed to mere obedience to laws: "*the good is justice, in other words, the common*

176. Faḍlallah, *Min Waḥy al-Qur'ān*, vol. 6, 343–48.

interest."[177] Adhering and working for the common good, which represents justice for Aristotle, is what keeps the community together. ʿAbduh, in chapter 2, regarded the act of "enjoining *maʿrūf* and deterring *munkar*" to be the main bond unifying the members of an *ummah*. Engaging in reform requires continuous deliberation or in some cases taking action to fix a situation.

Sometimes citizens' disposition to enforce standards of mutual obligation among community members does not result in peaceful social order; nonetheless, "it does give rise to the kinds of shared activity and identity that reinforce our sense of living in a community."[178] A closer analysis of the aforementioned verse (3:159) shows that holding a community together requires constant deliberation and consultation, which emphasizes the sense of equality between its members. In the battle of Uḥud, when a group of Muslims ignored the common interest and focused on their private interest, the whole *ummah* lost the battle. Despite their obvious error that had dire consequences for everyone, the Qurʾānic verse urged the Prophet to continue to consult with them on public matters; otherwise the verse warned: "they would break away from you."

Thus, we see a direct relationship between keeping the community together, that sense of sharing one destiny, and mutual consultation (*shūra*). That reciprocal deliberation process is similar to the concept of reciprocity (necessary for justice) argued by Aristotle. In that regard, Aristotle says: "In communities of exchange this sort of justice [reciprocity] does hold men together. . . . For it is the reciprocal return of what is proportional that holds cities together . . . Men seek to return either evil for evil—and if they cannot do so, think their position mere slavery—or good for good, and if they cannot do so there is no exchange."[179] Mutual exchange according to Aristotle is sort of a direct proof for the equality of citizens; hence fair exchange amounts to justice. Otherwise, unequal dealings reflect an unbalanced and unfair society. In the Qurʾān, this reciprocity between members of an *ummah* is expressed by different practices such as the practice of *shūra* and the act of "enjoining *maʿrūf* and deterring *munkar*," which are both regarded as unifying bonds for the *ummah*. Nevertheless,

177. Aristotle, *Politics* (1282b16).

178. Bernard Yack, *The Problems of a Political Animal*, 43.

179. Aristotle, *NE* (1132b31–40).

the Qur'ānic verse 3:159 ends by clarifying the role of the leadership, which is binding after conducting *shūra.* Aristotle differentiates between the rule of law and political power, for they are not equivalent—this difference is explored in the next section.

Ummah and Political Power

In this part, we reach the core of conducting this research, which is analyzing the relationship between the *ummah* and political power. Are they equivalent, or does one control the other? Do they exhibit a direct relationship, or are there intermediary agents that mediate or affect their relationship? Does law play a role in this relationship, or does it represent a third factor? In order to address these questions, we look at the existing scholarship on these issues in relationship to the Qur'ānic verses that address them.

Al-Farabi assumes that the *ummah* and its elite do not serve any political role.[180] However, he thinks that the *ummah* as a political association is of intermediate size between the city and the multinational empire. That would be the only political feature espoused by al-Farabi through which he interprets the Qur'ānic (*ummah wasaṭ*).[181] I have argued that *wasaṭ*, as a theoretical concept, is related to justice as a mean described by Aristotle. Justice could be attained as a political practice when the elite conduct *shūra.* However, I think that the status *wasaṭ* as a mean would defeat its purpose if it were limited to the elite. This invites a discussion of how the just leadership, law, and the community norms interact and are critical for the *ummah* to attain *wasaṭiyyah.* The following sections show how the latter is achieved, thereby proposing a new understanding of the *ummah wasaṭ* and clarifying its political role.

THE JUST LEADERSHIP VERSUS *ṬĀGHŪT*

The most common and controversial Qur'ānic verse directly addressing authority figures and their relationship to the *ummah* members is verse 4:59.

180. Alexander Orwin, *Redefining the Muslim Community: Ethnicity, Religion and Politics in the Thought of Alfarabi*, 179.

181. Ibid., 201.

Before delving into the interpretation of who represents those entrusted with authority, I would like to discuss the verses preceding and following verse (4:59) in light of the previous section's discussion of the concept of justice. The prior verse starts with the concept of justice (*ʿadl*) before introducing the idea of obeying law and figures of authority, which is then followed by the contrasting concept of *Ṭāghūt* (despotism) as shown:

> Surely Allah commands you to render back the trusts to their owners; and when you judge between people you judge with justice (*bil-ʿadl*); indeed Allah advises you with what is best; surely Allah is all seeing, hearing. (Qurʾān 4:58)

> O those who believe, obey Allah, and obey the Messenger, and those from among you who have been entrusted with authority (*ʾulī ʾl-amr minkum*); and if you are at variance over any matter, refer it to Allah and the Messenger, if you [truly] believe in Allah and the Last Day. This is best, and better interpretation (decision). (Qurʾān 4:59)

> Have you not seen those who pretend that they believe in what has been revealed to you and what was revealed before you; but their (real) wish is to resort together for judgment (in their disputes) to the *Ṭāghūt*, though they were commanded to reject it, but the devil desires to mislead them far astray. (Qurʾān 4:60)

The above verses present a clear picture to help us understand the function of *ʾulī ʾl-amr*. The first verse (4:58) speaks of a fair distribution of rights to respective owners, the fairness and equality earlier mentioned by Aristotle, and relates the practice to justice (*ʿadl*). The following verse (4:59) refers to the practical implementation of justice in society, and thereby addresses all believers to "obey Allah and the Messenger," which is equivalent to following the law. That the concept of abiding by the law is introduced before mentioning figures of authority and restated again afterward (that conflict should be resolved by referring to the common law) is critical to avoid misunderstanding the function and character of *ʾulī ʾl-amr*. This is because the verse places everyone under the same category, accountable to the law, and restricts the function of *ʾulī ʾl-amr* to the executive realm.

Relating the concept of fairness and justice in verse 4:58 with general obedience to law (4:59) confirms the Aristotelian understanding that the "just" exists only among those regulated by law. To stress the latter idea further, the subsequent verse (4:60) commands the rejection of *ṭāghūt*. The meaning of *ṭāghūt* in the encyclopedia of Arab and Islamic terminology is "transgressing against *sharīʿah* unjustly by a temporary unjust ruler whose transgression will disappear by his disposal."[182] In the Arabic lexicon, the root of the noun *ṭāghūt* is the verb *ṭaghā*, meaning to exceed the limit or transgress.[183] The verb is used in another Qurʾānic verse (69:11) referring to Noah's flood "when the water overflowed (*ṭaghā al-māʾ*) . . ." Thus, *ṭāghūt* represents the tyrannical rule of those who govern for the private interest; hence the root of the term refers to excess (taking more than what is due to you, which consequently usurps others of their rights) by acting against *sharīʿah*. Thereby, the term *ṭāghūt* stands by itself as the contrast of those who abide by law and conduct their affairs accordingly in order to fulfill justice. The individual or the group that practices *ṭāghūt* has no need to follow the law or use it as a means to resolve conflict because *ṭāghūt* entails seeking private gain only. Therefore, *ṭāghūt* acts against just law to oppress and gains in excess for itself against the rights of the *ummah*. Aristotle also relates injustice to excess: "the unjust person is guilty of "graspingness" or "overreaching" (*pleonexia*; literally "having more"). Such a man takes more than his fair share of the external goods involved in "good and bad fortune."[184] The compulsive desire to exceed one's fair share of resources creates a shortage or scarcity of resources for other people in society, thereby inviting conflict and a myriad of political problems. Moreover, intense competition and conflict beget the desire for mastery,[185] in Qurʾānic terms *ṭāghūt* or despotism.

Meanwhile, *ṭāghūt* is temporary like floodwater that rises against the balance of nature, destroys things, and eventually recedes, allowing

182. Jīrār Jihāmī, Samīḥ Daghīm and Rafīq al-ʿAjam, *Mawsūʿat Muṣṭalaḥāt al-Fikr al-Naqdī al-ʾArabī wal-ʿIslāmī al-Muʿāṣir* (Beirut: Maktabat Lubnān Nāshirūn, 2004), vol. 1, 1220.

183. Shaykh Abdullah Al-ʿAlāylī, *As-Ṣiḥāḥ fil-Lugha wal-ʿUlūm*, ed. Nadīm and Usāma Marʿashlī (Beirut: Dār al-Ḥaḍāra al-ʿArabiyya, 1974), vol. 2, 42.

184. As quoted in Thomas W. Smith, "Aristotle on the Conditions for and Limits of the Common Good," 626.

185. Aristotle, *NE* (1169121–2).

equilibrium to be restored. Tyrannical ruling resembles a flood that cannot last because it is against the natural equilibrium, which requires that justice prevail equally for everyone. *Ṭāghūt* makes its own law and rejects other revealed laws, as the verse shows, ". . . those who pretend that they believe in what has been revealed to you and what was revealed before you; but their (real) wish is to resort together for judgment (in their disputes) to the *ṭāghūt* . . ." (Qurʾān 4:60). *Thus, ṭāghūt does not prefer a specific divine revelation to another; rather it rejects them all because it is not interested in the common good but merely interested in its own good. Ṭāghūt is one-sided and independent; thereby it does not allow any opposition and eliminates all difference because that is the only means for it to thrive.* Hence, we see in the above verses that *ṭāghūt* (as a political power) in verse 4:60 is contrasted with the political community that abides by law whereby it mediates its conflicts as outlined in verse 4:59. The latter political community should reject *ṭāghūt.*

The preceding analysis also shows that *ʾulī ʾl-amr* could not be interpreted as authoritarian leaders governing according to private interest or devising their own law as they please. Moreover, the analysis shows that despotism could not be disguised by the cover of revealed religion because *ṭāghūt* rejects all revealed religions to make its own law that suits its private interests and propagates its despotism. This provides us with a security check for all ideological or political groups who claim to be ruling in the name of a specific revealed religion. The verses show that a just government abides by law, allows for opposition or the presence of difference, and mediates conflicts by means of law. That law should be targeted toward fair distribution and the common good of everyone and should reject *ṭāghūt*, or governing for private interest. The *ummah* of Medina did not exclude the Jews, whether as a social, religious group in society with rights to practice their own religion, or as a political entity with reciprocal rights and obligations toward their fellow Muslims. The pith of the law of the Medina Constitution was its organizing the mixed *ummah* of Medina with a view to the common good of all its members and groups, which as a result confirmed the equality of all before the law.

The following Qurʾānic verse highlights the coercive nature of *ṭāghūt*, which cannot sustain its power without force by contrasting it with the choosing nature of religion and *sharīʿa*, which is not based on compulsion:

> There is no compulsion in religion. Verily, truth stands out clear from error. Whoever disbelieves in *ṭāghūt* and believes

> in Allah, then he has grasped the most trustworthy handhold (*al-ʿurwat al-wuthqa*) that will never break. And Allah is all-hearing, all-knowing. (Qurʾān 2:256)

Shaḥrūr provides an interesting interpretation of *al-ʿurwat al-wuthqa* in relation to *ṭāghūt* and believing in God because believing in God is a personal choice, as the verse clearly says (there is no compulsion in religion), which in turn requires holding on firmly to human ethical values. Yet holding on to ethics (human *fiṭrah*) requires a simultaneous rejection of *ṭāghūt*, which leaves the human conscience victorious (as a result of balancing between human animalistic desires and rationality). Through the latter balance, a human can be in control and be freed from the chains of enslavement to desires or any societal pressures that would coerce him to act against his *fiṭrah* or will (i.e., *ṭāghūt*). Thus, Shaḥrūr interprets *al-ʿurwat al-wuthqa* as freedom, which is a direct result of the binary action (believing in God and rejecting *ṭāghūt*).[186] He sees freedom as a conscious, voluntary act that results from other deliberate choices that elevate parts of the human self (rationality, *fiṭrah*, conscience) and devalue others (selfish desires, greed, etc.). Belief is the foundational base for making such choices, because it is by itself a voluntary, rational choice that puts the human being on a path of continuously choosing ethical values and devaluing others.

ʾUlū ʾl-Amr (Those Entrusted With Authority)

The Qurʾānic verse "O those who believe, obey Allah, and obey the messenger, and those from among you who have been entrusted with authority (*ʾulī ʾl-amr minkum*) . . ." (Qurʾān 4:59)" represents one of the most controversial verses directly addressing authority figures and their relationship to the *ummah* members. The main controversy arising from this verse centers on who represents *ʾulī ʾl-amr* because the verse requires obedience to that person or entity. Obeying Allah and his messenger was never a controversial matter for Muslims because it represents abiding by Islamic law or *sharīʿah*. As previously mentioned, Aristotle hinted at the difference between following law and authority figures and clarified that law represents a less compulsive force for people than human coercion.

186. Moḥammad Shaḥrūr, *Ad-Dīn wal-Sulṭa: Qirāʾa Muʿāṣira lil-Ḥāimiyya* (Beirut: Dār al-Sāqī, 2014), 266–67.

Hence, exegetes differed in their understanding of who might be referred to as the authority figures of *ʾulī ʾl-amr.*

Afsaruddin did a thorough survey of the Qurʾānic exegesis of the latter verse from the early first two centuries of Islam until the modern period.[187] The Qurʾānic exegesis from the first two centuries had two main interpretations for *ʾulī ʾl-amr.* The first is related to the knowledge of Islamic ethics and law, and those would be "people of knowledge and insightful understanding," such as *ʿulamāʾ* ("religious scholars") and *fuqahāʾ* ("scholars of Islamic jurisprudence"), including righteous companions of the Prophet. The second interpretation is related to leadership during war, and those would be "military commanders" assigned by Prophet Muhammad. By the ninth century, exegetes such as at-Ṭabarī, in addition to the latter interpretations, started to associate the term with political leadership, such as the "sultan," a new term of that time used for political rulers. The twelfth century exegete Fakhr ad-Dīn al-Rāzī confined the term mainly to Jurists, called *ahl al-ḥal wal-ʿaqd* ("the people who loosen and bind"), who are capable of deciphering God's commandments from the Qurʾānic and Sunnah texts. A late medieval exegete, Ibn Kathīr, associated *ʾulī ʾl-amr* chiefly with political authority while reporting a few ambiguous *ʾaḥādīth* that mandated obedience to political authority irrespective of the legitimacy of the ruler. Similar was the argument offered by Al-Māwardī in his famous political treatise "*al-Aḥkām as-Sulṭāniyya*," which Afsaruddin argues propagated a culture of political quietism toward authoritarian rulers.

From the modern period, exegetes differed in their understanding of the term as well. For example, ʿAbduh and Riḍa stretched the term to include public figures who contribute to the welfare of the Islamic community, such as labor leaders and prominent journalists, in addition to scholars, jurists, and political figures. Nevertheless, obedience to them is merited as long as they follow God's law and the Prophet's *sunnah*; otherwise Muslims are forbidden to follow figures of authority if they are oppressive.[188] Similarly, Sayyid Quṭb asserts that *ʾulī ʾl-amr* should be believers who follow and implement *sharīʿah* because the Qurʾānic verse

---

187. Asma Afsaruddin, "Obedience to Political Authority: An Evolutionary Concept," in *Islamic Democratic Discourse*, ed. M. A. Muqtedar Khan (Lanham, MD: Lexington Books, 2006), 37–60.

188. Ibid., 37–47.

states "those ***from among you*** who have been entrusted with authority" (Qurʾān 4:59).[189] However, Quṭb did not clarify, like ʿAbduh and Riḍa, who are supposed to assume the role of *ʾulī ʾl-amr*, but only elucidated their attributes. Based on other political writings of Quṭb, Afsaruddin infers that Quṭb could have intended his *ṭalīʿa* to assume the role of *ʾulī ʾl-amr. At-ṭalīʿa* ("the vanguard") represents a group of rightly guided individuals who fully understand God's law and practice *shūra* to implement it. The vanguard represents the minority who are trying to bring the erring majority into conformity with *sharīʿa*.[190]

Most *Imāmī* Shīʿa interpret *ʾulī ʾl-amr* to represent the twelve *aʾimma* (pl. of *imām*) who were granted "*wilāya*" by the Prophet. Moreover, the Qurʾānic verse of purification,[191] sent on their behalf, signifies their infallibility, which in turn necessitates obedience to them. Faḍlallah says that it is possible that the verse refers to the infallible *aʾimma*; however, it is not restricted to them, and the concept of obedience does not necessitate that the leader is infallible because the Qurʾān applies to all times. On the other hand, what is necessary for obeying a leader is the latter's abiding by God's law and his messenger's teachings. Thus, it is not an independent leadership but one confined by *sharīʿah*. Faḍlallah adds that *ʾulī ʾl-amr* do not possess the eligibility of creating their own law or *sharīʿah*; rather they merely apply *sharīʿah* and are only flexible within the limits it defines. Thus, it is not incumbent on people to obey an authority that does not follow God's law and his messenger. In that sense he agrees with ʿAbduh and Quṭb in specifying what makes authority legitimate and deserving of obedience by the *ummah*. The same idea is discussed by Shaḥrūr, who says that the Qurʾānic usage of the word *minkum* rather than *ʿalaykum* ("over you") indicates that the relationship between *ʾulī ʾl-amr* and the people is based on obeying Islamic law rather than obeying them personally. If it were a personal obedience to people of authority, then it would be a tyrannical relationship between two different classes, and this is not what the verse implies. On the contrary, Shaḥrūr

189. Sayyid Quṭb, *In the Shade of the Qurʾān*, trans. and ed. ʿĀdil Ṣālaḥī and ʿĀshūr Shams (United Kingdom: The Islamic Foundation, 2001), vol. III, 196–98.

190. Asma Afsaruddin, "Obedience to Political Authority: An Evolutionary Concept," 45–46.

191. Qurʾān (33:33), ". . . and Allah only desires to keep away all abomination from you, *ahl al-bayt*, and purify you a (thorough) purifying."

continues that the word *minkum* implies a relationship of peers where each individual is guaranteed his rights.[192]

Faḍlallah then mentions other scholars who consider *ʾulī ʾl-amr* to be the whole *ummah* based on the *ḥadīth* that says, "my *ummah* does not unite upon error," which indicates that the *ummah*'s decision is infallible. However, he does not support this opinion because the scholars never had *ijmāʿ* ("unanimous agreement") on who should assume the position of *ʾulī ʾl-amr.*[193]

I do not think that *ʾulī ʾl-amr* refers to the whole *ummah* because the verse says "from among you" (*minkum*), which suggests that there is a group of people elected from the whole *ummah*. Second, it may be possible that the verse refers to the twelve *aʾimma*, companions of the Prophet, or the leaders assigned by the Prophet during his lifetime. However, the question arises, who would be entrusted with authority in their absence? Thus, I suggest that the verse needs to be interpreted in general for all times and not restricted to a specific time in history.

The concept of infallibility also does not resonate with the message of the verse because the verse continues to say, "and if you are at variance over any matter," which implies that conflict or disagreement can occur, and this is not a case that can be accepted when dealing with an infallible person or leader such as the Prophet. The Prophet mandates absolute obedience from the believers because obedience to him means obedience to Allah. In addition, the verse clarifies that in cases of conflict, matters should be referred to Allah and his prophet, the infallible sources. Therefore, there are three points raised so far. First, there are two parties involved: one is those entrusted with authority, and the other is those who are commanded to obey the latter; thus it is not talking about only one all-encompassing party that some scholars referred to as the *ummah*. Second, both parties are not infallible because conflict can arise between them. In addition, one party (those entrusted with authority) is chosen "from among" the rest of the *ummah*. Third, the infallible source and the only resort in case conflict arises between the two parties is Allah and his messenger, that is, the divine book and the *sunnah* (i.e., *sharīʿah*).

---

192. Moḥammad Shaḥrūr, Al-Dīn wal-Sulṭa: Qirāʾa Muʿāṣira lil-Ḥākimiyya (Beirut: Dār al-Sāqī, 2014), 374.

193. Faḍlallah, *Min waḥy al-Qurʾān*, vol. 7, 323–28.

Based on the above, there are the leaders (*ʾulī ʾl-amr*), the *ummah*, and obedience to God's message (*sharīʿah*). Both *ʾulī ʾl-amr* and the *ummah* should follow and implement *sharīʿah*. Islamic law becomes then the main bond between the *ummah* and its leaders in either conditions of peace or conflict. Islamic law is the foundation upon which the *ummah* elects its *ʾulī ʾl-amr*, which merits them obedience and power to resolve arising conflicts. Law limits the exercise of political power and regulates its interaction with the *ummah*. The Qurʾānic verse starts with the stipulation to obey God's law and ends with using it as a criterion to resolve conflicts. Giving law such a central function is similar to the Aristotelian depiction of the rule of law in the polis. Aristotle contends that there is no political community where laws do not rule. A lawful and just regime exists only among those regulated by law, that is, among people who are disposed to follow law.[194] "The rule of law for Aristotle represents a moral disposition, the disposition to follow and apply general rules rather than an adjudicative ideal."[195] Thus, everyone (rulers and people) should be disposed to follow the community's rules rather than merely respecting statuary and constitutional rule.

Similarly, by addressing everyone (people and leaders) with the general command to obey God and his messenger, the Qurʾānic verse establishes an equal authoritative base for everyone and urges the whole *ummah* to know and implement God's law in order to prosper. Hence, an *ummah* whose members are morally disposed and trained to follow rules is an *ummah* whose members enjoy equality and freedom without the oppression of authoritarian rulers or governments. The Qurʾānic referral to "arising conflict" confirms the latter point as well as Aristotle's contention that conflict is a characteristic feature only of political communities.

ʾUlū ʾl-amr are chosen "from among you"; thus leaders should not be separate from their people, isolated from their concerns, come from a different class and lifestyle, or hold different beliefs and ideologies. The word "*minkum*" (from you) implies more than "being chosen from you"; it also implies someone from your life, sharing your concerns, having complete knowledge of your situation, and vice versa. The same statement appears in the verse talking about the Prophet:

194. Bernard Yack, *The Problems of a Political Animal*, 199–200.

195. Ibid., 201.

> O our Sustainer! Raise up amongst them an apostle from among themselves[196] (*minhum*), who shall convey unto them your messages, and instruct them in scripture and wisdom, and cause them to grow in purity: for, verily, you are the exalted in might, the wise. (Qur'ān 2:129)

Then it is more clearly interpreted in the following verse: "Indeed, there has come unto you [O humankind] an Apostle from among yourselves (*min 'anfusikum*); heavily weighs upon him [the thought] that you might suffer; full of concern for you [is he, and] full of compassion and mercy towards the believers" (Qur'ān 9:128). This verse explains what the former verse describes as "an apostle from among themselves," which scholars interpreted as from his own people. However, the second verse signifies a deeper relationship with the Prophet, that he is "from yourselves," in a sense that he lives the full human experience and as a result has a genuine care and concern for humankind, is full of compassion and mercy toward others. Aristotle clearly states that the polis exists for the sake of achieving excellence for its members and making them good and just, which necessitates a just leadership, itself regulated by law. The Qur'ānic verse 2:129, which states ". . . an apostle from among themselves (*minhum*), who shall convey unto them your messages, and instruct them in scripture and wisdom, and cause them to grow in purity . . ." reflects an inherent connection between the ethical leadership and the ethical character of the people.

I think it is significant that the leaders are mentioned in plural form and not in singular. This reflects a distribution of duties and is more in tune with the spirit of *shūra* discussed in the previous section. If only one leader were entrusted with authority, then we would return to authoritarianism and personal rule. Obeying those entrusted with authority also shows that the results of *shūra* are "binding" rather than "infallible." After the *ummah* decides its leaders, it should conform to their decisions "as long as it does not contradict the law." The verse starts by describing the foundation of any political community. There should be specific principles upon which any community establishes itself and upon which it regulates the interaction between its members. It was already shown in this research that the *ummah* as a concept is based on the concept of the "book" that shapes its features or the law that governs its interactions. Figure 4.1 confirms the

196. In another translation, "of their own" by Yusuf Ali.

latter conclusions; *sharīʿah* is the main bond between different members of the *ummah*; legislators and the executive (plural form, thereby the need for practicing *shūra*) act as *ʾulī ʾl-amr* who are part of the *ummah* and follow and implement *sharīʿah*. Hence they act as liaisons between *sharīʿah* and the *ummah*. The *ummah*'s obedience to *ʾulī ʾl-amr* is binding as long as the latter follow *sharīʿah*. Conflict may arise between the *ummah* and its *ʾulī ʾl-amr* (hence the double-sided arrows in figure 4.1), and the means to resorting that conflict is through resorting to *sharīʿah*. This conflict is potentially reflective of an active *ummah* who is engaged in the political process through "enjoining *maʿrūf* and deterring *munkar*" to maintain active justice "*wasaṭiyyah*" for its members and hinder the rise of *ṭāghūt*.

ʾUlū ʾl-amr in the Medina Constitution

Looking at the Medina Constitution, we find three kinds of authority or *ʾulū ʾl-amr* who follow the law themselves and ensure its implementation in the *ummah*: first are the leaders of each tribe (whether Muslim or Jewish) selected by their own tribes who are in charge of managing their own internal affairs according to customary laws (which nonetheless do not contradict the law of the constitution); second is represented by the political power allocated to the practice of active justice in the *ummah* by its excellent members as shown in decrees 13 and 20. Aristotle describes "passive injustice" as "the behavior of those who do not oppose wrong when they have it in their power to do so."[197] Yack argues that passive injustice "bespeaks the absence of a kind of *active justice*, a kind of justice based on inherently disputable estimates of our capacity to prevent wrong rather than on determinate rules and principles."[198] This Aristotelian active justice resembles the Qurʾānic command for *ummah* members to enjoin righteousness and deter wrongness to be successful and in accord with the constitution's decrees that urge its members to actively oppose an aggressor, such as specified in decree 13.

Moreover, the Qurʾān adds that the practice of active justice should not be confined to the practice of those who have the power to prevent wrong (as Aristotle described), but is the responsibility of every

197. Bernard Yack, *The Problems of a Political Animal*, 161.

198. Ibid., 162.

single member who simply has the ability to verbally denounce unjust acts, even if they do not have the power to prevent them as discussed in the Qurʾānic verse (7:164).[199] What grants those active members of the *ummah* the position of *ʾulī ʾl-amr* is the very fact of their action to promote the common good of the *ummah*; hence they are described in the MC as "God conscious believers" in decree 13 and described in decree 20 as "God conscious believers [who] follow the best and the straightest path." Aristotle also affirms that the members who contribute most to the flourishing of their society should have the greatest share in it: "Political society exists for the sake of noble actions, and not of living together. Hence they who contribute most to such a society have a greater share in it than those who have the same or a greater freedom of nobility of birth but are inferior to them in political excellence."[200]

The third kind of *ʾulī ʾl-amr* in the MC is Prophet Muhammad, who assumes a central role in conflict resolution for all affiliated tribes as shown in decrees 23 and 42. The Prophet also acts as the common leader in case of war as shown in decree 36. Moreover, the Prophet acted as the legislator who drafted the constitution of Medina as shown in the first decree: "this is a book *from* Muhammad between the believers, Muslims, etc." The last decree reiterates the legislative function of the Prophet; however, it confines his power with two criteria. First, the last decree (47) specifies that the book (the constitution) will not protect acts of injustice, thereby placing everyone (including the Prophet) under the precepts of the common law that organizes the *ummah*. Second, whenever the judiciary or legislative function of the Prophet is mentioned, God is mentioned before him (in decrees 23, 42, 43, and decree 1, Muhammad is defined as "the messenger [prophet of Allah]") to reaffirm that the Prophet's judgment or legislation is shaped and confined by Qurʾānic teachings, in other words Islamic law and ethics. Only in decree 36 is Muhammad mentioned independently, without a title, which is likely related to the context of the decree. The decree specifies that the Jews could not conduct war without the permission of Muhammad as the common leader of the *ummah*, rather than as

---

199. The verse was discussed in detail in chapter 2: "And when an *ummah* from them said: "Why do you give advice to a people whom Allah is about to destroy or punish with a severe torment?" They replied: "To be free from blame before your sustainer, and perhaps they become God conscious (*yattaqūn*)" (Qurʾān 7:164).

200. Bernard Yack, *The Problems of a Political Animal*, 75.

his being the prophet. Thus, it may be possible that there was no need to emphasize his function as a prophet within that context.

If the Prophet as *waliy ʾl-amr* assumed the three positions of judiciary, legislative, and political/military leader in the *ummah* of Medina, it does not necessarily mean that one person should hold the three positions simultaneously after his model. After all, prophets are people who possess perfect integrity and complete virtue that is indispensable for their carrying out the mission demanded of them. This perfection was illustrated in the Qurʾānic description of Prophet Abraham as an *ummah* by himself. However, Aristotle reminds us that rarely do we find people who possess such complete virtue; rather people usually possess partial virtue, and thereby the need arises for the polis or the *ummah* in which individuals can cooperate for their common good. Therefore, the functions of the judiciary, legislative, and military should be performed by different people.

While Qurʾānic interpretations differed in their understanding of the function of *ʾulī ʾl-amr* and who should assume that position, the Medina Constitution helped us clarify their roles. So far, we have discussed five different roles assumed by *ʾulī ʾl-amr* in the MC: three functions (the judiciary, legislative, and political/military) were carried out by the Prophet; one related to customary laws was carried out by the leaders of the tribes; and the last one was performed by the excellent members of the *ummah* who actively partake in pursuing active justice in their community. Despite the different roles assumed by *ʾulī ʾl-amr* and the different authorities assuming those roles, the common factor is their being shaped and confined by Islamic law.

ʾUlū ʾl-amr in the Modern Period

Abd al-Raḥmān al-Kawākibī discusses this matter in his book *Um al-Qura*, saying that religious and political power should not be invested in the same person. He thinks that political power should be monitored by the *ʿulamāʾ* of the *ummah*; otherwise both the *ummah* and political power would be corrupt. An Arab *khalīfa* should take charge of religious matters, whereas a civic Arab ruler would rule where both should not interfere in each other's duties. The civic ruler (*ḥākim madanī*) should not interfere in religious rulings, but is subordinated to a *shūra* council that ensures that positive laws do not contradict basic *sharīʿah* principles.

Al-Kawākibī thinks that if religious and political authority were invested in one leader, then political power would corrupt religion or exploit it to promote its temporary political interests.[201] The latter results in tyranny (*al-istibdād*): a political power that is not monitored by the *ummah* and does not follow a constitution, but rather rules based on private interest. He adds that tyranny has many forms: an authoritarian ruler who came to power by force or hereditary rule, an irresponsible elected ruler or party, and a constitutional government that separates between legislative, executive and supervising authorities.[202] He separates between religious and political authorities yet subordinates the political ruling to a *shūra* religious council, a system quite similar to the Iranian *wilāyat al-faqīh* established after the revolution.

The core of Islamic thought is *tawḥīd*, an ideology that endorses acknowledging only God's power to be absolute. The fruit of such ideology is freeing the minds from servitude and slavery.[203] Al-Kawākibī mentions that Qur'ānic ideology is loaded with teachings and stories that fight tyranny and call for justice and equality. The story of the queen of Sheba[204] with her people is a perfect example of how political leadership consults the people and would not make a decision without their opinion. This keeps the strength and power in the hands of the people and acknowledges their contribution, while political leadership is merely vested in execution. On the other hand, tyranny is represented by the character of Pharaoh whose interaction with his people was based on

201. Abd al-Raḥmān al-Kawākibī, *Al-'A'māl al-Kāmila lil-Kawākibī*, ed. Mohammad Jamāl Ṭaḥḥān (Beirut: Markaz Dirāsāt al-Wiḥda al-ʿArabiyya, 1995), 80–81.

202. Ibid., 83.

203. Abd al-Raḥmān al-Kawākibī, *Um al-Qura* (Egypt: al-Taqadum Press), 61.

204. "(The Queen of Sheba) said (when she received the letter): "O chieftains! surely an honorable letter has been delivered to me. It is from Solomon, and is (as follows): (In the name of Allah, Most Gracious, Most Merciful. Saying: exalt not yourselves against me and come to me in submission.)" She said: "O chiefs! advise me in (this) my affair: no affair have I decided except in your presence." They said, "we are men of strength and of great military might, but the command is yours, so see what you will command." She said: "surely the kings, when they enter a town, corrupt it and make the noblest of its people to be low, *and indeed they do*." (Qur'ān 27:29–34) The last sentence is in italics because it is a confirmation from God that her opinion is right.

conflict and strife, the opposite of the *shūra* example implemented by the queen of Sheba.[205]

Hence, al-Kawākibī advocates Islamic reform (*Iṣlāḥ*) to develop and advance the *ummah*. This reform cannot occur without an intellectual awakening (*yaqaẓa ʿaqliyya*) that would free the mind from the burdens that have accumulated over the years and hindered it from speculation and discussion and rendered it incapable of taking charge of its own affairs, let alone the political and religious affairs. Religious thought should be freed from the additions that accrued over time, the fanatic restrictions imposed by some religious scholars, and sectarian differences that divided the *ummah*. He does not advocate imitation (*taqlīd*) except in religious rituals, and endorses *ijtihād* to allow the human mind to think and legislate in matters that were left unspecified by the wise divine legislator.[206] Al-Kawākibī thinks that the *ummah* and the ruler share equal responsibility in promoting tyranny because an ignorant *ummah* would be easily prone to tyrannical ruling.

Mohammad Shaḥrūr thinks similarly and clearly stipulates the coercive power of government and its limits. He says that a government has no right to interfere in the personal life of people in terms of belief, rituals, or ethics. However, the government can make it easy for people to practice their own faith by organizing religious institutions such as mosques and churches, and so forth. In addition, the government makes laws that regulate and protect human ethical values that are directly related to divine rulings (*al-ḥākimiyya al-ilāhiyya*) such as marriage laws, economic laws, and so forth. People obey the coercive laws of government, not for any symbol it may represent but because obeying the law would ensure the stability of the society and its progress. He makes a comparison between the power of religion and that of a government as shown in table 4.1.[207]

He differentiates between a government with a regulation power (*sulṭat ad-ḍabṭ*) whose mission is limited to achieving stability in society and securing a better life for its citizens and a dictatorial government (*sulṭat at-ṭughyān*) that transforms coercive power into violence (*ʿunf*) to subdue its people and ensure its power over them. The latter type of

205. Nazīh Kabbara, *Abd al-Raḥmān al-Kawākibī: Ḥayātuh wa ʿAsruh wa ʾĀrāʾuh* (Lebanon: Jarūs Press, 1994), 73.

206. Ibid., 103–6.

207. Moḥammad Shaḥrūr, *Al-Dīn wal-Sulṭa: Qirāʾa Muʿāṣira lil-Ḥākimiyya* (Beirut: Dār al-Sāqī, 2014), 279–83.

Table 4.1. Spheres of Governmental and Religious Authority

	Religion	Government (political authority)
Personal life	Interferes in human personal life through personal choice and will.	Does not interfere in personal life.
Religious allowances and prohibitions (*ḥalāl* and *ḥarām*)	Defines allowances and prohibitions, but leaves it up to the discretion of the people for implementation.	Organizes religious allowances and prohibitions through legal restrictions and laws.
Coercion	Has no coercive power.	Has coercive power.
Tool of coercion	Depends on the power of personal conscience. Religion specifies allowances and prohibitions but has no power of prevention.	Depends on power of coercion because it prevents and legalizes rather than specifying prohibitions only.
Effect on this life and the hereafter	Directs people (willingly) to happiness in this life and the hereafter.	Protects the dignity, security, and freedom of people in this life only.

government takes many forms, such as intellectual, ideological, religious, social, political, and economic tyranny.[208] What Shaḥrūr calls *ṭughyān*, Al-Kawākibī calls *istibdād*, but in essence both authors are discussing the same phenomenon and using Qurʾānic ideology to refute it.

While *ṭāghūt* is based on violence and subduing power, the civic government (*dawla madaniyyah*) is based on legitimacy (*sharʿiyya*) gained from its ethical orientation (*marjiʿiyya akhlāqiyya*), which ensures the rights and dignity of an individual. This government for Shaḥrūr is based on *al-ḥākimiyya al-ilāhiyya*, where the legislature belongs to *ulī al-amr* who only have the right to perform *ijtihād*. They ensure that the laws are governed by *sharīʿah* (or don't bypass it) as well as taking into consideration the customs and culture of a specific society.[209]

208. Ibid., 283–344.

209. Ibid., 345–73.

Both Al-Kawākibī and Shaḥrūr think that governmental laws should be legislated within the framework of *sharīʿah* and supervised by religious scholars. Yet religious scholars could also become tyrannical or influenced by government. There needs to be a continuous check on *ʾulī ʾl-amr*, both political and religious. This research showed that the distinctiveness of the Muslim *ummah* is its *wasaṭiya*, where justice is maintained through perseverance in maintaining a balanced environment. The status of *wasaṭ* can only be achieved through the *ummah* as a whole, which is less susceptible to error than the sole individual. The latter resonates with the Aristotelian concept of uniting partial virtues through deliberation. In the Qurʾān, deliberation should happen on two levels: *Shūra* (mutual consultation), which is usually performed by the elite, and *ʿamr bil-maʿrūf wa nahy ʿan al-munkar* (commanding civic virtue and forbidding injustice) performed by the people. Therefore, justice or *wasaṭiya* is implemented when the latter two levels of action are complementary. Members of *ummah wasaṭ* prevent the emergence of *at-ṭāghūt* by transforming laws into public norms, where people become innately disposed to lawfulness.

Concluding Remarks

The research carried out in this book is interdisciplinary across the disciplines of religion, history, philosophy, and political science. The book starts with examining an Islamic concept (*ummah*) through a systematic analysis of the word in the primary sources, the Qurʾān and the *sunnah*. By exploring how the concept has been interpreted historically (comparing premodern with modern interpretation), it was possible to propose a hermeneutical reinterpretation of the concept *ummah* that connects all its different meanings. The new understanding of the term was examined historically and then compared with the Aristotelean polis. This comparison highlights the political features of the *ummah*, thereby situating it within contemporary discourses on liberal politics and community and creating the space for an alternative vision to the nation-state (both as a local unit and a global system).

Comparing premodern with modern exegesis showed that there are many instances where the sociopolitical conditions of the exegetes' time affected their Qurʾānic interpretation. For example, premodern exegetes are more exclusive in interpreting the meaning of a united *ummah* (following one true religion), while the modern ones interpreted it as a universal concept (people having one *fiṭrah*). The modern exegesis embraces religious diversity and tolerance more than the premodern one.

Injustice is considered more critical in bringing God's wrath for modern exegetes, while *shirk* (associating partners with God) is considered more critical for premodern exegesis. In the Medinan verses, modern exegetes emphasized the individual responsibility as critical for the success of the *ummah*. Compared with premodern exegesis, there is less emphasis on the idea of cultural Islam or passive affiliation to the *ummah*. Premodern exegetes interpreted *khayr ummah* as a select group from the family of Prophet Muhammad or his companions for Shīʿī and Sunnī scholars respectively. On the other hand, modern exegetes considered *khayr ummah* a status that is achieved by those who choose to excel and lead; hence it is conditional rather than an intrinsic quality given to Muslims. Modern exegetes gave the Muslim *ummah* a sociopolitical function that requires the *ummah* to continuously engage in reform and establish justice. ʿAbduh and Quṭb even advocated the necessity of having strong political leadership. In addition, modern exegetes asserted that an *ummah* adhering only to religion, as a set of rituals, and abandoning sociopolitical reform in society will lead to its backwardness. Modern exegetes as well as Western scholars use the current condition of Muslims, as divided and conflicting states, to support their claim. The fall of the Muslim *ummah* as a united political entity and the rise of separate nation-states in the modern period not only affected the way Qurʾānic exegetes interpreted the verses but also their self-perception.

Another significant observation emanating from this research, and contrary to what is being propagated currently as major intrinsic differences, is the minor difference (if present at all) between Sunnī and Shiite exegesis. I frequently noticed intellectual similarities between ʿAbduh and Faḍlallah, despite their different sectarian affiliation, rather than between Faḍlallah and Al-Qummī (both Shiite) or between ʿAbduh and Quṭb (both Sunnī and modern). There are more pronounced differences between premodern and modern exegesis or between exegetes from the same sect.

The Meccan verses of the Qurʾān show that the core of *ummah* as a concept is choice and responsibility. Thus, *ummah* cannot be defined as ethnic, religious, or linguistic groups of people. Because belonging to an *ummah* is an individual choice and a responsibility, the concept of the *ummah* is grounded in the Book (*al-kitāb*) and not in religion (*al-dīn*). Individuals' understanding of the Book is personal and subjective and differs among different people; this amounts to people's religion. However, the Book is the unifying feature that gathers different subjective individuals into the body of one *ummah*. This is why the concept of the covenant is critical for the *ummah*, because different individuals belong and adhere to an *ummah* by either upholding a covenant with God to follow a specific divine revelation, or making a covenant with a leader and other people so that they can establish a particular way of life. Entering a covenant strengthens the awareness of responsibility associated with making choices.

Prophet Muhammad is described as the *ummī* prophet, which implies, I argue, that he is sent to a global *ummah* whose diverse communities are encouraged to seek unity through establishing covenants and competing in good works by following their respective laws. Another two terms are introduced that are characteristic of diverse societies. *al-ʾaḥzāb* ("confederates of evil") versus *al-muṣliḥūn* ("the reformers"). The Qurʾān hints that a process of continuous reform conducted by members of an *ummah*, which represents providing mutual advice and constructive action, is needed against the confederates of evil. The latter constantly try to divide the *ummah* based on their private interest, hence leading to the demise of the *ummah*.

While *ummah* in the Meccan verses is presented as a general concept with specific features, the Medinan verses present diverse *umam* across human history and introduce the Muslim *ummah* for the first time, clarifying its specific characteristics and function compared with preceding *umam*. Nonetheless, those attributes are usually acquired by specific actions rather than being inherited or culturally possessed. Therefore, the Medinan verses confirm the conceptual definition of the *ummah* described in the Meccan verses, that it is a term referring to a collectivity based on choice and action.

In the Medinan verses, the Qurʾān draws on the key figure of Prophet Abraham to explain the notion of Islam and consequently the Muslim *ummah*. Being before and outside the historical communities of Jews, Christians, and later Muslims (i.e., in the contemporary vernacular, followers of Prophet Muhammad), Prophet Abraham's life and character represent the core essence of submission to the one God, in Arabic terminology "Islam." All progeny of Prophet Abraham were described in the Qurʾān as Muslim, in other words submitting to and following the will of God. The Qurʾān portrays Prophet Abraham as praying for the rise of a Muslim *ummah* and for a prophet who would ultimately fulfill Abraham's vision of pure monotheism (who was later manifested in Prophet Muhammad). Therefore, while Muslims existed since the beginning of time as an attribute and a character with a specific ideology (*when one chooses, willingly and peacefully, to surrender their will to the will of their creator and follow his rulings*), the Qurʾānic verses imply that the "Muslim *ummah*" appeared only later in history after the coming of the last prophet Muhammad. Defining Islam or the Muslim *ummah* through

Prophet Abraham liberated the term from historical, ethnic, and cultural confines. Thereby, belonging to the Muslim *ummah* requires a choice, a specific orientation, and a resultant behavior, rather than merely belonging to a particular prophet or confessional community. *Submitting in peace (al-Islām) in that sense becomes a manifestation of one's trust in the divine wisdom rather than blind obedience to divine orders.*

The characteristic Muslim is an active term that has an essential meaning, yet is time contingent. Based on this understanding, being a Muslim today necessitates believing in Prophet Muhammad as well as all previous prophets. This may explain why the "Muslim *ummah*" appeared later in time, after the coming of the last Prophet, as it manifests a culmination of the experiences of previous prophets and *umam*.

The Medinan verses define the creed of the Muslim *ummah* by the *milla* of Abraham (*al-ḥanīf*), whose members follow the *qibla* of Abraham in ritual prayers. This *ummah* has an attribute of being *wasaṭ* compared with previous *umam*, acts as a witness (*shahīd*) to other *umam*, and performs a function "enjoining righteousness and deterring wrongness (*ya*ʾ*murūna bil-ma*ʿ*rūf wa yanhawna* ʾ*an al-munkar*)." Through performing the latter function, the Muslim *ummah* can acquire the attribute of *wasaṭ*, interpreted as moderation and connected to being just (ʿ*adl*), and consequently earn the best (*khayr*) *ummah* sent to humankind. This action resonates with the concept of continuous reform (ʾ*iṣlāḥ*) introduced in the Meccan verses and the mutual rights and obligations shared by members of an *ummah* toward each other in a virtuous and thriving society.

Modern exegetes such as Faḍlallah and ʿAbduh relate the concepts *wasaṭ*, *shahāda* ("witness"), and *qibla* together. As the concept of *wasaṭ* relates to the best of something, thereby the Muslim *ummah* has a leading role among nations. It should have the leading role in thinking, establishing justice, and guiding others, which in turn makes it a witness to (and of) other nations. Similarly, the Prophet was the model and the guide to humanity as well as the witness to them.

As the Qurʾān upholds diversity to be an indispensable result of the free will inherent in human nature, diversity is represented as the divine plan intended to enrich human life and foster human progress. This is reflective of the diverse series of prophets sent to humanity, who support each other in their mission and teachings, whereby each prophet completes the message of preceding prophets. Similarly, human beings are asked to emulate the prophetic model in understanding the meaning of diversity, which is not intended to create destructive conflict, but to foster fruitful collaboration and interaction. The Medinan verses introduce other monotheistic *umam*, Jews and Christians, as *ahl al-kitāb* ("people of the book") and, similarly to the Muslim *ummah*, describe a righteous *ummah* from them who holds specific attributes. Among the people of the book there is an *ummah muqtaṣida* and *ummah qā'ima*, which are both merited as righteous believers. Then the Qur'ān clarifies the means to establish a shared *ummah* that is multireligious and pluralistic in its makeup, but unified in its goal and orientation. Prophet Muhammad was granted the function of judging and leading this pluralistic *ummah*, reminiscent of his Qur'ānic attribute "the *ummī* prophet" and his creedal connection to his model Prophet Abraham, the common father of all monotheistic religions. The unified *ummah* seeks to settle their differences through a common book that outlines mutual rights and obligations of its different members, thereby establishing justice.

The characteristics and function of the Muslim *ummah* necessitated it being the last *ummah* sent to humankind because it is embracing of previous religions and accepts the different other as a divinely ordained reality. Its appearance later in history signifies that it has reached a level of mental and spiritual maturity that qualifies it to lead and embrace preceding *umam*. The Muslim *ummah*, in addition to sustaining itself, is asked to establish the wider, pluralistic Islamic *ummah*. While leadership is assigned to the Prophet and the last message as shown in the verse: "So judge between them by what Allah has revealed, and follow not their vain desires, diverging away from the truth that has come to you" (Qur'ān 5:48), the verse also addresses the Muslim *ummah* and clarifies its role with respect to other *umam*. Following the footsteps of Prophet Muhammad, the Muslim *ummah* is also asked to use its book as a guide to judge for itself as well as other people. Yet the verse speaks of legal pluralism (to each among you, We have prescribed a law and a clear way), so the Muslim *ummah* should not enforce its *sharī'ah* on other *umam*, that is, it is not a theocracy. Rather, the Muslim *ummah,* as a leading *ummah,* should allow each *ummah* to follow its own *sharī'ah* (book) based on the Qur'ānic injunction and the prophetic practice.

The prophetic practice was historically manifested through a treaty/book called the Medina Constitution (MC), which unified the first *ummah* in Islamic history. The first decree of the MC starts by defining the constitution as a book between the different communities comprising Medina.

The book, with its principles and values, represents the foundation that unites the diverse communities of the *ummah* into one shared whole, *ummah wāḥidah*. It is evident from the first decree that the Medina *ummah* is open to any individual or group who wishes to join it and abide by its inclusive principles and goals; hence from the outset choice manifests as a critical element behind the establishment of the *ummah*. Subsequent decrees continue to define its pluralistic stance. Religious and legal pluralism are manifested by inclusion of Muslims and Jews within the *ummah*, each following its own religion and law. Cultural pluralism appears through the mentioning of each tribe by its own name, thereby reinforcing the connection between the private and public spheres. Political pluralism is evident from the way the constitution details reciprocal rights and obligations for its diverse communities.

Starting from the first decree and proceeding through the rest of the document, we witness an expanding sequence of additions to the *ummah*, evidenced by the change of addressees' terms. First, believers are addressed, as they represent the basic element forming the *ummah* of Medina. The believers represent the Muslim *ummah*, which forms the nucleus from which the Islamic *ummah* grows, which is inclusive and pluralistic in character and has a global potential. The Islamic *ummah* expands to include Jews, allies, and protected persons, as figure 3.1 shows. This *ummah wāḥidah* is not a closed society as Orientalists, as well as some early Muslim scholars (e.g., Abū ʿUbayd), claim, and it does not merely represent a political confederation. While it is indeed a unifying political treaty, its core founding principles are based on Qurʾānic ethics, which stress the unity of humankind before God, connectedness between different prophets and divine messages, and common belief in one creator for all people.

Toward the end of the constitution, we see a new, encompassing term beyond religious, ethnic, and cultural affiliations: *Ahl al-Ṣaḥīfah* ("the people of the constitution"). Associated with the latter term, a new concept is introduced, *ḥaram* (sacred land), which is interrelated with the law of the constitution. This territorial term implies peace, security, and trust, which represent desired goals for the flourishing of the *ummah*, rather than boundaries that separate a nation from the "alien other." The book or the constitution establishes founding principles that resolve conflict and maintain a peaceful and righteous livelihood. Peace and security are indispensable for the flourishing of any *ummah* and the progress of its members. Its sacredness evolves from the sanctity of human life, a sanctity that should govern people's interaction with each other, foster mutual care, and benefit and ward off oppression and bloodshed.

Comparing the *ummah* as a concept with the nation-state, *ummah* is not merely a political concept nor solely territorial. It is an overarching concept with a specific outlook on difference or the "other" that contains political and territorial elements yet surpasses them. A nation-state sustains itself by creating a homogenous collective identity united by a political culture. Multicultural societies are held together based on a myth of false sovereignty. In an *ummah,* diversity is celebrated legally and publicly where political rights mirror social and cultural rights; hence there is no need to artificially create a homogenous culture through national symbols and values. Unity in an *ummah* is sustained by making covenants that secure multicultural communities their rights and define their obligations internally (within a specific territory) as well as externally. A global order based on nation-states is sustained by fear (tight security of borders), demonstration of power, and exploitation of the weak by the stronger nations. A global order based on *ummah* is sustained by constant interaction, interdependence based on covenants, porous borders, and tighter connection between the *umam* not merely within national borders.

From this perspective, I do not find validation for some traditional Muslim scholars who separate between Muslims and non-Muslims with the abstract notions of *dār as-salām* ("abode of peace") and *dār al-ḥarb* ("abode of war"). This dichotomy is reminiscent of modern liberal democracies that define the nation and keep its unity through demonizing the different other outside its borders. First, the need to create an outside enemy to maintain unity and cohesion in a modern nation-state is born out of a necessity: modern multicultural nations have lost common bonds that were sustained historically, such as religion, culture, or ethnicity. As individualism and secularism became the contemporary norm, alternative bonds need to be created to maintain national unity. Second, the characteristics of the Muslim *ummah* described in the Qurʾān show an *ummah* that is just, interactive, reforming, a witness to other people, and an intermediary as well as a leading *ummah* giving and contributing to prospering humanity as discussed by several scholars, despite their different intellectual orientations. The Qurʾānic description does not portray a closed society that maintains an aggressive or hostile attitude toward other nations. Third, the Qurʾān provided a general framework that organizes how the Muslim *ummah* deals with other *umam*, through the book; that is, through covenants and treaties. The *ummah* of Medina established by Prophet Muhammad provides a historical model that proves the practical efficacy of the latter ideas. Furthermore, what was established by the Prophet as a basic structure in dealing with diversity internally in Medina could be used externally with other non-Muslim sovereign *umam*. The latter idea is evident in the Meccan verses, which inspire the formation of a global *ummah* whose diverse communities are encouraged to seek unity through establishing covenants and competing in good works by following their respective laws.

The Qur'ānic verse "You were (*kuntum*) the best (*khayr*) *ummah* ever raised up for humankind for you enjoin righteousness and deter wrongness and believe in Allah, and if the people of the book were to believe it would have been better for them, among them are believers but most of them are transgressors" (Qur'ān 3:110) speaks to the modern allocation of religion into the private sphere and separating it from public life. Modern exegetes argue that the contemporary Muslim *ummah* has lost its leading role among other *umam* because Muslims, like the people of the book, have confined their religion to rituals and general ethics that barely influence practical life. *Proper belief should blossom right action in society; otherwise the belief is deficient.* In that regard, despite the transnational expansion of the Islamic religious community, the conflicting state of modern Muslim states is attributed to the Muslim *ummah* who forfeited its political role and only sustained its religious component by imitating the structure of modern nation-states.

The rapid transnational spread of the Arab uprisings in 2011 reflects a vibrant *ummah* that cuts across national boundaries. The uprisings unleashed the political power that the Islamic *ummah* could possess when it assumes its political role. In order to understand how the *ummah* functions politically, this book undertook a philosophical comparison between the Qur'ānic *ummah*, reinterpreted exegetically, and the Aristotelian polis.

Aristotle starts by defining the human being for whom the polis is created. Aristotle defines the human as a political animal who has an inherent need for political association. In the Qur'ān, the human being is given the role of a *khalīfa*, which requires interaction within a sociopolitical setting. *Khalīfa* is distinctive because he was taught the "names," which some exegetes interpreted as the names of all things, bespeaking the human's intellect, speech, and reason. Another interpretation discusses the human potential for spiritual growth and acquiring of virtue by emulating the divine names of God. Hence, while Aristotle reduced the human being to a political animal, the Qur᾽ān introduced the human being as a complex *khalīfa* whose need for social and political association is inherently connected to his need for spiritual growth. Social and political association become a means to a higher end: experiencing the attributes of the merciful and bettering life on earth. The *telos* (purpose) of the political animal is the perfect life based on choice and action, which should lead to happiness. However, the *telos* of *khalīfa* is using choice and action to enhance the life experience for oneself and other humans and all creation. While the Aristotelian human seems to be mainly concerned with his own happiness as an end goal, the Qur᾽ānic *khalīfa* is endowed with a responsibility and a duty whereby his own happiness cannot be realized without ensuring the happiness of others. Experiencing the mercy of the divine is enlivened by experiencing mercy toward the rest of his creation.

Aristotle regards the polis as the medium wherein humans deliberate about different conceptions of justice; hence the *telos* of the polis is to make human beings good and just. The polis, which is a provider of laws, is defined by its constitution, which Aristotle regards as the best form of government. While the *ummah* is defined by its book, which could be a constitution or a divine book, the Muslim *ummah* (specifically) is not a provider of laws, as is the Aristotelian polis. Al-Farabi provides an insight into uncovering the *telos* of the *ummah* by distinguishing the ethnic *ummah* and its "laws" from the virtuous *ummah* and its "ways of life." The way Al-Farabi describes the virtuous *ummah* is indicative of *khayr ummah* used in the Qur᾽ān to describe the Muslim *ummah*. Similar to the *khalīfa*, whose sociopolitical association is inherently tied to his spiritual growth, Qur᾽ānic exegesis shows that belief (ethical sphere) and sociopolitical action are inseparable in a thriving *ummah*. This concept was heavily discussed in the Medinan verses, which describe the best *ummah* (*khayr ummah*) as the one that enjoins active reform in society while believing in one God. Practically, the Medina Constitution translated the latter ideas through different forms of pluralism. The most prominent is legal pluralism, whereby a religious group abides by its own religious law publicly; hence, unlike the nation-state, the public mirrors the private. Adding this belief component makes moral action in society voluntary rather than compulsive, echoing al-Farabi's "voluntary traits" of the virtuous *ummah*, rather than "natural character" of the ethnic *ummah*. The latter uncovered the basic difference between the Muslim *ummah* and the polis, which is the Qur᾽ānic and Aristotelian understanding of law.

Law for Aristotle is externally enforced by moral educators so that they may internalize in people a disposition to lawfulness. With repeated performance, laws become familiar and no longer painful. Through habituation, laws become part of our character rather than merely being something we are asked to do. The latter reflects the Farabian "natural character" of the ethnic *ummah*. However, the Islamic perspective on religious law (*sharīʿah*) is that it is not externally imposed but originates inside individuals as a result of personal conviction. When people choose to repeatedly perform the rituals, a person attains purification. Ibn Khaldūn provides new insight into the difference between externally imposed laws and internally motivated adherence to religious law. He thinks that law imposed by external restraining influences develops in persons a sense of fear and docility, whereas exercising religious law motivated by a self-restraining influence improves human character in terms of courage, fortitude, self-reliance, and freedom to resist and act. This is what Al-Farabi probably meant by the "voluntary traits" of the virtuous *ummah* who choose to embody *sharīʿah*. When the latter is exercised as a norm in society, the virtuous *ummah* develops its "ways of life," rather than its "laws."

It is highly probable that Al-Farabi speaks of "ways of life" in a virtuous *ummah* specifically because it is pluralistic in its makeup and structure. When each religious group is invited to practice its own *sharīʿah* privately and publicly, this would result in an *ummah* that has different "ways of life." Thereby, the Islamic *ummah* provides its members with incentives using their own *sharīʿah* to participate in the welfare of the *ummah* and be politically active. The latter resolves a persistent issue in modern nation-states where minorities reside in a liberal society without feeling a sense of belonging; hence they do not sense the urge to contribute to its welfare, which ultimately results in threatening the stability and security of the nation.

Having a pluralistic legal system evades the problem of being alienated by the law of the majority that does not cater to one's needs or ideology. This may reflect Al-Farabi's description of the "voluntary traits" of the virtuous *ummah* rather than its "laws." When a member of the *ummah* does not feel obligated to follow an imposed central law through a coercive system, but instead the member follows his own law out of conviction, then the person would exercise the law voluntarily rather than coercively. Consequently, there will be no difference between the requirements of justice and those of citizenship, as is the norm in the nation-state, at least for minorities. In the Islamic paradigm, requirements of justice and citizenship are intertwined. Acceptance and public endorsement of difference respects the choices of a human being without imposition or coercion. This foundation creates a peaceful atmosphere for negotiation and makes it easier to reach a "binding legitimate" consensus, rather than an imposed coercive system with its own values.

Moreover, the *ummah* as an inclusive concept practically applied in seventh-century Arabia shows that there is no problem in having multiple affiliations. The Medina Constitution reflects different layers of affiliation. There is the tribal affiliation, the religious one, and the *ummah*, yet no affiliation negates nor opposes the other. One could be completely Jewish (in terms of religious affiliation and legally abiding by the Jewish law in the public sphere) and belong to a specific ethnic tribe, and be a member of the Islamic *ummah* (not only as a passive member possessing rights, but also as an active contributor carrying out duties). This is quite enlightening, not only for the seventh century, but more so for our modern time! There are many nation-states that do not accept multiple nationalities, let alone some religious groups that are being discriminated against only because they want to adhere to their religious values in the public sphere. The modern liberal nation-state, which claims itself to be civilized, has failed in these aspects. Accepting the other and expecting him or her to contribute and actively engage in the making of the public sphere (legally and politically) is still an unrealized dream. Fear and alienation are governing modern societies despite all the industrial advances, globalization, and fast connections the industrial revolution has achieved. We are still lacking in our understanding of human nature and how to establish healthy societies without creating marginalized people.

While the Aristotelian polis provides the laws that should train people to become good and just, the Qur᾽ānic *ummah* is invited to embody *sharī῾ah* for its own betterment and to develop better ways of living. The Aristotelian polis grants a lot of agency to the elite who make and enforce the law, who are as well responsible for making people good and just. The Qur᾽ānic *ummah* usurps that agency from the political elite and instead grants it to the human being (self-agency). Hallaq asserts that in Islamic history, political power (i.e., the state in modernity) was always transient and changing, termed *dawla* in Arabic, while the *ummah* and its organic ties to *sharīʿah* were fixed. This stability of the *ummah* and its *sharīʿah*, in comparison to the changing dynastic powers, made the Muslim *ummah* the main custodian of *sharīʿah*, not political power. The Arab uprisings prominently manifest the free will and capacity of human self-agency, thereby representing a vivid model of the Qurʾānic *khalīfa* who is ennobled for his ability to utilize choice and action to enhance the life experience for himself and others. The Arab uprisings shows how the *ummah* can be the main driver of change, not necessarily the political elite. This provides a new paradigm that is different from state-centric approaches endorsed by the modern nation-state.

If the nation is subordinate to the city in Aristotle's thought and to the state in modern thought, whereas the *ummah* is not subordinate to any political entity, how is it possible that the *ummah* has no political role? By highlighting the critical importance of the *ummah* in embodying and preserving *sharīʿah* as its way of life, this book uncovers the practical means through which the latter is realized in a political setting. The virtuous *ummah* is described as *wasaṭ* and ascribed a specific role in the Qurʾān, which is *ʿamr bil- maʿrūf wa nahy ʿan al-munkar* (commanding civic virtue and forbidding injustice). *Wasaṭ* was interpreted as an adjective by different scholars and exegetes, rather than an action and a role. For example, the Muslim *ummah* is described as moderate in faith, just, or the best by Qurʾānic exegetes; or intermediate in size (between the city and multinational empire) by Al-Farabi. This book uncovers how the *ummah* can actively and politically maintain the status of *wasaṭ* by engaging in a philosophical comparison with Aristotle's understanding of justice and the concept of the "mean," thereby reinterpreting *wasaṭ* politically.

Justice, as the chief virtue of the polis, is described as a "mean" that is achieved through the deliberative efforts of many individuals whose partial virtues coalesce to achieve complete virtue. Members of a polis, which Aristotle characterizes as heterogeneous, participate in administering justice through the medium of law. By exercising laws within a polis, justice is achieved whereby humans bond as well as perfect their character. Justice represented by the "mean" in Aristotelian thought is compared with the concept of *wasaṭ* in the Qurʾān. Similar to Aristotle, the status of *wasaṭ* can only be achieved through the *ummah* as a whole, which is less susceptible to error than the sole individual. The latter resonates with the Aristotelian concept of uniting partial virtues through deliberation. Nonetheless, unlike Aristotle, implementing justice in the Qurʾān is not confined to a specific elite group, whether religious or political, in charge of executing the law. Besides, it is not merely an Aristotelian political structure of taking turns ruling and being ruled. It is rather a comprehensive system (see figure 4.1) that prevents the monopoly of any group in society over the other.

Wasaṭiyyah thrives on parallel levels: *Shūra* is performed among the political elite to prevent the abuse of power by one side or person. Yet the binding authority that justifies the *ummah* to follow its political elite is their following and implementing *sharīʿah*, not their religious or political status. Simultaneously, the *ummah* should maintain its active role through *ʾamr bil- maʿrūf wa nahy ʿan al-munkar*. By depicting *at-ṭāghūt* as a term representing the one-sided private interest actor versus *wasaṭ*, which requires the collaboration of many actors to achieve the common good, the Qurʾān clarifies how justice can be implemented and sustained in a thriving *ummah*. Law is a good guarantee against power abuse; however, law is dormant or insignificant in an *ummah* whose members are not trained to implement law, in Aristotelian terms innately disposed to lawfulness. Being lawful requires training, not merely in law academies and firms, but in daily practice. This is what the Qurʾān refers to as *maʿrūf wa munkar*, public norms implemented by society for its own sake. In essence, the Qurʾān implies that law cannot be efficient unless it is transformed into public norms. *In that sense, the ummah becomes the means by which sharīʿah (legislation) is transformed into maʿrūf and munkar (community norm/Nomoi* in Aristotelean thought/*ways of life* in Al-Farabi's thought). The *ummah* should maintain "active justice"/*wasaṭiyyah* through *ʾamr bil- maʿrūf wa nahy ʿan al-munkar* to balance out any tyrannical tendencies from leaders. Alternatively, legislators and the executive should prevent the tyranny of the majority through the same means and by implementing *sharīʿah*.

For Aristotle, the polis is a provider of laws, as well as a provider of educators who train citizens to exercise those laws in public. The citizens assume the role of implementing the rules given to them by the political elite and the educators. However, the *ummah* does not provide laws/*sharīʿah*; neither do the legal experts or the rulers. Rather, the *ummah* embodies *sharīʿah* by actively and publicly engaging in enjoining *maʿrūf* and deterring *munkar*. The legal experts, organically produced by the *ummah*, interpret *sharīʿah*, and the rulers ensure its implementation. In this system (see figure 4.1), there is no place for the Farabian "first ruler" in the sense of an authority that legislates as well as ensures order and implementation. The ruler's role in an *ummah* is limited to the executive realm.

The ummah is the determining factor for the success or failure of a political government, not vice versa. Any delinquency on the part of the *ummah* in fulfilling its obligations will directly reflect on the behavior and performance of political ruling. When the *ummah* is politically passive and abandons its agency by not commanding civic virtue and forbidding injustice, a tyrannical political ruling develops (*at-ṭāghūt*), which rules for its private interest and usurps the *ummah* of its rights (which it abandoned in the first place!). The events of the Arab uprisings simply reflect a dormant *ummah* that suddenly assumed agency and resumed its inherent political role against its *ṭāghūt.* When the *ummah* reclaimed its role, balance was restored and the *ṭāghūt* was toppled; hence justice reigned and the *wasaṭ* status was achieved, even if temporarily. However, the *ummah* cannot maintain its *wasaṭiyyah* by merely toppling *ṭāghūt* because *wasaṭiyyah* thrives on a working system (as shown in figure 4.1) rather than on a onetime historical action/moment. This book shows that the *ummah* as a concept has specific attributes: a goal, a book that reflects that goal and accordingly establishes a covenant between its members, a leader, and possibly land (or geographical space). Disposing tyrannical rulers without having a book/constitution that clearly specifies rights and obligations of the different entities of the *ummah* could turn out to be futile. Therefore, a functioning and successful *ummah* needs to fulfill all its requirements and actively maintain its *wasaṭ* system. Disposing a dictator is a highly merited act; however, a system needs to replace the dictatorship. *Wasaṭiya* is a result of continuous public action, implemented through different venues, that discourages the rise of excess (different forms of extremism: political, religious, economic, etc.) The ideological framework of this system sketched in figure 4.1 and described in this book provides a basic foundation from which practical structures could be innovated to activate the system. Translating *Wasaṭiya* into a practical system, in which the *ummah* is its sociopolitical basis, viable for modern complex societies is the future research trajectory of this book.

The prevailing focus on the "Islamic state" as the solution for a thriving *ummah* in Islamic literature reflects the absence of critical political analysis. When the role of the *ummah* and *sharīʿah* is reduced to the role of a coercive state apparatus, the human being cannot fulfill his role as a *khalīfa*. Coercion is an obstacle that impedes the development of human virtue rather than a means to sustain it. Similarly, communitarians criticized the central control of the liberal state, a kind of control that hinders the moral development and integrity of human beings by suppressing their public deliberation about the common good.

This book provides a new paradigm not only on what the *ummah* represents in Islamic thought but also on its political role, which has been surprisingly neglected in the literature. This is critical for the contemporary period, as Muslim societies are confusingly struggling to deal with existing modern nation-states as well as their Islamic heritage. At the same time, the modern world is in desperate need of a fresh perspective on the role of citizens in a modern, globalized, diverse, and interconnected world, where the nation-state is losing its grasp on holding its multicultural societies together as well as securing its legitimacy as a viable political order.

Appendix

The Medina Constitution[1]

1- This is a book (*kitāb*) from Muhammad the prophet (the messenger of God) between the believers and Muslims of Quraysh and the people of Yathrib and those who follow them, join them, and strive along with them.

1- هذا كتاب من محمد النبي(رسول الله) بين المؤمنين والمسلمين من قريش و(أهل) يثرب و من تبعهم فلحق بهم وجاهد معهم.

2- They are one *ummah* (*ummah wāḥidah*) apart from the people.

2- أنهم أمة واحدة من دون الناس.

3- The *muhājirūn* (migrants) of Quraysh are in charge of the management of their affairs, they shall defray the cost of bloodshed among themselves and shall join in ransoming their war prisoners according to *ma῾rūf* and equity (justice) among the believers.

3- المهاجرون من قريش على ربعتهم يتعاقلون بينهم وهم يفدون عانيهم بالمعروف والقسط بين المؤمنين.

4- The Banī ῾Awf are in charge of the management of their affairs, they shall continue to pay the costs of their bloodshed among themselves as has been the custom, and each group shall ransom its war prisoner according to *ma῾rūf* and equity (justice) among the believers.

4- وبنو عوف على ربعتهم يتعاقلون معاقلهم الأولى، وكل طائفة تفدي عانيها بالمعروف والقسط بين المؤمنين.

5- The Banūl- Ḥārith (. . .)

5- وبنو الحارث(بن الخزرج) على ربعتهم يتعاقلون معاقلهم الأولى، وكل طائفة تفدي عانيها بالمعروف والقسط بين المؤمنين.

1. Muhammad Ḥamīdullah, *Majmū῾at al-Wathā᾿iq as-Siyāsiyya* (Cairo: Lajnat at-Ta᾿līf wat-Tarjama wal-Nashr, 1941), 1–7.

6- The Banū Sāʿida (. . .)

6- وبنو ساعدة على ربعتهم يتعاقلون معاقلهم الأولى، وكل طائفة تفدي عانيها بالمعروف والقسط بين المؤمنين.

7- The Banū Jashm (. . .)

7- وبنو جشم على ربعتهم يتعاقلون معاقلهم الأولى، وكل طائفة تفدي عانيها بالمعروف والقسط بين المؤمنين.

8- The Banū-Najjār (. . .)

8- وبنو النجار على ربعتهم يتعاقلون معاقلهم الأولى، وكل طائفة تفدي عانيها بالمعروف والقسط بين المؤمنين.

9- The Banū ʿAmrū bin ʿAwf (. . .)

9- وبنو عمرو بن عوف على ربعتهم يتعاقلون معاقلهم الأولى، وكل طائفة تفدي عانيها بالمعروف والقسط بين المؤمنين.

10- The Banū- Nabīt (. . .)

10- وبنو النبيت على ربعتهم يتعاقلون معاقلهم الأولى، وكل طائفة تفدي عانيها بالمعروف والقسط بين المؤمنين.

11- The Banūl- ʾAws (. . .)

11- وبنو الأوس على ربعتهم يتعاقلون معاقلهم الأولى، وكل طائفة تفدي عانيها بالمعروف والقسط بين المؤمنين.

12- The believers shall not leave a *mufrah*[2] (one under financial burden) among them without giving him what is (established by) custom for ransom or blood-wit.

12- وأن المؤمنين لا يتركون مفرحًا بينهم أن يعطوه بالمعروف في فداء أو عقل.

12 B- No believer shall oppose the *mawla* (client/ally) of another believer. (According to another reading: No believer may enter into an agreement with the *mawla* of another believer, so as to harm the latter.)

12ب- وأن لا يخالف مؤمن مولى مؤمن دونه.

13- All God-conscious believers shall be against the person who intends to commit an aggressive and unjust act among them, or who aims to infringe one's rights or to cause turmoil among believers. And even if this person is the offspring of one of them, they shall all raise their hands against him.

13- وأن المؤمنين المتقين (أيديهم) على (كل) من بغى منهم، أو ابتغى دسيعة ظلم، أو إثمًا، أو عدوانًا، أو فسادًا بين المؤمنين، وأن أيديهم عليه جميعًا، ولو كان ولد أحدهم.

14- No believer shall kill another believer for the sake of an infidel or shall assist an infidel at the expense of a believer.

14- ولا يقتل مؤمن مؤمنًا في كافر، ولا ينصركافرًا على مؤمن.

---

2. In another reading, *mufraj* (one turned Muslim among a people to whom he does not belong).

15- The security (*dhimmah*) of Allah (for life and property) is one; (a protection acknowledged by the least important of the believers) applies to them all. And the believers, some are allies of others apart from the rest of the people.

15- وأن ذمة الله واحدة يجير عليهم أدناهم، وأن المؤمنين بعضهم موالي بعض دون الناس

16- Among Jews, those who join (follow) us shall receive our assistance and equal treatment; they shall not be oppressed, nor shall we give assistance to their enemies.

16- وأنه من تبعنا من يهود فإن له النصر والأسوة غير مظلومين ولا متناصر عليهم.

17- Peace is one among believers. No believer, in a war fought in the path of God, may agree to a peace accord by excluding other believers. This peace shall only be made among them (believers) according to the principles of equity and justice/fair dealing between them.

17- وأن سلم المؤمنين واحدة، لا يسالم مؤمن دون مؤمن في قتال في سبيل الله، إلا على سواء وعدل بينهم.

18- Each raiding party which raids along with us—one shall succeed another.

18- وان كل غازية غزت معنا يعقب بعضها بعضًا.

19- Believers shall execute retribution on behalf of one another with respect to their bloodshed in the path of God.

19- وأن المؤمنين يبئ بعضهم عن بعض بما نال دماءهم في سبيل الله.

20- Surely, God-conscious believers follow the best and straightest path.

20- وأن المؤمنين المتقين على أحسن هدى واقومه.

20-B) No polytheist [affiliated with the community] may protect the life and property of a person affiliated with Quraysh nor can intervene with a believer in this matter.

20ب- وأنه لا يجيرمشرك مالاً لقريش ولا نفسًا، ولا يحول دونه على مؤمن.

21- If it is proven with certainty that one person has killed a believer (unjustly without a reason that necessitates killing), then it is his own responsibility unless the guardian of the victim grant him a pardon; and all believers shall be against him. And it is not permissible for the believers to fight for him.

21- وأنه من اعتبط مؤمنًا قتلاً عن بينة فإنه قود به، إلا أن يرضى ولي المقتول (بالعقل)، وأن المؤمنين عليه كافة و إنه لا يحل لهم الإقتتال عليه.

22- It is not lawful for any believer approving the contents of this sheet (document) and believing in God and the Day of Judgment, to support or shelter an aggressor; whoever supports or shelters him shall receive the curse and wrath of God on the Day of Judgment, when financial compensation or sacrifice shall no longer be accepted.

22- وانه لا يحل لمؤمن اقرّ بما في هذه الصحيفة، وآمن بالله واليوم الآخر ان ينصر محدثًا أو يؤويه، وأن من نصره، أو آواه، فإن عليه لعنة الله وغضبه يوم القيامة،ولا يؤخذ منه صرف ولا عدل

23- In whatever thing you are at variance, its reference back (*maradd*) is to Allah and to Muhammad.

23- وأنكم مهما اختلفتم فيه من شيء، فإن مردّه إلى الله وإلى محمد

Decrees addressing the Jews

24- Jews along with the believers shall bear (their own) war expenses as long as they are fighting.

24- وأن اليهود ينفقون مع المؤمنين ما داموا محاربين.

25- The Jews of Banī 'Awf, together with the believers constitute an *ummah*; the Jews having their religion/law (*dīn*) and the Muslims having their religion/law (*dīn*). This includes both their *mawla* and themselves personally. But whoever performs an unjust action or commits a crime shall harm solely himself and the people of his house.

25- وان يهود بني عوف أمة مع(من[3]) المؤمنين، لليهود دينهم وللمسلمين دينهم، مواليهم وأنفسهم إلا من ظلم وأثم، فإنه لا يوتغ إلا نفسه وأهل بيته.

26- The Jews of Banī Najjār shall have the same (rights) as the Jews of Banī ʿAwf.

26- وأن ليهود بني النجار مثل ما ليهود بني عوف.

27- The Jews of Banīl- Ḥārith shall have the same (rights) as the Jews of Banī ʿAwf.

27- وأن ليهود بني الحارث مثل ما ليهود بني عوف.

---

3. A different reading in Abū ʿUbayd Ibn sallām, *Kitāb al-Amwāl*, ed. M. Khalīl Harās (Cairo, 1968), 147. Also Ibn Kathīr, *Al-Bidāya wal-Nihāya* (Cairo, 1932), I, 43.

28- The Jews of Banī Sāʿida shall have the same (rights) as the Jews of Banī ʿAwf.

28- وأن ليهود بني ساعدة مثل ما ليهود بني عوف.

29- The Jews of Bin Jashm shall have the same (rights) as the Jews of Banī ʿAwf.

29- وأن ليهود بن جشم مثل ما ليهود بني عوف.

30- The Jews of Banīl- Aws shall have the same (rights) as the Jews of Banī ʿAwf.

30- وأن ليهود بني الأوس مثل ما ليهود بني عوف.

31- The Jews of Banī Thaʿlaba shall have the same (rights) as the Jews of Banī ʿAwf. But whoever performs an unjust action or commits a crime shall harm solely himself and the people of his house.

31- وان ليهود بني ثعلبة مثل ما ليهود بني عوف،إلا من ظلم وأثم، فإنه لا يوتغ إلا نفسه وأهل بيته.

32- The Jafna (family) is a branch of the Thaʿlaba [tribe] and because of this they shall be considered as the Thaʿlaba.

32- وأن جفنة بطن من ثعلبة كأنفسهم.

33- Banī Shuṭayba shall have the same rights as the Jews of Banī ʿAwf. Observation of one's undertakings eliminates treachery/breaking of treaties.

33- وأن لبني الشطيبة مثل ما ليهود بني عوف، وأن البر دون الإثم.

34- The clients/allies of Thaʿlaba shall be considered as Thaʿlaba themselves.

34- وأن موالي ثعلبة كأنفسهم.

35- Those associated with Jews (by alliance and bonds of mutual protection) shall be considered as Jews themselves.

35- وأن بطانة يهود كأنفسهم.

36- Among them (Jews) none may go (on a military campaign with the Muslims) without the permission of Muhammad.

36- وانه لا يخرج منهم أحد إلا بإذن محمّد.

36.B- It shall not be forbidden to take revenge of a wound. Surely if a person happens to kill another, both he and his family shall be responsible as a consequence, except if he kills one who acts wrongfully (*zalama*). God is with those who best obey this document.

36ب وانه لا ينحجز على ثار جرح، وأنه من فتك فبنفسه وأهل بيته إلا من ظلم وأن الله على أبر هذا.

37- In case of war Jews bear their expenses and the Muslims theirs. Surely they shall cooperate among themselves, in opposing those who wage war against the people designated on this sheet (document). There shall be good counsel and advice between them. Observation of one's undertakings eliminates treachery/breaking of treaties.

37- وأن على اليهود نفقتهم، وعلى المسلمين نفقتهم، وأن بينهم النصر على من حارب أهل هذه الصحيفة، وأن بينهم النصح والنصيحة والبر دون الإثم.

37.B- No one may commit a crime against his ally; surely the oppressed shall receive help.

37ب- وأنه لا يأثم امرؤ بحليفه، وأن النصر للمظلوم.

38- Jews along with Muslims shall bear the expenses of wars fought together.

38- وأن اليهود ينفقون مع المؤمنين ما داموا محاربين.

Decrees addressing *Ahl al-Ṣaḥīfah* (the people of the constitution)

39- On behalf of the people designated by this document (constitution), the Yathrib (*jawf*) constitutes a protected territory.

39- وأن يثرب حرام جوفها لأهل هذه الصحيفة

40- The protected person is like (one's) self, he shall not be oppressed nor shall he commit any crime.

40- وأن الجاركالنفس غير مضارّ ولا آثم.

41- A woman shall not be accorded protection except by permission of her people.

41- وأنه لا تجار حرمة إلا بإذن أهلها.

42- Whatsoever aggression/misdemeanor or quarrel that occurs between the people designated on this sheet, which is feared may cause dissension, will be referred to Allah and his messenger Muhammad. Allah is (surety) for the truest and most righteous observance of what is in this document.

42- وأنه لا ما كان بين أهل هذه الصحيفة من حدث، أو اشتجار يخاف فساده، فإن مردّه إلى الله وإلى محمد رسول الله (صلى الله عليه وسلّم)، وأن الله على أتقى ما في هذه الصحيفة وأبرّه

43- Neither Quraysh nor those assisting them shall receive protection.

43- وأنه لا تجار قريش ولا من نصرها.

44- There shall be cooperation among them (Muslims and Jews) against those who invade Yathrib.

44- وأن بينهم النصر من دهم يثرب.

45- If they (the Jews) are invited (by the Muslims) to make and adopt a peace agreement, they shall make that agreement and adopt it; and if they (the Jews) suggest the same thing (to the Muslims), they shall have the same rights from the Muslims; except in cases of war over religious issues.

45- وإذا دعوا إلى صلح يصالحونه ويلبسونه فإنهم يصالحونه ويلبسونه، وأنهم إذا دعوا إلى مثل ذلك، فإنه لهم على المؤمنين إلا من حارب في الدين.

45-B) Each group is responsible for the area belonging to it (with regard to defense and other needs.)

45ب-على كل أناس حصتهم من جانبهم الذي قبلهم.

46- The Jews of al-ʾAws, their *mawla* and themselves, shall have the same rights agreed upon on this sheet (document), with sincere/complete observation from the people designated on this sheet. Observation of one's undertakings eliminates treachery/breaking of treaties. He who commits a breach (of this treaty) commits it against himself alone. God is with those who best and truly observe the rules described on this sheet.

46- وأن يهود الأوس مواليهم وأنفسهم على مثل ما لأهل هذه الصحيفة مع البر المحض من اهل هذه الصحيفة، وان البر دون الاثم لا يكسب كاسب الا على نفسه، وان الله على اصدق ما في هذه الصحيفة وأبره.

47- This book (*al-kitāb*) shall not protect the perpetrator of an unjust act or crime from punishment. Whoever goes out shall have security and whoever remains in Medina shall also have security; except one who commits an unjust act or a crime. Allah protects the person who observes undertakings and keeps free of dishonorable acts and offences, and Muhammad the messenger of Allah, Allah bless and honor him.

47- وأنه لا يحول هذا الكتاب دون ظالم أو آثم، وأنه من خرج أمن ومن قعد آمن بالمدينة، إلا من ظلم وأثم، وأن الله جار لمن برّ واتقى، ومحمد رسول الله (صلى الله عليه وسلم).

Bibliography

Abduh, Muhammad, and Muhammad Rashīd Ridā. *Tafsīr al-Manār*, V. 1–12. Egypt: Dār al-Manār, 1954.

Abd al-Rāziq, Ali. *Al-Islām wa Uṣūl al-Ḥukm*. Cairo: Misr Press, 1925.

Ad-Darimi. *Sunan ad-Dārimī*. Beirut: Dār al-Kitāb al-ʿArabī, 1987.

Adraoui, Mohamed Ali. "Borders and Sovereignty in the Islamist and Jihadist Thought: Past and Present." *International Affairs* 93, no. 4 (July 2017): 917–35.

Afsaruddin, Asma. "The Hermeneutics of Inter-faith Relations: Retrieving Moderation and Pluralism as Universal Principles in Quranic Exegesis." *Journal of Religious Ethics* 37, no. 2 (2009): 331–54.

———. "Obedience to Political Authority: An Evolutionary Concept." In *Islamic Democratic Discourse*, edited by M. A. Muqtedar Khan, 37–60. Lanham, MD: Lexington Books, 2006.

Al-ʿAlāylī, Shaykh Abdullah. *As-Ṣiḥāḥ fil-Lugha wal-ʿUlūm*. Edited by Nadīm and Usāma Marʿashlī. Beirut: Dār al-Ḥaḍāra al-ʿArabiya, 1974.

Al-ʿAtī, Ibrāhīm. *Al-Insān fī Falsafat Al-Fārābī*. Beirut: Dār al-Nubūgh, 1998.

Al-Bukhārī. *Al-Jāmiʿ as-Ṣaḥiḥ*. Beirut: Dār ʾIḥyāʾ at-Turāth al-ʿArabī, 1980.

Al-Fārābī, Abū Naṣr Muhammad. *Arāʾ Ahl Al-Madīna Al-Fāḍila*. Edited by Albert Naṣrī Nādir. Beirut: Maṭbaʿat Al-Kāthūlīkiyya, 1959.

———. *Kitāb as-Siyāsa al-Madaniyya al-Mulaqqab bi-Mabādiʾ al-Mawjūdāt*. Edited by Fawzi al-Najjar. Beirut: Maṭbaʿat Al-Kāthūlīkiya, 1964.

Al-Faruqi, Maysam. "Umma: The Orientalists and the Quranic Concept of Identity." *Journal of Islamic Studies* 16, no. 1 (2005): 1–34.

Algar, Hamid. *Islam and Revolution*. Berkeley: Mizan Press, 1981.

Al-Hibri, Azizah. "Islamic and American Constitutional Law: Borrowing Possibilities or a History of Borrowing?" *University of Pennsylvania Journal of Constitutional Law* 1, no. 3 (Spring 1999): 492–527.

Al-Kawākibī, Abd al-Raḥmān. *Al-ʾAʿmāl al-Kāmila lil-Kawākibī*, edited by Mohammad Jamāl Ṭaḥḥān. Beirut: Markaz Dirāsāt al-Wiḥda al-ʿArabiyya, 1995.

———. *Um al-Qura*. Egypt: al-Taqadum Press.

Al-Khomeini, Ruhullah. *Al-Ḥukūma al-Islāmiyya*. Beirut: Beirut University College, 1974.

Al-Māwardī, Abul-Hassan. *al-Ahkam al-Sultaniya*. Cairo: Matba'at al-Watan, 1880.

Al-Muṭahharī, Murtada. *Ṭahārat al-Rūḥ*. Translated by Khalīl Zāil al-ʿAṣāmī. Beirut: Muʾassasat at-Tārīkh al-ʿArabī, 2004.

Al-Naysābūrī, Abī al-Ḥusayn Muslim Bin al-Ḥajjāj al-Qushayrī. *Ṣaḥīḥ Muslim*. Riyāḍ: Maktabat al-Rushd, 2001.

Al-Qāḍī, Wadād. "The Term "Khalīfa" in Early Exegetical Literature." *Die Welt des Islams*, New Series, Bd. 28. No. ¼ (1988): 392–411.

Al-Qummī, Abū al-Ḥasan ʿAli Bin 'Ibrahīm.*Tafsīr al-Qummī*. Edited by Ṭayyib al-Mūsawī al-Jaza'irī, V. 1–2. Beirut: Dār as-Surūr, 1991.

Al-Qurṭubī, Abī Abdullah Moḥammad Bin Aḥmad Al-Ansārī. *Al-Jāmiʿ li-'Aḥkām al-Qur'an*. Beirut: Dār 'Iḥyā' al-Turāth al-ʿArabī, 1985.

———. *Mukhtaṣar Tafsīr al-Qurṭubī*. Beirut: Dār al-Kitāb al-ʿArabī, 1987.

As-Sayyid, Riḍwān. *Al-Umma wal-Jamāʿa was-Sulṭa*. Beirut: Dār Iqraʾ, 1984.

Al-Waqidi, Muhammad b. 'Umar. *Kitab al-Maghazi*. Edited by Marseden Jones. London: Oxford University Press, 1966.

Aristotle. *The Politics and the Constitution of Athens*. Edited by Stephen Everson. Cambridge: Cambridge University Press, 1996.

———. *Politics*. Translated by C. D. C. Reeve. Indianapolis: Hackett, 1998.

———. *The Complete Works of Aristotle: The Revised Oxford Translation*. Edited by Jonathan Barnes. Oxford: Oxford University Press, 1982.

———. *Aristotle's Nicomachean Ethics*. Edited by Robert C. Bartlett and Susan D. Collins. Chicago: University of Chicago Press, 2011.

Arjomand, Said Amir. "The Constitution of Medina: A Sociolegal Interpretation of Muhammad's Acts of Foundation of the Ummah." *International Journal of Middle East Studies* 41 (2009): 555–75.

Asad, Muhammad. *The Message of the Qurʾān*. Bristol, UK: Book Foundation, 2003.

As-Ṣālihī, Shams ad-Dīn Bin Ali Bin Ṭūlūn. *Risāla fi Tafsīr Qawlihi Taʿāla: Inna Ibrāhīm Kāna Umma*. Edited by Muhammad Yūsuf. Beirut: Ibn Ḥazm Press, 1997.

At-Ṭabarī, Abū Jaʿfar Muhammad Bin Jarīr. *Jamiʿ al-Bayān*, V. 1–25. Beirut: Dār al-Fikr, 1995.

At-Ṭabaṭabāʾī, Muhammad Ḥusayn. *Al-Qurʾān fil-Islām*. Translated by Aḥmad al-Ḥusaynī. Tehran: Dār az-Zahrāʾ, 1973.

———. *Al-Mīzān fi Tafsīr al-Qurʾān*. Beirut: Muʾasassat al-ʾAʿlamī lil-Maṭbūʿāt, 1983.

At-Tirmithī. *Sunan at-Tirmithī* (*Al-Jāmiʿ as-Ṣaḥīḥ*). Beirut: Dār al-Kitāb al-ʿArabī, 2005.

Bearman P. et al., ed. *Encyclopedia of Islam, Second Edition*. Brill: 2009, American University of Beirut, http://www.paulyonline.brill.nl/subscriber/entry?entry=islam_COM-1133.

Bin Nabiy, Mālik. *Mushkilat Al-Afkār fī Al-ʿĀlam al-Islāmī*. Damascus: Dār Al-Fikr, 2002.

Borgatta, Edgar F., ed. *Encyclopedia of Sociology*. New York: Macmillan Reference USA, 2001.

Bulac, Ali. "The Medina Document." In *Liberal Islam,* edited by Charles Kurzman, 169–78. New York: Oxford University Press, 1998.

Claeys, Gregory, ed. *Encyclopedia of Modern Political Thought*. CQ Press, 2013.

Collins, Susan D. *Aristotle and the Rediscovery of Citizenship*. Cambridge: Cambridge University Press, 2009.

Del Sarto, Raffaella A. "Contentious Borders in the Middle East and North Africa: Context and Concepts." *International Affairs* 93, no. 4 (July 2017): 767–87.

Denny, Frederick. "Community and Salvation: The Meaning of the Ummah in the Qurān." PhD diss., University of Chicago, Illinois, 1974.

———. "The Meaning of Ummah in the Quran." *History of Religions* 15, no. 1 (August 1975): 39–42.

———. "Ummah in the Constitution of Medina." *Journal of Near Eastern Studies* 36, no. 1 (January 1977): 39–47.

Donner, Fred M. *Muhammad and the Believers: At the Origins of Islam*. Cambridge: The Belknap Press of Harvard University Press, 2010.

Eliade, Mircea, ed. *The Encyclopedia of Religion*. New York: Macmillan Publishing Company, 1987.

Emon, Anver. "Reflections on the Constitution of Medina: An Essay on Methodology and Ideology in Islamic Legal History." *UCLA Journal of Islamic and Near Eastern Law* 1, no. 1 (Fall/Winter 2001–2002): 103–33.

Enayat, Hamid. *Modern Islamic Political Thought*. London: Macmillan, 1982.

Esposito, John, ed. *The Oxford Encyclopedia of the Islamic World*. Oxford: Oxford University Press, 2009.

———., ed. *The Oxford Encyclopedia of the Modern Islamic World*. New York: Oxford University Press, 2001.

Etzioni, Amitai. "The Attack on Community: The Grooved Debate." *Society* 32, no. 5(July/August 1995): 12–17.

———., ed. *New Communitarian Thinking: Persons, Virtues, Institutions and Communities*. London: University Press of Virginia, 1995.

———. *The Spirit of Community: Rights, Responsibilities, and the Communitarian Agenda*. New York: Crown Publishers, 1993.

Faḍlallah, Muhammad Ḥusayn. *Min Waḥy al-Qurʾān*, V. 1–24. Beirut: Dār al-Malāk, 1998.

Fisher, R. "Fractioning Conflict." In *Conflict Resolution: Contributions of the Behavioral Sciences,* edited by C. G. Smith, 157–69. Notre Dame, IN: University of Notre Dame Press, 1971.

Fletcher, G. P. "The Case for Tolerance." *Social Philosophy and Policy* 13, no. 1 (1996): 229–39.

Fukuyama, Francis. "The End of History?" *The National Interest*, Summer 1989.

Ghannouchi, Rached. *The Islamic Conception of the State*, Conference of the Young Muslims in London, April 1992.

Giannakis, Elias. "The Concept of Ummah." *Graeco-Arabica* 2 (1983): 103–4.

Gibb, H. A. R., and J. H. Kramers, eds. *The Shorter Encyclopedia of Islam*. Leiden: E. J. Brill, 1954.

Gil. "The Medinan Opposition to the Prophet." *JSAI* 10 (1987): 65–96.

Gottlieb, Paula. *The Virtue of Aristotle's Ethics*. Cambridge: Cambridge University Press, 2009.

Habermas, Jurgen. "The European Nation-State: On the Past and Future of Sovereignty and Citizenship." Translated by Ciaran Cronin. *Public Culture* 10, no. 2 (1998).

Hallaq, Wael B. *The Impossible State*. New York: Columbia University Press, 2013.

Halper, Edward. "Aristotle and the Liberal State." In *Aristotle's Politics Today*, edited by Lenn E. Goodman and Robert Talisse, 33–44. Albany: State University of New York Press, 2007.

Ḥamīdulla, Muhammad. *Majmūʿat al-Wathāʾiq as-Siyāsiyya*. Cairo: Lajnat at-Taʾlīf wat-Tarjama wal-Nashr, 1941.

Ḥanafī, Ḥasan. *Al-Wāqiʿ Al-ʿArabī Al-Rāhin*. Cairo: Dār al-ʿayn lil-Nashr, 2012.

Hodgson, Marshall. *The Venture of Islam*, V. 3. Chicago: University of Chicago Press, 1974.

Hourani, Albert. *Arabic Thought in the Liberal Age*. London: Oxford University, 1962.

Hoyland, R. "Sebeos, the Jews and the Rise of Islam." In *Medieval and Modern Perspectives on Muslim-Jewish Relations.* Edited by R. L. Nettler, 89–102. Oxford: Harwood Academic Publishers, 1995.

Ibn Abī Ṭālib, Ali. *Nahjul Balāgha*. Edited by Muhammad ʿAbduh. Beirut: Muʾassasat al-ʾAʿlamīlil-Maṭbūʿāt, 2003.

Ibn an-Nadīm. *Al-Fahrast*. Translated by Ayman Sayyid. London: Muʿassasat Al-Furqāan lil-Turāth, 2009.

Ibn Hisham, Abou Mohammad Abd al-Malek. *Al-Sīra Al-Nabawiyya*. Edited by Suhail Zakkar. Beirut: Dār al-Fikr, 1992.

Ibn Kathīr, Abīl-Fidāʾ Al-Ḥāfiẓ. *Tafsīr Al-Qurʾān Al-ʿAẓīm*. Beirut: Dār Al-Fikr, 1997.

———. *Al-Bidāya wal-Nihāya*. Beirut: Maktabat al-Maʿārif, 1966.

Ibn Khaldun. *Muqaddimat Ibn Khaldūn*. Cairo: Lajnat Al-Bayān Al-ʿArabī, 1962.

———. *The Muqaddimah: An Introduction to History*. Translated by Franz Rosenthal. Princeton, NJ: Princeton University Press, 1967.

Ibn Maja. *Sunan Ibn Māja*. Beirut: Dār al-Fikr, 1995.

Ibn Manḍhūr. *Lisān al-ʿArab*. Beirut: Dārʾ Iḥyāʾ at-Turāth al-ʿArabī, 1993.

Ibn Sallām, Abūʿ Ubayd. *Kitāb al-Amwāl*. Edited by M. Khalīl Harrās. Cairo: Maktabat al-Kullīyāt al-Azharīyah, 1968.

ʿImāra, Mohammad. *Nathariyat al-Khilāfa*. Cairo: Dār al-Thaqā al-jadīda.

———. *Ad-Dīn wal-Dawla*. Cairo: Maṭābiʿ al-Hayʾa al-Miṣriyya al-ʿĀmma lil-Kitāb, 1986.

———. *Ad-Dawla al-Islāmiyya bayna al3ilmāniyya wal-Sulṭa ad-Dīniyya*. Cairo: Dār al-Shurūq, 2007.

Jackson, Roy. *Mawlana Mawdudi and Political Islam*. London: Routledge, 2011.

Jackson, Sherman. "Islamic Reform between Law and the Nation-State." In *The Oxford Handbook of Islam and Politics*, edited by John Esposito and Emad El-Din Shahin, 42–53. Oxford: Oxford University Press, 2013.

Jihāmī, Jīrār, and Samīḥ Daghīm. *Al-Mawsūʿa al-Jāmiʿa li-Muṣṭalaḥāt al-Fikr al-ʾArabīwal-ʿIslāmī*. Beirut: Maktabat Lubnān Nāshirūn, 2006.

———, and Rafīq al-ʿAjam. *Mawsūʿat Muṣṭalaḥāt al-Fikr al-Naqdī al-ʾArabī wal-ʿIslāmī al-Muʿāṣir*. Beirut: MaktabatLubnānNāshirūn, 2004.

Kabbara, Nazīh. *Abd al-Raḥmān al-Kawākibī: Ḥayātuh wa ʿAsruh wa ʾĀrāʾuh*. Lebanon: Jarūs Press, 1994.

Khadduri, Majid. "Translator's introduction." In *The Islamic Law of Nations: Shaybānī's Siyar*. Baltimore, MD: John Hopkins University Press, 1966.

Krämer, Gudrun, et al., eds. *Encyclopedia of Islam* III. Brill: 2009, American University of Beirut, http://www.paulyonline.brill.nl/subscriber/entry?entry=ei3_SIM-0323.

Lang, Jeffrey. *Even Angels Ask: A Journey to Islam in America*. Beltsville, MD: Amana Publications, 2014.

Lecker, Michael. *The "Constitution of Medina": Muhammad's First Legal Document*. Princeton, NJ: The Darwin Press, 2004.

Liew, Han Hsien. "The Caliphate of Adam: Theological Politics of the Qur'ānic Term Ḫalīfa." *Arabica* V. 63, nos. 1–2 (2016): 1–29.

MacIntyre, Alasdair C. *After Virtue: A Study in Moral Theory*, 2nd ed. London: Duckworth, 1985.

———. *Whose Justice? Which Rationality?* Notre Dame, IN: University of Notre Dame Press, 1988.

Madigan, Daniel. *The Qur'an's Self-Image*. Princeton: Princeton University Press, 2001.

Mahdi, Muhsin S. *Al-Farabi and the Foundation of Islamic Political Philosophy.* Chicago: The University of Chicago Press, 2001.

Mahoney, James, and Dietrich Rueschemeyer. *Comparative Historical Analysis in the Social Sciences.* Cambridge: Cambridge University Press, 2003.

Maritain, Jacques. *Man and the State.* Chicago: University of Chicago Press, 1968.

March, Andrew. "Liberal Citizenship and the Search for an Overlapping Consensus: The Case of Muslim Minorities." *Philosophy and Public Affairs* 34, no. 4 (2006): 373–421.

Martin, Vanessa. *Creating an Islamic State: Khomeini and the Making of a New Iran.* London: I.B. Tauris, 2007.

Mawdūdī, Sayyid Abul ʿAlāʾ. *The Islamic Way of Life*, edited by Khurshid Ahmad and Khurram Murad. United Kingdom: The Islamic Foundation, 1986.

Meier, Daniel. "Bordering the Middle East." *Geopolitics* 23 (2018): 495–504.

Miller, Fred D., Jr. "Aristotelian Statecraft and Modern Politics." In *Aristotle's Politics Today*, edited by Lenn E. Goodman and Robert Talisse, 13–32. Albany: State University of New York Press, 2007.

Minar, David, and Scott Greer. *The Concept of Community; Readings with Interpretations.* Chicago: Aldine Publishing Company, 1969.

Moses, Jonathon W. "The Umma of Democracy." *Security Dialogue* 37, no. 4 (2006): 489–508.

Mūsa, Faraḥ. *Ad-Dīn wad-Dawla wal-Umma ʿand al-Imām Muhammad Mahdī Shams Ad-Dīn.* Beirut: Dār al-Hādī, 2001.

Muʾnis, Ḥusayn. *Dustūr Ummat al-Islām.* Cairo: ad-Dār al-Miṣriyya al-Lubnāniyya lil-nashr, 1993.

Mulhall, Stephen, and Adam Swift. *Liberals and Communitarians.* Cambridge: Blackwell Publishers, 1996.

Nasr, Seyyed Hossein. *The Essential Seyyed Hossein Nasr.* Edited by William Chittick. Canada: World Wisdom Press, 2007.

Nasr, Seyyed Vali Reza. *Mawdudi and the Making of Islamic Revivalism.* Oxford: Oxford University Press, 1996.

Naṣṣār, Naṣīf. *Mafhūm al-Umma bayna ad-Dīn wal-Tārīkh.* Beirut: Dār at-Talīʿa, 1978.

Nietzsche, Friedrich. *Beyond Good and Evil: Prelude to a Philosophy of the Future.* Translated by R. J. Hollingdale. Harmondsworth, UK: Penguin, 1974.

Orwin, Alexander. *Redefining the Muslim Community: Ethnicity, Religion and Politics in the Thought of Alfarabi.* Philadelphia: University of Pennsylvania Press, 2017.

Perry, Glenn E. "The Islamic World: Egypt and Iran." In *Politics and Religion in the Modern World*, edited by George Moyser, 97–134. London, New York: Routledge, 1991.

Pickthall, Mohammad. *The Glorious Quran: Text and Explanatory Translation*. New York: Mostazafan Foundation of New York, 1984.

Quṭb, Sayyid. *Fī Ẓilāl al-Qur'ān*. Cairo, Beirut: Dār al-Shurūq, 2005.

———. *In the Shade of the Quran*. Translated and edited by Adil Salahi and Ashur Shamis. United Kingdom: The Islamic Foundation, 2001.

Rahman, Fazlur. *Major Themes of the Qurān*. Minneapolis: Bibliotheca Islamica, 1980.

Rawls, John. *Political Liberalism*. New York: Columbia University Press, 1993.

———. "The Domain of the Political and Overlapping Consensus." *New York University Law Review* 64, no. 2 (May 1989): 233–55.

Riḍa, Rashīd. *Al-Khilāfa wal Imāma al-Uẓma*. Cairo: Manār Press, 1923.

———. "Bayān Ḥaqiqat al-Khilāfa wa Shurūṭ al-Khalīfa fil-Islām." *Al-Manār* 27, no. 3 (1926): 226–32.

Roy, Olivier. *Globalized Islam: The Search for a New Ummah*. New York: Columbia University Press, 2004.

Rubin, Uri. " 'The Constitution of Medina' Some Notes." *Studia Islamica* 62 (1985): 5–23.

Sadiki, Larbi. "The Arab Spring: The 'People' in International Relations." In *International Relations of the Middle East*, edited by Louise Fawcett, 324–55. Oxford: Oxford University Press, 2016.

Serjeant, R. B. "The Sunnah Jami'ah, Pacts with the Yathrib Jews and the Tahrim of Yathrib: Analysis and Translation of the Documents Comprised in the So-Called 'Constitution of Medina.' " *Bulletin of the School of Oriental and African Studies, University of London*, V. 41, no. 1 (1978): 1–42.

———. "The Constitution of Medina." *The Islamic Quarterly* VIII (1964): 3–16.

———. "Haram and Hawtah, the Sacred Enclave in Arabia." In *Melanges Taha Hussein*, edited by Abdu-r-raḥmān Badawī, 41–58. Cairo: Dār al-Maʿārif, 1962.

Shaḥrūr, Moḥammad. *Dirāsāt Islāmiyya Muʿāṣira fi al-Dawla wal-Mujtama*. Damascus: Al-Ahālī lil-Ṭibāʿa wal-Nashr wal-Tawzīʿ, 1994.

———. *Al-Kitāb wal-Qur'ān: Qirā'a Muʿāṣira*. Damascus: Al-Ahālī lil-Ṭibāʿa wal-Nashr wal-Tawzīʿ, 1990.

———. *Ad-Dīn wal-Sulṭa: Qirā'a Muʿāṣira lil-Ḥāimiyya*. Beirut: Dār al-Sāqī, 2014.

Shakir, H. M. *Holy Qur'an: al-Qur'ān al-Ḥakīm*. Elmhurst, NY: Tahrike Tarsile Qur'an, 1984.

Shams ad-Dīn, Muhammad Mahdī. *Fil-Ijtimāʿ as-Siyāsī al-Islāmī*. Beirut: Al-Mu'a-sassa al-Jāmiʿiyalil-Dirāsātwal-Nashr, 1992.

———. *Bayna al-Jāhiliyya wal-Islām*. Beirut: Al-Mu'assasa al-Jāmiʿiyya lil-Dirāsāt wal-Nashr, 1975.

———. *At-Tajdīd fil-Fikr al-Islāmī.* Beirut: Dār al-Manhal al-Lubnānī lil-Ṭibāʿa wal-Nashr, 1997.

Simonsen, J. B. *Studies in the Genesis and Early Development of the Caliphal Taxation System.* Copenhagen: AkademiskForlag, 1988.

Smith, Thomas W. "Aristotle on the Conditions for and Limits of the Common Good." *The American Political Science Review* 93, no. 3 (September 1999): 625–36.

Ṭaḥḥān, Mohammad Jamāl. *al-Ru'a al-Iṣlāḥiyya lil-Mufakkir al-Nahḍawī Abd al-Raḥmān al-Kawākibī.* Damascus: Ittiḥād al-Kuttāb al-ʿArab, 2007.

Taylor, Charles. *The Ethics of Authenticity.* Cambridge: Harvard University Press, 1992.

Thiry, Leon. "Nation, State, Sovereignty and Self-Determination." *Peace Research* 13, no. 1 (January 1981).

Tibawi, A. L. "Second Critique of English-Speaking Orientalists and Their Approach to Islam and the Arabs." *Islamic Quarterly* 23 (1979): 3–50.

Walbridge, John. *God and Logic in Islam: The Caliphate of Reason.* Cambridge: Cambridge University Press, 2011.

Walzer, Michael. *Obligations: Essays on Disobedience, War and Citizenship.* Cambridge, MA: Harvard University Press, 1970.

Watt, W. Montgomery. *Muhammad at Medina.* Oxford: Clarendon Press, 1956.

———. *Islamic Political Thought.* Edinburgh: Edinburgh University Press, 1987.

———. *Islam and the Integration of Society.* Illinois: Northwestern University Press, 1961.

———. "The Conception of the Charismatic Community in Islam." *Numen* VII (1960): 77–90.

———. "Conditions of Membership of the Islamic Community." *Studia Islamica* XXL (1964): 5–12.

Wellhausen, Julius. "Excursus: Muhammad's Constitution of Medina." In *Muhammad and the Jews of Medina*, translated by Wolfgang Behn. Freiburg im Breisgau: K. Schwarz, 1975.

Wolin, Sheldon S. "The Liberal/Democratic Divide, on Rawl's Political Liberalism." *Political Theory* 24 (February 1996): 103–8.

Yack, Bernard. *The Problems of a Political Animal: Community, Justice and Conflict in Aristotelian Political Thought.* Berkeley: University of California Press, 1993.

Yafeh, Hava Lazarus. "Is There a Concept of Redemption in Islam?" In *Types of Redemption*, edited by Werblowsky and Bleeker, 168–80. Leiden: E.J. Brill, 1970.

Yildrim, Yetkin. "The Medina Charter: A Historical Case of Conflict Resolution." *Islam and Christian-Muslim Relations* 20, no. 4 (2010): 439–50.

Yusuf Ali, Abdullah. *The Meanings of the Illustrious Qur'ān: English Translation with Introduction.* New Delhi: KitabBhavan, 2000.

Index

Pages in **bold** indicate illustrations.

Abbasid Caliphate, 8, 194
Abd al-Rāziq, Ali, 177, 193–94, 196
ʿAbd al-Razzāq al-Sanʿānī, 104
ʿAbduh, Muhammad (modern exegete), 15, 17–18, 22–23, 33, 51, 119
on Abraham, 97
on becoming *khalīfa*, 184, 190
colonial experiences of, 26, 27–28
on enforcing *sharīʿah*, 126
on enjoining (*maʿrūf*) and deterring (*munkar*), 244
on God judging people by what they know, 114
on good and evil, 68, 185, 190
of *ḥanīf*, 94–95
on *hijrah* ("migration"), 27–28
on injustice, 72
intellectual similarites between ʿAbduh and Quṭb, 264
on *khayr ummah* as the best *ummah*, 116, 117–18
and *mīthāq* (Covenant), 43–44
on Muhammad as "*al-ummī*," 51
on "names" taught by God to Adam, 184
on oneness of God's religion (*tawḥīd*), 44–45
on one *ummah* (*ummah wāḥidah*), 22–23, 69, 70, 122
on people of the book (*Ahl Al-Kitāb*), 110, 118
on perfection of human beings, 235
on political community, 225–26
on political leadership, 128, 264
on the Qurʾān, 78, 97, 110–11, 124–25, 126–27, 175
relating concepts of *wasaṭ*, *shahāda*, and *qibla* together, 266
on religious tolerance, 64
responsibility of calling people to goodness, 117
on *sharīʿah*, 125
on *shūra*, 241–42
on *sibṭ* and *ummah*, 56
on stages of human development, 123
on those in power related to followers, 26
on *ʾulī ʾl-amr*, 250–51
on *ʾūlū baqiyya*, 67–68
on *ummah muqtaṣida*, 112

ʿAbduh, Muhammad (continued)
  on *ummah muslimah* (Muslim *ummah*), 85–86, 105–106, 118
  on *ummah's* survival, 119
  unity reflecting God's mercy, 71
  using reason in interpreting religious texts, 16, 31
  on *wasaṭ*, 105, 106, 112
Abode of covenant (*dār al-ʿahd*), 121
Abode of peace (*dār as-salām*), 92, 120, 167, 269
Abode of reconciliation (*dār al-ṣulḥ*), 121
Abode of war (*dār al-ḥarb*), 120, 167, 269
Abraham (Prophet) or *Ibrāhīm* (Prophet), 45, 77, 93, 100, 103, 131
  Abrahamic *sharīʿah*, 89
  as *al-ḥanīf*, 93–100
  and concept of *ḥanīf*, 129
  and the covenant with God, 87
  as exemplary model of the Muslim individual, 82, 103, 129, 237, 265
  and the house (*Kaʿba*), 86, 101, 103
  Medinan verses on, 77, 129, 265, 266
  millat Ibrāhīm (creed of Abraham), 93–100, 238, 266, 267
  monotheistic message of, 87, 89, 90, 95, 97, 265
  and the Muslim *ummah*, 85, 86, 87, 89, 104, 108, 129, 265–66
  and *nusuk* (ritual), 103
  prayer of, 161–62
  qibla of, 103, 104, 109, 236, 238, 266
  as the Qurʾānic model, 137
  submission to the will of God, 83, 86, 87, 90, 93, 96, 99, 101, 103, 108, 129, 265
  trial of, 83
  as an *ummah*, 80–83, 93, 108, 237–38, 257
  as an '*ummah 'qānitan lillah*,' 103
Abū l-Jārūd, 16
Abū ʿUbayd al-Qasim b. Sallam. *See* Ibn Sallām, Abūʿ Ubayd
Active justice (*wasaṭiyyah*). See *Wasaṭiyyah* (active justice)
Active or dynamic Islam (*al-Islām al-ḥarakī*), 79, 117
Adam, 22, 23
  angels and Satan ordered to prostrate before, 185, 186, 189–90
  "names" taught by God to Adam, 180, 181, 184–85, 189, 192–93
  as a political ruler and viceregent of God, 183
Ad-dalīl (proof), 107
ʿAdl (just), 104, 235, 246, 266. *See also* Justice
Adraoui, Mohamed Ali, 14
Afsaruddin, Asma, 104–105, 111, 112, 250, 251
ʾAḥadīth (prophetic sayings), 111, 250. See also *Ḥadīths*
Ahl al-ḥal wal-ʿaqd ("the people who loosen and bind" or Jurists), 2, 120, 121, 167, 173, 174, 250
Ahl al-Kitāb ("People of the Book"), 68, 109–14, 117, 129, 130, 131
  Medina Constitution addressing, 267
  Qurʾān addressing, 109, 110, 111, 115, 118, 120, 140, 141, 225, 270
  See also Christians; Jews
Ahl al-ṣaḥifa (people of the Medina Constitution), decrees addressed to, 49, 138, 143, 158–59, 160, 164, 168, 171, 225, 268

A'imma. See *Imām*
Ajal (appointed term) and *ummah*, 24–30, 73
Al-Afghānī, Jalāl al-Dīn, 17–18
Al-Ahkam al-Sultaniya (Al-Māwardī), 250
Al-aḥzāb (confederates of evil), 65–66, 68, 74, 265
'Ala 'imma (kingship or luxury), 34
Al-'anbiyā (*sūrat*), 62
Al-'aql (reason/cognition), 32, 185
  hidāyat al-'aql (guidance derived of reason), 23, 122
  "instrumental reason," 214
Al-'A'rāf (*sūrat*), 24, 25–26, 27, 36, 50–54, 55, 78
'Ala ummah, 32–33, 34
'Alaykum ("over you"), use of *minkum* instead, 251
Al-bayyināt (clear proofs), 122, 123
Al-Bukhārī, 81, 165
Al-Fārābī, Abu Nasr Muhammad, 174–75, 177
  on cities, 179, 200, 211–12, 222–23, 274
  on finding the mean, 235
  on limiting conflict, 212
  on Muslim *ummah*, 271, 274
  on need for a convention to fulfull goals, 232
  on need for human association, 178–79
  on political roles, 245
  on *ummah*, 199–200, 201, 203, 211–12, 245, 271
  on virtuousness, 200, 222–23, 271
  on "voluntary traits," 203, 271–72
  on ways of life, 199–200, 205, 212, 272, 275
  See also Farabian political philosophy
Al-Faruqi, Maysam, 29–30, 50
Al-fikra al-aṣliya (originial idea) vs. *al-fikra al-fa'āla* (effective idea), 4–5
Al-ghalaba (dominance) as pillar of *khilāfa*, 193
Al-Ḥaj (*sūrat*), 100
Al-ḥākimiyya al-ilāhiyya (divine rulings), 259–60
Al-ḥanīf. See *Ḥanīf*
Al-Ḥasan al-'Askarī (*Imām*), 16
Al-Ḥijr (*sūrat*), 25
Al-Hussein (*Imām*), 181
Ali Bin Abī Ṭālib (*Imām* Ali), 37, 40, 42, 239
'Alī b. Mūsā al-Riḍā, 16
Alien, 217
  alien "other," 1, 62, 268
  resident alien, 218, 219
Al-Islām (submitting in peace), 103, 129, 266
Al-Islām al-ḥarakī (active or dynamic Islam), 79, 117
Al-Islām al-mas'ūl (as a responsible Islam), 85
Al-jamā'a al-islāmiyya, 46, 191
Al-janīf (inclined toward excess and carelessness), 95
Al-Jāthiya (*sūrat*), 34, 35
Al-Kawākibī, Abd al-Raḥmān, 6, 177, 257–59, 260, 261
al-Khandaq, battle of, 165
Al-Kitāb ("the Book"), 84
  as the backbone of the concept of *ummah*, 121
  function of the Book and governance, 122–28
  and leadership and justice, 55–57
  in the Medina Constitution, 41, 167–68, 169, 170
  polis and constitution versus *ummah* and *al-Kitāb*, 222–23

Al-Kitāb (continued)
Qur'ān as *al-Kitāb* ("the Book"), 34–38, 55–57, 122, 124
umam interconnection of based on covenants, sovereignty based on the Book, **60**
and *ummah*, 34–38, 73, 121, 122–28, 264
ummah of the Book (*Al-Kitāb*), 122–28
See also *Ahl Al-Kitāb* (people of the book); Qur'ān
Allah/God
Adam as a political ruler and viceregent of God, 183
Allah alone having the Truth, 48
as All-Knowing, All-Aware, 70
al-wadūd (the loving) as one of God's names, 189
belief in God, 68, 96, 117, 119, 141, 144, 146, 152, 157, 161–62, 203, 268. *See also* Monotheism
God conscious believers (*mu'miniūn*), 88, 256
God not favoring one people over another, 97
God's authority, 37, 192
God's mercy, 1, 8, 69, 70–71, 79, 91, 92, 114, 189, 191, 241, 271
God's punishment of corruption, 67–68, 72
God's *sharī'ah* or divine *sharī'ah*, 2, 117, 192, 210, 253. *See also* Divine law; *Sharī'ah*
khalīfa representing Godly attributes, 238
khilāfa 'an Allah (*khalīfa* on behalf of God), 184–85
mīthāq (covenant) between God and the Prophets, 54, 87, 96
and "names" taught by God to Adam, 180–81, 183–85, 192–93, 270
obedience to God, 82, 97, 107, 173, 194, 252–53
Prophet Muhammad as messenger (prophet of Allah), 41, 53, 135, 164, 167, 169, 256
Qur'ān as direct communication with God, 37–38
raḥmān (one of the names of Allah, the merciful), 186
submission to God, 22, 27, 62, 100, 101, 103. *See also* Abraham (Prophet) or *Ibrāhīm* (Prophet), *millat Ibrāhīm* (creed of Abraham), submission to the will of God
taqwa (piety of God consciousness/awareness), 70, 102
Allies, 143, **144**, 149, 159, 160, 169, 171, 268. See also *Mawla/mawālī* (client/ally)
Al-Madīna Al-Fāḍila (virtuous city), 179, 222
Al-Māwardī, Abul-Hassan, 250
Al-milla al-ḥanīfiya of Abraham. *See* Abraham (Prophet) or *Ibrāhīm* (Prophet), *millat Ibrāhīm* (creed of Abraham)
Al-Muṭahharī, Murtada, 95
Al-Mutrafūn (blind followers), 26, 33–34
Al-Qāḍī, Wadād, 182
Al-Qaeda, 11
Al-Qaṣaṣ (*sūrat*), 25, 47–48
Al-Qummī, Abū al-Ḥasan 'Ali Bin 'Ibrahīm (premodern exegete), 15, 16, 26, 31
on *'ala ummah*, 32, 42

on *al-Kitāb* and the book of the *Ummah*, 35
on angels fear of humans and role of *khalīfa* (human being), 181
on arrogance (*istikbār*), 186
on the best *ummah*, 115
on historical context of the Qur'ān, 175
on *imām*, 38, 39, 40, 41–42
intellectual similarites between Faḏlallah and Al-Qummī, 264
interpreting Qur'ānic citations, 64, 78, 101, 186
on literal nature of, 31, 32, 39, 40, 44, 64, 85
on *nadhīr*, 38–39
on "names" taught by God to Adam, 184
on *sibṭ* and *ummah*, 55
on *ummah*, 41–42, 44, 55, 81, 106, 115
on *ummah muqtaṣida*, 113
on *ummah wāḥidah*, 46
on *wasaṭ*, 106
Al-Qurṭubī, Abī Abdullah Moḥammad Bin Aḥmad Al-Ansārī (premodern exegete), 15, 27
on *Imams*, 39
interpreting Qur'ānic citations, 51, 64, 66
on *khalīfa*, 183
literal interpretation of, 64, 85
on *nadhīr*, 38
on Prophet Abraham, 85, 97, 237
on *qiyāman*, 162
on Qur'ān as divine revelation, 36
on *shirk* and God's punishment for corruption, 67
on *sibṭ* and *ummah*, 55–56
on *ummah*, 56, 58, 66, 82, 85
on *ummah muqtaṣida*, 112
on *ummī*, 51, 52–53
Al-Rāzī. *See* Fakhr ad-Dīn al-Rāzī
Al-ummah maṣdar as-Sulutāt as source of delegating powers, 7
Al-ʿUrwa al-Wuthqā (journal), 18
Al-ʿurwat al-wuthqa (Qur'ānic interpretation), 249
Al-wadūd (the loving) as one of God's names, 189
Al-Waqidi, Muhammad b. 'Umar, 134, 165
Al-yahūd. See Jews
Al-Zamaḵhšharī, Mahmud ibn 'Umar, 112, 183
Al-Zuhri, Muhammad ibn Muslim, 134
Al-Zukhruf (*sūrat*), 32
Amma or *amama* (lead or go intentionally) as a root verb for *ummah*, 25, 29
Angels, 26, 35, 70, 175–76, 182, 183, 184, 189–90, 191, 192–93
creation of, 180
on humans' destructive potential, 180, 181, 185–87, 189, 190, 235
relationship to *khalīfa*, 181
An-Naḥl (*sūrat*), 36
An-Naml (*sūrat*), 57
Appointed term (*ajal*) and *ummah*, 24–30, 73
"Approximist" describing an Aristotelian statesman, 224
Arab uprisings in 2011 (the Arab spring), 11–13, 270, 274, 276
Aristotle, 2–3, 174, 186, 227
Abraham representing the Aritotelian man of perfect integrity, 237

Aristotle *(continued)*
on common good, 216, 222, 227, 244
on conflict, 253
contrasted to Plato, 176
on democracy, 226
on injustice, 233–34, 247, 255
on judgment of many versus a single person, 239
on justice, 236–37, 243–44, 245, 246
on law, 203–204, 207, 229, 249, 275
on limiting deliberation, 242
on nation being subordinate to the city, 200, 274
on the need for a political community, 177–78
on not considering what is best but what is possible, 223–24
on polis, 197–212, 232, 254, 271, 273, 275
on the political animal, 189–91, 270–71
on politics, 211, 216, 256
on public deliberation, 216–17
on reciprocity and "hitting the mean," 233–35
resolving conflict by ignoring virtues in Aristotle and the Qur᾿ān, 208–12
on rule of law, 245, 253
on the salvation of the community, 229
on *telos*, 177–78, 179, 186, 189–90, 191, 197, 208, 228
on unity of virtues, 237–38
on virtue and virtuous activity, 201, 202, 232, 233, 236, 237–38, 257, 261, 274

Arjomand, Said Amir, 137, 139, 141, 147, 150, 155–56, 165, 166
Arrogance (*istikbār*), 186
Asad, Muhammad, 69–70, 71
᾿Asbāb an-nuzūl, 27
᾿Aslimū (surrendering to God), 83, 84, 87, 89, 90, 93–94, 96–97, 98, 100, 101, 238, 265
As-Ṣadiq, *Imām*, 186
As-Sayyid, Riḍwān, 21
As-sulṭān al-a῾ẓam (supreme ruler), 183, 223, 240
At-Ṭabarī, Abū Ja῾far Muhammad Bin Jarīr (premodern exegete), 15, 16, 17, 26
on Abraham, 85, 237
on *῾ala ummah*, 32, 34
on the book of the *Ummah*, 35
on historical context of the Qur᾿ān, 175
on *Imām*, 40, 237
interpreting Qur᾿ānic citations, 27, 39, 55, 64, 78, 81, 85, 101, 115
on leadership, 241, 250
literal interpretation of, 31, 39, 40, 44, 64, 85, 101
on meaning of *khalīfa*, 182–83
on meaning of *ummī*, 51
and *mīthāq* (Covenant), 43
on *muhaymin* (guardian), 124
on *muslimūn*, 97
on *nadhīr*, 38
on "names" taught by God to Adam, 184
on political leadership, 250
on *qiwām*, 162
on the Qur᾿ān, 36, 125
on retribution for a murdered or wounded person, 158
on *sharī῾ah*, 125

on *shūra*, 239
on *sibṭ* and *ummah*, 55
on the Torah, 122, 124
on *ʾūlū baqiyya*, 67
on *ummah*, 22, 51, 55, 56, 66, 78, 81, 122
on *ummah qāʾima*, 109
on *ummah wāḥidah*, 46, 122
on *wasaṭ*, 104
At-Tabarsī, 15
At-Ṭabaṭabāʾī, Muhammad Ḥusayn (modern exegete), 15, 98, 106, 107, 163, 184
Authoritarian rule, 11, 19, 208, 217, 223, 241, 248, 250, 253, 254, 258
Authority
absolute authority, 223
authority figures, 249–55
God's authority, 37, 192
governmental versus religious authority, 4, 6–7, 140, 192, 204, 259–60, **260**
making authority legitimate, 251
marjaʿīyat at-taqlīd ("authority of the source of imitation"), 20
of Prophet Muhammad, 155, 167, 193
scholarly authorities (*Isnād*), 18
See also *ʾUlī ʾl-amr*

Badr, battle of, 165, 243
Balance, 106, 153, 234, 239, 249, 261
and active justice, 275
balanced position of Islamic thought, 105, 235
communitarianism, liberalism and Islamic *ummah* on, 217–21
Faḍlallah on, 105, 236
between individual rights and social responsibility, 3
and least intervention of central power, 153
between religious message and politics, 7
and toppling of *ṭāghūt*, 247–48, 276
and *umma wasaṭ*, 151, 235, 236
and the virtuous city, 179
Banī ʿAwf (addressed in the Medina Constitution), 135, 136, 139, 140, 145, 169
all tribes treated the same as Banī ʿAwf, 156–57
See also Jews
Behavioral conduct and *ummah*, 6
Belief, system of, 30, 93–94, 118, 121, 123, 142, 249
belief in God, 68, 96, 117, 119, 141, 144, 146, 152, 157, 161–62, 203, 268. *See also* Monotheism
complete belief, 140
diversity of, 47, 64–65, 67, 80, 253
proper belief blossoms right action, 118, 149, 203, 270
true belief (*al-īmān as-ṣaḥiḥ*), 123
and *ummah*, 36, 46, 54, 65, 86, 203
Believers (*Muʾminiūn*). See *Muʾminiūn* (believers)
Belonging and "imagined community," 58
Best *ummah*. See *Khayr ummah* as the best *ummah*
Bin Nabiy, Mālik, 4–6, 177
Blind followers (*al-Mutrafūn*), 26, 31, 33–34
"The Book." See *Al-Kitāb* ("the Book")
Borders, 58–59, **60**, 61–62, 74, 79, 165, 166, 171, 269
alternate conceptualization of, 14
artificial, 11, 59
bordering, 58, 61

Borders *(continued)*
defining of in Medina Constitution, 160, 166–67, 168
securing of, 1
trans-border, 12
Brotherhood (*mu'ākhā*), 147–48
Bulac, Ali, 143

Caliphates, 8, 11, 71, 72, 79, 119, 167
Abbasid Caliphate, 194
Rightly-Guided Caliphs, 8, 183
Umayyad Caliphate, 182, 193
Capitalism, 5
Centralized institutions and bureaucracies, 11, 214, 216
Christians and Christianity, 23, 51, 91, 96, 104, 125
Coptic Christians, 220–21
Islamic *ummah* including, 90, 109–14, 129
in Medina, 90, 136, 225, 265, 267
and Prophet Abraham, 95, 96, 97
Qur'ān on, 66, 96, 97, 99–100, 140
See also *Ahl Al-Kitāb* (people of the book)
Cities
Al-Fārābī on, 179, 199, 222–23, 245
and Greek thought, 176, 200, 244, 274. *See also* Aristotle; Polis
and *ummah*, 2, 199–200, 211, 245, 274
Virtuous ciry (*Al-Madīna Al-Fāḍila*), 179, 222
ways of life and laws, 199, 200, 203, 271, 272, 275
See also Mecca; Medina
Citizenship, 61, 218, 219, 220, 227, 273
Civic (*madaniyyah*), 6, 7, 205, 260
Civic ruler (*ḥākim madanī*), 257
civic virtue, 202, 206, 261, 274, 276
Clear proofs (*al-bayyināt*), 122, 123
Coercion, 103, 192, 193, 201, 249, 276–77
in spheres of religious and government authority, **260**
without coercion, 98, 220, 273
Collective identity, 58, 61–62, 166, 198, 269
Collective judgment
common good resulting from, 243–45
of *khulafā'*, 238–43
Common good, 3, 75, 210, 214–15, 221, 231, 236, 275, 277
Aristotle on, 216, 224, 227, 244
justice manifested in, 243–45
a state being neutral to, 227, 228
of the *ummah*, 218, 224, 248, 256, 257
Common interest, 222, 244
Communitarians and Communitarianism, 3, 14, 176–77, 216–18, 277
Communities
active community, 41, 73
Aristotle on why people engage in, 209–10
chosen community, 87
closed community and *ummah*, 72, 74, 89, 90, 114, 118, 131, 136, 137, 142
community and its religious path, 23–24. *See also* Religious communities
community and state in contemporary political theory, 212–21. *See also* Poliktical community
community "being," 211
community norm, 229–32, 245, 275
community salvation, 89, 91–92, 93, 229

confessional community, 88, 114, 260
constitutional law transformed into community norm, 229–32
diverse communities, 60–61, 170, 171, 177, 210, 216, 217, 265, 268, 270
forgiving community, 107
God's select community, 104
Holy community, 91, 92
and homogenous culture, 58, 73–74, 269
and identity, 119, 135, 142, 166, 198, 215, 244, 269
imagined community, 1, 58, 73
Islamic community, 15, 173, 250
of Jews and believers and *ummah*, 88, 90, 96, 129, 135, 136, 137, 139, 140, 143, **144**, 152, 157, 170, 171
and justice, 245, 255, 257
majoritarian communities, 217
Muslim community and *ummah*, 1, 21, 91–92, 116, 118, 131, 171. *See also* Muslim *ummah*
nation-state as a community compared to *ummah*, 58, 120–21, 166
new community, 136, 138, 164
and organization, 105, 116, 147, 176, 224, 235
and *qawm*, 29, 55, 73
relationship of keeping the community together and *shūra*, 244
ritualistic community, 89, 131
role of community, 105
salvific community and *ummah*, 72, 74
shared community, 216, 217
and *sharīʿah*, 14, 22, 211, 242
and social exclusion, 216
and *ummah*, 23–24, 40, 41, 47, 63, 73, 91–92, 147, 211
uniting of diverse communities, 210
universal community as global *ummah*, 58, 120–21
Companions of Prophet Muhammad, 16, 81, 110, 112, 115, 128, 243, 250, 252, 263–64
Confederates of evil (*al-aḥzāb*), 65–66, 68, 74, 265
Conflict resolution, 256
and competing virtues in Aristotle and the Qurʾān, 208–12
Constitution
and Aristotle's polis, 176, 222–24, 226, 229, 232, 242, 253, 255, 271
character of and its citizens mirror each other, 226–29
constitutional law transformed into community norm, 229–32
introducing reforms through a constitution, 223–26
polis and constitution versus *ummah* and *al-Kitāb*, 222–23
shūra as a constitutional principle, 241
See also Medina Constitution
Continuous reform (*ʾiṣlāḥ*), 68, 79, 119, 121, 148, 265, 266
Coptic Church in Egypt, treatment of, 220–21
Corruption, 67, 74, 79, 116, 117
God's punishment of, 67–68, 72
humans causing, 180, 181, 190, 235
Covenant (*mīthāq*). See *Mīthāq* (covenant)
Creation (by God), 22, 70, 179, 184, 189, 192–93
human creation as a *khalīfa*, 181, 183, 188, 190–91, 192, 202
main purpose of, 69, 187–88

Creed (*millah*), 95, 98, 99–100, 266. *See also* Abraham (Prophet) or *Ibrāhīm* (Prophet)
Cultural pluralism, 157, 170, 268

Daʿesh, 11
Dār al-ʿahd (abode of covenant), 121
Dār al-ḥarb ("abode of war"), 120, 167, 269
Dār al-Islām, 28
Dār al-ṣulḥ (abode of reconciliation), 121
Dār as-salām ("abode of peace"), 92, 120, 167, 269
David (Prophet) as a *khalīfa*, 182, 190–91, 235
Dawla, 206, 273
Day of Judgment, 36, 52, 81
  mentions of in the Medina Constitution decress, 153, 154, 157
  and the people of the book (*ahl al-Kitāb*), 109, 120, 140
Del Sarto, Raffaella A., 14
Democracy, concept of, 58, 119, 176
  character of democracy creates democracy, 226
  Western democracy compared to Islamic democracy, 120, 192
Denny, Frederick, 24, 211
  on Jews, 136, 139
  on *khayr ummah* and Qurʾān 3:113–115, 120
  on Muslim *ummah*, 92, 96
  on nature of salvation, 92
  on Prophet Muhammad's leadership, 155
  theory of rupture, 138, 141–42
  on *ummah*, 91, 92–93, 142, 145
  on *ummah wasaṭ*, 107
  on the word *ummi*, 51
Despotism (*ṭāghūt*). See *Ṭāghūt*
Deterring (*munkar*). *See* Enjoining (*maʿrūf*) and deterring (*munkar*)
Deterritorialization, 12
Dialectic/dialectical, 14, 15, 21, 23–24, 187
  dialectical reasoning, 2–3
  dialectical relationships, 6, 23
  dialectic contradictions, 186
Dialogue, 8, 14, 15, 16, 20, 30, 33, 34, 97
Dīn (religion), 56, 99–100, 125, 264
  best religion is following *al-milla al-ḥanīfiya* of Abraham, 93–100
  as individual identity, 73
  Jews allowed to practice their own *dīn* in Medina, 139, 228, 230
  of the Jews and Christians, 99–100
  meaning of in Qurʾānic terms, 98
  in the Medina Constitution, 135–36, 139, 142, 156, 228, 230
  millah (creed) as the essence of, 99
  and *ummah*, 56
Direction or orientation (*qibla*). See *Qibla*
Diversity, 6, 40, 63, 70, 71, 72, 212–13, 220, 263
  in Aristotelian polis, 198
  dealing with religious diversity, 64–65
  diverse communities, 60–61, 170, 171, 177, 210, 216, 217, 265, 268, 270
  exploiting diversity, 64
  intrinsic diversity of humans, 127
  in the Medina Constitution, 135, 136, 270
  Medina Constitution recognizing, 171, 220

in nation-states, 1, 47
need for recognition of diverse communities, 216
in Qurʾānic verses, 57, 63, 266
Qurʾān upholding, 266–67
and tolerance as means to limit conflict, 212
and *ummah*, 60, 61, 62, 74, 135, 166, 171, 269
Divine guidance, 23, 38, 42, 57, 67, 70, 99–100, 122, 123, 238
Divine justice, 110, 123
Divine law, 23, 60, 123, 126, 129, 173, 192. See also *Sharīʿah*
Divine mercy, 122
Divine messages, 36, 49, 82, 98, 106, 112, 113, 123, 126, 127, 144, 154, 268
Divine order (*taklīf ʾilāhī sharʿī*), 242
Divine revelation, 19, 23, 38, 47, 63, 98, 137, 248, 264
Qurʾān as, 36
and Truth, 57
on *ummah*, 47
Divine rulings (*al-ḥākimiyya al-ilāhiyya*), 259
Divine will, 50, 83, 86, 101, 102, 103
Divine wisdom, 90, 102, 103, 123, 129, 193, 266
Dominance (*al-ghalaba*) as pillar of *khilāfa*, 193
Donner, Fred, 88, 89, 90
Dynamic or active Islam (*al-Islām al-ḥarakī*), 79, 117

Elites, 168, 174, 231, 245, 261, 273, 275
politically elites, 4, 11, 59, 60, 207, 208, 232, 241, 273, 274, 275
Enjoining (*maʿrūf*) and deterring (*munkar*)
as a community norm, 231, 275
to maintain active justice ("*wasaṭiyyah*"), 255
in Medina Constitution, 230
in the *ummah*, 202, 203, 207, 232, **233**, 244, 275
Ennahda party (Tunisia), 10, 11
Equality, 150, 151, 168, 192, 212, 233, 244, 246, 248, 253, 258
Equilibrium, achieving, 233–35, 239, 248. *See also* Mean, hitting a (achieving equilibrium)
Ethical orientation (*marjiʿiyya akhlāqiyya*), 260
Ethics, 7, 40, 118, 125, 167, 241–42, 259, 270
and Aristotle, 208, 210
human *fiṭrah*, 249
importance of a book, 40, 41, 73
Islamic ethics, 9, 20, 28, 71, 85, 90, 129, 196, 219, 250
and the Medina Constitution, 41, 134, 142, 150, 231
Qurʾānic ethics, 130, 131, 134, 142, 144, 150, 152–53, 256, 268
Etzioni, Amitai, 14, 214, 215, 218
European Union, 8
Evil. *See* Good and evil
Excess or carelessness, inclination toward (*al-janīf*), 95
Exegesis and exegetes
exegetical references, 15–20
general comparisons of modern and premodern exegesis interpretations, 28, 44, 50–51, 63, 68–69, 71–72, 128, 176, 263–64, 270

Exegesis and exegetes *(continued)*
Khalīfa in early, classical, and modern exegesis, 181–91
modern exegetes. *See* ʿAbduh, Muhammad (modern exegete); At-Ṭabaṭabāʾī, Muhammad Ḥusayn.; Faḍlallah, Muhammad Ḥusayn (modern exegete); Quṭb, Sayyid (Sayyid Quṭb Ibrāhīm Ḥusayn Shādhilī) (modern exegete)
premodern exegetes. *See* Al-Qummī, Abū al-Ḥasan ʿAli Bin 'Ibrahīm (premodern exegete); Al-Qurṭubī, Abī Abdullah Moḥammad Bin Aḥmad Al-Ansārī (premodern exegete); At-Ṭabarī, Abū Jaʿfar Muhammad Bin Jarīr (premodern exegete)

Faḍlallah, Muhammad Ḥusayn (modern exegete), 15, 16, 19–20, 35, 127
on Abraham, 82, 83, 95, 97
on *ala ummah*, 33
on *al-Islām al-ḥarakī,* 117
on angels and Satan ordered to prostrate before Adam, 185
on collective responsibility, 35
on concepts of *wasaṭ*, *shahāda*, and *qibla* together, 105–106, 266
on conventional Islam versus a responsible one, 85
on diversity in belief, 47
on diversity of humans, 71, 127
on divine laws, 126
on divine order (*taklīf ʾilāhī sharʿī*), 242
on divine revelation, 36
on false argument, 66
on God not favoring one people over another, 97
on *Imām*, 39–40, 42, 251
intellectual similarites between Faḍlallah and Al-Qummī, 264
interpreting Qurʾānic citations, 23, 39, 40, 79–80, 101–102, 110, 112, 112–13, 127, 175
on the *Kaʿba*, 163
on *khilāfa*, 184, 185, 187, 190
on *kitāb* ("book"), 45
on *kufr* (denying the truth), 26
on *mīthāq* (Covenant), 43
on the Muslim *ummah*, 106, 118
on *nadhīr*, 39
on "names" taught by God to Adam, 184
on necessity of emigration from countries of oppression, 28
on the people of the book, 111, 112, 118
on prophets, 45
on the Qurʾān, 36, 97–98, 125, 175
on reason, 31, 185, 190
on religious tolerance, 64
on rituals, 101–102
on *shūra*, 239, 242, 243
on *sibṭ*, 56
on sovereignty, 58
on supercession, 113
on *ʾulī ʾl-amr*, 251, 252
on *ummah*, 25, 26, 29, 42, 46, 56, 58, 66, 70, 79–80, 101, 110, 117
on *ummah wāḥidah*, 46, 122
on *ummah wasaṭ*, 105, 106, 147, 235–36
on unity reflecting God's mercy, 70–71
Fakhr ad-Dīn al-Rāzī, 104, 112, 250
Falāḥ (success), 92, 202

False argumentation, 66
Falsehood, determining truth from, 97, 186
Family of Prophet Muhammad, 16, 52, 115, 128, 263–64
Farabian political philosophy, 174–75, 240, 275–76
on "first ruler," 275–76
on "natural character" of the ethnic *ummah*, 272
See also Al-Fārābī, Abu Nasr Muhammad
Firqa nājiya ("saved group"), 92
First ruler, 232, 275–76
Fiṭrah (innate nature), 23, 54, 63, 72, 98, 122, 249, 263
Fī Ẓilāl al-Qur'ān (Quṭb), 18
Forbidden (*ḥarām*), 102
Forefathers, 30–34, 58, 82, 84, 99, 148, 152
Freedom, interpreting *al-ʿurwat al-wuthqa* as, 249
Free Officers, 18–19
Fukuyama, Francis, 3, 5
Fuqahā' ("scholars of Islamic jurisprudence"), 250

Ghannouchi, Rached, 10
Giver of laws (*wāḍiʿ ashsharī ʿah*), 199
Globalization, 10, 13, 14–15, 23, 59, 72, 273
Global order, alternative to, 1. See also *Ummah*
Global *ummah*, 53, 54, **63**, 73, 265, 270
composed of different *umam*, 48–65
networked global structure of, **48**
and *ummah* and *ummī* prophets, 50–54
Good and evil, 176, 178, 185, 190, 202
Gospel, 50, 53–54, 88, 111, 112–13
on coming of Prophet Muhammad, 54
as *sharīʿah* for Christians, 125
See also Scripture
Gottlieb, Paula, 234
Governance
Islamic governance, 9, 14, 177, 220
of a modern state, 196
shūra as basis for *ummah's* governance, 241–42
ummah and political governance, 173–261
and *ummah* of the Book, 122–28, 167
See also Polis; Political power
Government, 175, 195, 214, 258
Aristotle on, 222, 226, 271
coercive or authoritarian governments, 253, 259, 261
correlation between character of government and character of individual, 226–29
governmental versus religious authority, 4, 6–7, 140, 192, 204, 259–60, **260**
Islamic government, 7, 128
khilāfa as, 193, 194
society choosing and shaping its government, 28, 227
Spheres of Governmental and Religious Authority, **260**
ummah as determining factor for success or failure, 276
See also Governance; Political authority
Greek philosophy's influence on Muslim and Arabic philosophy, 174

Guardian (*muhaymin*). See *Muhaymin*
Guidance, 31, 39, 194, 225, 230
  and Abraham, 82, 97
  book of guidance, 41, 73, 230
  derived of reason and cognition, 23, 32, 122
  path of guidance, 46, 95
  in Qur'ānic verses, 32, 33, 36, 57, 70, 113, 148, 152
  sent by a messenger, 62
  See also Divine guidance
Guilt of offense, 146, 148

Habermas, Jurgen, 10, 13–14, 61
Ḥadīths, 49, 52, 81, 110, 188, 238, 239, 252. See also *'Aḥādīth*
Ḥakīmīyah lillah (sovereignty of God theory of Quṭb), 19
Ḥākim madanī (civic ruler), 257
Hallaq, Wael, 8–9, 14, 205–206, 231, 232, 273
Ḥanafi, Ḥasan, 8–9, 177
Ḥanīf
  al-ḥanīf or *ḥanīfan*, Abraham as, 81, 93–100, 102, 129, 266
  following creed of Abraham as best religion (*millat Ibrāhīm ḥanīfan*), 93–100, 238, 266
  meaning of, 94–95
  monotheistic implication of, 94, 97
  ritual dimension of, 100
Ḥarām (forbidden), 102, 118, **260**
Ḥaram (sacred), 62, 146, 160–69, 171, 268
  in the Medina Constitution, 160, 163, 165–66, 168
Ḥarām and the sacred house (*Ka'ba*), 162, 163
Hāshim, Abraham b., 16
Hermeneutic, apprehending *ummah* in, 177
Hidāyat al-'aql (guidance derived of reason), 23, 122
Hijrah ("migration"), 27–28, 29
Hodgson, Marshall, 14–15
Holy rite (*mansakan*), 100
Homeland (*waṭan*) and *ummah*, 57–58
Homogenous culture, 58–59, 73–74, 269
  homogenous collective identity, 269
Human history, 45, 87, 90, 125, 205
  Al-Ummah al-Wāḥidah differentiated across, 62–65
  Qur'ān describing evolution of, 74
  umam across, 48–65, 265
Humble (*mukhbitīn*), 100, 101
Hypocrisy, 91, 114

Iblīs (later called *Shayṭān* or Satan), 180, 186, 191. *See also* Satan (*Shayṭān*)
Ibn 'Abbas, 'Abdulla, 134, 183
Ibn al-Jawzī, 183
Ibn Hishām, Abu Muhammad 'Abd Al-Malik Ibn Hisham, 134, 135
Ibn Isḥāq, Muhammad, 134
Ibn Kathīr, Abīl-Fidā' Al-Ḥāfiz, 15, 81, 104, 182–83, 237, 250
Ibn Khaldūn, 119, 177, 272
  on externally applied laws and religious law, 204–205, 206, 207
  on *khilāfa*, 192
  on land of origin, 57–58
Ibn Sallām, Abū'Ubayd, 134–35, 144, 268
Ibrāhīm (Prophet). *See* Abraham (Prophet) or *Ibrāhīm* (Prophet)
Ijtihād (independent exercise of judgment), 17, 195, 259, 260
Imām
  Imām Ali, 37, 40, 42, 239

a'imma (plural of), 34, 42, 106, 181, 251, 252
Prophet Abraham as an *Imām*, 237
and *ummah*, 38–42, 73, 81
Imāmī traditionalists (*muḥaddith*), 16, 251
ʿImāra, Mohammad, 6–7, 177
Imitation (*taqlīd*). See *Taqlīd*
The Impossible State (Hallaq), 205–206
Independence, 9–10, 11, 15, 57, 59, 125, 195
intellectual independence, 26, 125
in the Medina Constitution, 147, 159, 171
Individualism, 6, 121, 236, 269
Infallibility, 251, 252
Injustice, 28, 67, 72, 205, 209, 235, 261, 263, 276
Aristotle on, 233–34, 247, 255
justice as median between two injustices, 7
in the Medina Constitution, 41, 149, 157, 230, 256
not surviving injustice, 68, 72
passive injustice, 255
in the Qur'ān, 55, 274
and the *ʿulamā'*, 194–95
ummah stopping, 116
See also Justice
Innate nature (*fiṭrah*), 23, 54, 63, 72, 98, 122, 249, 263
Instrumental reason, 214
Integrity, 1, 15, 27, 49, 149, 215, 221, 277
moral integrity, 216
perfect integrity, 237, 257
Intellectual awakening (*yaqaẓa ʿaqliyya*), 259
Intercession (*shafāʿa*), 52
Interpretation (*ta'wīl*) of *ummah*, 22
Isaac (*Isḥāq*), 84, 87, 95
Ishmael (*Ismāʿīl*), 84, 86, 87, 91, 95, 101
'Iṣlāḥ (continuous reform), 68, 79, 119, 121, 148, 259, 265, 266
Islam, 14, 23, 28, 33, 101, 102
active or dynamic Islam (*al-Islām al-ḥarakī*), 79, 117
al-Islām al-mas'ūl (as a responsible Islam), 85
conventional Islam versus a responsible one, 85
cultural Islam, 128, 263
dār al-Islām, 28
as final religion sent to humanity, 113
historical Islam, 2, 17, 82, 112, 134, 250
Islam of Abraham, 93–94, 97, 102–103, 129, 265
meaning of *khayr* in Islam, 116
as monotheistic, 88
as the one true religion, 72
Pan-Islam, 17–18
pluralism in, 137, 157
and the Prophet Muhammad, 86, 113, 193
in Qur'ānic verses, 86, 90, 93–94
and submitting in peace (*al-Islām*), 103, 129, 266
and *ummah*, 7, 24, 85, 110, 225, 263, 265–66
ummat al-Islam, 135
values of, 14
See also Islamic ethics; Islamic law; "Islamic state"; Islamic thought
Islam and Liberal Citizenship: The Search for an Overlapping Consensus (March), 219
Islamic civilizations comparing with Western civilizations, 4–6
Islamic ethics, 9, 20, 28, 71, 85, 90, 129, 196, 219, 250
moral principles, 195

Islamic law, 4, 158, 195, 249, 251, 256, 257
  aims of (*maqāsid al-sharī'ah*), 7
  as foundation of *ummah*, 253
  See also *Sharī'ah*
Islamic modernism, 17
Islamic reform (*Iṣlāḥ*). See *Iṣlāḥ* (continuous reform)
Islamic state, 19, 46, 47, 231, 276–77
  concept of, 8, 205
  contradictions in the term, 9, 205–206
  political Islam, 4, 8, 19, 205
Islamic thought, 1, 14, 91, 98, 105, 225, 258, 277
  and "middle status" (*wasaṭiyyah*), 7
Islamic *ummah*, 88, 119, 131, 143, 200, 273
  comparing democracy with, 120
  embracing united *ummah*, **144**
  established by the Prophet Muhammad, 129
  inclusivity of, 90, 129, 130, 267, 268
  Muslim *ummah* as nucleus of, 90, 129, 143, 268
  political roles, 270, 272
  unity of, 11, 194
Islamists, 10, 11, 14, 19, 80, 196, 205
  oposition between Islamists and secularists, 8
  opposition between Qur'ānic *ummah* and Islamists, 206, 208
Istikbār (arrogance), 186

Jackson, Sherman, 220, 221
Jacob (Prophet), 84, 86, 87–88, 95
Jāhiliyya (ignorance or barbarism), 19
Jamā'a, 117
  jamā'a kabīra, 56
  jamā'a Muslima, 117
  jamā'at al-Muslimīn, 27
  Jamā'at-i-Islāmī (the Islamic revivalist party), 46, 191
Jāmi' al-bayān 'an ta'wīl al-Qur'ān (At-Ṭabarī), 17
Jarīriyya, 17
Jawf, 160, 163, 165
Jesus, 23, 89, 96, 100, 113
Jews
  cooperation between Jews and Muslims, 168. *See also* Tolerance
  and cultural plluralism, 170
  in the early *ummah* of Medina, 88, 90, 136–37, 140–41, 150–51, 153
  embracing united *ummah*, **144**
  as followers of Moses, 96
  Islamic values specified as nonbinding to, 157
  Jewish affiliation, 273
  in the Medina Constitution, 49, 135–36, 139–40, 155–60, 225
  Medina Constitution giving equal treatment to all tribes, 156, 169, 223–24
  not conducting war without permission of Muhammad, 256
  not in battle of Badr, 165
  pride in their ethnic origin, 142
  Prophet Muhammad's treaty with the Jews of Medina, 134
  and religious identity of Prophet Abraham, 97
  sharī'ah of as the Torah, 125. *See also* Torah
  ways Jewish and Islamic laws differ, 157–58
  See also *Ahl Al-Kitāb* (people of the book)
Jinn, 25, 175–76, 180, 189
  relationship to *khalīfa*, 181, 182, 183, 187, 191

Judgment, 35, 246, 248, 256
 Aristotle on, 222
 collective judgment, 40, 238–45
 common good resulting from collective judgment, 243–45
 ijtihād (independent exercise of judgment), 17, 195, 259, 260
 and *khalīfa* (*khulafā'*), 183, 238–43
 passed equally, 62
 political judgment, 235
 subjective judgment, 40, 73
 tools of, 46
Jurists (*ahl al-ḥal wal-ʿaqd*), 2, 120, 121, 167, 173, 174, 250
Just (*ʿadl*), 104, 235, 246, 266
Justice
 Aristotle on, 236–37, 243–44, 245, 246
 and citizenship, 3, 199, 218, 273
 common good resulting from collective judgment, 243–45
 as communal bond between citizens of polis, 198
 conception of, 198, 213, 228
 divine justice, 110, 123
 enjoining (*maʿrūf*) and deterring (*munkar*) to maintain active justice ("*wasaṭiyyah*"), 255
 and equity, 62, 63, 145, 150, 151, 224
 established by the messenger, 62, 63, 112
 establishing justice, 55, 74, 105, 128, 266, 267
 judicial authority of Prophet Muhammad, 155, 167–68, 267
 justice as median between two injustices, 7
 justice through *shūra*, 238–43
 just leadership versus *tāghūt* (despotism), 245–49
 khalīfa implenting justice on earth, 235
 laws as means and justice as result, 210
 and leadership and the Book, 55–57
 as a "mean" and the concept of *wasaṭ*, 232–37, 245
 in the Medina Constitution, 148, 153
 need for a continuour appeal for justice, 119
 in polis, 198–99, 232, 271, 272, 273–74, 275
 and politics, 198, 207, 213, 245
 in the Qur'ān, 274–75
 reciprocal justice, 197
 religious groups having own conception of, 228
 requirements of justice, 218, 220, 228, 273
 and *sharīʿah*, 19, 225
 translating human virtue into justice, 208
 and truth, 7, 55, 56, 119, 182, 183, 188, 190, 235
 for *ummah* and believers, 74, 105, 128, 230
 as a virtue, 236, 274
 and *wasaṭ*, 109, 232–37, 245
 See also Injustice; *Wasaṭiyyah* (active justice)

Kaʿba, 86, 101, 103, 109, 162–63
Khalīfa, 179–80, 276–77
 attaining a human's full potential, 190, 205, 226
 on becoming a *khalīfa*, 190–91, 205, 237
 developing a "way of life," 205
 in early classical and modern writings, 181–91

Khalīfa (continued)
implenting justice on earth, 235
jinn as early version of, 181
"*khalīfa bil-ʿilm*" ("successor by knowledge"), 184
khilāfa ʿan Allah (*khalīfa* on behalf of God), 183, 184–85
khulafāʾ as plural of, 181, 192, 238–43
meaning or source of, 182–83
and Muslim *ummah*, 194, 271
and "names" taught by God, 180–81, 183–85, 270
and the political animal, 177–79, 271
Qurʾānic *khalīfa*, 180, 182, 190, 191, 208, 235, 237, 271, 274
as representing God as an administrator, 192
representing Godly attributes, 238
role of, 180, 184, 190, 191, 206, 208, 229, 257, 270, 276
Satan seeing self better than, 189
taking charge of religious matters, 257
and *telos* (purpose of any creation or institution), 181, 187–88, 191, 203, 271
Khalīfat Allah, 182, 183
Khayr (virtue) and virtuous activity, 205, 208, 212–13, 234, 257, 271
Al-Madīna Al-Fāḍila (virtuous city), 179
Aristotle on virtue, 201, 202, 232, 233, 236, 237–38, 257, 261, 274
civic virtue, 202, 206, 261, 274, 276
competing virtues in Aristotle and the Qurʾān, 208–12
duty of making citizens virtuous, 205, 223
and justice, 233–34, 236
moral virtue, 197, 206, 232
obstacles to virtue, 206, 276–77
striving for all virtues, 124, 126, 198
Tazkiya (virtuous disposition), 201, 203
and *ummah*, 201–203
unity of virtues, 237–38
virtuous ruler in a virtuous city, 222–23
Khayr ummah as the best *ummah*, 114–22, 128, 129, 148, 266, 271
differing interpretations of, 263–64
and proper belief, 118, 131, 270
virtuous *ummah* (*khayr ummah*), 200, 201, 202, 203, 205, 271, 272, 274
Khilāfa
dominance (*al-ghalaba*) as pillar of, 193
in Islamic literature, 191–96
khuḍūʿ (submission to human beings), 185
and political *khilāfa*, 191, 194, 196
reflecting the duty and role of human race, 187
and religious *khilāfa*, 196
as a religious or political state, 7
Khilāfa ʿan Allah (*khalīfa* on behalf of God), 184–85
Khomeini, Ruhollah, 19
Khomeini Revolution in Iran (1979), 12
Khūʾī, Abu al-Qasim, 19
Khulafāʾ (plural of *khalīfa*). See *Khalīfa*
Kingship (*ʿala ʾimma*), 34
Kitāb ("the Book"). See *Al-Kitāb* ("the Book")
Kitāb al-Amwāl (Abu ʿUbayd al-Qasim ibn Sallam), 134

Kitāb al-Kharāj (Abu Yusuf Ya'qub), 134
Kitāb al-Ṭabaqāt (ibn Sa'd), 134
Kitāb maʿlūm, 25

Land and the concept of *ummah*, 57–58. See also *Ḥaram* (sacred); Territory
Lang, Jeffrey, 187, 188–89, 190
Language
 and deterritorialization, 12
 development of, 199–200
 and meaning, 184, 185
 purpose of, 178, 190
 shared language, 6, 58, 73, 211
 and *ummah*, 199, 200
Laws
 Aristotle on, 203–204, 207, 229, 249, 272, 275
 constitutional law transformed into community norm, 229–32
 difference between law and *sharīʿah*, 200, 203–207, 208, 211. See also *Sharīʿah*
 equality as basis of law, 233, 248
 externally applied laws and religious law, 204–205, 206, 207
 giver of laws (*wāḍiʿ ash sharī ʿah*), 199
 Ibn Khaldūn on, 204–205, 206, 208
 internalizing a disposition to lawfulness, 206
 introducing new laws in the Medina Constitution, 223–26
 Islamic ethics and the law, 250
 law as means and justice as result, 210
 maʿrūf and *munkar* (law accepted and practiced by people), 202
 nature of law from a Qurʾānic perspective, 230
 Nomoi as general rules or norms that a community follows, 229, 230, 275
 obedience to laws, 173, 195, 230, 247
 in polis, 198–99, 201, 232, 271, 272, 273–74, 275
 Qurʾānic law, 7, 127, 242
 ways Jewish and Islamic laws differ, 157–58
 and ways of life, 199, 200, 203, 271, 272, 275
 See also Divine law; Islamic law; Legal; Religious law; Rule of law
Leadership, 129, 174, 251
 civic ruler (*ḥākim madanī*), 257
 ethical leadership, 254
 just leadership, 245–49, 254
 and *khayr ummah*, 116–17, 128
 leadership, the Book, and justice, 55–57
 political leadership, 1, 58, 119, 128, 191, 192, 194, 250, 258, 264
 of Prophet Muhammad, 88, 155, 193, 267
 in Qurʾānic verses, 126, 245
 sociopolitical leadership, 131
 ʾulī ʾl-amr (those trusted with authority), 248, 249–55
 and *ummah*, 1, 41, 58, 73, 79, 80, 131, 164, 240–43
 during war, 250
 See also Political authority
Legal
 Islamic legal pluralism, 221
 legal experts of the *ummah*, 206, 231, 232, 275–76
 legal order and social order in Islamic *sharīʿah*, 231
 legal pluralism, 74, 126, 129, 137, 158, 171, 220, 221, 267, 268, 271, 272, 273

Legal *(continued)*
legal structure of *ummah*, 61, 158
See also Laws; Rule of Law; *Sharīʿah*
Legislator, 200, 205, 226, 256, 259
Leviticus 24:17–20, 158
Liberalism and liberal societies, 3, 216, 217
central control in liberal societies, 277
Rawlsian liberalism, 215–16
relation of citizen to modern liberal state, 227
requirements of justice and those of citizenship, 218
and resident alienage, 218–19
Liew, Han Hsien, 182–83
Lisān al-ʿArab (Ibn Manḍhūr), 149
Literal interpretations, 71, 86, 247
of al-Qummi, 31, 32, 39, 40, 44, 64, 85
of al-Qurṭubī, 64, 85
of at-Ṭabarī, 31, 39, 40, 44, 64, 85, 101
Literature
khilāfa in Islamic literature, 191–96
of prophetic sayings, 16
ummah in, 3, 21–24, 128, 276

MacIntyre, Alasdair, 176–77, 213, 215, 218, 227
Madaniyyah (civic), 6, 7, 205, 260
civic ruler (*ḥākim madanī*), 257
civic virtue, 202, 206, 261, 274, 276
Madhhab, 17
ʿala madhhab, 32, 42
madhhaban yadhhabūna fīh, 101
Madigan, Daniel, 2, 37–38, 230
Majority
law of the majority, 220, 272
and minority, 61, 74, 113, 251
tyranny of the majority, 275
Manāsik (rituals), 86, 100–103, 128, 130
and attaining purification, 204
internalizing a disposition to lawfulness, 206
manāsikanā, 84, 91, 100, 188
ṣalāt (ritual prayers), 52, 101, 103
and *ummah*, 86, 101
Mansak/mansakan (holy rite), 100, 130
Maqāsid al-sharīʿah (aims of Islamic law), 7
March, Andrew, 218–20
Maritain, Jacques, 9, 59
Marjaʿīyat at-taqlīd ("authority of the source of imitation"), 20
Marjiʿiyya akhlāqiyya (ethical orientation), 260
Maʿrūf
enjoining (*maʿrūf*) and deterring (*munkar*), 202, 203, 207, 230, 231, 232, **233**, 244, 255, 275
as a Qurʾānic concept on actions of the best *ummah*, 145–47
as Qurʾānic equivalent of *Nomoi*, 230
Maʿrūf wa munkar (public norms), 275
Mawālī (allies), 171, 268
Mawdūdī, Sayyid Abul ʿAlāʾ, 15, 177, 191–92, 195–96, 205
Mawla/mawālī (client/ally), 136, 143, 147, 156, 169. *See also* Allies
MC. *See* Medina Constitution
Mean, hitting a (achieving equilibrium), 233–35, 238, 239. *See also* Equilibrium, achieving; *Wasaṭ*
Mecca
taḥrim of Mecca, 165
as *Umm al-Qura* ("the mother of the villages"), 51

Meccan verses of the Qur᾿ān, 2, 21–75, 126
conceptual meaning of *ummah*, 21–75
and continuous reform (*᾿iṣlāḥ*), 148, 266
description of *ummah*, 77–78, 129, 264, 265, 270
layers of interpretations of *ummah*, 72–73
Qur᾿ānic theme in, 129
using term *al-aḥzāb*, 68
Medina
defense of, 168–69
formation of the Muslim *ummah* in, 28–29, 126
and the formation of the polical movement in, 225–26
Islamic *ummah*, 268
issues raised by political theories, 217–18
Jews in the early *ummah* of Medina, 88, 90, 136–37, 140–41, 150–51, 153
pluralism in, 230
Prophet Muhammad establishing the first "*jamā῾a Muslima*" in, 117
taḥrim of Medina (making Medina a *ḥaram*), 165
ummah in, 134, 135, 208, 225, 228, 270
ummah wāḥidah established in, 121–22
using term *jawf* to describe Medina, 163–64, 165–66
Medina Constitution, 2, 77, 78, 133–71, 225, 267–68
allowing for freedom for religious groups, 204, 218, 228, 248, 268
calls for collaboration and protection of all, 149
on cases of war or aggression against the *ummah*, 152–54, 155–56, 158–59, 166, 167, 171
and common good, 248
complete text of, 279–85
and the concept of "minority," 220
as the Covenant of Unity, 139
decrees addressing believers (*al-mu᾿minīn*), 49, 138, 144–55, 225
decrees addressing Jews (*al-yahūd*), 49, 138, 155–60, 225
decrees addressing people of the Medina Constitution (*ahl al-ṣaḥifa*), 49, 138, 143, 159, 160, 164, 168, 171, 225, 268
decrees relating to the concept of *ḥaram* (sacred enclave or land), 160–69
defining borders, 160, 166–67
inspired by Qur᾿ānic ethics, 134, 142
and interplay between written rules and established norms, 230–31
introducing reforms through, 223–26
layers of affiliation in, 273
and pluralism, 170–71, 230, 271
and the Prophet Muhammad, 40–41, 134, 135, 169, 256
seeing law as a collective duty and activated by *ummah*, 206–208
showing high level of reciprocity between communities, 229
structuring of decrees in, 138
summary of, 169–71
three representations of *ummah* in, 48
᾿ulī ᾿l-amr in, 255–57
ways Jewish and Islamic laws differ, 157–58

Medinan verses of the Qur᾽ān, 2, 42, 129, 265, 271
conceptual meaning of *ummah*, 77–131, 148, 265, 267
defining creed of the Muslim *ummah*, 266
describing *khayr ummah* as the best *ummah*, 148, 266, 271
on individual responsibility, 263
monotheistic *uman*, 267
not using term *al-aḥzāb*, 68
sociopolitical context, 74–75
Mercy
to believers, 36, 57, 70–71, 79
God's mercy, 1, 8, 69, 70–71, 79, 91, 92, 114, 189, 191, 241, 271
in Qur᾽ānic verses, 36, 69, 70, 188, 189, 241, 254
Messenger (*rasūl*), 23, 33, 45, 47, 54, 63, 64, 67, 106, 181, 251, 252
nadhīr as a messenger, 38–39
Prophet Muhammad as, 41, 53, 135, 164, 167, 169, 256
in Qur᾽ānic verses, 36, 38, 44, 53, 62, 104, 142–43, 246, 249, 253
rasūl versus *nabī*, 63
ummī Prophet as a messenger, 50, 51, 53, 54
Middle East boundaries imposed by Colonial powers, 10–11, 13
Middle *ummah* (*Ummah Wasaṭ*). See *Ummah Wasaṭ*
Migration (*hijrah*), 27–28, 29
Millah (creed), 95, 98, 99–100, 266
meaning of, 99
See also Abraham (Prophet) or *Ibrāhīm* (Prophet)
Miller, Fred, 224
Minkum (from you), 115, 116, 251–52, 253
᾽ulī ᾽l-amr minkum, 246, 249
Minority, 61, 219, 220
and majority, 61, 74, 113, 251
Mīthāq (covenant), 75, 126, 265
faithful covenanters (*mu᾽minīn*), 139
between God and the Prophets, 54, 87, 96
in the Medina Constitution, 49, 121–22, 134, 135, 139, 149–50, 151–55, 169–70, 230
and nation-states, 74
Qur᾽ān as form of, 73
and *ummah*, 42–48, **48**, 53, **63**, 74, 121, 129, 143, 264, 269, 276
and *umman*, **60**, 61, 121, 126, 270
Modern depiction of *ummah*, 79
Modern exegetes. *See* ʿAbduh, Muhammad (modern exegete); At-Ṭabaṭabā᾽ī, Muhammad Ḥusayn (modern exegete); Exegesis and exegetes; Faḍlallah, Muhammad Ḥusayn (modern exegete); Quṭb, Sayyid (Sayyid Quṭb Ibrāhīm Ḥusayn Shādhilī) (modern exegete)
Modernity, 18, 195–96, 205, 206
post-modernity, 273
Modern period
and corruption, 67, 68
and globalization, 10, 13, 14–15, 23, 59, 72, 273
human reason and *fiṭrah* in, 23, 72
and marginalization, 3, 196, 273
modern Muslim states, 270, 272
modern societies addressing conflict, 212, 227–28, 273
nation-states in the modern period, 8, 13–14, 264
nation subordinate to the state in, 200
᾽ulī ᾽l-amr in the modern period, 257–61

and *ummah*, 1, 3, 12–13, 21, 22, 79, 114, 264
Modern world, 2, 9, 14, 59, 195, 196, 277
Monotheism, 265
Islamic monotheism, 50, 88
monotheistic beliefs versus *shirk*, 153
monotheistic *uman*, 267
pure monotheism of Abraham, 87, 89, 90, 95, 97, 265
Moses, 23, 100
people of, 55–56, 96, 243
sharīʿah of, 89
Moses, Jonathon, 119, 120, 128
The mother of the villages (*Umm al-Qura*), 51
Muʾākhā (brotherhood), 147–48
Muḥaddith (*Imāmī* traditionalists), 16
Muhājirūn (migrants) of Quraysh (in the Medina Constitution), 144–45
Muhammad (Prophet), 77, 130, 193
and conflict resolution, 256
and the Constitution of Medina, 40–41, 134, 135, 169, 256
on definitions of *ummī ummah*, 51
establishing the first "*jamāʿa Muslima*" in Medina, 117
establishing the *ummah* of Medina, 223, 225, 270
as the first *shahīd*, 108–109
followers of, 96
on greatest acts of worship, 188
having a covenant with God, 54
judicial authority of, 155, 167–68, 267
as the last of the Prophets, 49, 53, 86, 87, 89, 90, 93, 265, 266
as messenger (prophet of Allah), 41, 53, 135, 164, 167, 169, 256
as perfect model for *wasaṭ*, 105
Prophet Abraham hinting at coming of, 86, 265
sent to all humankind, 53
those who migrated from Mecca to Medina as the best *ummah*, 115
and time that the Qurʾān was revealed, 225–26
ummah as mediator between the Prophet and humankind, 107
as *ummī*, 51–52, 53, 54, 137, 265
as *waliy ʾl-amr*, 257
on Zayd bin ʿAmrū as an *ummah*, 81
Muhammad al-Bāqir, 16
Muhaymin (guardian), Qurʾān as, 124–25, 126, 131
Mujāhid ibn Jabr, 104, 182
Mukhbitīn (humble), 100, 101
Multiculturalism, 10, 59, 61, 74, 121, 269, 277
Muʾmin (someone secure or granted security), 139, 141
Muʾminūn (believers), 70, 139–44
addressed in decrees 3–23 in the Medina Constitution, 138, 142, 144–55
also in singular form *muʾmin*, 141, 152
carrying out continuous reform (*ʾiṣlāḥ*), 148
God conscious believers, 88, 256
Munkar. *See* Enjoining (*maʿrūf*) and deterring (*munkar*)
Muqaddimah (Ibn Khaldūn), 204
Muqātil b. Sulaymān, 104, 182
Muqtaṣida. See *Ummah muqtaṣida*
Mushrik (polytheist), 94, 152
Muṣliḥūn (reformers), 66–71, 74, 195, 265
Muslim Brotherhood, 11, 18–19, 47, 79

Muslims
characteristic of, 266
as a community (*jamāʿat al-Muslimīn*), 27
and cultural pluralism, 170
defining character and attributes, 83–93, 96
and Jews, 141, 157. See also *Ummah muqtaṣida*
mentions of in the Medina Constitution decrees 25 and 37, 138, 141
origin of term and its derivatives, 86
and proper belief, 118, 121, 270
Qurʾānic perception of term, 89, 193
use of term believers rather than Muslims in Medina Constitution, 141–43
Muslim societies, 4–6, 8, 16, 77, 195, 196, 231, 277
Muslim *ummah*, 24
appearance of after the coming of Prophet Muhammad, 90, 265–66
asked to follow the creed of Abraham, 238
as the best *ummah*, 104
characteristics and functions of, 267, 269
compared to other *ummah*, 101
compared to the people of the book, 139
described as *wasaṭ*, 95
described through its religious rituals (*manāsik*), 128
fall of as a united political entity, 264
as *firqa nājiya* ("saved group"), 91
forging unity among members, 121
as a "holy community" or "community of salvation," 91, 92
inclusiveness of towards earlier prophets, 96
as inheritor of all divine messages, 98
as last *ummah* sent to humankind, 130, 267
losing its way, 118–19
not a closed community, 89, 90, 114, 121
and Prophet Abraham, 85, 86, 87, 89, 104, 108, 129, 265–66
propspering in the medieval period, 120
Quṭb's warning to, 117
united by one book and following one *sharīʿah*, 129, 131
Muslimūn, 84, 97

Nabī (a prophet), 63
Abraham on, 84, 95, 97
Nadhīr (warners), 32, 38–39, 122
"Names" taught by God to Adam, 180–81, 183–85, 189, 192–93, 270
Naskh (supersession), 113
Naṣṣār, Naṣīf, 13, 21, 23–24
Nasser, Gamal Abdel, 18–19
Nation-state, 273
alternatives to, 1–2, 3, 13–14, 263–77
challenges to, 10, 11, 13–14, 46, 47, 121, 272–73
comparing *ummah* with, 166, 269
difference between nation-states and *umam*, **60**
differences between the Islamic and modern nation-state paradigms, 220–21
efforts to imitate, 270
Egyptian society as, 80
impact of globalization, 10

legal pluralism not present in, 271
nation-state system imposed by colonialism, 10–11, 13, 47
obsession with sovereignty and borders, 166, 167, 171
and "political Islam," 8
process of creating, 73–74
rise of, 1–2, 9, 17, 20, 221, 264
secularism as forming ideology of, 3, 71, 72
and *ummah*, 58–62
ummah as alternative to, 1–2
See also State
Nation subordinate to city according to Aristotle, 200, 274
Nietzsche, Friedrich, 227–28
Noah's flood, 247
Nomoi as general rules or norms that a community follows, 229, 230, 275
Norms
constitutional law transformed into community norm, 229–32
Islamic values and norm, 154
in Muslim scholarship, 18
public norms, 261, 275
societal norms, 208, 217
tribal norms, 153, 154
Nusuk and rituals, 101, 103

Obedience, 249, 250, 251, 255
of Abraham, 82
blind obedience, 103, 129, 192, 266
to God, 82, 97, 107, 173, 194, 252–53
to laws, 230, 243, 247
mindless obedience, 31
slavish obedience, 195
See also Surrendering to God (*ʾaslimū*)
Obligations of *ummah*, 74, 78–80, 129, 138, 148–49, 151, 153, 170, 248, 266, 267, 269, 276
One *ummah*. See *Ummah wāḥidah*
Orange Revolution in Ukraine (2004), 12
Orientalists on *ummah*, 29–30, 92, 128
seeing *ummah* as a closed society of Muslims, 72, 89, 114, 118, 135, 144, 268
Original idea (*al-fikra al-aṣliya*) vs. effective idea (*al-fikra al-faʿāla*), 4–5
Orwin, Alexander, 201, 212, 232
Other, 59, 61–62, 213, 269
accepting the other, 273
alien "other," 1, 62, 268
"foreign other," 73–74

Pan-Arabism or pan-Islamism, 13, 17–18
Paret, Rudi, 29
Passive injustice, 255
Peoplehood, concept (*al-ḥarāk*), 11, 12
People of the book (*Ahl Al-Kitāb*). See *Ahl al-Kitāb* ("People of the Book")
People of the Medina Constitution (*ahl al-ṣaḥifa*), 49, 138, 143, 159, 160, 164, 168, 171, 268
People's Power revolution in Philippines (1986), 12
Piety or God consciousness/ awareness (*taqwa*), 70, 102
Pilgrims and pilgrimages (*al-ḥāj*), 101, 118, 133, 163
Plato, 174, 176, 223
Pluralism, 1, 20, 131, 170, 271
cultural pluralism, 157, 170, 268
legal pluralism, 74, 126, 137, 158, 171, 220, 221, 267, 268, 271

Pluralism *(continued)*
political pluralism, 170, 268
religious pluralism, 137, 170
Polis, 198, 244, 254, 273
Aristotelian polis and Qur'ānic *ummah*, 2–3, 177–79, 257
concept of justice and laws in, 198–99, 232, 271, 272, 273–74, 275
defining, 176
nation subordinate to city according to Aristotle, 200, 274
polis and constitution versus *ummah* and *al-Kitāb*, 222–32
polis and justice versus *ummah* and *wasaṭiyyah*, 232–37
polis existing for the sake of the good life, 209–10
and rule of law, 207–208, 245, 253
telos of the polis, 178, 179, 197, 271
and virtuous activity, 201–203
virtuous city (*Al-Madīna Al-Fāḍila*), 179, 222
See also Governance; Political power
Political animal
humans as political animals, 270–71
and *khalīfa*, 177–79, 191
Qur'ānic ideas compared to Aristotelian on political animal, 189–91
telos of, 191, 271
Political authority, 102, 119, 192, 193, 250
authority not invested in single leader, 257–58
civic (*madaniyyah*) vs. religious authority (*dīniyyahh*), 6–7
and *khilāfa*, 191–96
See also Government; Leadership
Political community, 136–37, 155
ummah and political governance, 173–261
ummah as equivaltent to, 149
Political culture, 61, 74, 216, 227, 269, 2147
Political Islam, 8
Politically elites, 4, 11, 59, 60, 208, 232, 241, 273, 274, 275
Political philosophy
community and state in contemporary political theory, 212–21
ummah and governance, 173–261
Political pluralism, 170, 268
Political power, 3, 4, 117, 127–28, 206, 214, 241, 273–74
not invested in single leader, 257–58
power of religion versus power of government, 259–61, **260**
and rule of law, 207–208, 245, 248, 253, 255
and *ummah*, 13, 167, 245–49, 270, 274
See also Governance; Tyranny (*al-istibdād*)
Politics (Aristotle), 177
Post-modernity, 273
Prayer, 52, 110, 161, 162, 239, 240
direction of, 86, 104, 108, 109
ritual prayers (*ṣalāt*), 52, 101, 103
Premodern
and an emphasis on exclusivity, 23
religious and political institutions in the West, 4
scholars, 1, 20, 25
ummah in the premodern period, 4
Premodern exegetes
early premodern exegetes, 104, 112
See also Al-Qummī, Abū al-Ḥasan ʿAli Bin 'Ibrahīm (premodern exegete); Al-Qurṭubī, Abī Abdullah Moḥammad Bin Aḥmad Al-Ansārī (premodern exegete); At-Ṭabarī, Abū Jaʿfar

Muhammad Bin Jarīr (premodern exegete); Exegesis and exegetes
Private interest, 59, 217, 222, 241, 244, 247, 248, 258, 265, 275, 276
Private life and public political, connection between, 206, 215, 217, 218
Private sphere, 270
Proof (*ad-dalīl*), 48, 107, 244
  clear proofs (*al-bayyināt*), 123
Prophetic sayings (*ʾaḥadīth*), 16, 111, 176
Prophets
  last Prophet, 49, 53, 86, 87, 89, 90, 93, 265, 266
  nabī, 63
  possessing perfect integrity and complete virtue, 257
  before the Prophet Muhammad, 130
  ummah of, 62–63
  ummī prophet, 50–54, 137, 265, 267
  See also Names of specific prophets
Public concern, 240, 241
Public deliberation, 198, 217, 218, 227, 228, 277
Public discourse, 65, 175, 216
Public norms (*maʿrūf wa munkar*), 261, 275
Public political and private life, connection between, 206, 215, 217, 218
Public sphere, 3, 170, 214, 268, 273
Purification, 92–93, 204, 251, 272
  purification of the soul (*tazkiya*), 92, 203

Qabīla ("tribe"), 29
Qawm (a group of people or community), 29, 55, 73
  and the difference with *ummah*, 55
Qibla (direction of ritual *ṣalāt*)
  qibla of Abraham, 103–104, 109, 236, 238, 266
  relating concepts of *wasaṭ*, *shahāda*, and *qibla* together, 105–106, 266
Qiwām, 162
Qiyāman, importance of in exploring *ḥaram* (sacred enclave or land), 162
Qurʾān, 7, 88
  as *al-Kitāb* ("the Book"), 34–38. See also *Al-Kitāb* ("the Book")
  Aristotelian Polis and Qurʾanic *Ummah*, 197–203
  and concept of a covenant, 42–48
  conceptual meaning of in Meccan verses of the Qurʾān, 21–75
  conceptual meaning of in Medinan verses of the Qurʾān, 77–131
  describing evolution of human history, 74
  as direct communication with God, 37–38
  the function of, 124
  meaning of the term "book" in, 230
  as *muhaymin* (guardian), 124–25, 126, 131
  and non-human creatures (angels and Jinn), 175–76
  purpose of the human being in, 175–76
  Qurʾānic ideas compared to Aristotelian on political animal, 189–91
  as a rationale for different communities' coexistence, 65
  recognizing the peoplle of the book, 140, 225. See also *Ahl al-Kitāb* ("People of the Book")
  resolving conflict by competing virtues in Aristotle and the Qurʾān, 208–12

Qur'ān *(continued)*
as a revealed book, 39
on *telos* of the human being, 179. See also *Khalīfa*
time of being revealed to the Prophet, 225–26
understanding Qur'ānic concepts, 16
upholding diversity, 266–67
See also Qur'ānic citations index
Qur'ānic ethics, 130, 131, 134, 142, 144, 150, 152–53, 268
Qur'ānic law, 7, 127, 242
The Qur'ān's Self-Image (Madigan), 37
Quraysh, 81
addressed in Medina Constitution, 41, 135, 144–45, 152, 168
Prophet Muhammad persecutors coming from, 88, 152, 168
Quṭb, Sayyid (Sayyid Quṭb Ibrāhīm Ḥusayn Shādhilī) (modern exegete), 15, 33, 35, 39, 67–68, 177, 256
on Abraham as an *ummah*, 82
on *al-jamā'a al-islāmiyya*, 46
on a believer's manners and behavior, 65
on the Book (*Al-Kitāb*), 124
dealings with political power and European colonialism, 47, 127
on diversity of humans, 127
on false argument, 66
on groups included in Qur'ān 7:164, 78–79, 80
on intellectual freedom, 33
intellectual similarites between 'Abduh and Quṭb, 264
interpreting Qur'ānic citations, 102, 113, 114, 127
on *khayr ummah*, 116–17, 125
on Muslim *ummah*, 106, 111, 117
on *nadhīr*, 38
on political leadership, 128, 264
on the Qur'ān as last divine message, 36–37
on ritual and sacrifice, 102
support of *hijrah* to the house of Islam (*dār al-Islām*), 28
on the Torah and the Gospel, 125
on *'ulī 'l-amr*, 250–51
on *ummah*, 54, 56, 66, 106, 119
on the *ummī* prophet, 54
on unity, 98
on *wasaṭ*, 106
Quṭb, Sayyid (Sayyid Quṭb Ibrāhīm Ḥusayn Shādhilī) (modern exegete) (modern exegete), 18–19

Raḥmān (one of the names of Allah, the merciful), 186
Rahman, Fazlur, 66, 68
Rasūl (messenger), 63
Rawls, John, 176
political conception of, 212–14, 215
Rawlsian liberalism, 215–16
Rawlsian method of tolerance, 216, 219
Reason (meaning intellect/cognition)
'Abduh on, 18, 23, 31, 85, 122
cognition as foundation for true knowledge, 32
dialectical reasoning, 2–3
Faḍlallah on, 31, 185, 190
guidance derived of reason (*hidāyat al-'aql*), 122
humans united by reason, 23
humans use of intellect and reason, 173, 174, 184, 185, 186, 190, 197, 214, 215, 270
instrumental reason, 214
in Qur'ānic verses, 32

and revelation, 18
Riḍa on, 195
Satan falsifying reality in human intellect, 187
supremacy of reason, 71, 72
At-Ṭabarī on, 67
use of in interpreting religious texts, 16, 31
value of, 31
See also *Al-ʿaql* (reason/cognition)
Reformers (*muṣliḥūn*), 66–71, 74, 195, 265
Religious authority vs. governmental authority, 4, 6–7, 140, 192, 204, 259–60, **260**
Religious communities, 1, 6, 66, 137
and *ummah*, 30, 60, 109, 119, 201, 270
Religious law, 22, 23–24, 123, 192, 196, 208, 271, 272
externally applied laws and religious law, 204–205, 206, 207
in the Medina Constitution, 142, 157, 171
See also *Dīn*; *Sharīʿah*
Religious pluralism, 137, 170
Religious scholars (*ʿulamāʾ*), 18, 19, 27, 195–96, 250
Religious versus governmental authority, 259–60
Resident alien, 218–19
Revolutionary Command Council (RCC), 18
Riḍa, Rashīd, 18, 177
on *khilāfa*, 194
on need for a preparation phase for forming a political community, 225–26
on religious scholars (*ʿulamāʾ*), 195–96
on *ʾulī ʾl-amr*, 250
Right and wrong, 70, 110, 118, 121, 145, 148, 270
Rightly Guided Caliphs, 8, 183
Rights, 105, 146, 218
of allies, 159, 169
in a centralized system, 216
community rights, 3, 169, 228–29, 269. *See also* Communitarians and Communitarianism
of the community vs. individual rights, 105, 147, 236
cultural and social rights, 60, 61, 74, 269
divine right, 137
equal or same rights, 8, 150, 156, 157, 159, 168, 169, 225
fair distributiion of, 246
individual rights, 3, 14, 61, 105, 151, 212, 215, 216, 235–36, 252, 260
of the least privileged or oppressed, 150, 159
in the Medina Constitution, 129, 138, 144, 146, 147, 148, 149, 150, 151, 156, 157, 159, 168–69, 170, 218, 228–29
of multicultural communities, 269
mutual rights, 6, 74, 218, 266, 267
political rights, 60, 61, 170, 208, 216, 248, 259, 268, 269
reciprocal rights, 170, 248, 268
religious rights, 60, 221, 248
rights and obligations, 74, 78–80, 129, 138, 147, 151, 159, 170, 198, 218, 223, 228–29, 248, 266, 267, 268, 269, 276
of sovereignty, 57
and *ummah*, 60, 74, 78–80, 129, 138, 151, 208, 235, 247, 248, 266–67, 269, 273, 276
usurping or not usurping rights of others, 57, 68, 148, 215, 217, 247

Rituals (*manāsik*). See *Manāsik* (rituals); Sacrifices
Roy, Oliver, 6
Rubin, Uri, 139, 164, 165
Rule of law, 9
Aristotle on, 197, 245, 253
polis and *ummah*, 207–208, 245, 253
and political power, 207–208, 245, 248, 253, 255
See also Laws

Sacred enclave or land (*ḥaram*). See *Ḥaram* (sacred); Land and the concept of *ummah*; Territory
Sacrifices, 101, 102, 103
in the Medina Constitution, 153. *See also* Rituals (*manāsik*)
Sadiki, Larbi, 11–13
Ṣalāt (ritual prayers), 52, 101, 103
Salvation, 29, 89, 90, 118
community salvation, 229
Muslim *ummah* as a community of salvation, 91, 92
personal or private salvation, 174
various concepts of defined, 90–93
Satan (*Shayṭān*), 36, 175, 180, 186, 187, 193
as Jinn, 175, 189
seeing self as *khalīfa*, 189
See also *Iblīs*
Saved group (*firqa nājiya*), 92
Sayyid Quṭb. *See* Quṭb, Sayyid (Sayyid Quṭb Ibrāhīm Ḥusayn Shādhilī) (modern exegete)
Scholars of Islamic jurisprudence (*fuqahā'*), 250
Scripture
abiding by, 42
Allah/God sending, 22, 54
codified scripture, 38
divine scripture, 125, 137
earlier scriptures (non-Muslim), 41, 50–51, 53–54, 96, 112, 113, 124, 131, 137, 225. *See also* Gospel; Torah
ethical values of, 112
Holy Scripture as truth, 55
instruction in scripture, 84, 86, 254
in Qur'ānic verses, 22, 32, 38, 84, 124, 254
unscriptured, 50, 51. See also *Ummī*
See also *Al-Kitāb* ("the Book"); *Muhaymin* (guardian), Qur'ān as; Qur'ān
Secularism, 3–4, 6, 7, 8, 10, 121, 193, 204, 221
as a contemporary norm, 121, 269
secular nation-states and secular nationalism, 3, 68, 71–72
Self-agency, 273
Self-determination, 10, 212
Self-sufficiency, 9, 59, 107, 198, 230, 238
Serjeant, R. B., 139, 141, 146, 165, 168–69
Sha'b ("nation"), 29
Shafā'a ("intercession"), 52
Shāfi'ī madhhab, 17
Shāfi'ism, 17, 121
Shahīd or *shahāda* (witness), 47–48, 103–109, 130, 266
relating concepts of *wasaṭ*, *shahāda*, and *qibla* together, 105–107, 266
Shaḥrūr, Moḥammad, 5–6, 177, 186
on *al-'urwat al-wuthqa* and *ṭāghūt*, 249
on power of government, 259–61
on *'ulī 'l-amr*, 251–52
Shams ad-Dīn, Muhammad Mahdī, 177
on characteristics of believers, 240

on concept of the witness in relationship to *wasaṭ*, 106–107
considering *ummah* as a political community, 149, 155
on decrees of the Medina Constitution, 136–37, 159, 207
on the equality of all people in the Medina Constitution, 150–51
on Medina Constitution addressing different tribes, 147
on Medina Constitution addressing peace, 151
on religiosity and religion, 98
on *shūra*, 241, 242
on the *ummah's* guardianship over itself, 153
Shanoudah (Pope), 221
Sharīʿah, 19, 54, 89, 98, 101, 116, 171, 186, 195, 226, 275–76
as bond between members of the *ummah*, 255
difference between law and *sharīʿah*, 200, 203–207, 208, 211
and *dīn*, 125, 142
each of the holy books having its own, 89, 125
giver of laws (*wāḍiʿ ashsharī ʿah*), 199
God's *sharīʿah* or divine *sharīʿah*, 2, 117, 192, 210, 253. *See also* Divine law
and governance, 194, 196, 242, 260–61
and human development, 123, 127
implementing of in Indonesia, 9–10
and justice, 19, 225
legal experts of the *ummah* interpreting, 206, 231, 232, 275–76
maqāsid al-sharīʿah (aims of Islamic law), 7
and *maʿrūf* and *munkar* (community norm), 231, 255, 275
meaning and practice of, 15, 93–94
and Muslim *ummah*, 89, 126, 131, 267
one *ummah* following one *sharīʿah*, 126, 129, 209
as part of diagram of an *ummah*, **233**
and political communities, 14
and Prophet Muhammad, 54, 90, 93, 105
and *Qiyām*, 162
and the Qurʾān, 43, 93–94, 125, 131, 137, 158, 209, 210, 248–49
as religious law, 22, 272
and rituals, 101, 103, 118, 130
and *shūra*, 241, 242, 255, 257, 275
and *tāghūt*, 247, 248–49
and *ʾulī ʾl-amr*, 250–51, 255
and *ummah*, 206, 272, 273, 274
ummahs abiding by own *sharīʿah*, 125, 130, 131, 137, 158, 210, 211, 218, 221, 251, 267, 272
values of embodied in the moral fabric of society, 231
Shayṭān. *See* Satan (*Shayṭān*)
Sheba, queen of, 258–59
Shīʿī, 15, 16, 19, 31, 42, 264
Shirk, 67, 68, 72, 95, 152, 153, 263
Shūra, 7, 150, 151, 244–45, 251, 261
and common good, 243
as a constitutional principle of *ummah*, 241
and *sharīʿah*, 241, 242, 255, 257, 275
spirit of, 254
ummah attaining justice through *shūra*, 238–43
Sibṭ, 55–56

Single *ummah*. See *Ummah wāḥidah*
Sīrat ibn Hishām (Ibn Hishām), 134
Sovereignty, 9–10, 19, 192
  absolute sovereignty, 60
  false sovereignty, 269
  in the Medina Constitution, 155, 166
  of Prophet Muhammad, 193
  umam (interconnected based on covenants, sovereignty based on the Book), **60**
  and *ummah*, 55–62
State
  avoiding oppressive use of state power, 213
  community and state in contemporary political theory, 212–21
  See also Nation-state
Subjectivity, 3, 40, 42, 56, 264
  and the law, 168
  subjective choices, 73
  subjective judgment, 40, 73
  subjective rulings, 41
Submission, 129
  blind submission, 31, 193
  essence of, 103
  followers of Muhammad submit by believing in all preceding prophets, 96
  *khuḍū*ʿ, 185
  submission to divine law, 103
  submission to God, 22, 27, 62, 100, 101, 103. *See also* Abraham (Prophet) or *Ibrāhīm* (Prophet), submission to the will of God
  submitting in peace (*al-Islām*), 103, 129, 266
Success (*falāḥ*), 92, 202
Sufyān al-Thawrī, 182
Sulṭat ad-ḍabṭ versus *sulṭat at-ṭughyān*, 259
Sunnah, 7, 175
Sunnī, 15, 16, 17, 38, 115, 182, 183, 264
Supersession (*naskh*), 113
Supreme ruler (*As-sulṭān al-aʿẓam*), 183, 223, 240
Surrendering to God (*ʾaslimū*), 83, 84, 87, 89, 90, 93–94, 96–97, 98, 100, 101, 238, 265
Sykes-Picot Agreement, 10

Tafsīr (Abū l-Jārūd), 16
Tafsīr (At-Ṭabarī), 17
Tafsīr al-Manār (ʿAbduh), 18
Tafsīr al-Qummī (Al-Qummī), 16
Tafsīr methodology, 17
Tafsīr Mujāhid, 182
Tafsīr Muqātil b. Sulaymān, 182
Tafsīr Sufyān al-Thawrī, 182
Ṭāghūt (despotism), 194, 239, 246, 260, 275, 276
  just leadership versus *tāghūt*, 245–49
  and *sharīʿah*, 247, 248–49
  "soft despotism," 214
  at-ṭāghūt, 261, 275, 276
  toppling of, 247–48, 276
Taḥannuf, 94
Taḥrim of Medina (making Medina a *ḥaram*), 165
Taklīf ʾilāhī sharʿī (divine order), 242
Taqlīd (imitation), 18, 259
  blind imitation, 33, 195
  source of imitation, 20
  of tradition, 31, 85
Taqwa (piety of God consciousness/awareness), 70, 102
Taṣdīq, 137, 187

Tawḥīd, 36–37, 45, 191, 205, 237, 238, 258
Taylor, Charles, 214
Tazkiya (purification of the soul), 92, 203
Telos (purpose of any creation or institution)
Aristotle on, 177–78, 179, 186, 189–90, 191, 197, 208, 228
of the citizen, 217, 227
of the human being, 179, 181, 187, 189–90, 191, 203, 271
of polis, 197, 208, 229, 271
of the political animal, 191, 271
of the *ummah*, 179, 197, 200, 201, 271
Territory, 61–62, 160, 161, 164, 166, 171, 268, 269
deterritorialization, 12
territorial society, 58
See also *Ḥaram* (sacred); Land and the concept of *ummah*
Tolerance
as means to limit conflict, 212
Medina Constitution allowing for freedom for religious groups, 204, 218, 228, 248
Rawlsian method of tolerance, 216, 219
religious tolerance, 64, 65, 72, 155, 263
Torah, 50, 53, 88, 111–12, 122, 157–58
on coming of Prophet Muhammad, 54
Jewish *ummah* as covenant based on, 49
as a revealed book or divine message, 39, 112–13, 124
as *sharīʿah* for Jews, 125
See also Scripture
Transnational, 1, 2, 11, 12
Treaty, 126
Medina Constitution, 41, 49, 134, 169, 267
political treaty, 119, 129, 144, 268
and the Qurʾān, 42, 47, 73, 152–53
See also *Mīthāq* (covenant)
Tribes
Prophet Muhammad making changes in tribal practices, 231
treatment of in Medina Constitution, 223–24, 230
tribal affiliation, 273
Truth, 65–66
al-ḥanīf as being inclined toward the truth, 95
al-Ḥaq ("the Truth"), 34
al-Kitāb ("the Book") sent in Truth, 113, 122, 123, 124
bearing witness to truth, 104, 106, 109, 119, 236
believers guided by, 123
confirmation (*taṣdīq*) of truth, 187
denying the truth (*kufr*), 26, 65, 161, 180
determining truth from falsehood, 34, 66, 95, 97, 125, 186, 190
as divine revelation, 57
emotional attachments not equivalent to, 32
inclined toward the truth (*al-janīf*), 95
and justice, 7, 55, 56, 119, 182, 183, 188, 190, 235
objective truth, 33, 34
religion of truth, 22
ummah who guides others with truth, 55, 56, 57
unitary truth, 66

Tyranny (*al-istibdād*), 258
sulṭat ad-ḍabṭ versus *sulṭat aṭ-ṭughyān*, 259–60
ṭughyān as another term for tyrannical rule, 260

Uḥud, battle of, 52, 240–41, 244
ʿUlamāʾ ("religious scholars"), 18, 19, 27, 194, 195–96, 250, 257
ʾUlī ʾl-amr, 246, 248
and the *aʾimma*, 251
in the Medina Constitution, 255–57
in the modern period, 257–61
those entrusted with authority, 249–55
ʾulī ʾl-amr minkum, 246, 249
ʾUlū baqiyya, 67, 68
Um al-Qura (Al-Kawākibī), 257
Umam (plural of *ummah*). See *Ummah*
Umayyad dynasty, 118, 119
Umayyad Caliphate, 8, 182, 193–94
Ummah
and *ajal* (appointed term), 24–30, 73
amma or *amama* (lead or go intentionally) as a root verb for *ummah*, 25, 29
Aristotlian polis and Qurʾānic *ummah*, 197–212
concept of, 23–24, 34, 100, 147, 167
conceptual meaning of in Meccan verses of the Qurʾān, 21–75, 129
conceptual meaning of in Medinan verses of the Qurʾān, 77–131, 129
defining, 5–6, 29, 35, 40–41, 54, 57, 63, 72–73, 78, 79, 83, 92, 134, 160, 264
difference between nation-states and *umam*, **60**
differentiating ethnic and religous *ummah*, 200
differentiation of the one *ummah*, **63**
different parts of an *ummah*, **233**
first *ummah*, 88, 129
importance of *muʾākhā* (brotherhood) to formation of, 147–48
looked at through lens of modern liberal democracies, 121
of Medina, 28–29, 88, 121–22, 126, 134
in the Medina Constitution, 133–71
monotheistic *uman*, 267
Muhammad granting *shafāʿa* ("intercession") to, 52
networked global structure of, **48**
obligations of, 74, 78–80, 129, 138, 148–49, 151, 153, 170, 248, 266, 267, 269, 276
organization of, 147
Orientalists seeing *ummah* as a closed society of Muslims, 72, 89, 114, 117–18, 135, 144, 268
as an original idea, 5
polis and constitution versus *ummah* and *al-Kitāb*, 222–23
of the Prophets, 62–63
reassessing meaning of, 15
religion and forefathers, 30–34
and rights within it, 60–61
shared *ummah:* rights and obligations, 78–80
as a sociopolitical realization, 13
stability of, 274
tested in its submission to the creator, 108

three definitions of, 50–51
thriving *ummah*, 203, 226, 266, 271, 275, 276
time when all peoples were one *ummah*, 22–23
umam before the coming of Muhammad, 72
umam interconnected based on covenants, sovereignty based on the Book, **60**
as understood in the Qur'ān, 1, 15, 114
the whole *ummah*, 252
See also Specific types (i.e., *ʿAla ummah, Global* ummah, *Khayr ummah,* Muslim *ummah, Ummah muslimah,* etc.)
Ummah muqtaṣida, 111–13, 131, 139, 140, 267
Ummah muslimah, 77, 83, 84, 85, 86, 91, 100
Ummah qā'ima, 109, 110, 131, 140, 267
Ummah wāḥidah (single *ummah*), 46, 70, 121–22, 170, 268
achieving unity (one *ummah* and its differentiation), **63**
different interpretations of, 23, 72, 122
embracing united *ummah*, **144**
and its differentiation across human history, 62–65
in the Medina Constitution, 135, 137, 139, 142, 143–44, 147, 150
on one *ummah*, 22–23, 69, 70, 122
Ummah wasaṭ (middle *ummah*), 68, 104, 107, 112, 125, 149, 235, 245, 261
as *'a'immat ʿadl*, 42
al-ummah al-wasaṭ, 103–109
and balance, 151, 235, 236
as a communal organization, 105, 147, 235
preventing the emergence of *at-ṭāghūt*, 261
and *ummah muqtaṣida*, **111–12**
and the witness (*Shahāda*), 103–109
as "witness" before humankind, 236
See also *Wasaṭ*
Umm al-Qura ("the mother of the villages"), 51
Ummat al-Islam, 135
Ummī
meaning of, 51
ummī prophet, 50–54, 137, 265, 267
'Unās, 55
Unity
achieving unity (one *ummah* and its differentiation), **63**
embracing united *ummah*, **144**
unity of virtues, 237–38
Universal
Qur'ānic universal ethics, 152–53
At-Ṭabarī as supreme universal historian, 17
ummah as a universal concept, 53, 54, 263
ummah wāḥidah some seeing as a universal concept, 72
universal community as global *ummah*, 53
universal interdependence, 10
universal principles of conduct, 112
universal *ummah*, 136
'Unāsin, 39, 40

Virtue (*khayr*) and virtuous activity. See *Khayr* (virtue) and virtuous activity
Virtuous ciry (*Al-Madīna Al-Fāḍila*), 179, 222

Wāḍiʿ ash sharī ʿah (giver of laws), 199
Walbridge, John, 175
Waliy ʾl-amr, 257
Warners (*nadhīr*), 32, 38–39, 122
Wasaṭ
  achieving through the *ummah* as a whole, 261
  implying justice and the best of something, 109
  interpretation of, 7–8
  justice as a "mean" and the concept of *wasaṭ*, 232–37
  multiple interpretations of, 104
  Muslim *ummah* described as, 95
  Prophet Muhammad as perfect model for, 105
  relating concepts of *wasaṭ*, *shahāda*, and *qibla* together, 266
  resembling Aristotelian concept of mean, 235–36, 238, 239, 245, 274
  virtuous *ummah* as, 274
  See also *Ummah wasaṭ*
Wasaṭiyyah (active justice), 7, 245, 255, 257, 261, 275, 276
  polis and justice versus *ummah* and *wasaṭiyyah*, 232
  See also Justice
Waṭan (homeland) and *ummah*, 57–58
Wathīqa (binding document), 43
Watt, Montgomery, 89, 90–91, 145
"Way of life" and *ummah*, 199–200, 205, 275
Ways of life, 199, 200, 203, 271, 272, 275
Wealth
  and liberal sociopolitical order, 5
  striving with wealth and self, 143
Western civilizations compared with Islamic civilization, 4–6
Westphalian paradigm, 11, 13
Widdis, Randy, 166
Wilāyat al-faqīh ("rule of the jurisconsult"), 20, 258
Witness (*shahīd* or *shahāda*), 47–48, 103–109
  ummah wasaṭ as a witness before humankind, 236

Yack, Bernard, 198, 207, 209, 255
Yarn, 45, 61, 150
  interwoven yarn, 48

Zayd bin ʿAmrū, 81–82, 93

Index of Qur'anic Citations

2. *Al-Baqarah*
2:30–34, 180, 182
2:83-84, 42–43
2:120, 99
2:125, 162
2:126, 161, 162
2:127–134, 84
2:128, 100
2:128–129, 90–91
2:129, 254
2:129–130, 93–94
2:135, 95
2:135–136, 96
2:142–143, 104, 108, 236
2:143, 42
2:170, 30
2:171, 31
2:213, 22, 122, 126, 225
2:256, 248–49
2:258, 83
2:260, 83
3:3, 113
3. *ʾĀl-ʿImrān*
3:64, 141
3:81, 44
3:103, 66
3:104, 6, 115, 203
3:110, 4, 51–52, 115, 140, 202, 203, 270
3:113–115, 109–110, 120
3:159, 240, 241, 244, 245
4. *An-Nisāʿ*
4:58, 246–47
4:59, 245–47, 248, 249
4:60, 246–47, 248
4:97–98, 26–27
4:125, 93, 238
5. *Al-Māʿidah*
5:3, 90
5:46, 113
5:48, 6, 124, 126, 127, 131, 137, 158, 167–68, 209, 210, 267
5:66, 111
6. *Al-ʾAnʿām*
6:74–80, 82
6:108, 64
7. *Al-ʾAʿrāf*
7:12, 186
7:34, 25
7:38–39, 25–26, 30
7:97–98, 36
7:157, 50, 51
7:158, 53
7:159, 55, 56, 57
7:160, 55, 57, 58
7:164, 78, 256
7:181, 55

8. *Al-'Anfāl*
8:62, 52
9. *At-Tawbah*
9:101, 91
9:128, 254
10. *Yūnus*
10:19, 62, 64
10:47, 62
11. *Hūd*
11:116–117, 67
11:118–119, 69, 188
15. *Al-Ḥijr*
15:4–5, 25
15:28–29, 186
16. *An-Naḥl*
16:63–64, 36
16:91, 47
16:91–93, 45–46, 48
16:92–93, 49, 149–50
16:120-121, 80–81
17. *Al-'Isrā'*
17:71, 39, 40
19. *Maryam*
19:41–48, 82
21. *Al-'anbiyā'*
21:52–74, 82
21:92, 62, 64
22. *Al-Ḥaj*
22:34, 100, 101
22:36–37, 102
22:67, 100–101
23. *Al-Mu'minūn*
23:52, 70
27. *An-Naml*
27:76–78, 57
28. *Al-Qaṣaṣ*
28:23, 25
28:75, 48
29. *Al-'Ankabūt*
29:48, 51
29:67, 161, 162
35. *Fāṭir*
35:24–25, 38
37. *As-Ṣāffāt*
37:99–111, 83
38. *Ṣād*
38:26, 182, 183, 184, 190, 235
40. *Ghāfir*
40:4–5, 65
42. *As-Shūra*
42:38, 239
43. *Az-Zukhruf*
43:21, 34
43:21–24, 32, 42, 148
43:23, 152
45. *Al-Jāthiyah*
45:28–29, 34
49. *Al-Ḥujurāt*
49:13, 6, 70
49:14–15, 142–43
51. *Adh-Dhāriyāt*
51:56–58, 187
69. *Al-Ḥāqqah*
69:11, 247
91: *As-Shams*
91:7–10, 202
91:9, 203

www.ingramcontent.com/pod-product-compliance
Lightning Source LLC
Chambersburg PA
CBHW030127240426
43672CB00005B/56
* 9 7 8 1 4 3 8 4 8 2 0 4 0 *